Regional Powerhouse: The Greater Pearl River Delta and the Rise of China

Regional Powerhouse: The Greater Pearl River Delta and the Rise of China

Michael J. Enright
Edith E. Scott
Ka-mun Chang

John Wiley & Sons (Asia) Pte Ltd

While this publication is designed to provide accurate information in regard to the subject
matter covered, it is sold with the understanding that neither the author, the publisher nor any
Citigroup entity is engaged in rendering legal, tax or accounting advice and is giving no
professional advice with respect to the subject matter covered in this publication. Before
making any investment, the services of a competent professional person should be sought.

Other Wiley Editorial Offices
John Wiley & Sons, Inc., 111 River Street, Hoboken, NJ 07030, USA
John Wiley & Sons Ltd, The Atrium, Southern Gate, Chichester PO19 BSQ,
   England
John Wiley & Sons (Canada) Ltd, 22 Worcester Road, Rexdale, Ontario
   M9W ILI, Canada
John Wiley & Sons Australia Ltd, 33 Park Road (PO Box 1226), Milton,
   Queensland 4046, Australia
Wiley-VCH, Pappelallee 3, 69469 Weinheim, Germany

Library of Congress Cataloging-in-Publication Data:

ISBN-13   978-0-4708-2173-2
ISBN-10   0-4708-2173-6

Typeset in 10/13 point, Photina by Cepha Imaging Pvt Ltd
Printed in Singapore by Saik Wah Press Pte Ltd

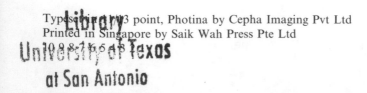

Contents

Preface

China is increasingly the focus of analysts, business people, and policy-makers around the world. While much is known about China's economic rise over the last two and a half decades, much less is known about the regional patterns of China's development and the mechanisms by which China's regions are developing. As a result, the understanding of China's economic rise is at best incomplete. This is particularly true of the Greater Pearl River Delta region, a complex, multi-faceted region with an enormously dynamic economy. Having lived and worked in the region for many years, we were anxious to delve into the sources of this dynamism in detail.

The 2022 Foundation, a Hong Kong-based, non-profit foundation dedicated to improving understanding of the long-term economic trajectories of Hong Kong and the Chinese mainland, afforded us the opportunity to realize this aim by sponsoring the research upon which this book is based. We wish to thank the Foundation as well as its constituent organizations: CLP Holdings Ltd.; Dah Sing Bank; Esquel Group; Hang Seng Bank; Hong Kong Dragon Airlines Limited; The Hong Kong Pearl River Delta Foundation; Hongkong Land Ltd.; Hysan Development Co., Ltd.; iTVentures Limited; Kerry Holdings Ltd.; Li & Fung Group; and Sun Hung Kai Properties Ltd. Special thanks go to Dr. Victor Fung, Chairman of the Li & Fung Group, who first saw the need for the project and has helped us in countless ways throughout, and Mr. Po Chung, Chairman of The Hong Kong Pearl River Delta Foundation, who encouraged and backed our efforts to make the results accessible to international audiences. We would also like to thank Dr. Saimond Ip, formerly Executive Director of The Hong Kong Pearl River Delta Foundation, for his support throughout the research and writing process.

We wish to acknowledge the members of the project team that undertook the research in Hong Kong, Macao, and the Chinese mainland. Dr. Zhu Wen-hui performed substantial mainland-based research, contributed data, insights, and perspectives to the book's analysis of the Pearl River Delta region, and made significant contributions to Chapters 3 and 4. Ms. Jo Wilson contributed significantly to the Hong Kong-based field research effort, worked extensively on the overall manuscript, and made significant contributions to Chapters 3 and 5. Helen Chin and Francis Ng provided detailed research support; their hard work is reflected in the facts and figures that appear throughout the text. We also wish to acknowledge the research support provided by Zhongshan University.

Finally, we would like to thank the hundreds of executives, managers, public officials, community activists, industry experts, and others throughout the Greater Pearl River Delta region who generously donated their time for interviews. It is to them that we owe our greatest debt and much of our own understanding of the dynamic interactions that have created a regional powerhouse that continues to play a crucial role in the rise of China.

The views expressed in this book and any remaining errors are those of the authors.

Michael J. Enright
Edith E. Scott
Ka-mun Chang
Hong Kong
March 2005

Foreword

China's meteoric rise over the last two and a half decades has captured imaginations the world over. During that period, China has become one of the world's largest and most dynamic economies, as well as a leader in international trade and investment. Rarely does a day go by that China does not figure prominently on the business pages of the world's major newspapers. Policy makers, business people, analysts, and others follow developments in China with great attention, focusing on the opportunities and challenges associated with China's emergence.

Nowhere is China's dynamism greater than in the Greater Pearl River Delta region, an area encompassing Hong Kong, Macao, and the Pearl River Delta Economic Zone of Guangdong Province. This region became the leading edge of the reform program initiated by Deng Xiaoping in 1978, and the leading edge of the international portion of China's economy. Since then, the Greater Pearl River Delta region has become a manufacturing center of global importance as well as one of the world's fastest growing economic regions.

As a businessman operating in the region, I have been able to witness this development first hand, development that has transformed the Pearl River Delta region into one of the world's leading manufacturing centers and workshops, and Hong Kong into an international financial and supply chain management center of global importance. As the interaction within the region has intensified, its economy has deepened and broadened to encompass light manufacturing, high-technology industries, transportation equipment, basic industries, heavy manufacturing, and trade-related services.

Despite the increasing emphasis on China, in recent years, the story of the Greater Pearl River Delta region has received surprisingly little attention. As observers have focused on political and economic developments in Beijing and the Yangtze River Delta, the Greater Pearl River Delta region has continued to prosper. However, today, it is the Greater Pearl River Delta that is home to the largest regional economy in China, a fact that companies, analysts, and policy makers overlook. No one can understand China's economic rise or project its future without understanding the Greater Pearl River Delta region.

To advance the state of knowledge about the Greater Pearl River Delta region, the 2022 Foundation sponsored a research project under the direction of Professor Michael Enright of the University of Hong Kong and Edith Scott of Enright, Scott & Associates, with strong support from Zhongshan University, Ka-mun Chang of Li & Fung Development (China) Ltd. and the Li & Fung Research Centre, and Dr. Zhu Wen-hui. The intent was to understand the dynamism and economic potential of this important region. The initial conclusions and recommendations from the project were released in 2003 and quickly found their way into the policies and strategies undertaken around the region.

In the present book, Enright, Scott and Chang have expanded and refocused their research and analysis for an international audience. The resulting work explores the complex economic interactions that have shaped the development of this regional powerhouse. It shows how combinations, complementarities, and competition within the Greater Pearl River Delta region have fostered the emergence of a wide range of internationally competitive industries and industry clusters. Within the context of a rapidly changing China, it examines how national and regional forces can create new opportunities, challenges, and horizons for companies, investors, and policymakers the world over. For those of us who live in the Greater Pearl River Delta region, this book captures for the first time the full magnitude and complexity of the strength that has emerged from our unique interactions. For those living elsewhere, it makes a compelling case for why the Greater Pearl River Delta region should be in the forefront of their own understanding of an emerging China.

Dr. Victor K. Fung
Chairman, The Greater Pearl River Delta Business Council
Chairman, The Li & Fung Group
March 2005

List of abbreviations

CAD	Computer-aided design
CEPA	Closer Economic Partnership Arrangement
GDP	Gross domestic product
GPRD	Greater Pearl River Delta
HKSAR	Hong Kong Special Administrative Region
ICT	Information and communications technology
ICTI	International Council of Toy Industries
IPO	Initial public offering
ODM	Original design manufacturer
OEM	Original equipment manufacturer
PPRD	Pan-Pearl River Delta
PRC	People's Republic of China
R&D	Research and development
SAR	Special Administrative Region
SARS	Severe Acute Respiratory Syndrome
SEZ	Special Economic Zone
TDC	Hong Kong Trade Development Council
PRD	Pearl River Delta
WTO	World Trade Organization
USTR	United States Trade Representative
YRD	Yangtze River Delta

CHAPTER ONE

China, its Regions, and the Greater Pearl River Delta

China's emergence on the world stage was one of the most important stories in the world economy in the latter portion of the twentieth century and promises to continue to be one of the most important stories in the twenty-first century. China has gone from an economic backwater to become the world's most dynamic large economy. Since China's economic opening began in 1979, its economy has been growing at a real rate of over 9%, while its trade has been growing at more than 20% per year (see Figure 1.1). China's development since the onset of its economic reform program in 1979 has lifted more people out of poverty than in any other place over a comparable period of time.

By 2002, China was the world's sixth-largest economy (see Table 1.1) and its GDP grew another 9.1% in 2003. Given current growth rates, China will soon be the world's fourth-largest economy. Also in 2002, China was the world's fifth leading merchandise exporter and sixth leading importer (see Table 1.2). This reflects the fact that China has become the last stop in a pan-Asian production system, in which capital goods and advanced components are imported from Japan, Korea, and Taiwan; other inputs are imported from other Asian economies, mostly in South-east Asia; and final assembly takes place in China.[1] This system has resulted in explosive growth in China's exports and

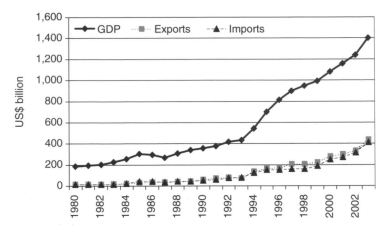

Sources: World Bank 2003; China State Statistical Bureau

Figure 1.1   China's GDP, exports, and imports in current US$

Table 1.1   Leading economies, gross national income (GNI) 2002

Economy	GNI US$ billion	Share %
United States	10,110	32.1
Japan	4,266	13.5
Germany	1,870	5.9
United Kingdom	1,486	4.7
France	1,343	4.3
China	1,210	3.8
Italy	1,098	3.5
Canada	700	2.2
Mexico	597	1.9
India	502	1.6

Source: World Bank, 2003

imports in recent years. In 2003, China's exports and imports both grew in excess of 30%. Recognising the opportunities developing in China as both a production platform and a market, international investors have made it the world's second-leading destination for foreign direct investment (see Table 1.3). China's position is even more impressive when one realises that most investment into Luxembourg, which registered as the leading destination, represents financial transactions. Also, most of the inward investment in the large OECD countries like France, Germany, the United States, and the United Kingdom, involves mergers and acquisitions; that is, the trading of existing assets rather

Table 1.2 Leading merchandise exporters and importers, 2002

Exporters	Value US$ billion	Share %	Annual change %	Importers	Value US$ billion	Share %	Annual change %
United States	693.9	10.7	−5	United States	1202.4	18.0	2
Germany	613.1	9.5	7	Germany	493.7	7.4	2
Japan	416.7	6.5	3	United Kingdom	345.3	5.2	4
France	331.8	5.1	3	Japan	337.2	5.0	−3
China	325.6	5.0	22	France	329.3	4.9	0
United Kingdom	279.6	4.3	3	China	295.2	4.4	21
Canada	252.4	3.9	−3	Italy	243	3.6	4
Italy	251.0	3.9	4	Canada	227.5	3.4	0
The Netherlands	244.3	3.8	6	The Netherlands	219.8	3.3	5
Belgium	214.0	3.3	12	Hong Kong[a]	207.2	3.1	3

Note: (a) Includes imports for domestic consumption and re-exports.
Source: World Trade Organization 2003

Table 1.3 Leading destinations for foreign direct investment, 2002

Economy	Investment US$ million	Share %
Luxembourg	125,660	19.3
China	52,700	8.1
France	51,505	7.9
Germany	38,033	5.8
United States	30,030	4.6
The Netherlands	29,182	4.5
United Kingdom	24,945	3.8
Spain	21,193	3.3
Canada	20,595	3.2
Ireland	19,033	2.9

Source: UNCTAD 2003

than the creation of new assets. In China, on the other hand, most foreign direct investment actually involves commitments for new assets.

In the first years of the twenty-first century, China's growth has been one of the beacons of the world economy, accounting for a substantial portion of total world economic growth. However, in the rest of the world, China's economic rise has been viewed with a mixture of admiration and alarm. In industry after industry, China is obtaining a substantial if not dominant portion of world production. This, in turn, has caused dislocation in competitor countries. In some developing countries, like Mexico and several ASEAN countries, hundreds of thousands of jobs have been lost or placed at risk. Even

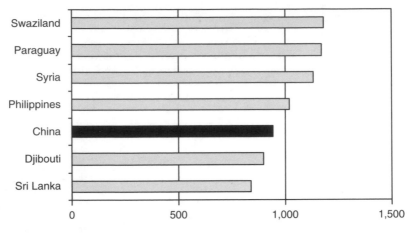

Source: World Bank 2003

Figure 1.2   Per capita GDP, 2002, US$

governments in the advanced economies of the United States, Western Europe, and Japan have voiced concern that China will take jobs away.

While the outside world sees a strong and growing China, within China itself, the picture is rather different. In China, the country is viewed as a progressing but poor country that has a long way to go before it will be able to achieve prosperity. In 2002, for example, China's per capita income ranked near Swaziland, Syria, the Philippines, Djibouti, and Sri Lanka, not economies that one typically thinks of as world beaters (see Figure 1.2). According to the World Economic Forum, China ranked 44th and 46th out of 82 economies on their two competitiveness indices.[2] Within China, one sees not just the development and growth, but also the challenges that arise in attempting to foster development in a traditionally backward economy: the challenge of changing from a planned economy to a market-oriented economy, the challenge of developing social security systems to take the place of state employment and subsidies, and the challenge of creating the institutions capable of governing a modern market economy.

For many of the world's companies, China's emergence is likely to represent the single largest opportunity this decade if not this century. Economic reforms have opened the way for vast new business opportunities. China's population, growth rates, and the fact that its reform process means that competitive positions are not yet entrenched, have placed China at the top of the list for companies from around the world. Even companies that do not compete in China itself will have to worry about competition from China, or its potential to influence world prices in a wide range of commodities.

For many of the world's governments, China's emergence has created both challenges and opportunities. As China develops, it is increasingly coming into competition with other developing economies in Asia and elsewhere, which are finding it more and more difficult to compete with China in export markets for light manufactured goods. For more advanced economies, China has become a production location that allows their firms to stay competitive. For a wide range of economies, China represents an enormous potential market for everything from commodities, to raw materials, to capital goods, to advanced components, to services, to niche manufactures.

THE REGIONAL BASIS OF CHINA'S ECONOMY

Despite the fact that understanding China and the Chinese economy has become a must for firms, governments, and investors around the world, China remains a mystery to many. One reason is that China is far from transparent and another is that China is a land of huge disparity. Instead of a single, national economy, for example, the Chinese mainland has a set of loosely coupled regional economies with some regions experiencing rampant growth and others stagnation. China is not a monolith politically either. Competition between regions and between individual jurisdictions has been played out in the corridors of power in Beijing, as well as in the regions themselves. The fact of the matter is that most opportunities and challenges in China today are driven as much by regional issues and regional concerns as they are by national issues and national concerns. Many of the best opportunities and toughest challenges for China are regional in nature. Companies, governments, and investors that are serious about China need to understand China's regions.

The regional nature of China's economy has a long history. China's topography, with deserts, mountain ranges, major rivers, and coastal planes, has always provided a certain amount of separation for China's regions. In the nineteenth and early twentieth centuries, the coastal regions, particularly around the so-called 'Treaty Ports' developed much more rapidly than the interior. After the end of the Chinese Civil War in 1949, Mao Zedong and other Chinese leaders decided to set up a 'cellular' economic system in which self-sufficient local economies would make the country less vulnerable to attack by foreign powers, reduce the potential for challenges to the nation's leadership, have plants near sources of raw materials, and distribute industries to match the population base. State-owned enterprises were mostly locally administered concerns and other than raw materials and some commodities, there was relatively little inter-provincial trade. Industries were decentralised away from the coasts, creating heavy industrial centres in the western part of the country to supplement those in the traditional heavy industrial areas in the north-east, as the country was divided into three 'fronts', approximately corresponding to coastal, central, and western regions. In the 1970s, as fears of attack abated, there was a shift of emphasis back to the coast, due to its more advanced economic base, labour skills, technical capabilities, and managers. Despite government efforts, the gap in income levels between the richest and the poorest regions in China actually increased between 1952 and 1978.[3]

As China began to open its economy in 1979, reforms were first limited to designated Special Economic Zones in Guangdong and Fujian. In 1984, coastal cities were allowed to set up their own Economic and Technological Development Zones. The policy was continued by the establishment of Coastal Open Economic Zones in 1985, an Open Coastal Belt in 1988, and the Shanghai Pudong New Area in 1990. In 1992, new open economic zones were started in major cities along the Yangtze River, capital cities of inland provinces and autonomous regions, and border regions. The coastal provinces, having strategic, export-friendly geographic locations, and most of the economic zones, received most of the foreign direct investment (FDI), generated the most trade, and grew much faster than the interior. In the late 1990s and 2000s, regional policies in China began to favour the western provinces, particularly Sichuan and Chongqing, as well as the north-eastern provinces, particularly Liaoning, as the Central Government focused attention on the lesser developed regions of the country.[4]

In any case, regional disparities remain, as can be seen in Figures 1.3, 1.4, and 1.5. Guangdong Province had the highest GDP among provinces and listed cities in the Chinese mainland in 2002, followed by Jiangsu, Shandong, and Zhejiang provinces.[5] Not surprisingly, three of the listed cities had the highest per capita GDP figures, followed by Zhejiang and Guangdong. Guangdong, however, registered by far the highest exports for 2002 and the first half of 2003. The figures show that there are some stark differences between different areas in China. The same country that is developing gleaming cities with burgeoning economies still has hundreds of millions of people in a state of severe poverty. Modern, forward-looking segments of the economy coexist with primitive, backward segments.

Uneven development in China actually has been a great advantage in many ways. As a relatively poor country, China could not build the complete infrastructure to connect the entire nation to the rest of the world. Instead, it started by providing infrastructure in the coastal regions sufficient to link to major seaports, such as Hong Kong, Shenzhen, Shanghai, Ningbo, and Tianjin. Areas within a few hundred kilometres of these cities have accounted for the

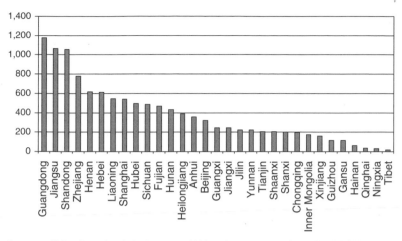

Sources: China State Statistical Bureau 2003, *China Statistical Yearbook 2003*

Figure 1.3   Provincial GDP, 2002, billion RMB

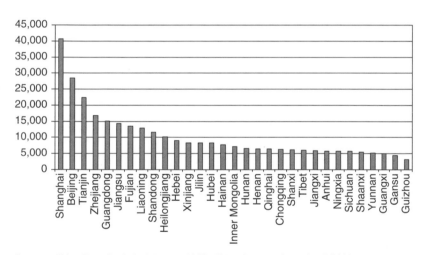

Sources: China State Statistical Bureau 2003, *China Statistical Yearbook 2003*

Figure 1.4   Provincial GDP, 2002, RMB

vast majority of China's inward investment and exports. As the coastal areas become wealthier, China is able to tap some of that wealth to fund infrastructure and development further inland. At the same time, many people from the interior provinces have gone to work for a few years in coastal regions and then have returned home, with money and experience in working in a more advanced economy. Finally, the growing economies of the coastal region are

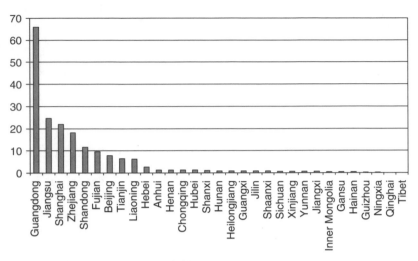

Source: China State Statistical Bureau 2003a

Figure 1.5   Provincial exports, first half of 2003, US$ billion

providing markets that can stimulate the development of producers in other parts of the country.

The regional disparities in China's economic development has created numerous issues and a host of policy challenges that only become apparent when one looks at China's regions in detail. An economy in which some parts are growing at 12 to 15% per year creates enormous challenges associated with providing the hard and soft infrastructure necessary to accommodate such rapid growth and deal with its consequences, such as labour migration, environmental degradation, and resource constraints. An economy in which some parts are stagnating and in which it is difficult to provide alternative employment for people that have been displaced by the reform process creates other challenges, such as unemployment, social dislocation, the need for massive public spending, and managing the impact and pace of reform.

China faces the challenge of creating national policies in the face of stark regional differences. Macroeconomic policies that might make sense in the rapidly growing coastal regions, such as a tight monetary and limited fiscal spending in order to prevent inflation, could be totally counterproductive for stagnating regions. On the other hand, spending and lending policies designed to help the western and north-eastern parts of the country may well postpone needed reforms in the banking sector in particular and the economy in general. In China, even the exchange rate is as much a micro-regional issue as it is a macro-national issue. While policymakers in the West and Japan have claimed China has kept its currency pegged against the US dollar in order to ensure the competitiveness of China's light manufacturing exports, it is far more likely that the peg has been kept to try to ensure that uncompetitive heavy industries in regions that have experienced social disruption and riots are afforded some measure of protection from imports into the domestic market. By averaging out the regional differences, the aggregate numbers tend to mask what might be the greatest challenges and the best opportunities to be found within China. It is only when one examines China's regions that the picture becomes clear.

THE PEARL RIVER DELTA REGION

The Pearl River Delta region has emerged as one of the most important economic regions in China. It has been one of three regions, the other two being the Yangtze River Delta region (around Shanghai) and the Bohai Rim (including Beijing, Tianjin, and Hebei Province) that have been driving much of China's development. The Pearl River Delta Economic Zone, as specified by Guangdong Province, includes Guangzhou, Shenzhen, Dongguan, Foshan, Jiangmen, Zhongshan, Zhuhai, and the urban areas of Huizhou and Zhaoqing. The Pearl River Delta Economic Zone was first defined by Guangdong Province in 1984 and was expanded to its present dimensions in 1987 (see Figure 1.6). In this book, we will use this official definition for what we will call the 'Pearl River Delta region'. We will define the 'Greater Pearl River Delta region' to include the Pearl River Delta Economic Zone plus the Hong Kong

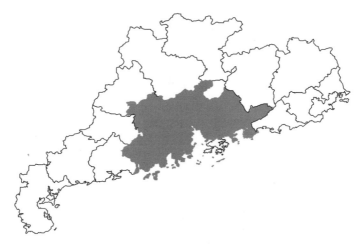

Figure 1.6   The Pearl River Delta Economic Zone in Guangdong Province

Figure 1.7   Main jurisdictions in the Greater Pearl River Delta region

Special Administrative Region and the Macao Special Administrative Region (see Figure 1.7).

As of 2002, Guangdong Province had the largest GDP and second-highest GDP per capita among the provinces of the Chinese mainland (excluding the listed cities in the latter case). This was not always the case. Historically, Guangdong Province and the Pearl River Delta region were economic backwaters that lagged behind other parts of the Chinese mainland in terms of industrial development and income levels. This situation continued until China began its economic opening in 1979. Soon, the Pearl River Delta started to attract export-oriented foreign investment and began to engage in export-led development. The region came to dominate Chinese production in an increasing range of industries. By 2002, the Pearl River Delta region accounted for less than half a percent of the land mass of the Chinese mainland and 1.8% of the registered population, but 9% of GDP, and around a third of the international trade and inward foreign investment (see Table 1.4).

In many ways, the Pearl River Delta region has been one of China's best kept secrets. While several scholars have written about Guangdong Province and the Pearl River Delta region,[6] it is a story that is not well known to people throughout the world. As the Central Government and foreign observers have focused on the rise of Shanghai, Beijing, and other centres, the Pearl River Delta region has quietly continued to exhibit growth rates that have outstripped every other part of China. One reason for the relative lack of focus on the Pearl River Delta has been the nature of the region's development. Instead of

Table 1.4　Pearl River Delta compared to Guangdong and Chinese mainland, 2002

	PRD portion of Guangdong %	PRD portion of Chinese Mainland %
Land area	23.2	0.4
Registered population (2002)	30.9	1.8
Census population (2000)	47.8	3.2
GDP	80.0	9.0
Total trade (2002)	95.0	33.8
Exports (2002)	94.2	34.3
Imports (2002)	95.9	33.0
Foreign direct investment (2002)	88.6	22.0

Sources: Calculated from data in *China Statistical Yearbook 2003; Guangdong Statistical Yearbook 2003*

skyscrapers and large-scale vanity projects, the Pearl River Delta region has grown through the emergence of hundreds of thousands of factories in what once was a rural setting, many producing for export markets. Only relatively recently have visible large-scale investments been made to serve the region itself. Much of the development in the Pearl River Delta region has been in the private sector, linked with Hong Kong, Taiwanese, foreign, and increasingly indigenous firms, and not controlled by the State.

One reason for the relative lack of attention on the region has been the nature of Chinese control of reporting and news coverage. The largely autonomous development of the region has not relied on massive state-sponsored projects that tend to be praised in the Chinese media. This was particularly the case in the 1990s when Central Government leaders with connections to Shanghai pushed the development of the Yangtze River Delta region. In addition, it has been very difficult for foreign news organisations to set up bureaus outside of Beijing and Shanghai. For example, reporters based in Hong Kong were not allowed to enter the Pearl River Delta region from Hong Kong to act as reporters until 2003. What this meant was that when an editor wanted a China political story, he or she called up the Beijing office, while if the editor wanted an economic story, he or she called up the Shanghai office. One of the great ironies in the coverage of China is the focus on Beijing and the Central Government when two of the most important trends in China have been the decentralisation of responsibility and greater private-sector and market-oriented development. Development through foreign investment and the private sector in the Pearl River Delta region has continued to take place almost beneath the radar screen of many observers, a fact that local authorities were keen not to alter until recently.

HONG KONG AND THE GREATER PEARL RIVER DELTA

One of the most salient features of the development of the Pearl River Delta region has been its links with Hong Kong. The Pearl River Delta region was chosen to take the lead in China's reform program partly due to its proximity to Hong Kong. The idea was to use Hong Kong's links to the rest of the world to foster a process of step-by-step reform in which Hong Kong would learn from the world, South China would learn from Hong Kong, and the rest of China would learn from South China. While not highly publicised, since the onset of China's reform program, the Pearl River Delta region has received a constant stream of study groups and officials from elsewhere in China.

The economic interaction is only one type of link between Hong Kong and the Pearl River Delta region. Most of Hong Kong's residents or their families origically came from Guangdong Province. As a result, numerous ties of family and friendship have always existed between Hong Kong and the Pearl River Delta region. Even though decades of formal separation has resulted in different levels of affluence, and differences in lifestyle, cultural and linguistic ties remained. Once China began to open, these historical ties were quickly turned into business relationships.

The world received a stark reminder of the extent of the interaction between Hong Kong and the Pearl River Delta region in early 2003. South China has long been known as a hotbed of infectious diseases. In particular, the interactions among wild and domesticated poultry, domesticated pigs, and human beings living in close proximity has made Guangdong Province one of the world's leading incubators of new influenza viruses. In 2002, when a new virus started affecting people in Guangdong Province, the outbreak was kept secret from outsiders. In March 2003, a doctor that had been treating patients with the unidentified virus in Guangzhou came to Hong Kong, where he eventually died. Once the disease, eventually named 'SARS' (for Severe Acute Respiratory Syndrome) reached Hong Kong, it was spread globally. Individuals infected through contact with the Guangdong doctor spread the disease to Vietnam, Singapore, and Canada in a matter of days. By August 2003, when the disease had run its course, there had been 8,098 people infected in 29 nations (or regions in the case of Hong Kong and Macao) and 774 deaths. Hong Kong accounted for 1,755 of the infections and 299 of the deaths, while the Chinese mainland accounted for 5,327 of the infections and 349 of the deaths.[7]

During the height of the SARS outbreak, in March through to May of 2003, many activities ground to a halt in Hong Kong and Guangdong. Most notably, tourism into the region collapsed. For example, Hong Kong's visitor arrivals in May 2003 were 70% lower than they had been in February and hotel occupancy was only 18%. By August, arrivals were back above February levels and hotel occupancy rates were back at 88%.[8] Retail sales in Hong Kong in April and May of 2003 were actually higher than they had been in January and February (though they were down 15% and 11% from the previous year). Restaurant receipts were down 19% in the second quarter of 2003 from the same quarter in 2002. Even so, Hong Kong's GDP grew at a real rate of 3.3% in 2003, up from 2.3% growth in 2002.[9] Despite the rapid rebound from the SARS outbreak, officials and the public in Hong Kong and Guangdong remained on alert in case the disease returned.

In a sense, the SARS outbreak was a metaphor for the links between Hong Kong and the Pearl River Delta region. The virus was a local matter in Guangdong until it hit Hong Kong, but Hong Kong's connections to the rest of the world soon made it an international issue. Similarly in economic terms, it has been Hong Kong that has connected the Pearl River Delta region to the rest of the world, driving its transformation into a production platform and regional economy of global importance.

The high levels of interaction between Hong Kong and the Pearl River Delta region mean that it is actually the Greater Pearl River Delta region that should be compared to other regions in China and elsewhere in the world. When it is, the Greater Pearl River Delta region comfortably outstrips the other leading economic regions in China, the Yangtze River Delta, and the Bohai region in GDP, exports, and inward investment (see Figure 1.8), a fact that is not generally known, usually because the statistics are not gathered according to true regional economies. Thus, the Greater Pearl River Delta region is not just the most internationally oriented part of China's economy, it is also the largest regional economy in China. If it were a country, the Greater Pearl River Delta would have been the world's sixteenth-largest economy and its tenth-leading exporter in 2002.

UNDERSTANDING THE REGIONS

If China's development path and its rise as an international economic power-house is to be understood, it is essential to understand the progress of China's different regions. In this regard, the prominence of the Pearl River Delta region looms particularly large. How after all did one of the more backward regions of one of the world's most backward economies achieve a position of global importance in just a few short decades? Part of the answer rests in the potential of China that had remained unrealised for so many years, but part of the answer

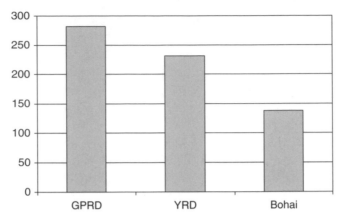

Notes: GPRD = Hong Kong + Macao + Pearl River Delta Economic Zone
        YRD = Yangtze River Delta Economic Zone
        Bohai = Beijing + Tianjin + Hebei

Source: Enright and Scott 2004

Figure 1.8   GDP of selected Chinese regions, 2002, US$ billion

rests in the distinctive features of the Greater Pearl River Delta region. Hong Kong's political history, as a British colony for over 150 years before its return to Chinese administration, and its unique economic history, as one of the freest capitalist economies in the world now part of a reforming socialist country, have created a unique set of circumstances. These have contributed to the emergence of the Greater Pearl River Delta region, the home of a mix of systems and attributes that is not matched anywhere else in the world. How this mix of systems has combined to create one of the world's most dynamic regional economies is the focus of the present volume.

CHAPTER TWO

The Economic Development of Hong Kong

T he economies of Hong Kong and the Pearl River Delta region have developed rapidly since the onset of China's economic reform program in different, but closely related ways. While Hong Kong has emerged as a leading centre for management, coordination, finance, information, and business services, the Pearl River Delta region has developed into a manufacturing powerhouse with few rivals worldwide. Before going into the details of the nature of the interaction between the economies of Hong Kong and the Pearl River Delta region, it is useful to first outline these economies. In this chapter we will sketch some of the major developments in the evolution of Hong Kong's economy: its composition, clusters of competitive industries, economic decision-making, and roles in the world economy. In Chapter 3 we will do the same for the economy of the Pearl River Delta region.

HISTORICAL DEVELOPMENT

Hong Kong's economic development has been influenced by its unique history. For over 150 years, Hong Kong was under British administration. During this time it became a free port, a manufacturing enclave, an international financial centre, a regional centre for management in Asia, and a place where the economies of the East and the West came together. While under British administration, Hong Kong's economy developed numerous attributes that it has retained since its return to Chinese administration in 1997. Under the 'one country, two systems' mechanism, Hong Kong retains its separate economic system, including its own currency and customs zone, and autonomy in most areas that influence the economy.[1]

For over a century after the British took possession of Hong Kong Island in 1842 its primary economic role was as an entrepôt for trade into and out of China, and a way station for ships sailing to or from Asia. In the 1950s, after the founding of the People's Republic of China, as the PRC became isolated from the rest of the world economy, Hong Kong's entrepôt role faded. Instead, the colony became a maritime and trade centre for Asia. In addition, numerous refugees from the Chinese mainland provided both the know-how and the cheap labour that allowed Hong Kong to obtain a strong position in a range of light-manufacturing industries. Hong Kong became a leading exporter in garments, textiles, footwear, plastic products, simple electronics goods, and related products. Hong Kong's economy in the 1960s and 1970s was based largely on labour-intensive light manufacturing and the services directly related to trade and transportation. These had grown to supplement Hong Kong's maritime role. Over time, its position as a free port, its openness, and its legal and administrative systems allowed Hong Kong to develop into a business service centre for a growing Asian region.[2]

By the late 1970s, rising wages and land costs were rapidly making Hong Kong uncompetitive as a manufacturing location. The opening of the Chinese economy in 1979, and particularly the ability of Hong Kong firms to move their manufacturing activities into the Pearl River Delta region, meant that they could concentrate the knowledge-intensive activities associated with manufacturing in Hong Kong. The knowledge worker portion of Hong Kong's workforce (represented by 'managers and administrators', 'professionals and related', and 'clerical') increased from 21% in 1981, to 46% in 1996, and to well over 50% by 2001.[3] Hong Kong firms found it far more valuable to manage and coordinate from Hong Kong than to actually produce in Hong Kong. A large number of firms in knowledge-intensive professional service industries also came to use Hong Kong as a base to serve Hong Kong, China, and the rest of Asia.

Growth and adjustment

Hong Kong experienced rapid economic growth for several decades. Annual real GDP growth averaged 8.5% from 1975 to 1985 and 6.5% from 1985 to 1995.

As a result, from 1975 to 1995, Hong Kong's real GDP quadrupled, and its real GDP per capita tripled. In the run-up to the return of administration to China, Hong Kong's economy grew at a real rate of 4.5% in 1996 and 5% in 1997. The Asian Economic Crisis, which started in the middle of 1997, hit Hong Kong in 1998 when its real GDP fell by 5.3%. Many people underestimated the links between Hong Kong's economy and that of South-east Asia, and therefore the impact that the Crisis would have on Hong Kong's economy.[4] In addition, Hong Kong went through the bursting of its own asset price bubble. Like many economies in Asia, Hong Kong saw its property prices and stock market index increase dramatically in the early and mid-1990s. Both increased in the order of 50% in 1996 and 1997 alone. As prices fell throughout Asia, they could not be maintained in Hong Kong, particularly as business throughout the region suffered. While growth returned, particularly in 2000, Hong Kong's unemployment, which had been 2.2% in 1997, climbed to 7.9% in 2003 (see Table 2.1).[5]

As of 2004, Hong Kong had been going through a period of economic adjustment following the onset of the Asian Economic Crisis. Even though property prices fell by 50% or more, attempts by the Hong Kong government to prop up the market by reducing land supply (the Hong Kong government owns virtually all land in Hong Kong) only prolonged Hong Kong's period of deflation, which reached six years in 2004. Hong Kong was still facing adjustments due to the aftermath of the Asian Crisis, China's accession to the World Trade Organization, the rise of other cities in China, the improvement of skills and capabilities in the Chinese mainland, and its own home-grown challenges, such as substantial budget deficits. Though the economy was starting to pick up, these adjustments were likely to continue for some time. Even so, Hong Kong remained one of Asia's more remarkable and wealthiest economies, with per capita income approaching US$24,000 in 2002 (see Table 2.2).

Such income levels make Hong Kong a sizeable market in its own right. Hong Kong is known as a relatively sophisticated market, and as a relatively large market for luxury goods and other consumer products.[6] In 2002, Hong Kong, with a population of just under seven million people, had a GDP substantially

Table 2.1 Real GDP growth, inflation, and unemployment in Hong Kong, 1999–2003

	1999	2000	2001	2002	2003
Real GDP growth (%)	3.4	10.2	0.6	2.3	3.3
Inflation (%)	−4.0	−3.8	−1.6	−3.0	−2.6
Unemployment rate (%)	6.2	4.9	5.1	7.3	7.9

Sources: Hong Kong Trade Development Council 2002g and 2004c; Hong Kong Special Administrative Region Government, Census and Statistics Department 2004b and 2004d

Table 2.2   Economic indicators for Hong Kong, 1980–2002

	1980	1985	1990	1995	2000	2001	2002
Population (million)	5.039	5.456	5.705	6.156	6.665	6.725	6.7861
GDP, at factor cost (HK$ billion)	135.04	255.42	563.52	1,041.07	1,228.90	1,215.35	1,208.94
– Primary (%)	1.0%	0.6%	0.3%	0.2%	0.1%	0.1%	0.1%
– Secondary (%)	31.7%	29.9%	25.3%	16.1%	14.2%	13.4%	12.4%
– Tertiary (%)	67.3%	69.5%	74.4%	83.7%	85.7%	86.5%	87.4%
Per capita GDP (US$)	5,268	6,134	13,092	22,831	24,782	24,211	23,797
Exports (US$ billion)	19.10	30.15	82.04	172.32	201.63	189.87	200.07
Total Trade (US$ billion)	40.80	59.82	164.41	363.49	414.19	390.92	407.68

Source: Hong Kong Special Administrative Region Government, Census and Statistics Department, various years

larger than that of Guangdong Province, with a population in excess of 86 million people. As of 2002, per capita income in Hong Kong was more than 10 times that of Guangdong Province.[7] Hong Kong also has had a history as a substantial market in a variety of industries. In the mid-1990s, for example, when the Hong Kong International Airport and related projects were underway, Hong Kong had more major infrastructure construction in process than most large countries. Hong Kong's position as a trade and transportation centre has made it a very large market for goods and services related to these industries. Hong Kong's position as a major financial centre also has made its markets for financial services and related items substantially larger than one might expect given its small population.

Composition of the economy

Hong Kong's economy has always been dominated by the service sector. In the 1950s, 1960s, and 1970s, Hong Kong's central location in Asia, its open economy, and its transparent business environment helped attract financial and business service activities. Hong Kong also grew as a tourism centre with its unique blend of Eastern and Western cultures. Even at the height of the importance of Hong Kong's manufacturing sector, services still accounted for more than two-thirds of GDP. As China began to open its economy and as the manufacturing activities of Hong Kong firms were moved into the Pearl River Delta region, the portion of Hong Kong's GDP in the service sector increased to over 85%, a figure typical of major city economies like London and New York (see Tables 2.2 and 2.3).[8]

Table 2.3   Composition of Hong Kong's economy, 2002

Industry or sector	Percentage of GDP
Primary	0.1
Secondary	12.4
– Manufacturing	4.6
– Construction	4.4
– Utilities	3.4
Services	87.4
– Wholesale, retail, import–export trade, restaurants, hotels	27.0
– Transportation, storage, communications	10.7
– Financing, insurance, real estate, business services	21.9
– Community, social, and personal services	22.2
– Ownership of premises	13.1
Less: adjustment for financial intermediation services indirectly measured	7.5

Source: Hong Kong Special Administrative Region Government, Census and Statistics Department 2004d

Table 2.4   Hong Kong's trade performance, 2000–2002, US$ billion

	2000	2001	2002
Total exports	201.6	189.9	200.1
– Domestic exports	23.2	19.7	16.8
– Re-exports	178.4	170.2	183.3
Imports	212.6	201.1	207.6
Total trade	414.2	390.9	407.7
Trade balance	−10.9	−11.2	−7.6

Source: Hong Kong Trade Development Council 2004c

Particularly noteworthy are the prominence of producer services in Hong Kong's economy, and the extent to which the service sector is linked to economic activities that take place outside.[9] Hong Kong is a major exporter of services, ranking ninth in the world in the early 2000s.[10]

Hong Kong is one of the most trade-dependent economies in the world. In 2002, Hong Kong's total trade equalled 252% of its GDP.[11] The vast majority of Hong Kong's trade involves re-export trade with China. During the years 2000–2002, Hong Kong's re-exports were in the range of seven to 10.5 times its domestic exports (see Table 2.4). Most of this trade involved manufactured goods imported into Hong Kong from the Chinese mainland and then re-exported, or industrial inputs imported into Hong Kong and then re-exported to factories in the Chinese mainland. Hong Kong's leading manufactured goods are mostly produced for export.

HONG KONG'S ECONOMIC ROLES

Hong Kong has an influence in the global economy that goes far beyond what would be expected, given its tiny geographical size and its small population. Hong Kong firms act as packagers and integrators of business activities, matching supply and demand from East to West and West to East. Hong Kong is a major source of foreign investment and a home to one of the world's larger contingents of overseas firms. Hong Kong and its firms have been drivers of the modernisation of the mainland Chinese economy and its emergence into world markets, as well as a leading force in regional development.

Hong Kong as packager and integrator[12]

Hong Kong is often described as a bridge or a gateway, but neither metaphor conveys the extent to which Hong Kong and its firms actively set up, direct, and manage activities for the local, regional, and global economies. Hong Kong firms are instigators and initiators of economic activity, matching demand and supply on a local, regional, and global basis. The role of Hong Kong firms as packagers and integrators may be seen among Hong Kong's manufacturers and export trading companies which match demand, often in North America or Europe, with sources of supply throughout Asia and beyond. A Hong Kong company, for example, might help a United States apparel company design its autumn collection and then organise purchasing, manufacturing, and logistics to get the product onto retail shelves on time, meeting the right quality and product specifications, and on budget. This involves a complex set of roles that goes well beyond that of the traditional view of a 'middleman'.

Hong Kong's role as a packager and integrator extends beyond manufacturing and into the service sector. As a major business service centre, Hong Kong and its firms package financial and business deals for corporate and private clients from Hong Kong, from the region, and from the rest of the world. Hong Kong is the centre where fund managers and private bankers put together Asian investment funds, portfolios, and financial vehicles. Hong Kong financiers are involved in some of the largest capital raising efforts in the region. Hong Kong also is the leading centre for packaging infrastructure projects in Hong Kong, the mainland, and elsewhere in South-east Asia. With its long history of private sector-financed infrastructure, Hong Kong is the leading location for integrating skills in architecture, design, construction, civil engineering, law, and finance.

Hong Kong as foreign investor[13]

Despite its small size, Hong Kong is one of the world's leading sources of foreign direct investment. It was sixth in the world in 2000, accounting for outflows of more than US$59 billion, surpassed only by the United Kingdom, France, the United States, Luxembourg, and the Netherlands (see Table 2.5). As of 2002, Hong Kong ranked tenth worldwide, with more than US$17 billion in outward foreign direct investment, behind economies with much larger economies and populations. There are many reasons why Hong Kong has emerged as the region's largest foreign investor after Japan. First is its relationship with the Chinese mainland. Also crucial are its large and liquid capital market, the absolute freedom with which capital can enter and leave the economy, and the fact that such a large number of the world's leading firms, whether European, American, or Asian, coordinate regional operations from their bases in Hong Kong.

China has been the dominant destination for Hong Kong investment and such investment has been extremely important in China. At the end of 2002, Hong Kong entities accounted for a cumulative US$373 billion in contracted investment in mainland China – more than 45% of the total US$828 billion contracted since 1979 (see Table 2.6). While this investment is concentrated in Hong Kong's Pearl River Delta hinterland, it has been so substantial that Hong Kong investors remain by far the largest investors in virtually every province in mainland China. For example, China's Jiangsu Province, which is not in

Table 2.5 Top 10 sources of FDI outflows by home economy, 2000 and 2002, US$ billion

Economy	2002	Ranking	Economy	2000	Ranking
Luxembourg	154.07	1	Luxembourg	86.36	4
United States	119.74	2	United States	142.63	3
France	62.55	3	France	177.45	2
United Kingdom	39.70	4	United Kingdom	249.78	1
Japan	31.48	5	Japan	31.56	12
Canada	28.79	6	Canada	44.67	9
The Netherlands	26.27	7	The Netherlands	73.54	5
Germany	24.53	8	Germany	56.85	7
Spain	18.46	9	Spain	54.68	8
Hong Kong	17.69	10	Hong Kong	59.38	6

Note: Figures for Luxembourg for 2000 include Belgium.
Source: UNCTAD 2003

Table 2.6   Selected foreign investors in the Chinese mainland

	Contracted FDI (US$ billion)							
	Cumulative 1979–1995		Cumulative 1996–2002		1997		2002	
Country/region	US$ bn	%	US$ bn	%	US$ bn	%	US$ bn	%
Total	395.86	100.0	431.95	100.0	51.00	100.0	82.77	100.0
Hong Kong	233.60	59.0	140.01	32.4	18.22	35.7	25.20	30.4
United States	33.06	8.4	48.02	11.1	4.94	9.7	8.16	9.9
Virgin Islands	n/a	n/a	46.84	10.8	5.16	10.1	12.65	15.3
Taiwan	28.75	7.3	32.01	7.4	2.81	5.5	6.74	8.1
Japan	27.52	7.0	28.27	6.5	3.40	6.7	5.30	6.4
Singapore	18.53	4.7	22.84	5.3	4.47	8.8	2.79	3.4

Sources: Enright, Scott, and Dodwell 1997, p. 73; *China Statistical Yearbook 2003*, p. 671; and China Foreign Economic and Trade Press, various years

Hong Kong's immediate hinterland, has received substantial press attention due to the investments of Singapore in the Suzhou and Wuxi township projects. In fact, Hong Kong is a much larger investor in the province than Singapore. Out of contracted investment in Jiangsu Province totalling US$98.7 billion between 1985 and 2002, Hong Kong investors accounted for about one-third – US$29.5 billion. In 2002, when Hong Kong investors accounted for investment of just under US$4 billion, Taiwan accounted for investment of nearly US$2.6 billion, Japan for US$1.7 billion, the United States for US$1.5 billion, Singapore for just over US$1.3 billion, and Korea for US$900 million.[14]

Hong Kong as a location for overseas firms

Hong Kong plays very specific roles for multinational firms active in the Asia Pacific. Hong Kong serves as the pre-eminent management and coordination centre for the Asia Pacific, the North Asia Pacific, and Greater China, across all industry sectors. In its role as the regional headquarters capital for the Asia Pacific, Hong Kong has no equal. One of the world's great business cities, Hong Kong combines world-class hard and soft infrastructure with proximity to, and a high degree of integration with, the region's largest markets including the Chinese mainland. As one multinational executive observed, 'if Singapore is where you go to build production facilities, Hong Kong is where you go to build markets.'[15]

According to a multiyear study of multinational firms in the Asia Pacific region carried out by Enright, Scott & Associates Ltd that included 1,100 survey responses and 450 interviews from leading multinational executives, Hong Kong is the most important city in the Asia Pacific for regional coordination, central management, market planning, regional strategy setting, regional finance, and senior personnel management activities of multinational companies.[16] The study showed that in the early 2000s Hong Kong was the regional headquarters capital of the AsiaPacific by a wide and growing margin over Singapore. Hong Kong also had more than three times the number of regional headquarters as Tokyo, nine times that of Sydney, and roughly twelve times that of Shanghai or Beijing.[17] Updates have shown that Hong Kong's position has been expanding and that Hong Kong offices had by far the widest geographic span of control in the region.[18]

Hong Kong: Modernisation and internationalisation of the mainland Chinese economy

Hong Kong has played a critical role in the modernisation of the Chinese economy, providing capital, logistical support, access to world markets, management know-how, technology, equipment, design and research, marketing skills, procurement services, and quality assurance. These inputs have helped China, a nation cut off from the international economy for decades, to emerge as a major trading nation since the early 1990s.[19] Hong Kong and Hong Kong firms handle about 30% of mainland China's foreign trade. Not counting re-exports to and from the Chinese mainland, Hong Kong is the Chinese mainland's third-largest trading partner.[20] In 2002, there were about 600 scheduled flights weekly between Hong Kong and some 40 mainland cities, and more than 33,000 vehicles crossed the Hong Kong/mainland boundary daily.[21]

Hong Kong companies have helped build the infrastructure property projects necessary to modernise the Chinese economy. Hopewell Holdings' investments include the 123 kilometre, US$2.3 billion Guangzhou–Shenzhen superhighway and four other toll road projects in the Pearl River Delta region. New World Development and its affiliates have infrastructure projects across the mainland, including roads and bridges in Guangdong, Guangxi, Hubei, and Shanxi provinces, as well as in Tianjin; power plants in Guangdong and Sichuan provinces; and water plants in Guangdong, Hebei, Henan, Jiangxi, Jilin, Liaoning, Shandong, and Zhejiang provinces, and Shanghai. The Hutchison group has invested in ports and related services in Shanghai, Ningbo, and several South China locations, including Yantian and Zhuhai, as well as power plants in Henan, Jilin, and Guangdong provinces, and highways and bridges in Henan, Hunan, and Guangdong provinces. The Shui On Group and its affiliates have assumed a leading role in urban redevelopment in the mainand and are developing a 52-hectare project in downtown Shanghai, as well as projects in the urban centres of Hangzhou and Chongqing.

Hong Kong also acts as a business and financial service hub for China. While traditionally these services were provided within Hong Kong, the geographic scope of services provision by Hong Kong firms is radiating outwards. In the 1980s and 1990s much of the investment by Hong Kong firms in the Chinese mainland was in manufacturing, often by smaller investors. Since 2000, private Hong Kong-based investment has been expanding rapidly into services, retail, wholesale and distribution, and logistics and transportation. China is liberalising access to these sectors by Hong Kong service providers pursuant to the Closer Economic Partnership Arrangement (CEPA) between China and Hong Kong. Many Hong Kong law, accountancy, and consulting firms have office networks across mainland China that are set to expand substantially under CEPA.

Hong Kong's clusters

Hong Kong is the home of a number of dynamic clusters – groups of industries that are related to each other, that draw upon common skill bases or inputs, and reinforce each others' competitive positions through dynamic interaction.[22] This is particularly true in industries or activities that bundle, integrate, or package different aspects to create unique combinations. Among Hong Kong's leading clusters are the property, infrastructure, and development cluster; the financial and business services cluster; the transport and logistics cluster; the light manufacturing and trading cluster; and the tourism cluster (see Figure 2.1). In each case, several related businesses in which Hong Kong is world class feed off each other and contribute to each other's advantage.[23]

Financial and business services cluster

Hong Kong's extensive financial and business services cluster is unique in Asia for its breadth, depth, sophistication, and mix of international and local firms. This cluster includes private banking, fund management, corporate finance, currency trading, insurance, venture capital finance, direct corporate investment, and stock broking, as well as business services such as law, accounting, management consulting, executive search, public relations, advertising, and communications and IT support.

Hong Kong, one of the world's major international financial centres, has one of the most liberal and liquid securities markets anywhere. As of June

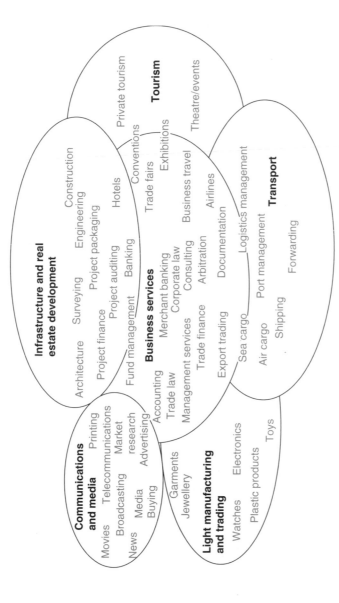

Figure 2.1 Localised industries in Hong Kong

Source: Enright, Scott, and Dodwell 1997, p. 107

2003, the Hong Kong Stock Exchange, with 824 listed companies, had the ninth-largest capitalisation worldwide (US$501 billion) and the second largest in Asia after Tokyo.[24] At the same time, the Growth Enterprise Market (GEM), established in November 1999 on the NASDAQ model, had a market capitalisation of US$7.82 billion, with 175 listed companies. The Hong Kong stock market offers international investors greater depth and liquidity than any other Asian market outside Japan.

In 2003, Hong Kong's banking system ranked third in Asia by volume of external transactions.[25] In that year, a large majority of the world's biggest banks – 73 out of the world's top 100 – were present in Hong Kong.[26] Hong Kong also was Asia's leading centre, after Japan, for the syndication of bank loans and debt issues. As of June 2003, Hong Kong accounted for 29% of the Asian syndicated loan market, excluding Japan.[27] Hong Kong was also Asia's leading centre, after Japan, for raising venture capital, with total assets under management of more than US$26 billion as of year end 2001.[28] According to the Bank for International Settlements, in 2001, Hong Kong's foreign exchange market ranked seventh in the world and its international derivatives market ranked eighth in the world.[29]

Since 1979, Hong Kong has established itself as the major financial intermediary for transactions involving the Chinese mainland, and as the leading centre for raising foreign funds for it. As of July 2003, 81 China-incorporated enterprises ('H-shares'), 73 China-affiliated enterprises ('red chips'), and 88 other Chinese enterprises incorporated outside the Chinese mainland were listed in Hong Kong. From 1986 to July 2003, the 'red chip' and 'H-share' firms had raised over US$100 billion on the Hong Kong market. Total initial public offering (IPO) funds raised by Chinese mainland enterprises accounted for 84% of the funds raised on the Hong Kong Stock Exchange in the first seven months of 2003.[30] Major IPOs of mainland firms in Hong Kong have included Beijing Datang Power Generation Co Ltd, Beijing Enterprises Holdings, BOC Hong Kong, China Petroleum & Chemical Corporation, China Telecom Corporation Ltd and China Telecom (HK) Ltd, China Unicom Ltd, CNOOC Ltd, Jiangsu Expressway Co Ltd, PetroChina Co Ltd, PICC Property and Casualty Co Ltd, and Zhejiang Expressway Co Ltd.

Hong Kong has become a leading hub for business services, including law, accountancy, advertising, engineering, and consulting.[31] Business services generated an estimated 4.5% of Hong Kong's GDP in 2002 and that year the sector employed 201,994 people.[32] In terms of Hong Kong's competitive positioning, the breadth of services offered by this sector matters as much as its size. The complete menu of world-class business services readily available in Hong Kong is an advantage compared with most other cities in Asia and on the mainland.[33] Hong Kong's advanced judicial, legal, and regulatory systems have underpinned its strengths as a services platform. As a result, Hong Kong-based professional service providers have been uniquely equipped to design, protect, and implement sophisticated business strategies for their clients, strategies that often span the Chinese mainland and the larger Asia Pacific region.[34] Hong Kong also has had particular advantages with respect to services for small businesses due to the ease of outsourcing activities to independent service providers, and for business on the Chinese mainland due to the high concentration of mainland-related expertise across a wide range of professions. In addition to China-related expertise, Hong Kong's international legal and accounting communities have offered world-class expertise in tax strategy and advice, international tax laws and treaties, shelf and offshore companies, corporate formation, and corporate structuring.

Infrastructure and real estate development cluster

Hong Kong's infrastructure and real estate development cluster links property development and construction groups with engineers, architects, surveyors, and interior designers. In mid-2003, Hong Kong had around 432 firms engaged in a wide range of engineering and technical services, more than 400 firms active in real estate surveying, valuation, and consultancy, and more than 200 architectural design firms, with these three sectors as a whole employing almost 20,000 persons.[35]

In the mid-1990s, very large investments in infrastructure and real estate throughout the Asia Pacific region were being made and coordinated from Hong Kong. Region-wide investment by Hong Kong-based firms experienced a downturn with the onset of the Asian Crisis. Between 1998 and 2004, some Hong Kong firms, such as Hopewell Holdings, pulled back from large infrastructure projects in South-east Asian countries including Indonesia and Thailand, while pursuing investments on the Chinese mainland. Other Hong Kong firms have maintained a pan-Asian focus despite the regional downturn, such as Hutchinson Whampoa's Hutchison Port Holdings, which has expanded its presence in port operations throughout the Asia Pacific.

Hong Kong's property and infrastructure companies are very significant developers on the Chinese mainland, involved in projects ranging from hotels and shopping complexes to housing projects and port construction. Hong Kong's property and construction firms have brought Hong Kong contractors and architects with them throughout the Chinese mainland. As a result, Hong Kong contractors have two decades of experience in operating on the mainland. Many Hong Kong contractors have acquired licences issued by China's Ministry of Construction. As of 2004, activities by Hong Kong contractors in the mainland were expected to expand in the future under the CEPA, which permits Hong Kong construction firms to set up wholly owned operations in the mainland subject to licensing requirements.

Transport and logistics cluster

Hong Kong has an extensive transport and logistics cluster, comprising air cargo, sea cargo, tourism, freight forwarders, and logistics-related services. In 2002, Hong Kong's sea port was the world's busiest container port, handling approximately 19.1 million TEUs (20-foot equivalent container units, a measure of container throughput), up more than 7% from the year before, and more than triple its throughput in 1991.[36] Hong Kong International Airport (HKIA) was the busiest in the world in international air cargo throughput in 2002. In that year, Hong Kong International Airport handled 33.45 million passengers, up 4.4% from 2001, and 2.48 million tonnes of cargo, up 19.5% from 2001.[37]

Hong Kong is home to one of the world's largest and most technologically sophisticated community of sourcing companies, freight forwarders, and trade financiers. Members of the Hong Kong Shipowners' Association control a significant portion of the world's cargo fleet. Service providers in this cluster also include banks, maritime lawyers, adjusters, shipbrokers, shipbuilders, insurers, and surveyors. Hong Kong firms have substantial expertise in trade documentation, trade finance, and associated communications.

Both the air and sea cargo sectors derive advantage from Hong Kong's specialised pool of legal expertise in the area of air and maritime regulations and dispute resolution (Hong Kong is an international arbitration centre for maritime disputes), as well as financial expertise in supplying finance and insurance for air and sea cargo. Hong Kong's logistics services also provide specialised support. Hong Kong's advanced communications infrastructure is another important source of advantage for the transport and logistics cluster, because shippers and customers often want up-to-the-minute information on the whereabouts and arrival times of aircraft and ships.

Light manufacturing and trading cluster

Hong Kong's light manufacturing and trading cluster comprises the four largest manufacturing industries in Hong Kong by domestic export value – clothing, electronics, textiles, and jewellery – as well as watches and clocks, plastics, toys, footwear, and other consumer goods. This cluster derives powerful advantage from its critical mass. In 2003, Hong Kong was headquarters to numerous garment, electronics, watches, jewellery, and toy manufacturers, as well as more than 100,000 export trading firms.[38] In 2002, the import–export trading sector alone employed almost 500,000 people out of a workforce of 3.49 million.[39] The manufacturing, trading, and logistical expertise of these firms has reinforced itself in a virtuous circle. However, this cluster has been built more around activities or functions, such as organising the production chain, designing fashion-sensitive goods, and packaging and integrating inputs and components, than around specific product lines or even industries per se. What has linked together, and generated the extraordinary dynamism of Hong Kong's light manufacturing clusters, is not so much industry-specific investments or positioning, but the ability to develop supplier and customer relationships, as well as the common ability to manage a particular type of operation. What might look like opportunism and improvisation, hopping from industry to industry, in individual cases is, in the aggregate, the developing of a set of skills that can be applied within and across industries and, when viewed across the economy as a whole, reveals a meaningful pattern of competitive advantage.

In many light manufacturing sectors (for example, electronic goods and electrical appliances, garments and accessories, watches and clocks, jewellery, travel goods, and toys and games) Hong Kong firms have developed sources of cost-sensitive mass production and assembly activities on the Chinese mainland and elsewhere in Asia, transforming themselves into 'trading' companies specialising in a complex of knowledge-intensive creative activities along the length of the manufacturing value chain. This is not a traditional 'middle person' function of the stereotypical trader or intermediary. It is part of a far more complex set of functions that allow the Hong Kong firms to add value through their knowledge of source and destination markets, through their familiarity with production capabilities of literally thousands of factories scattered throughout Asia, through advanced capabilities in logistics, and through expertise in managing subcontractors.

The skills set typical of the Hong Kong light manufacturing and trading cluster includes the ability to organise flexible and efficient production, based on a preponderance of small- and medium-sized firms linked by efficient sub-contracting networks. It includes strong interpretative design skills; that is, the ability to interpret and anticipate consumer trends in major foreign markets, and world-class packaging and integrating skills; the ability to integrate far-flung sources of demand and supply worldwide into successful consumer products; and to create logistical solutions to sourcing, production, and distribution needs.

Tourism and travel cluster

Another cluster of importance in the Hong Kong economy is centred on tourism, the hotel industry, and a range of tourism-oriented services like retailing and restaurants. Tourism earnings were estimated at US$9.9 billion in 2002, or 6.1% of GDP, making Hong Kong the world's ninth-leading tourism destination by receipts.[40] In 2002, Hong Kong visitor arrivals reached an all-time high of nearly 16.6 million, second in Asia only to the PRC.[41] Between January and April 2003, as a result of the SARS health crisis, monthly visitor inflows to Hong Kong fell by nearly 75% on a year-on-year basis. Once SARS came under control, the rebound was almost as swift as the downturn. Monthly visitor arrivals returned close to 2002 levels as early as July 2003. Hong Kong visitor arrivals reached 21.8 million in 2004, surpassing the record set in 2002.[42]

Hong Kong's position as a major exhibition and convention centre has generated substantial tourism revenue. In 2002, Hong Kong was host to around 70 major trade fairs attended by 350,000 buyers from around the world.[43] The Summer Sourcing Show for Gifts, Houseware and Toys organised by the Hong Kong Trade Development Council (TDC) in July 2003 registered the highest attendance ever for a TDC-sponsored trade show, as overseas buyers and sellers returned to Hong Kong to transact deferred business and pushed ahead with their trading cycles. The tourism industry also has included related industries such as hotels and retail trade. Hong Kong is a leading centre for hotel management.

In the early 2000s, Hong Kong was becoming increasingly popular among visitors from the Chinese mainland as a holiday and shopping destination, especially for gold and other jewellery items, Chinese and Western pharmaceuticals, consumer electronics, cosmetics, and fashion. Mainland visits to Hong Kong climbed almost 45% in 2004 over 2003, to 12.24 million, under the mainland's liberalised regime for mainland visits to Hong Kong on individual travel visas (see Chapter 4). The Walt Disney Company's launch of a Disneyland theme park on Hong Kong's Lantau Island, scheduled for 2005, is likely to boost mainland visitor arrivals in 2005 and thereafter.

Communications and media cluster

Hong Kong is the leading centre for international telecommunications in the Asia Pacific. Due to superior marine cable and satellite access, Hong Kong has more international call capacity than Australia or Japan, largely because of immense private-sector investment in land lines to China, submarine cables, and communications satellites.[44] Hong Kong is Asia's optical fibre hub, giving it huge regional advantages in terms of capacity, and is also a major hub for regional and mainland Internet connections, and teleconferencing and hosting services. Deregulation of Hong Kong's telecommunications sector has resulted in broadband and mobile communications costs that are among the lowest in the world.[45]

Hong Kong is a leading centre for the media as well. It is the home of the regional headquarters of many international news and information organisations, as well as a centre for broadcasting, printing, and publishing. In 2003, around 100 international media organisations had offices in the Hong Kong Special Administrative region (HKSAR). International newspapers that printed editions in Hong Kong included the *Financial Times*, *International Herald Tribune*, and *USA Today*.[46] Hong Kong has also been a leading centre for motion picture production and distribution. As of 2004, Hong Kong was considered the capital of Asia's advertising industry, and was also a major regional centre for market research and intelligence.

Links among Hong Kong's clusters

One of the interesting aspects of Hong Kong's clusters is the extent to which they interact. The points of greatest overlap between Hong Kong's largest clusters tend to be sectors of the economy with very strong competitive positions in the relevant international markets. In trading, Hong Kong firms take advantage of the transportation and logistics cluster, the financial and business services cluster, and the light manufacturing cluster. The fact that Hong Kong is strong in all three clusters greatly strengthens the position of the Hong Kong traders. Trade finance is another activity that draws upon all three of the leading clusters. Tourism, particularly related to travel involving business or shopping or conventions, would be another. Again the interactions and intersections among Hong Kong's clusters provide substantial sources of competitive strength and make the individual industries more robust than they would be otherwise.

ECONOMIC DECISION-MAKING IN HONG KONG

The most salient feature of Hong Kong's economy is its traditional market orientation. Hong Kong has repeatedly topped lists of the world's freest economies put together by organisations such as the United States' Heritage Foundation and

Canada's Fraser Institute.[47] Hong Kong has prided itself on its low tax rates, light-handed regulation, and entrepreneurial culture. In addition, many of the activities typically taken on by governments in other jurisdictions, such as container ports and tunnels, are taken on by the private sector. Hong Kong's system, in which government generally acts as a neutral party that sets and enforces rules of the economic game comparable with those in many other advanced economies, has been one of its critical strengths. For most types of economic decisions, Hong Kong relies on private actors operating within a framework set by government policy.[48]

Hong Kong was returned to Chinese administration on 1 July 1997 when Hong Kong became a Special Administrative Region of the PRC. Under this arrangement, Hong Kong is to be administered according to the principles set out in the Sino–British Joint Declaration of 1984. This agreement formed the basis for the 'Basic Law of the Hong Kong Special Administrative Region of the People's Republic of China', which lays out the parameters by which Hong Kong is to be governed after its return to the mainland. Aside from foreign affairs and defence, the provisions of the Basic Law give Hong Kong autonomy over its own affairs.[49] It provides a framework, within the 'one country, two systems' parameters, for the protection of individual rights and freedoms, as well as for increasing democratisation and moving towards direct elections. However, its provisions on Hong Kong's electoral framework do not extend beyond 2007, or 10 years beyond the hand over. Though the expectation at the time of drafting was that Hong Kong would embrace a system of direct, universal suffrage, no timetable or mechanisms were prescribed.

According to Hong Kong's Basic Law, most governmental power lies in the office of the Chief Executive. This mirrored the situation in the British colonial administration in which the Governor exercised executive and administrative authority. Historically, the Governor was supported by a politically neutral civil service, which over the years had taken on a major role in generating policy options and deciding policy issues.[50] As of 1 July 1997, Hong Kong's Chief Executive was at the top of a similar system. This system was replaced in July 2002 by a ministerial system in which ministers appointed by the Chief Executive share responsibility for decisions and are responsible for particular portfolios. Although Hong Kong's Legislative Council has certain powers in economic affairs, such as the right to approve or disapprove the government expenditures, in reality its lack of power means that it tends only to react to initiatives from the government or from the general public.[51] As a result, the civil service policy bureau and departments retain substantial power to shape governmental options and agendas. They are supported by a series of advisory committees and commissions, mostly staffed with people from the private sector and other groups on a pro-bono basis with government officials participating in an ex-officio manner.

Once policies are generated in Hong Kong, there often is a lengthy consultation process in which the government solicits views from members of the public on specific initiatives. The tradition of consultation was initiated by the colonial administration as a means of vetting initiatives that were generated by a non-representative government. The process has evolved into one that tries to take various views into account and to build acquiescence, if not support, for government initiatives. The result is an often complex process that can result in decisions being drawn out as special interests either are accommodated or attempts are made to use political influence to delay or reverse unpopular decisions. Once decisions are made, bureaucratic inertia can make it difficult to change tack, even when circumstances change. This is particularly true in infrastructure planning and land usage, where it can take years for changes to be made, and where numerous departments and bureaus can be involved in a single decision.[52]

Hong Kong's complex decision-making process has caused some frustration in its relations with counterparts in the Chinese mainland. The governmental decision process, with the accompanying consultation, can be complex and lengthy. With respect to business matters, the emphasis on private-sector decision-making in Hong Kong means that the Hong Kong government cannot commit local companies to act and does not have the ability to bring the 'Hong Kong private sector' to the table in the same way that Chinese mainland jurisdictions can.[53]

HONG KONG'S ECONOMY

Hong Kong has evolved into a modern management, coordination, and financial centre for local and overseas companies. Local firms have branched out from Hong Kong to play major roles in the Chinese mainland and the rest of Asia. Foreign multinationals use Hong Kong as a service centre, as well as a centre to manage and coordinate their activities in the Asia Pacific region. The dominance of services and the knowledge-intensive portions of the manufacturing value-added chain in Hong Kong reinforces the mutual dependence between services and manufacturing. The division of labour between Hong Kong and the Chinese mainland results in Hong Kong companies coordinating and providing support services to manufacturing production undertaken across the border. Taken together, these facts underline Hong Kong's

economic roles, roles that have much in common, not just with other metropolitan economies, but with major international centres such as London,
New York, and Tokyo.[54] However, it is the interaction with its hinterland in
the Pearl River Delta region of Guangdong Province that is the focal point of
this book and it is to this part of China that we next turn.

CHAPTER THREE

The Economic Development of the Pearl River Delta Region[1]

T he Pearl River Delta region of Guangdong Province has been the most dynamic economic region in the PRC since the onset of China's reform program in 1979. Since then, the region has become a leader in terms of development, exports, and attracting foreign investment. It developed from a backward agricultural economy, to a domestic manufacturing centre, to an export-oriented production platform of global importance. In the process, it has developed into a sizeable industrial and consumer market. The importance of the Pearl River Delta region to China goes well beyond its own economic performance. As the vanguard of reform in China, it has served as a test bed for reform and has provided numerous lessons for other jurisdictions in China.

HISTORICAL DEVELOPMENT[2]

The development of the Pearl River Delta region, and Guangdong Province as a whole, took a marked turn with China's economic opening and reform program. Before the economic reform program in 1979, the Pearl River Delta region, and Guangdong Province as a whole, was not very important in China's overall economy. Guangdong's geographic position as a peripheral province on the southern coast meant that it was far from China's industrial heartland. Guangdong's lack of natural resources limited the ability of the province to contribute to the development of heavy industries, which were the focal points of China's five-year plans in the 1950s, 1960s, and 1970s. The lack of convenient transportation links with the rest of China also hindered Guangdong's development, as did an emphasis on the development of industrial facilities in the interior of China. All of these compounded Guangdong's historical position as something of an agricultural backwater.[3]

As Table 3.1 indicates, Guangdong accounted for around 5% of the PRC in terms of population and most economic aggregates. Guangdong lagged behind in terms of gross industrial output, capital construction, and investments in innovation. The most outstanding feature of the Guangdong economy was its relatively high share (7.7%) of China's trade. Much of this was due to Guangdong's proximity to Hong Kong and the fact that the province exported agricultural produce to Hong Kong.

Vanguard of reform

China's economic reform program placed Guangdong Province in the vanguard of reform. Guangdong was chosen for special treatment due to its proximity to Hong Kong and Macao, its distance from the heartland of the Chinese mainland, and the fact that it was lagging behind other provinces in the Chinese mainland in economic terms.[4] In 1979, the Central Government announced that Guangdong and Fujian provinces would be allowed to follow less restrictive economic policies and would be allowed to create Special Economic Zones (SEZs) in Shenzhen, Zhuhai, Shantou, and Xiamen.[5] The Special Economic Zones were formalised in a set of regulations promulgated in 1980. The Shenzhen SEZ comprised an area of 327.5 square kilometres just north of Hong Kong. The Zhuhai SEZ, initially only 6.81 square kilometres adjacent to Macao, was eventually expanded to 121 square kilometres. Preferential policies in the SEZs included a 15% corporate tax rate, tax holidays of up to five years, the ability to repatriate corporate profits, the ability to repatriate capital investments after a contracted period, duty-free imports on raw materials and intermediate goods destined for exported products, no export taxes, and a limited ability to sell into the domestic market.[6]

The SEZs also were given greater political and economic autonomy than other jurisdictions in the Chinese mainland. The main areas of greater autonomy were finance and fiscal matters, foreign trade and investment, commerce

Table 3.1   Major indicators of Guangdong's economic development in 1978

Indicator	Guangdong	National total	Proportion of Guangdong in the PRC (%)
Population (million persons)	50.64	962.59	5.3
Employment (million persons)			
– Employment	22.76	401.52	5.7
– Staff and workers	5.16	94.99	5.4
National accounting at current prices (RMB billion)			
– GDP	18.59	362.41	5.1
– Primary industry	5.53	101.84	5.4
– Secondary industry	8.66	174.52	5.0
– Tertiary industry	4.39	86.05	5.1
Investment in fixed assets (RMB billion)			
– Capital construction	1.79	50.10	3.6
– Investment in innovation	0.22	16.77	1.3
Government revenue (RMB billion)	3.95	95.65	4.1
Government expenditures (RMB billion)	2.70	59.00	4.6
Gross output value of agriculture at current price (RMB billion)	8.59	139.70	6.1
Gross output value of industry at current price (RMB billion)	20.03	423.70	4.7
Total retail sales of consumer goods (US$ billion)	7.72	126.49	6.1
Total value of imports and exports (US$ billion)	1.59	20.64	7.7

Source: Guangdong Provincial People's Government, Development Research Centre 1998

and distribution, allocation of materials and resources, the labour system, and prices. Guangdong was allowed to keep a larger share of its output and foreign exchange than other provinces, and it was required to be self-sufficient in terms of capital investment. The province was given greater control over economic planning, approval of foreign investments, and foreign trade. Guangdong also took over control of several state-owned enterprises located in the province. After Deng Xiaoping's southern tour of 1984, Guangzhou, along with 13 other coastal cities, was given greater autonomy in foreign trade and investment. In 1988, Guangdong asked for, and received, expanded powers to set its own economic direction and designation as a 'comprehensive economic reform area' (*zonghe jingji gaige qu*). Included in these policies were the privatisation of some housing, the development of a land lease system, the creation of the Guangdong Development Bank, and the creation of the Shenzhen Stock Exchange. A second southern tour by Deng Xiaoping in 1992 reaffirmed Guangdong's role as a leader in China's economic reform process.[7] Deng suggested that the province accelerate its reforms in order to catch up with other developing Asian economies.[8]

The local governments in Guangdong took advantage of their greater autonomy to run a number of experiments that were eventually repeated elsewhere. Control over trade was devolved to local levels, control over land was devolved to local communities or households, prices were freed, toll roads were built, and bonds issued. By allowing foreign banks to operate, Shenzhen became a leader in terms of foreign exchange markets. Shenzhen also took the lead in terms of land reform and stock market development. While the Central Government initiated and encouraged reform, entrepreneurial local governments have been credited with accelerating the reform process in the Pearl River Delta region.

Despite a consistent direction of reform, the process has been anything but smooth. There have been several cycles of reform and retrenchment in the Pearl River Delta region since 1979, mostly due to local abuses and changes in national government policy. Gradually, preferential policies have spread to other parts of the Chinese mainland, reducing Guangdong's policy advantages. However, Guangdong's early experience with reform has allowed a market-oriented culture to develop earlier than in other places in the Chinese mainland and has allowed the province to develop a variety of mechanisms to deal with greater opportunity and greater competition.[9]

Economic development

The economic development of Guangdong Province took off after the reform program was instituted. Most of this development took place in the Pearl River Delta region, the area immediately north of Hong Kong and Macao and surrounding the Pearl River. From 1979 to 1984, the industrial development of the Pearl River Delta region was mainly geared towards the domestic market. Years of a command economy had left enormous pent-up demand for a wide range of consumer products, particularly for light-manufactured goods. Much of the development in the region took place in Guangzhou and in nearby areas, such as Foshan, Nanhai, and Shunde. Goods from the Pearl River Delta region, such as drinks, packaged foods, clothes, and appliances, began to penetrate mainland Chinese markets. Retailers from as far away as North-east China and Inner

Mongolia would drive their cars to the Pearl River Delta region in order to buy goods in bulk.

Export processing began to develop in the late 1970s in the eastern part of the Pearl River Delta region and accelerated substantially in the late 1980s when the Chinese Government relaxed restrictions on FDI. The eastern part of the Delta soon became a manufacturing powerhouse, which became largely responsible for China's emergence on export markets. The western part of the region also began to export, particularly in home appliances, though the western part of the region remained primarily focused on the domestic market. A study by the Guangdong Economic and Trade Commission in April 1997 found that 25.3% of the sales of Guangdong's products were inside Guangdong Province, while 43% of the sales were to other provinces in the Chinese mainland, and 31.7% were to other countries or regions.[10] As other areas of the Chinese mainland opened up, however, the growth of sales of Pearl River Delta-based facilities in other provinces slowed.

The GDP of the Pearl River Delta region grew from just under RMB 12 billion (US$8.0 billion) in 1980 to over RMB 941 billion (US$113.6 billion) in the year 2002 (see Table 3.2 for a summary of the major economic indicators of the Pearl River Delta). During that period, the average real rate of GDP growth in the Pearl River Delta region was 16.1% per year, well above that of Guangdong

Table 3.2 Pearl River Delta region major economic indicators (at current prices)

Indicator	1980	1985	1990	1995	2000	2001	2002
Registered population (million persons)	16.27	17.57	19.28	21.38	23.07	23.37	23.65
GDP (RMB billion)	11.92	30.39	87.22	389.97	737.86	836.39	941.88
Primary industry (RMB billion)	3.07	5.73	12.94	31.49	42.85	44.52	46.50
Secondary industry (RMB billion)	5.40	14.87	40.46	195.71	365.73	413.90	468.81
Tertiary industry (RMB billion)	3.45	9.79	33.82	162.77	329.29	377.98	426.56
Total amount of investment in fixed assets (RMB billion)	1.66	12.84	23.14	149.10	229.16	256.68	288.66
Total amount of retail sales of consumer goods (RMB billion)	7.07	19.80	44.57	154.47	278.14	312.01	348.13
Total amount of exports (US$ billion)	0.62	1.63	8.14	46.11	84.74	90.83	112.61
Amount of foreign capital actually utilised (US$ billion)	0.10	0.74	1.54	8.58	12.54	14.19	15.02
Government revenue (RMB billion)	2.34	4.99	9.59	31.53	59.91	74.57	76.87
Government expenditure (RMB billion)	0.82	2.61	7.64	31.66	68.54	82.27	96.36
Savings deposits by urban and rural residents at year-end (RMB billion)	2.10	11.20	55.27	281.04	664.10	767.06	924.02

Sources: Guangdong Provincial Statistics Bureau 1995; and China Statistics Press (*Guangdong Statistical Yearbook 2001, 2002,* and *2003*)

Table 3.3   The relative importance of the Pearl River Delta region in Guangdong Province and in the PRC, 1980–2002

Year	PRD proportion of the Guangdong total (%)			PRD proportion of the PRC total (%)		
	GDP	Exports	Realised foreign capital	GDP	Exports	Realised foreign capital
1980	47.7	28.4*	47.2	2.6	3.4	3.3*
1985	52.6	55.2*	70.4*	3.4	6.0	16.5
1990	55.9	76.7*	76.0	4.7	13.0*	14.9
1995	68.0	81.5	70.9	6.7	31.0	17.8
2000	76.4	92.2	86.0	8.2	34.0	21.1
2001	78.6	95.2	90.1	8.7	34.1	28.6
2002	80.0	95.1	90.5	9.0	38.2	27.3

Sources: *The Centre for Urban and Regional Studies 2002a, pp. 1 and 34. All other data are taken from *Guangdong Statistical Yearbook 2001*, pp. 538 and 626; *Guangdong Statistical Yearbook 2002*, pp. 30 and 410; and *China Statistical Yearbook 2001*, pp. 586 and 599

Province (13.4%), and the PRC as a whole (9.5%). In 1980, the Pearl River Delta region accounted for 47.7% of Guangdong's GDP and 2.6% of the Chinese mainland's GDP. By 2002, the Pearl River Delta region's share had grown to 80% of Guangdong's GDP and 9% of the Chinese mainland's GDP. Similarly, in 1980, the Pearl River Delta region provided 3.4% of the Chinese mainland's exports and 3.3% of realised inward investment. By 2002, the Pearl River Delta region accounted for 38.2% of the Chinese mainland's exports and 22% of the realised foreign capital in the mainland, despite having only 3.2% of the mainland's population (see Table 3.3). Over the entire period from 1980 to 2002, the Pearl River Delta region was the fastest growing portion of the fastest growing province in the fastest growing large economy in the world.[11]

Composition of economy

The composition of the Pearl River Delta region's economy has changed substantially since China's reform program. In 1978, the relative proportions of agriculture, industry, and services in the Pearl River Delta region economy were 30%, 47%, and 23%. By 2000, the figures were 6%, 50%, and 45%, respectively.[12] Ownership also has been evolving. In 1978, state-operated and collective enterprises respectively accounted for 64% and 36% of the total gross industrial output in the region. By 1991, state-operated enterprises and collective enterprises accounted for 31% and 33% of Pearl River Delta region enterprises. By 2000, the figures were 7% and 10% for wholly owned state and collective enterprises, though enterprises with some kind of state-owned or state-controlled shareholding amounted to 23% of the region's enterprises. Firms with investments from Hong Kong, Macao, and Taiwan ranked first in importance in the region followed by those with investments from non-Chinese locations.[13]

As Jiang Zemin proposed in his 'Three Represents' (a guiding policy whereby the Communist Party should represent advanced production systems, advanced culture, and the best interests of the people of China), the development environment for privately owned enterprises has been greatly relaxed in China. Many enterprises, which once were listed as collectives, have been revealing their privately owned status, especially in the Pearl River Delta region. In this regard, Shenzhen, Dongguan, Nanhai, and other portions of the region have been at the forefront in China.[14] It is foreseeable that privately owned enterprises will play an even more important role in the economy of the Pearl River Delta region in future.

The composition of trade of the Pearl River Delta region has also changed substantially over time. In 1980, for example, agricultural products accounted for nearly 40% of the region's exports. Manufactured goods, mainly low value-added textile, garment, and other light-industrial products, accounted for some 60%. By 1999, manufactured goods accounted for 96.1% of the Pearl River Delta region's exports, and primary goods only around 4%. Electronics, electrical goods, and machinery accounted for 49.7% of total exports. Nearly half of this portion consisted of electrical equipment and machinery, television sets, and audio-visual apparatus. The aggregate composition of the Pearl River Delta region's imports remained roughly similar over the period. Primary goods accounted for 8.5% of imports in 1990 and 10.3% of imports in 1999. Manufactured goods accounted for 91.5% of the region's imports in 1990 and 89.7% of its imports in 1999.[15]

Industrial and consumer markets

As one of the most dynamic economic regions in the Chinese mainland, the Pearl River Delta region is increasingly important as a market. The region is clearly important as an industrial market for all sorts of inputs, materials, and capital goods. It is also a major market for transportation and trade-related services. Rapid urbanisation in the Pearl River Delta region has created demand for infrastructure, building materials, transportation services, housing, and other goods and services associated with urban development.[16]

Increasingly, the region is becoming an attractive consumer market as well. According to the 2000 National Census, the Pearl River Delta Economic Zone had a population of 40.8 million people. This contrasts with the official

Table 3.4   Living standards of local residents in major cities of the Pearl River Delta, 2002, RMB

City	Disposable income	Annual consumption per capita	Food consumption expenditure/total consumption expenditure (%)	Annual accommodation expenses (including rent and utilities)
Shenzhen	24,941	18,926	27.4	2,606
Dongguan	16,949	15,157	31.8	1,060
Zhuhai	15,320	11,988	36.9	1,403
Guangzhou	13,380	10,672	41.0	981
Foshan	**13,582**	**10,937**	**33.9**	**1,554**
Zhongshan	14,208	10,989	39.4	1,022
Huizhou	10,691	8,603	39.2	977

Note: Figures for urban households only except in the case of Foshan. The Foshan figures (in bold) include urban and rural households.
Sources: *Shenzhen Statistical Yearbook 2003, Dongguan Statistical Yearbook 2003, Zhuhai Statistical Yearbook 2003, Guangzhou Statistical Yearbook 2003, Foshan Statistical Yearbook 2003, Zhongshan Statistical Yearbook 2003, Huizhou Statistical Yearbook 2003*, and Jiangmen Statistical Bureau, 2003, pp. 128–130

registered population of 23.6 million that was recorded for the region in 2002.[17] As a result of this difference, actual per capita income (using the Census figures) for the region was RMB 18,098 (US$2,186 at the exchange rate of RMB 8.28 to US$1), as opposed to the 'official' figure of RMB 31,983 (US$3,863). Regardless of the figure used, per capita income has been growing substantially in recent years, as have consumer expenditures.

A survey by the Guangdong Provincial Statistical Bureau shows that residents in eight cities in the Pearl River Delta region (Shenzhen, Dongguan, Zhuhai, Shunde, Guangzhou, Foshan, Zhongshan, and Huizhou) are at the stage of 'relatively comfortable living standards'. Average per capita consumption expenditures surpassed RMB 10,000 (US$1,208) in six cities in 2002 (see Table 3.4). In one measure of consumption, the number of registered cars per 100 households in 2001 was Dongguan (16), Shunde (14), Shenzhen (14.5), and Zhongshan (10).[18]

JURISDICTIONS IN THE PEARL RIVER DELTA REGION

Since 1979, there have been tremendous advances in the economy of the Pearl River Delta region. Different parts of the region, however, have emerged as leaders in different categories of economic activity as can be seen in Tables 3.5 and 3.6.

Table 3.5 Selected economic statistics, Pearl River Delta region cities, 2002

City	Census population 2000 (000)	GDP (RMB billion)	GDP in industry (RMB billion)	GDP in services (RMB billion)	Retail sales (RMB billion)	Utilised FDI (US$ million)	Exports (US$ billion)
Guangzhou	9,943	300.15	106.90	167.13	137.07	2,284	13.78
Shenzhen	7,008	225.68	107.66	100.31	68.96	3,191	46.56
Zhuhai	1,236	40.63	18.97	16.60	14.35	698	5.20
Huizhou	3,216	52.52	28.16	14.90	16.10	1,082	5.89
Dongguan	6,446	67.29	34.66	27.28	22.50	1,459	23.74
Zhongshan	2,364	41.57	22.68	14.32	13.43	639	5.73
Jiangmen	3,950	66.08	31.02	27.09	24.84	735	2.95
Foshan	5,338	117.59	59.54	47.80	41.98	984	7.89
Shunde	N/A	43.73	23.25	17.23	12.67	240	4.05
Zhaoqing	3,371	45.02	15.17	15.84	15.46	546	0.90

Sources: *Guangdong Statistical Yearbook 2003*; and Jiangmen Statistical Bureau 2003, pp. 12–13, 16–17, 96–97, 112–113, and 120–121

The Eastern and Central Delta

The eastern and central portions of the Pearl River Delta are the most familiar to international businesspeople and researchers. Building from close links with Hong Kong, this part of the region was largely responsible for China's emergence into international markets in the 1980s and early 1990s. The eastern and central Delta cities of Shenzhen, Dongguan, and Guangzhou became first the sites of export-oriented production in relatively simple light manufacturers, such as garments and footwear, before expanding into electrical and electronics products. The eastern cities of Shenzhen and Dongguan ranked first and third as exporters among the cities of the Chinese mainland in 2002. Meanwhile, Guangzhou, the capital of Guangdong Province, had by far the most diversified of the economies among Pearl River Delta cities, with expanding automotive and heavy industrial sectors to go with its traditional light manufactured goods and growing service sectors.

Guangzhou

Guangzhou, located at the apex of the Pearl River Delta, is the capital of Guangdong Province, as well as the political and economic centre of the Pearl River Delta region. In the period from 1949 to 1979, Guangzhou was by far the leading city in Guangdong Province. Guangzhou, and nearby Foshan and Nanhai, were home to much of the manufacturing that existed in the province. The most significant economic function that Guangzhou played for the entire

Table 3.6   Gross industrial output, selected industries, Pearl River Delta region cities, 2002, RMB million

City	Textiles	Garments	Chemicals	Plastic products	Iron/ steel	Transport equipment	Electrical/ machinery	Electronics/ telecom equipment
Guangzhou	10,509	14,352	34,827	12,040	8,161	42,179	22,519	30,357
Shenzhen	2,655	3,851	5,006	9,756	1,225	4,125	18,385	209,607
Zhuhai	1,935	3,576	2,671	3,052	–	1,009	12,686	20,949
Huizhou	1,566	1,911	1,350	3,062	582	1,862	7,550	54,737
Dongguan	4,051	3,921	3,930	6,019	499	1,122	9,391	50,334
Zhongshan	7,864	4,725	4,718	6,181	584	472	11,623	16,695
Jiangmen	8,169	7,499	8,648	4,016	1,577	5,109	13,257	5,625
Foshan	9,824	7,847	5,756	11,174	910	4,886	51,492	15,924
Zhaoqing	3,576	3,202	2,540	966	99	851	884	6,015
Guangdong Province	65,868	65,724	82,133	64,560	20,630	64,488	154,659	416,442

Source: *Guangdong Statistical Yearbook 2003*, p. 270

PRC was related to the 'Chinese Export Commodities Fair', also known as the 'Canton Fair', which was held in Guangzhou. In the decades following 1949, this trade fair was the only real link between China's economy and that of the rest of the world. Guangzhou was chosen for this fair due to its proximity to Hong Kong, as well as its traditional role, dating back to the Qing Dynasty, as being China's only officially sanctioned trading port.[19]

In the years following China's initial opening, Guangzhou and its immediate surroundings continued to play a leadership role in traditional industries, with much of the output geared towards the domestic market. In the 1980s and 1990s, Guangzhou attracted substantial foreign investment from companies looking to serve the South China market.[20] The city also saw a large influx in investment in the real estate sector, as new office complexes were built in the city centre and residential communities were developed on its outskirts. In 2002, Guangzhou had the third-largest economy among cities in the Chinese mainland after Shanghai and Beijing. Guangzhou also had the largest population and the largest and most diversified economy of any city in the Pearl River Delta region. That year, Guangzhou led the cities of the Pearl River Delta region in population, GDP, GDP in the tertiary sector, and retail sales (see Table 3.5).[21] Although its private sector was thriving, a larger percentage of the Guangzhou economy was state-owned than is the case in most other cities in the Pearl River Delta region. In 2002, Guangzhou's retail sales exceeded those of any other city in the Pearl River Delta region by a wide margin and was driving demand for related services. In 2002, Guangzhou residents were among the most affluent urbanites in the Chinese mainland, and spending on housing and cars showed strong growth.

In 2002, Guangzhou's leading manufacturing industries by gross industrial output were transport equipment (US$5.09 billion), raw chemical materials and chemical products (US$4.21 billion), electronic and telecommunications equipment (US$3.67 billion), and electrical equipment and machinery (US$2.72 billion). Guangzhou provided a strong base for light manufactures, including garments and textiles, leather goods, and plastic products.[22] Other leading industries included shipbuilding, food processing and sugar-refinery, iron and steel production, and rubber products.

Guangzhou is the leading centre in Guangdong Province for a range of services, including software and domestically oriented logistics and distribution. In 2002, Guangzhou's foremost service sectors were transportation, storage, post and telecommunications, and wholesale and retail trade and catering services. Banking, insurance, and real estate were also significant.

Guangzhou is also a leading trade and exhibition centre. The city's Pazhou International Convention and Exhibition Centre covers an area of 10.5 square kilometres. Modern shopping centres, such as Teem Plaza in Tianhe, were likely to be replicated as the city government supported the establishment of large-scale chain store operations and themed shopping streets.[23]

Since the 1980s, Guangzhou has attracted substantial foreign investment from multinational firms seeking to serve the South China market. As of 2002, there were more than 8,700 registered multinational companies in Guangzhou. These include Alcatel, Amway, Avon, BASF, Bosch, BP, Colgate Palmolive, Compaq, DEC, Dupont, General Electric, Hitachi, Honda, IBM, ICI, Intel, Kellogg, Lotus, Lucent, Microsoft, Mitsui, Olympus, Owens Corning, Pepsico, Philips, Procter & Gamble, Ricoh, Samsung, San Miguel, Sanyo, Siemens, Toshiba, Toyota, Wrigley, and Xerox. Proctor & Gamble runs a sizeable and highly successful consumer products operation out of Guangzhou. As of 2004, Toyota was joining Honda, Nissan, and Isuzu in auto production in the city. Toyota was also investing in a large auto engine plant and Nissan's joint venture was setting up a research and development centre for passenger cars in Guangzhou.[24] Also in 2004, Japanese manufacturers, such as JFE Steel and Denso, were making sizeable investments in plants for auto-related production in galvanised steel and auto parts.

Multinationals active in Guangzhou's service sector as of 2004 included Adecco, AIA, Allianz, American Express International, Bank of America, Bax Global, Deacons, Dentsu, Deutsche Bank, DTZ Debenham Tie Leung, HSBC, Federal Express, KPMG, Marriot International, UPS, and Young and Rubican. International retailers attracted to Guangzhou by its affluent consumer base include Carrefour, Circle K, Jusco, Makro, Seven Eleven, Starbucks, Trust-mart, and Wal-Mart.[25] In 2004, Shangri-La Asia was planning a five-star hotel next to Guangzhou's Pazhou International Convention and Exhibition Centre.

In many ways, Guangzhou has been trying to re-establish its leading economic position in the Greater Pearl River Delta region including Hong Kong.[26] Substantial provincial and city funds have been invested in Guangzhou, resulting in large infrastructure projects, as well as completely new developments in Nansha, south of the urban centre, and elsewhere around the city. The successful Ninth National Games held in Guangzhou in the autumn of 2001 further strengthened Guangzhou's position as the leading city in the Pearl River Delta region and as a leading city in China. As of 2004, ambitious investments in port facilities, a new airport and train station, completely new urban districts, new industrial and science parks, a light rail system, and cultural facilities were being made in an attempt to extend this position and win selection as the venue of the 2010 Asian Games.[27]

Shenzhen

Shenzhen, the jurisdiction just north of Hong Kong, was designated as a Special Economic Zone in 1979. This designation allowed Shenzhen to enjoy preferential policies and made it relatively independent of the Guangdong provincial government, both politically and economically.[28] Shenzhen has used its status to develop a dynamic and vibrant economy that attracts workers, scientists, and engineers throughout China. It is a world-leader in the export of a wide range of electronics products, including computers, telecommunications products, and electronic components. Its residents have the highest average educational achievement in the Chinese mainland, and are highly concentrated in the wage-earning age bracket. The city's long-term residents are among the most affluent consumers in the mainland.

Shenzhen emerged rapidly in the years following 1979. Its population rose from 321,000 in 1980 to more than seven million in 2000. Most of the newcomers were immigrants from other parts of China who came to work in Shenzhen's burgeoning factories. As a result of immigration, the most common language spoken in Shenzhen is Mandarin (not Cantonese as in most of the rest of Guangdong). The portion of the population below 14 years of age and above 65 years of age is far smaller than anywhere else in Guangdong Province and in the Chinese mainland, with the exception of Dongguan, which approaches similar demographics (see Table 3.7).

In the 1980s, a large number of foreign-invested export processing enterprises were attracted to Shenzhen. In fact, over the reform period, Shenzhen has had the highest cumulative utilised foreign direct investment among Pearl River Delta region cities. The initial investments were mostly in traditional industries, such as garments, textiles, footwear, plastic products, and other labour-intensive industries. However, due to rising land and labour costs after 1990, Shenzhen began to put great emphasis on developing what it called its 'high-technology' industries, mostly the relatively simple assembly manufacturing of electronics products.[29] From 1992 to 2000, Shenzhen's output in such 'high-technology' industries grew at an annual rate of 53.2% per year, reaching almost RMB 106.5 billion (US$12.9 billion), or 42.3% of Shenzhen's total industrial output value.[30] Since 1999, Shenzhen has hosted China's annual Hi-Tech Fair, the nation's leading exhibition of electronics and related products. Shenzhen's technology-based investment initially came from Hong Kong, Taiwan, Japan, Europe, and the United States. Over time, these companies have moved more and more sophisticated activities into Shenzhen. In addition, in recent years, local companies, such as Huawei Technologies, Kingdee International Software Group, and ZTE Corporation, have become some of the leading technology-based companies in China.[31]

Table 3.7   Age distribution of populations living in major cities in Guangdong according to the Fifth National Census, 2000

Jurisdiction	Total population (000 persons)	Proportion of population aged 14 or below (%)	Proportion of population aged 65 or over (%)
Guangdong Province	86,421.7	24.17	6.06
Guangzhou	9,943.0	16.44	6.02
Shenzhen	7,008.4	8.50	1.11
Dongguan	6,445.7	8.68	2.00
Zhanjiang	6,072.9	34.72	6.98
Foshan	5,337.9	16.40	4.85
Maoming	5,239.7	36.26	7.44
Jieyang	5,237.4	34.11	6.50
Shantou	4,671.1	31.18	6.55
Jiangmen	3,950.3	22.60	8.52
Meizhou	3,802.0	30.86	9.11
Zhaoqing	3,371.4	29.59	7.67
Huizhou	3,216.3	23.13	6.10
Qingyuan	3,147.7	30.36	8.24
Shaoguan	2,735.1	25.75	7.37
Shanwei	2,453.1	37.72	5.87
Chaozhou	2,402.2	27.02	7.79
Zhongshan	2,363.5	16.15	4.54
Heyuan	2,265.2	32.19	8.66
Yangjiang	2,170.4	28.23	8.43
Yunfu	2,152.9	32.43	8.10
Zhuhai	1,235.6	17.38	3.92

Source: *Guangdong Statistical Yearbook 2001*, p. 156

In 2002, Shenzhen ranked first in exports among all cities in the Chinese mainland, was the mainland's fourth-largest city in terms of GDP. Among the cities in the Greater Pearl River Delta region, Shenzhen ranked third in GDP to Hong Kong and Guangzhou, and second to Hong Kong in total trade and utilised foreign direct investment. That year, it had the highest gross industrial output among the cities of the Greater Pearl River Delta region. One of the Chinese mainland's leading cities in high-technology industries, Shenzhen exported US$15.7 billion in such products in 2002 out of total exports of US$46.5 billion.[32] It accounted for around 20% of the Chinese mainland computer products and 15% of its semiconductor integrated circuits.[33]

In 2002, electronic and telecommunications equipment was by far the leader among Shenzhen's manufacturing industries, with gross industrial output of US$25.31 billion. Other top manufacturing industries included office equipment, instruments, and meters (US$2.22 billion); electrical equipment and machinery (US$2.22 billion); plastic products (US$1.18 billion); and metal products (US$1.09 billion).[34] Shenzhen also is a leading centre for watches, clocks, gifts, and souvenirs and other light manufactures, many of which dominate world output. For example, in 2002, Shenzhen claimed to produce 45% of the world's output of watches and clocks, and in the following year around 80% of the world's artificial Christmas trees.[35]

In the service sector, Shenzhen's port and logistics industries have emerged as leaders within China and worldwide. Shenzhen's ports made it the world's fourth leading city in terms of container port throughput in 2003. Some of the world's largest distributors have set up buying offices in the city. In 2002, Wal-Mart alone sourced US$12 billion in goods (an amount equal to roughly 1% of China's GDP) mostly through its offices in Shenzhen; this rose to an estimated US$15 billion in 2003.[36] Shenzhen is also home to a number of international trade fairs and exhibitions covering a wide range of industries from nuclear power to high technology. Shenzhen's software industry has attracted key national and international companies to the city. Shenzhen is home to one of two stock exchanges in the Chinese mainland and has been a leader in the opening of China's finance and insurance sectors.[37] Shenzhen's tourism infrastructure includes a variety of theme parks and numerous golf courses.

In 2004, there were thousands of foreign invested enterprises in Shenzhen. International firms were prominent in the high-technology sector, with Compaq, DuPont, Epson, Hitachi, Hon Hai Precision, IBM, Intel, Lucent, Olympus, Oracle, Ricoh, Samsung, Sanyo, Seagate, and Sony all having operations in Shenzhen. IBM has claimed that its PC factory in Shenzhen is among its best in the world, and since 2004, Olympus has based its Asia Pacific headquarters out of Shenzhen. Both Intel and Oracle have chosen Shenzhen for their first design centre in China. In 2004, there was also significant international presence in other fields. These include banking, finance, insurance (AIG, ABN Amro, Bank of Tokyo, BNP Paribas, Dresdner Bank, HSBC, IDG, and Standard Chartered), shipping and logistics (Maersk and Federal Express), business services (Ernst & Young, KPMG Peat Marwick, and PricewaterhouseCoopers), and retailers (B&Q, Carrefour, Jusco, McDonald's, and Wal-Mart). Along with Wal-Mart, other major companies, such as IBM, Sony, and Target were sourcing billions of dollars worth of commodities through their Shenzhen-based offices each year. In addition, leading firms from all over the Chinese mainland have set up in Shenzhen to take advantage of the infrastructure, workforce, and links to Hong Kong.

Dongguan

Dongguan, located between Guangzhou and Shenzhen, has become the leading centre for export processing in labour-intensive, light-manufacturing industries in the Chinese mainland. Since the early 1980s, Dongguan's industrialisation has been dominated by foreign investment and exports. Utilised foreign investment in Dongguan increased from US$1.7 million in 1979 to US$1.5 billion in 1998. Over that time period, the total amount of foreign capital actually used in Dongguan was US$9.6 billion. In 1998, foreign-invested enterprises accounted for 77.5% of all industrial enterprises and 74.5% of total industrial output value in Dongguan.[38] A study by the Dongguan government showed that, from 1978 to 1995, Hong Kong was the source of 80% of the utilised foreign capital that came into Dongguan (US$5.1 billion).[39]

In the early 1980s, Dongguan's foreign-invested facilities (largely involving Hong Kong investment) were mainly engaged in labour-intensive processing industries such as textiles, clothing, and plastic products. As Shenzhen began to move up the technology ladder in the early 1990s, many facilities that focused on lower value-added activities moved to Dongguan. In the mid-1990s, traditional foreign-invested processing facilities in Dongguan were joined by newer facilities that focused on electronics, telecommunications equipment, electrical equipment, and machinery, largely involving Taiwanese and then Japanese investment. In 1998, electronic and telecommunications equipment accounted for 29.1% of Dongguan's industrial output, while electrical equipment and machinery accounted for another 8.2%.[40] Although Dongguan's output in textiles, clothing, and plastic products industries continued to increase in absolute terms, they lost ground in relative terms. Even so, Dongguan and some parts of neighbouring Huizhou remain one of the world's major production bases for labour-intensive products.

Since the mid-1990s, Dongguan has also become a base for operations selling to the Chinese domestic market. Dongguan's Humen, for example, has developed into a national wholesale centre for garments and textiles. More importantly, Dongguan has become home to thousands of component and input suppliers for the city's electronics industry. Taiwanese and local component firms in particular have become major component and input suppliers to the Dongguan-based facilities of mainland Chinese, Taiwanese, Japanese, and North American computer and electronics companies. This has facilitated the development of dense clusters of electronics firms and industries in Dongguan in particular, and the Pearl River Delta region in general.[41]

In 2002, Dongguan was the third-leading export city in the Chinese mainland behind Shenzhen and Shanghai. In that year, the city had a total export value of US$23.73 billion.[42] As of 2004, Dongguan was one of the world's leading production bases for PCs and accessories and it accounted for a significant share of global output of PC drivers, scanners, displays, power supply units, mini motors, motherboards, computer magnetic heads, and quartz clock chips. In addition, Dongguan was one of the world's leading producers of mobile phones, household appliances, textiles, garments, toys, footwear, leather products, paper products, and plastic products. As a manufacturing platform, Dongguan stands out among Greater Pearl River Delta locations, both for its dense concentration of light-manufacturing firms and suppliers, and its large pool of migrant factory workers from other regions of China.[43]

Also in 2002, the leading manufacturing industries in Dongguan by gross industrial output were electronic and telecommunications equipment (US$6.08 billion), tobacco processing (US$1.38 billion), electrical equipment and machinery (US$1.13 billion), plastic products (US$0.73 billion), and paper products (US$0.70 billion).[44] Transportation, storage, post, and telecommunications services ranked first in terms of output in Dongguan's service sector. Although substantial portions of these industries are linked to Dongguan's export-oriented manufacturing sector, Dongguan also is an important distribution centre for mainland Chinese markets. In 2004, Dongguan was taking steps to strengthen its distribution and exhibition services and was holding regular trade fairs for the light manufacturing sectors. The retail sector was experiencing significant growth.

By 2002, approximately 13,500 foreign-invested companies had accounted for US$8 billion in foreign investment in Dongguan. Active companies included Akzo Nobel, Canon, DuPont, Duracell, Framatone, General Electric, Hitachi, Hoechst, Kraft, Mattel, NEC, Nestlé, Nippon Steel Corporation, Nokia, Philips, Samsung, Sony, TDK, and Thomson. Nokia was producing more mobile phones in Dongguan than anywhere else in the world. Leading computer giants, such as IBM and Dell, were using Dongguan as a base for sourcing computer parts and components. The vast majority of Taiwan's top computer and computer components manufacturers had facilities in the city. Both Wal-Mart and Carrefour have established large shopping outlets in Dongguan, while McDonald's has opened fast-food restaurants.

Huizhou

Huizhou, on the eastern edge of the Pearl River Delta Economic Zone to the north-east of Shenzhen, has a diversified manufacturing economy that includes electronic components, petrochemicals, audio-visual equipment, and traditional industries such as garments and textiles. As of 2004, Huizhou was home to the Chinese mainland's largest single foreign investment, a US$4.3 billion petrochemical joint venture between CNOOC and Shell Petrochemicals. In 2002, Huizhou was the world's largest producer of laser diodes and also a leading producer of DVD and VCD players. It is also a global player in the production of batteries, telephones, computer circuit boards, and other electronic components.

In 2002, Huizhou's top manufacturing industries by gross industrial output were electronic and telecommunications equipment (US$6.61 billion), electrical equipment and machinery (US$0.91 billion), plastic products (US$0.37 billion), metal products (US$0.35 billion), and garments (US$0.23 billion).[45] Huizhou's service sector was relatively underdeveloped when compared to its manufacturing sector. In that year, its leading service sectors were transportation, storage, post, and telecommunications, as well as wholesale and retail trade and catering services. Much of the service sector focused on the local market.[46]

There were also nearly 8,000 foreign-invested enterprises in Huizhou. In 2001, CNOOC and Shell Petrochemicals signed a contract to build a US$4.3 billion petrochemical complex at Daya Bay, representing the single largest foreign investment in the history of the Chinese mainland. This fuelled foreign participation in large-scale construction projects in the area. Multinational investment has also proved popular in the electronics field where firms such as General Electric, Hitachi, LG Electronics, Matsushita, Philips, Primax, Samsung, Sony, Tandy, and Toshiba all had operations as of 2004. Samsung and LG have moved much of their audio-visual equipment production to Huizhou. In addition to foreign companies, five major domestic producers of home electronics – TCL, Desai, Maikete, Huayang, and Bailuabao – were located in Huizhou. China's leading computer-maker, Legend, also had production facilities in the city.

The Western Delta

The western part of the Pearl River Delta region, encompassing the cities of Foshan, Zhuhai, Jiangmen, Zhongshan, and Zhaoqing, has had a distinctly different economic profile than the eastern part of the region. In the early days of China's economic reform program, the major driving force of industrial development in the Pearl River Delta region came from Guangzhou and towns and cities on the western bank of the Pearl River. These areas, which benefited from some pre-existing industrial development, focused on production for the Chinese domestic market. Factories in the western part of the Pearl River Delta region soon began selling products to meet growing demand in other provinces. The area took advantage of access to raw materials, equipment, parts, and product designs through Hong Kong, as well as preferential foreign exchange policies that allowed the import of needed equipment, inputs, and components. Collectively owned firms in the area were able to establish large-scale production lines for the import substitution of light-manufactured goods and home appliances.

In the late-1990s, the western part of the Pearl River began to participate actively in international markets. Shunde's total exports rose by 69.5% between 1999 and 2001.[47] Zhuhai and Foshan also registered substantial export growth in the late 1990s, though not as great as Shunde. Jurisdictions in the western part of the Pearl River Delta region have also increasingly sought out investment from Hong Kong and Taiwan. These developments indicate that there is substantial scope for the development of the international economy of the western part of the Pearl River Delta region.

Foshan

Foshan, one of the traditional manufacturing centres in the western part of the Greater Pearl River Delta region, is just to the south-west of Guangzhou and north of Jiangmen and Zhongshan. Foshan, the fourth-largest economy in the region after Hong Kong, Guangzhou, and Shenzhen in 2002, has evolved into a major centre for OEM processing and for manufacturing facilities serving the Chinese mainland. Foshan's well-established production areas attract an abundant supply of workers from all over China. In 2004, particularly prominent were Shunde's appliance manufacturers, such as Midea, Kelon, and Galanz, which had achieved substantial market share in the Chinese mainland and increasingly were seeking out foreign customers. Foshan also has been emerging as an important consumer market within the Greater Pearl River Delta region. To meet competitive pressures from other parts of China and demand from international markets, Foshan jurisdictions such as Shunde and Nanhai have accelerated changes in the management and ownership structures of local firms, employing consultants and professionally trained staff, and privatising enterprises by listing them on the domestic stock exchanges.

In 2002, Foshan's top manufacturing industries by gross industrial output were electrical equipment and machinery (US$6.22 billion), non-metal mineral products (US$2.24 billion), electronic and telecommunications equipment (US$1.92 billion), metal products (US$1.81 billion), and plastic products (US$1.35 billion).[48] Some of Foshan's traditional industries date back hundreds of years. In the household electronics and ceramics sectors, some of Foshan's brands occupied 50% or more of the market share within the Chinese mainland.[49] In services, Foshan's leading sectors in 2002 were in transportation, storage, post and telecommunications, and wholesale and retail trade and catering services. A significant part of Foshan's service economy served its growing manufacturing and export base.

There were roughly 5,000 foreign-invested enterprises in Foshan. DuPont runs China's largest polyester film factory in Foshan and companies such as 3M, Bayer, Bosch, DuPont, General Electric, Hoechst, Laeis Bucher, Northern Telecom, Osram Lighting, Pohang Steel, Sanyo, Siemens, Tetrapak, Thomson Multimedia, and Toshiba have all invested in the area. Along with foreign investors, there was a strong presence of local brand names, such as Kelon, one of the world's top manufacturers of refrigerators; Midea, China's number one producer of electric fans; and award-winning soft drinks manufacturer, Jianlibao.

Zhuhai

Between 1980 and 1992, Zhuhai, on the Pearl River Delta's western bank, saw its population grow by a factor of 10 and its industrial output in US dollar terms by a factor of 500. In 2002, based on actual population, Zhuhai City had the highest per capita income in the Pearl River Delta region.[50] In that year, the city's top manufacturing industries by gross industrial output were electronic and telecommunications equipment (US$2.53 billion); electrical equipment and machinery (US$1.53 billion); office equipment, instruments, and meters (US$0.69 billion); garments and other fibre products (US$0.43 billion); and medical and pharmaceutical products (US$0.38 billion). Other prominent industries included plastic products, raw chemical materials and chemical products, papermaking and paper products, textiles, and metal products.[51]

Wholesale and retail trade and catering services topped Zhuhai's service sector output in 2002. Zhuhai's annual international air show has become a venue for sealing major aviation-related deals. In 2003, construction was under way of a 50,000 square metre site to host the air show. The area was also developing its tourist attractions, as well as promoting specialised real estate developments, such as retirement communities and sports facilities. In recent years, Zhuhai has taken steps to strengthen its high-technology capability and its education sector. The city has invested in software parks and has established a university campus park.

At the end of 2002, there were over 7,000 foreign-invested enterprises active in Zhuhai. These included Arco, BP Amoco, Canon, Casio, Cheung Kong Holdings, Coca-cola, Daimler-Chrysler, Flextronics, Fosters, General Electric, Iwatani, Matsushita, Mitsubishi, Mitsumi, Mobil, Phillips, Siemens, and Union Carbide. In 2003, BP opened a world-scale purified terephthalic acid (PTA) facility in Zhuhai. Flextronics was planning to expand its two million-plus square foot electronics production complex. Retailers Carrefour and Jusco have opened stores in Zhuhai, while fast-food chains KFC and McDonald's both had outlets in the city.

Jiangmen

Located on the western side of the Pearl River Delta, Jiangmen covers nearly one-quarter of the land area of the Greater Pearl River Delta region. Jiangmen was a centre for international commerce in the early 1900s and has developed a manufacturing base that serves both local and international markets. As some costs have risen in other parts of the Pearl River Delta region, several companies have found Jiangmen to be an attractive alternative. Jiangmen is expected to be a major beneficiary of the expansion of the road and rail networks planned for the Greater Pearl River Delta region.

In 2002, Jiangmen's leading industries by gross industrial output were metal products (US$1.65 billion), electrical equipment and machinery (US$1.60 billion), raw chemical materials and chemical products (US$1.04 billion), textiles (US$0.99 billion), and garments and other fibre products (US$0.91 billion). Jiangmen also produced electronic and telecommunications equipment, transport equipment, plastic products, shipping containers, high-energy batteries, circuit boards, and cameras.[52] Jiangmen also has been a leader in the production of motorcycles, television sets, and washing machines for the domestic market.

Jiangmen's leading tertiary sector was wholesale and retail and catering services. Jiangmen's tertiary sector was expanding, particularly in the area of distribution services for its motorcycles, household electrical products, stainless steel items, and building materials. Foreign investment in the city has greatly boosted Jiangmen's real estate trade, leisure services, and logistics sectors. The city has been particularly keen to attract investment in its commerce, trade, tourism, education, banking, and insurance sectors.[53]

There were also more than 4,000 foreign-invested enterprises in Jiangmen. Notable foreign investors in Jiangmen included ABB, Allied Signal, BP, Danone, Eastman Kodak, Emerson Electric, Foster Wheeler, Honeywell, Hyundai, Mitsubishi, RGM International, and Sumitomo. Rousselot, a French producer of gelatine products for photographic, pharmaceutical, and edible items had a large gelatine production facility in Jiangmen. Singaporean paper company Golden Eagle Group announced plans to increase its investment in Jiangmen to US$1.92 billion, which would enhance Jiangmen's position as a leading production base for office and stationery paper. The city was already home to some of the largest domestic brands in paper products, Weida and Vinda. As of 2004, Jiangmen was attracting new investment projects in auto sales services, electrical appliances, and auto parts.

Zhongshan

Zhongshan is located in the western part of the Pearl River Delta, north of Zhuhai and south of Guangzhou. The city has a number of distinctive towns under its jurisdiction that have well-established manufacturing bases. In addition to its export-oriented facilities, Zhongshan is also home to a large number of factories that supply the Chinese domestic market. In 2002, Zhongshan's top manufacturing industries by gross industrial output were electronic and telecommunications equipment (US$2.02 billion), electrical equipment and machinery (US$1.40 billion), textiles (US$0.95 billion), metal products (US$0.94 billion), and plastic products (US$0.75 billion).[54] In that year, Zhongshan's leading tertiary sectors were wholesale and retail trade and catering services; transportation, storage, post and telecommunications; social services; and real estate trade.

As of 2004, numerous foreign investors had invested in Zhongshan, including ABB Transformers, Acer, Canon, Detroit Diesel, Glaxo-SmithKline, Toshiba, Union Carbide, and Wistron. In 2001, Canon invested in a laser printer production facility in Zhongshan. Hong Kong real estate developers, such as Sun Hung Kai, have invested in large-scale residential projects in the city. In 2003 and 2004, mainland manufacturing giants such as Galanz, Midea, and Gree have committed to setting up large-scale production facilities in Zhongshan to make air-conditioners, electric fans, and other household electrical products.[55]

Zhaoqing

Zhaoqing, located in the mountains around 100 kilometres from Guangzhou, is an outlying locality falling in part within the official definition of the Pearl River Delta Economic Zone. In 2004, as its highway connections continued to improve, Zhaoqing was poised for urban growth and industrialisation. While the area's limestone mountains, hot springs, and golf courses were attracting an increasing number of visitors, providing a significant boost to the area's tourism and related industries, Zhaoqing was aiming to be more than a 'garden city'.

In 2002, Zhaoqing's leading industries by gross industrial output were electronic and telecommunications equipment (US$0.73 billion), timber processing and related industries (US$0.46 billion), metal products (US$0.44 billion), textiles (US$0.43 billion), and garments and other fibre products (US$0.39 billion).[56] Other industrial specialities included machinery and auto parts, cement, nylon, vacuum equipment, and redwood processing. Primary output included rice, vegetables, livestock and aquatic products, turpentine, cinnamon, bamboo, tapioca, sugar cane, and fruit, as well as gold from the Hetai Goldmine, one of the largest in China. Though services remained relatively underdeveloped, output from services had more than tripled between 2002 and 1997, with research and development, medical services, education, and social services leading this growth. The tourist industry also has provided a significant boost to the local economy.[57]

As of 2002, there were more than 1,400 foreign-invested enterprises in Zhaoqing. Foreign investors included Aker of Taiwan (a leading designer and manufacturer of quartz crystal), Blue Ribbon Brewery, and Korea's SK Group. As of 2004, Henkel produced cosmetics in Zhaoqing, while Honda had a foundry producing aluminium light metal parts for high-performance vehicles. In 2004, Korea Engine Tech agreed to invest US$500 million to produce train engines, engine parts, auto and auto parts, and related electronics in Zhaoqing.

CLUSTERS IN THE PEARL RIVER DELTA

The different jurisdictions in the Pearl River Delta region have different industrial profiles. Several of the jurisdictions are home to vibrant regional clusters of firms and industries. National and regional economies tend to develop, not in isolated industries, but in clusters of industries related by buyer–supplier links, common technologies, common channels or common customers.[58] The economies of the Pearl River Delta region are no exceptions. The region has developed a broad range of clusters in garments and textiles, footwear, plastic products, electrical goods, electronics, printing, transportation, logistics, and financial services. The Pearl River Delta region's electronics and electrical cluster is particularly strong and accounts for the vast majority of Chinese production in a wide range of industries in the cluster as seen in Table 3.8.

In addition to producing finished goods, the region's clusters increasingly are developing deep supply networks to provide critical inputs to the finished goods producers. Figures 3.1, 3.2, 3.3, and 3.4 show some of these clusters. Figure 3.1 represents only some of the inputs and components that can be sourced in the Pearl River Delta region that support its world-leading toy industry, an industry that has a world production share in excess of 60% in some categories. Figure 3.2 shows a range of inputs and components available in the region that supports its footwear industry, another industry in which the Pearl River Delta region has become a world leader. Figure 3.3 shows a number of electrical and electronics industries in which the region is a leader in Asia or in the world. Figure 3.4 shows some of the components and inputs that can be sourced from highly competitive suppliers in the region. The point is that rather than isolated industries, the Pearl River Delta region has been developing a set of industry clusters that are mutually reinforcing. In addition, as more and more of the inputs and components are made locally, the clusters become stronger and more embedded into the local economy. Competitors or potential competitors, therefore, have to compete not just with a set of end-product manufacturers, but with entire production chains, and in some cases subcultures, found in the region.

Table 3.8 The Pearl River Delta region's share of PRC output, selected industries, 2000, %

Industry	Share of PRC output
Electrical fans	88.2
Hi-fi equipment	80.4
Electric rice cookers	79.0
Telephones	78.8
Microwave ovens	72.1
Cameras	64.3
Printers	60.2
Gas water heaters	58.4
Fax machines	55.8
Digital switches	50.7
Video recorders	43.6
Air-conditioners	37.5
VCD players	35.5
Colour televisions	34.8
LS semiconductors	31.1
Refrigerators	25.1
Vacuum cleaners	24.9
Cathode ray tubes	24.3
Personal computers	23.0
Mobile phones	19.1

Source: Bu Xinmin, Ye Jianfu, Huang Defa, Zhang Hanchang, Ma Jianqiang, Meng Shenbao, and Chen Lifen in *Guangdong Statistical Yearbook 2001*, pp. 34–52

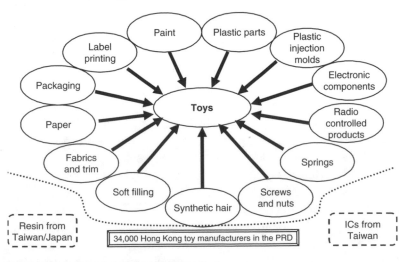

Source: Enright, Scott & Associates Ltd research

Figure 3.1 The Pearl River Delta region toy cluster

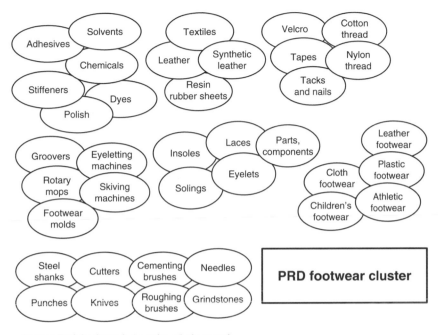

Source: Enright, Scott & Associates Ltd research

Figure 3.2   The Pearl River Delta region footwear cluster

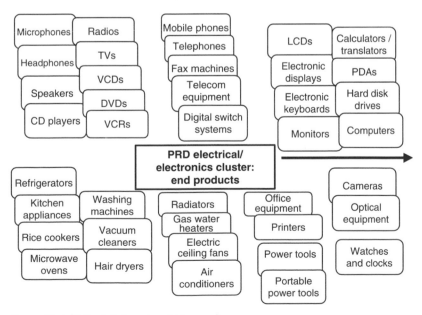

Source: Enright, Scott & Associates Ltd research

Figure 3.3   The Pearl River Delta region electronics cluster, end products

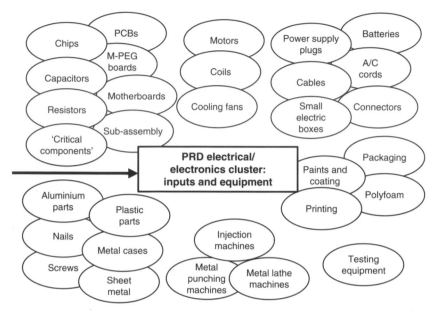

Source: Enright, Scott & Associates Ltd research

Figure 3.4   The Pearl River Delta region electronics cluster, inputs and components

Geographic concentration

The production for many of these clusters can be found in relatively small geographic areas. Figure 3.5 shows a wide range of industries in which there is a strong geographic concentration in individual cities or towns in the Pearl River Delta region. In such cases, the tight concentration of firms facilitates linkages with suppliers and buyers, as well as fostering a mixture of competition and cooperation that can give rise to vibrant local economies. Whereas some of these industries have emerged relatively recently, others date back hundreds of years.[59]

Guangzhou, for example, is developing its own automotive district, with Nansha as its focal point. As of 2004, the city was home to Honda, Isuzu, Nissan, and Toyota. Honda was expected to build more than 70,000 cars in 2003 and increase capacity to 200,000 cars in 2004. Nissan's plant was designed to reach an annual capacity of more than 200,000 cars within three to five years.[60] Toyota was constructing a plant to produce Camry sedans with a 500,000 cars per year capacity. Denso, Japan's biggest car parts maker had set up a joint venture in Guangzhou to make auto air-conditioners and other car parts.[61] Toyota's engine joint venture with Guangzhou Automobile Group was planned to have an initial capacity of 300,000 engines, of which 200,000

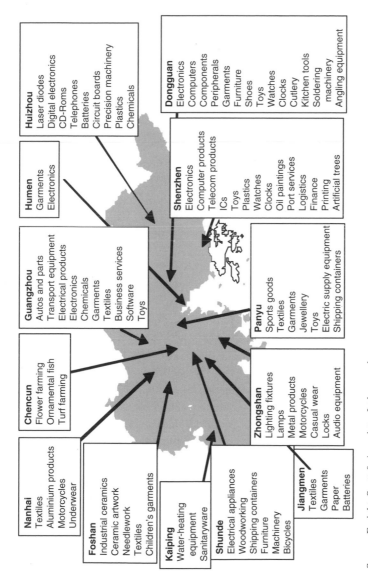

Huizhou
Laser diodes
Digital electronics
CD-Roms
Telephones
Batteries
Circuit boards
Precision machinery
Plastics
Chemicals

Dongguan
Electronics
Computers
Components
Peripherals
Garments
Furniture
Shoes
Toys
Watches
Clocks
Cutlery
Kitchen tools
Soldering machinery
Angling equipment

Humen
Garments
Electronics

Shenzhen
Electronics
Computer products
Telecom products
ICs
Toys
Plastics
Watches
Clocks
Oil paintings
Port services
Logistics
Finance
Printing
Artificial trees

Guangzhou
Autos and parts
Transport equipment
Electrical products
Electronics
Chemicals
Garments
Textiles
Business services
Software
Toys

Chencun
Flower farming
Ornamental fish
Turf farming

Panyu
Sports goods
Textiles
Garments
Jewellery
Toys
Electric supply equipment
Shipping containers

Nanhai
Textiles
Aluminium products
Motorcycles
Underwear

Foshan
Industrial ceramics
Ceramic artwork
Needlework
Textiles
Children's garments

Zhongshan
Lighting fixtures
Lamps
Metal products
Motorcycles
Casual wear
Locks
Audio equipment

Kaiping
Water-heating equipment
Sanitaryware

Shunde
Electrical appliances
Woodworking
Shipping containers
Furniture
Machinery
Bicycles

Jiangmen
Textiles
Garments
Paper
Batteries

Source: Enright, Scott & Associates Ltd research

Figure 3.5   Localised industries in the Pearl River Delta region

would be for export.[62] Japanese steel giant JFE Holdings had entered into a joint venture to build a plant to make steel sheets for the automobile and appliance industries.[63] Nansha also was rapidly growing as an area for the chemical, machinery, and logistics sectors.

Guangzhou also has a number of geographic concentrations in traditional industries. Panyu County, just south of Guangzhou's city limits, provides a major base for light manufacturing for the city. Fangcun has become known for its cut flowers. Zengcheng has developed as a major production and distribution centre for jeans and casual wear, accounting for 60% of China's total output by volume in 2002, while Huadu boasted about its yearly output of 1.8 million ironing boards.

In the Shenzhen township of Nanshan, high-technology goods accounted for over 50% of total production in 2003. The area has attracted big foreign firms, such as IBM, Compact, Lucent, and Oracle, as well as local technology companies Huawei and Zhongxing. Elsewhere in Shenzhen, the Futian district has become one of the main sites for warehousing and trade facilities and is the site of one of South China's major free trade zones. In 2002, Dafen, well known for its replica art, had a population of 300, but had 60 workshops that reproduced the works of great masters, such as Monet and Van Gogh, to sell to European and Japanese markets.[64] Shekou and Yantian have become major port and logistics areas. Shekou also has developed a significant petrochemical sector. More than 900 watch and clock manufacturers were registered in Shenzhen, producing 830 million watches in 2003. These accounted for 55% of the domestic market and more than 40% of the global market.[65]

As of 2004, Dongguan's Qingxi Township was one of the largest computer production bases in China. The town has specialised in the output of monitors, motherboards, keyboards, PC boxes, as well as the assembly of computers. The area was so important to the computer industry that the Deputy Director of IBM Asia was quoted as saying, 'If there is a traffic jam between Dongguan and Hong Kong, 70% of the world's computer market will be affected.'[66] Dongguan's Humen Township has developed into a national wholesale centre for garments and textiles. In 2001, the town had over 1,000 garment enterprises, with more than 400,000 of the town's 700,000 population engaged in garment manufacturing. As of 2004, the 2,000-plus knitwear factories in Dalang accounted for more than 60% of the area's GDP. Investment from the Hong Kong business community had fuelled the growth that brought 400,000 migrant workers into an area which had a native population of just 60,000.[67] Nearby Hongmei has focused on a variety of textile- and leather-related products, such as garments, bags, dyeing and finishing products, packaging materials, zippers, and threads. The township of Zhangmutou has branded itself 'Little Hong Kong' and since 1992 has taken steps to develop its real estate industry. As of 2003, more than 150,000 Hong Kong people had invested in property there and more than 50,000 housing units had been sold in markets outside of mainland China.

In Huizhou, as of 2004, Henan's industries included electronics, hardware, kitchen utensils, leather products and plastic items, Huicheng-made garments, shoes, hats, and toys; Huidong had a predominance of shoe and knitting factories; Qiuchang produced tiles, material for curtains, industrial gloves, bamboo furniture, and shoes; and Shatianzhen produced tins, furniture, garments, and mattresses. The nuclear and petrochemical facilities at Daya Bay also represented substantial industrial concentrations in their own right.

Many areas within Foshan are known for particular industries. As of 2004, Shunde was a major hub for the production of household appliances, including refrigerators, microwave ovens, electric fans, and air-conditioners. DaLiang was well known for plastics, Leilu for bicycles, Chencun for flowers and horticultural products, Lecong for furniture distribution, Lunjiao for wood-working machinery, Gaoming for garments and textiles, Yanbu for underwear, Jun'an for jeans, and Shiwan for ceramics. In 2002, Foshan had more than 2,300 registered manufacturers of children's clothes, accounting for 31.3% of China's total.[68] Yanbu, in the Foshan district of Nanhai, for instance, was a centre for underwear manufacture. In 2002, there were more than 100 underwear manufacturers in the town, which also boasted an underwear design centre, and runway shows in the town's leading restaurant. As of 2003, Jun'an Town in Shunde had a 20-year history of jean making and more than 95% of the town's 1,000 or so garment manufacturers made jeans. The township government had invested more than 123 million yuan to build a special jeans exhibition centre.[69] As of 2004, Nanhai had more than 150 aluminium extrusion enterprises, centred in the township of Dali. Collectively they produced 520,000 tons of aluminium products in 2003, accounting for 40% of the national production and 60% of Guangdong's total. In 2004, 10 of China's top aluminium products manufacturers were located in the Nanhai Industrial Zone. The Nanhai government was backing the development of this industry through the construction of the Nanhai Non-Ferrous Metal Industry Park, an exhibition and trading centre and a distribution centre.[70]

In Zhongshan, as of 2004, the township of Xiaolan was noted for its hardware products, such as locks, stoves, and electrical appliances. The township had also established itself as a base for the manufacture of audio equipment. Among other Zhongshan towns, Shaxi was known for its production of garments; Dachong had a high concentration of rosewood furniture factories; Dongfeng was noted for domestic appliances, and Huangpu for cured food.

In 2002, Shaxi had more than 500 clothing manufacturers employing 30,000 people and producing around 60 recognised mainland brands, particularly for sportswear. There were approximately 300 cloth shops on one of the main streets in Shaxi and two large rag markets that were said to process 100 tonnes of textile off-cuts every day. Shaxi had also become a major base for clothing distribution, with a sportswear mall housing some 200 retailers. In 2002, the suburb of Guzhen claimed to produce around half of the lights and light fittings in China.[71] In Jiangmen, the township of Siquan in the city of Xinhui obtained 80% of its industrial value from metal kitchen products in 2002, while Kaiping in the south-west has been known for its water heaters and ceramic sanitary ware.

The presence of these dense clusters of firms enhances the competitiveness of the region's economy in many ways. The presence of multiple companies in an industry tends to embed the industry in a particular location, making it more difficult to compete against it or to displace it. At the same time, such clusters are not reliant on a single company for success, but rather take advantage of the skills, capabilities, and resources of many companies sharpened by local competition. The result is a far deeper and more competitive situation than in the case of single firm development.

ECONOMIC DECISION-MAKING IN THE PEARL RIVER DELTA REGION

The existence of multiple, sometimes overlapping jurisdictions in the Pearl River Delta region can create a tangled web of economic decision-making. At the Guangdong provincial level, there are departments involved in economic strategy and planning, departments that monitor and examine operations, and departments that focus on specific industries. The Development and Planning Commission is responsible for annual economic plans, as well as plans for the province's medium- and long-term social and economic development. This remit includes the formulation of industrial policies, budgeting for fixed asset investments, and planning large-scale infrastructure projects. The Economy and Trade Commission manages the provincial economy, including industrial and transportation policies, as well as general rules and regulations. It also participates in macroeconomic forecasting and monitoring, in formulating and monitoring economic plans, and in developing solutions to economic problems. The Department of Finance sets and manages the provincial budget, tax policies, and accounting rules. It also monitors government revenue and expenditures. General monitoring functions are carried out by the Provincial Department of Auditing, the Administration of Industry and Commerce, the Bureau of Prices, the Bureau of Local Taxation, and the Bureau of the State-Owned Property of China, among others. Provincial departments concerned with specific sectors include the Department of Construction, the Department of Water Resources, the Department of Agriculture, the Department of Trade and Economic Cooperation, the Department of Information Industry, and the Provincial Tourism Administration.

Guangdong also is the home of numerous lower level jurisdictions. As of the end of 2003, it contained three Special Economic Zones (in Shenzhen, Zhuhai, and Shantou), all of which have the right to develop their own economic plans; one provincial capital, Guangzhou; 21 prefecture-level cities; 31 county-level cities; 42 counties; 48 districts; three autonomous counties; and 1,529 towns. Instead of a top-down process, development throughout much of the Pearl River Delta region is more bottom-up, with local jurisdictions developing their own plans and seeking to expand their rights of approval and economic reach. The Guangdong government has usually been supportive of such efforts, often lobbying the Beijing government on behalf of greater flexibility and autonomy in economic policymaking. The bottom-up, decentralised decision-making process has proven a benefit to the province as a whole. However, such a process leaves open the possibility that local jurisdictions will engage in destructive competition for the same or similar types of industries. This seems to be the case in the Pearl River Delta region where multiple jurisdictions all seem to make the same investments in pursuit of the same industries, without regard to the plans of neighbouring jurisdictions or a clear sense of specialisation and division of labour.[72] In addition, devolution of authority to lower levels of government creates challenges in terms of governmental capacity to plan, to provide social security and public safety, or to implement strategies.

The roles of different economic actors are changing in the Pearl River Delta region. Local government and party officials increasingly are taking on the role of facilitators for private and collective firms, rather than acting as managers of state-owned enterprises. They often act to develop infrastructure, attract foreign investment, seek out business advice, and negotiate with other levels of government on behalf of local firms. The Central Government's State Planning and Development Commission is much more a gatekeeper, passing judgement on plans from below, than a proactive decision-maker for local level activities.[73]

THE IMPORTANCE OF THE PEARL RIVER DELTA REGION

The Pearl River Delta region has played several economic roles. For China, the region has been the vanguard of economic reform, the place where economic experiments could be carried out, the place that showed the Chinese leadership that greater openness could lead to greater prosperity, the place that showed the value of foreign investment, and the place that showed that reform could progress without causing systemic failure in the political and economic system. The Pearl River Delta region's impact, however, has not been limited to China. The region's emergence has affected the global economy in profound ways. The Pearl River Delta has become a manufacturing base that cannot be ignored by companies or governments elsewhere in the world.

Close connections with Hong Kong have fostered much of the development of the Pearl River Delta region. As we will see, the economies of Hong Kong and the Pearl River Delta region have become inextricably intertwined. It is difficult to even discuss the economy of Hong Kong without discussing that of the Pearl River Delta region and it is difficult to discuss the economy of the Pearl River Delta region without discussing that of Hong Kong. The next two chapters will focus on the economic interaction between Hong Kong and the Pearl River Delta region that has led to the development of perhaps the world's most dynamic economic region.

CHAPTER FOUR

Economic Interaction between Hong Kong and the Pearl River Delta Region[1]

Since 1979, Hong Kong has been an important driver of modernisation of the Pearl River Delta region and all of the Chinese mainland. Hong Kong has provided capital, logistical support, access to world markets, management know-how, technology, and marketing skills. The Pearl River Delta region has provided labour, land, and natural resources. It is this interaction that has allowed the Greater Pearl River Delta region to emerge in a relatively short period of time as one of the world's major manufacturing bases and has allowed China to emerge as a major trading nation.

The economic interaction between Hong Kong and the Pearl River Delta region has evolved substantially over time. Before China's opening, the interaction was rather limited. Hong Kong received water and staples from the Pearl River Delta region and provided limited services linked with China's imports and exports. In the late 1970s and early 1980s, as China began to open, Hong Kong investors and businesses began to explore possibilities in the Pearl River Delta region. As of the mid-1980s, Hong Kong investment in the Pearl River Delta region grew dramatically and it could be said that Hong Kong was the leader of Pearl River Delta development at least in terms of burgeoning foreign investment and exports.[2] By the mid- to late 1990s, Hong Kong was playing more of a strong supporting role in the region's development. In the 2000s, the prospects are for a much more even-handed and integrated development.

INVESTMENT IN THE PEARL RIVER DELTA REGION

Foreign investment has been critically important to the development of the Pearl River Delta region. In 2000, for example, foreign-funded enterprises, including Hong Kong-invested enterprises, generated RMB 730.83 billion (US$88.26 billion) in total output value, accounting for 59.46% of the gross industrial output value of Guangdong Province.[3] Foreign investors have also been responsible for the bulk of Guangdong's exports. Much of this investment has come from Hong Kong itself. Firms from other places have used Hong Kong as a base to make and manage their investments in the region. The interaction has driven the region's growth in trade as well as infrastructure and a range of related services.

Hong Kong investment

Hong Kong investment has been a particularly important part of the interaction between Hong Kong and the Pearl River Delta region. Hong Kong has been the source of over 70% of the cumulative foreign direct investment in the region since 1979, or roughly eight times the investment of North America, Japan, and Europe combined. One reason Hong Kong has played such an important role is because it links the region with the rest of the world, handling more than 70% of its seaborne exports and an even greater percentage of its airborne exports in the early 2000s. In addition to the tens of thousands of small and medium-sized Hong Kong firms active in the Pearl River Delta region are several large players, such as Hutchison in port services, VTech in electronics, Hopewell in highways, Jardines in retailing, HSBC and Bank of East Asia in banking, CLP in power generation, and several Hong Kong developers in property and hotels.[4]

Given its location, the Pearl River Delta region boasts a natural advantage in attracting funds from Hong Kong. Hong Kong and the Pearl River Delta region share a long history, family ties, and close relations among residents. Since the onset of China's reform program, the economic contacts and cooperation between Hong Kong and the Pearl River Delta region have become closer and closer, fostering a relationship of mutual dependence and mutual support. The Pearl River Delta region has become the first choice for Hong Kong investors, while Hong Kong has become a showcase for the Pearl River Delta region's efforts to open to the outside and to attract overseas funds. Hong Kong investment has evolved in three broad stages, each characterised by a somewhat different investment mix: a start-up stage, which lasted from 1979 until the mid-1980s; a rapid growth stage, which lasted from the mid-1980s to the early 1990s; and a steady development stage, which has broadly continued from the mid-1990s to 2004.[5]

When the Pearl River Delta region began to open in 1979, there was considerable uncertainty about the rules governing inward investment and how the economy would evolve. At this time much of the investment into the region involved Hong Kong business people investing to contribute to their ancestral hometown and to take advantage of family connections to reduce the risk of investment.[6] Most of the investment involved labour-intensive export processing facilities attracted by very low land and labour costs[7] located in the Shenzhen Special Economic Zone and in Dongguan along the Guangzhou–Shenzhen railway line at a time when travelling to adjacent cities in the Pearl River Delta region could take hours. Investment in the service sector was mainly in the provincial centre of Guangzhou and in nearby Shenzhen.

By the mid-1980s, early successes, higher levels of comfort and familiarity, and better transportation infrastructure attracted increasing investment from Hong Kong into the eastern portion of the Pearl River Delta, still mostly in export-oriented processing facilities. By the end of 1992, two-thirds of the exports from the Pearl River Delta region had direct links to Hong Kong-invested enterprises.[8] Many of these enterprises had moved pre-existing production activities into the Pearl River Delta region. As they recognised the potential of the region, Hong Kong companies began to employ many times the number of workers in the Pearl River Delta region than they had in Hong Kong previously.

After Deng Xiaoping's South China tour in 1992, China launched a second round of reforms and economic opening. This in turn stimulated a new round of inward investments from Hong Kong. The number of Hong Kong companies investing in their first factory facility in Guangdong Province reached an all-time high in 1992.[9] Deng's tour and subsequent developments heralded greater opening in the service sector within the Pearl River Delta region. Hong Kong investment also became more diversified, with Hong Kong firms investing in finance, insurance, real estate, and other services. Although the geographic focus remained in the eastern portion of the Pearl River Delta region, some investments also started to be made in the western portion of the Delta and in the mountainous areas of Guangdong. By 2002, the vast majority of factories controlled by or doing work for Hong Kong firms in the Pearl River Delta remained concentrated in the eastern Pearl River Delta cities of Dongguan (an estimated 18,100 factories) and Shenzhen (15,700 factories), while the cities on the western side of the Pearl River had far fewer. Zhongshan, for example, had only 3,000 such factories.[10] The different stages coincided with increasing investment commitments. The average contract value grew from US$36,800 from 1979 to 1984, to US$177,000 from 1985 to 1992, to US$811,000 from 1992 to 2003.[11]

Hong Kong firms were the earliest investors in the Pearl River Delta region and Hong Kong has continued to be the dominant source of foreign capital in the Pearl River Delta region. Hong Kong and Macao were the source of 90.8% of the total foreign capital used in the Pearl River Delta region in 1985, 73.6% from 1986 to 1990, 74.5% from 1991 to 1995, and 67.6% from 1996 to 1999, according to figures built up from the statistical yearbooks of different jurisdictions in the Pearl River Delta region (see Table 4.1). The figures may be understated given the fact that much of the capital recorded as coming from the Virgin Islands was probably due to Hong Kong firms routing capital through corporate entities in the Virgin Islands. Despite the diversification of investment sources, Hong Kong (which represented nearly all of the investment in the Hong Kong and Macao category) remained the dominant source of foreign capital.

It is hard to overstate the impact of Hong Kong investment on the Pearl River Delta region. Many of the Hong Kong companies interviewed for this study indicated that they employed far more people in the Pearl River Delta region than in Hong Kong. The ratios ranged from 1 to 6 in the software industry to 1 to 55 in the toy industry (see Table 4.2). Based on figures like these, and those we have obtained for other industries in the course of hundreds of interviews, we estimate that Hong Kong manufacturing and trading companies employ in the order of 10 million to 11 million people in the Pearl River Delta region.[13] The 10 million to 11 million figure is similar to that estimated in a study carried out by the Hong Kong Centre for Economic Research for the Hong Kong Federation of Industries in Guangdong Province.[14] It also represents in the order of one-quarter of the entire population of the Pearl River Delta region.

Hong Kong firms have invested in a wide range of sectors in the Pearl River Delta region. Table 4.3 shows the industrial structure of the utilisation of foreign capital in the Pearl River Delta region from all sources from 1979 to 2002. It shows that secondary industries, including manufacturing, accounted for the lion's share of investment, followed by the tertiary sector. Only a small portion of the investment has been in the primary sector. Although precise figures are not available, experts estimate that the importance of Hong Kong investment has meant that the Hong Kong investment into the region has followed a similar pattern.

Table 4.1 Main sources of foreign funds in the Pearl River Delta Region, US$ million

Source region/country	1985		1985–1999		1986–1990		1991–1995		1996–1999	
	Amount	%	Amount	%	Amount	%	Amount	%	Amount	%
Total	738.95	100.00	80,473.82	100.00	6,133.61	100.00	29,453.64	100.00	44,147.62	100.00
Hong Kong and Macao	671.14	90.82	56,941.10	70.76	4,514.79	73.61	21,932.37	74.46	29,822.80	67.55
South-east Asia	7.83	1.06	1,846.89	2.30	48.20	0.79	476.26	1.62	1314.6	2.98
Taiwan, China	0	0	2,662.99	3.31	75.62	1.23	884.03	3.00	1,703.34	3.86
Japan	31.33	4.24	4,758.73	5.91	789.75	12.88	1,807.23	6.14	2,130.42	4.83
Korea									280.09	0.63
Europe	6.57	0.89	4,122.97	5.12	299.96	4.89	1,032.76	3.51	2,783.68	6.31
North America	20.08	2.72	2,955.22	3.67	374.66	6.11	901.51	3.06	1,657.97	3.76
Australasia	0.5	0.07	356.97	0.44	34.79	0.57	114.23	0.39	207.42	0.47

Sources: Derived from *Guangdong Statistical Yearbooks* and the statistical yearbooks of different Pearl River Delta region cities[12]

Table 4.2   Ratios of Hong Kong firm employment in Hong Kong and the PRD, 2002

Industry	HK : PRD employment
Toys	1 : 55
Electronics	1 : 50
Giftware	1 : 30
Plastics	1 : 27
Printing	1 : 24
Garments	1 : 15
Watches and clocks	1 : 9
Software	1 : 6
Simple average	1 : 26

Source: Enright, Scott & Associates Ltd research

Hong Kong investment in the Pearl River Delta's secondary sector has concentrated in manufacturing, with the focus on export-oriented processing of a wide range of products, including electronic products, textiles, garments, plastics, machinery, and household electric appliances.[15] By 2000, some 70% of the Hong Kong-invested enterprises in the Pearl River Delta region were engaged in production of textiles, garments, electronics, toys, metal products, plastics, and other labour-intensive light industrial products. Some 80 to 90% of Hong Kong's plastic industry, roughly 85% of its electronic industry, and 90% of its watch and toy industries had moved to the Pearl River Delta region. The vast majority of these facilities were engaged in export activities in export-processing original equipment manufacturer (OEM) or original design manufacturer ODM arrangements.[16] The Hong Kong Chinese Manufacturers' Association estimated that 86.1% of its members had set up factories in the Chinese mainland by 2001.[17] Looking at manufacturing and traders more broadly, the Hong Kong Centre for Economic Research estimated that in 2002, 52% of all manufacturing and import-export firms in Hong Kong had manufacturing operations in the Chinese mainland, overwhelmingly in Guangdong Province.[18] Over 96% of these firms had a facility in Guangdong. Also according to the Hong Kong Centre for Economic Research estimates, by 2002, Hong Kong-based firms had invested in and had management control of some 53,300 factories in Guangdong Province. Of these, 21,300 were factories in which Hong Kong-based firms had invested in, and had management control of, as foreign-funded enterprises, and 32,200 factories provided manufacturing operations for Hong Kong-based firms.[19]

Of particular importance have been arrangements whereby Hong Kong companies contract with township or village enterprises that supply land and

Table 4.3 Utilised foreign funds in Guangdong Province by industry, selected years, percent

Industry	1979–2002	1981	1985	1990	1995	2000	2002
Total	100.00	100.00	100.00	100.00	100.00	100.00	100.00
Primary industry total	1.23	3.33	2.68	1.87	0.88	0.99	0.96
Farming, forestry, animal husbandry, and fisheries	1.23	3.33	2.68[a]	1.87[a]	0.88	0.99	0.96
Secondary industry total	73.18	41.19	66.21	77.58	69.29	75.13	77.01
Mining and quarrying	0.15	–	–	–	–	0.16	0.16
Manufacturing	66.56	41.19[b]	61.16[b]	77.54[b]	65.71	67.13	71.38
Production and supply of power, gas, and water	3.86	–	–	–	–	5.47	4.86
Construction	2.62	–	5.05	0.04	3.58	2.38	0.61
Tertiary industry total	25.59	55.46	31.12	20.56	29.85	23.88	22.03
Geological prospecting and water conservancy	0.01	–	–	–	–	0.02	–
Transport, storage, post and telecommunication services	3.76	13.84	4.14	1.69	4.43	1.84	2.86
Wholesale, retail, trade, and catering services	1.94	4.95	3.87	2.03	2.37	1.65	1.47
Finance and insurance	1.12	–	–	2.92	0.39	0.16	3.67
Real estate	10.94	25.31[c]	22.38[c]	4.53[c]	13.46	13.92	8.47
Social services	2.05	–	–	–	–	4.10	3.77
Health care, sports, and social welfare	0.47	–	0.05	–	1.29	0.54	0.21
Education, culture, arts, radio, film, and television	0.16	0.00	0.05	0.11	0.34	0.07	0.02
Scientific research and polytechnic services	0.08	–	0.01	–	0.04	0.09	0.18
Government agencies, Party agencies, and social organisations	–	–	–	–	–	–	–
Others	5.06	11.36	0.62	9.28	7.53	1.48	1.37

Notes:
(a) including water conservancy
(b) including mining and excavating sector
(c) including power, coal, gas, and water production and supply, as well as social service trade.
Source: *Guangdong Statistical Yearbook*, various years

workshops, while the Hong Kong entity organises production and logistics. As long as the products are exported, inputs and capital goods can enter China duty-free. Historically, most of the arrangements were for 'single-step' export processing, in which a single production step, usually assembly, took place in the Pearl River Delta workshop. This system has created challenges in recent years as the development of a denser supplier base in the Pearl River Delta region has caused more and more companies to wish to do multi-stage processing that mixes foreign and locally produced inputs. In addition, as China's domestic market grows, more and more companies wish to use their Pearl River Delta production capacity to meet local demand. According to the Hong Kong Centre for Economic Research, in 2002, 71% of output 'produced in Mainland factories with connection to Hong Kong' was exported, 19% was transferred to other facilities for further processing, and 10% was sold domestically.[20] To reduce the coordination requirements with customs officials, many firms that wish to do multi-stage processing ship partially processed goods to Hong Kong to ensure they clear customs and then re-import the same goods for further processing. Furthermore, customs officials usually demand that firms completely separate the production lines and inventory stocks associated with production of goods destined for the local market as opposed to foreign markets.

In general, the Hong Kong manufacturing companies have kept their pre-production and post-production activities, including design, development, marketing, sales, and logistics management in Hong Kong, along with senior management and finance, while decentralising production and activities closely related to production.[21] Low labour costs have been the primary driver of the move of production-related activities across the border into Guangdong Province, followed by the availability of low-cost land.[22] Within this general model, the geographic distribution of activities across the corporate value chain has varied by industrial sector (see Chapters 5 and 8). This ongoing division of labour between Hong Kong and the Pearl River Delta region has allowed Hong Kong manufacturing firms to expand their global presence.

Hong Kong as an investment platform for international firms

Other investors use Hong Kong as a base of operations for the Pearl River Delta region as well. The Hong Kong Trade Development Council performed a series of surveys of foreign companies operating in the Pearl River Delta. In one survey, 87% of the Japanese companies with investments in the Pearl River Delta

Table 4.4   Reasons for foreign firms to set up PRD operations, by origin, %

	Japan	Korea	EU	United States
Proximity to Hong Kong	40	45	24	22
Lower production costs	36	34	24	24
Better services to PRD clients	34	5	23	31
Opportunities in the PRD	31	37	60	59
Better infrastructure than elsewhere in the mainland	26	16	24	12
Availability of raw materials, parts, and components	18	39	21	10
Greater openness than other places in the mainland	17	21	16	14
Presence of countries from the same country	13	3	10	14

Note: Percentage of companies indicating the main reasons they set up in the Pearl River Delta.
Source: Hong Kong Trade Development Council 2003l

region claimed those investments had strong links to Hong Kong.[23] The Dutch Chamber of Commerce in Guangzhou also reports that accessibility to Hong Kong is one of the most important factors associated with foreign investments in the Pearl River Delta region.[24] In fact, proximity to Hong Kong was listed as the number one factor that influenced both Japanese and Korean firms to invest in the Pearl River Delta region as opposed to other locations (see Table 4.4). Proximity to Hong Kong was also important to the European Union (EU) and the United States, though somewhat less so than opportunities in serving Pearl River Delta markets, reflecting the fact that the majority of the Japanese and Korean companies were engaged in manufacturing for export, while the EU and United States firms either manufactured for the domestic Chinese market or were service firms.[25] In many cases, foreign investments in the Pearl River Delta region are managed or supported from a Hong Kong base, or the managers themselves live in Hong Kong and commute into the Pearl River Delta region to oversee operations.

The absence of direct links between Taiwan and the Chinese mainland means that nearly all of the Taiwanese firms active in the Pearl River Delta region use Hong Kong to facilitate their investments and to gain access to the Chinese mainland. In a Hong Kong Trade Development Council survey, 82% of the Taiwanese companies with investments in the Pearl River Delta region reported that they had a Hong Kong office.[26] A survey of Taiwanese enterprises in Hong Kong conducted by the China Business Centre of the Hong Kong Polytechnic University shows that Taiwanese firms use their Hong Kong branches to market their products, receive orders, procure raw material and parts, coordinate production in the Chinese mainland, arrange for transportation, collect money, and operate their financial activities.[27] Many Taiwanese enterprises use Hong Kong as a financial base to avoid risks on the Chinese mainland and regulations in Taiwan. Since the renminbi is not freely convertible and Taiwanese authorities intentionally restrict Taiwanese investment on the Chinese mainland, Hong Kong has become the prime facilitator for Taiwanese businesses on the Chinese mainland.[28]

In general, foreign companies claimed that Hong Kong's financial services, location, tax system, information flows, and legal system were strong reasons for using Hong Kong as a base for investing in the Pearl River Delta. The services that they obtain in Hong Kong vary somewhat by industry and nationality. According to the Trade Development Council surveys, regional headquarters or regional office services, import–export, banking and financial services, financial control and auditing services, and transportation and logistics services were among the most common services that foreign companies active in the Pearl River Delta region sourced from Hong Kong (Table 4.5). These results indicate that Hong Kong is a management, finance, control, and business service centre for the Pearl River Delta activities of firms from a wide range of nationalities.

Table 4.5   Types of services acquired from Hong Kong to facilitate PRD operations, %

	Japan	Korea	EU	United States	Taiwan
Import–export trade	56	53	34	43	NA
Business negotiations and liaison	41	21	24	37	NA
Hong Kong regional headquarters or regional office	40	44	54	57	NA
Transportation and logistics	38	47	24	43	80
Banking and financial services	38	53	37	54	77
Material procurement	29	21	15	17	30
Financial control, accounting, auditing	25	29	34	54	25
Marketing and sales	24	23	37	37	34
Insurance	15	2	22	14	17
Others	8	5	NA	NA	NA
Quality control, testing, inspection	7	5	12	17	NA
Legal and arbitration	5	2	20	17	12
Research and development	3	NA	7	14	NA
Other professional services	6	5	7	11	NA
Equity investment/fundraising	NA	NA	NA	NA	13

Note: percentage of companies indicating that they acquired or performed specific services in Hong Kong for Pearl River Delta operations.
Source: Hong Kong Trade Development Council 2003l

TRADE BETWEEN HONG KONG AND THE PEARL RIVER DELTA REGION

Hong Kong investment in the Pearl River Delta region has largely determined the patterns of trade between the two sides. Much of the trade between Hong Kong and the Pearl River Delta region has been prompted by Hong Kong investment in export processing activities in this region. Hong Kong firms export semi-finished products and raw materials made locally or purchased on the international market to the Pearl River Delta region. After they are processed in Hong Kong-invested enterprises in the Pearl River Delta region, Hong Kong companies export the finished products to various parts of the world. This has greatly increased the volume of entrepôt trade between Hong Kong and the Pearl River Delta region, as well as the export of semi-finished products and raw materials made locally.[29]

According to Guangdong statistics, the value of Guangdong's exports to Hong Kong, most of which were re-exported, more than doubled from 1995 to 2002 (see Table 4.6). The majority of Hong Kong's trade with the Chinese mainland involves export processing (see Table 4.7), most of it concentrated in the Pearl River Delta region. According to Guangdong statistics, export processing represented 3.75% of provincial exports in 1980, 72.04% in 1990, 78.09% in 2000, 80.17% in 2001, and 78.67% in 2002. Export processing also accounted for 62.23% of provincial imports in 2001 and 63.84% in 2002 (see Table 4.8).

Trade between the Pearl River Delta region and Hong Kong (including re-export via Hong Kong) accounts for the vast majority of the total trade of the Pearl River Delta region. The main form of trade between the Pearl River Delta region and Hong Kong is import and re-export. Only a small portion is produced in or consumed in Hong Kong. According to a 2001 survey by the Hong Kong Trade Development Council, 86.9% of the products exported by

Table 4.6   Guangdong–Hong Kong trade, 1995–2002, US$ million

Year	Total value of Guangdong exports	Exports to Hong Kong		Total value of Guangdong imports	Imports from Hong Kong	
		Value	(%)		Value	(%)
1995	56,592	22,255	39.3	47,380	6,055	12.8
1999	77,705	26,891	34.6	62,663	4,139	6.6
2000	91,919	32,105	34.9	78,187	5,335	6.8
2001	95,421	33,683	35.3	81,066	5,093	6.3
2002	118,458	42,386	35.8	102,634	5,229	5.1

Source: *Guangdong Statistical Yearbook*, various years

Table 4.7 Hong Kong's trade involving outward processing in the Chinese mainland, 1991–2002

	1991	1994	1996	1998	2000	2002
Estimated value of outward processing (HK$ million)						
Domestic exports to the mainland of China	40,369	41,959	43,089	42,184	39,304	28,848
Re-exports to the mainland of China	73,562	139,221	179,235	179,089	242,929	248,801
Total exports to the mainland of China	113,931	181,179	222,324	221,273	282,233	277,650
Imports from the mainland of China	197,384	354,912	452,890	477,743	567,000	531,034
Re-exports of the mainland of China origin to other places	221,450	422,544	552,822	559,726	647,338	594,708
Estimated proportion of outward processing trade (%)						
Domestic exports to the mainland of China	76.5	71.4	72.8	77.4	72.7	69.8
Re-exports to the mainland of China	48.2	43.3	43.2	44.1	49.7	43.6
Total exports to the mainland of China	55.5	47.7	46.9	48.1	52.0	45.3
Imports from the mainland of China	67.6	75.9	79.9	82.7	79.3	74.0
Re-exports of the mainland of China origin to other places	74.1	82.0	86.0	87.6	85.1	82.8

Source: Hong Kong Special Administrative Region Government, Census and Statistics Department, various years

Table 4.8 Imports and exports of Guangdong by forms of trade and by types of economic units

Exports (%)

| Year | Total | By forms of trade | | | By economic units | | | | |
		General trade	Export processing trade	Others	State-owned units	Collective-owned units	Private-owned units	Foreign-funded units	Other types of ownership
1980	100	95.94	3.75	0.30					
1985	100	82.99	16.72	0.29					
1988	100	32.89	66.05	1.06	87.22			12.27	0.51
1990	100	26.79	72.04	1.17	74.91			24.67	0.43
1993	100	20.90	77.92	1.18	60.10	1.05	0.00	38.42	0.43
1995	100	24.03	74.70	1.26	52.42	1.62	0.01	45.52	0.43
1997	100	24.07	73.54	2.39	47.93	2.27	0.01	49.35	0.44
1999	100	19.84	77.73	2.44	46.02	2.63	0.22	50.73	0.41
2000	100	18.97	78.09	2.94	42.39	2.75	0.67	53.86	0.33
2001	100	17.29	80.17	2.54	37.86	3.61	1.48	56.98	0.08
2002	100	18.33	78.67	3.01	33.91	3.79	3.50	58.77	0.02

(Continued)

Table 4.8 Continued

Imports (%)

| Year | Total | By forms of trade | | | | By economic units | | | | |
		General trade	Export processing trade[a]	Imports of equipment[b]	Others	State-owned units	Collective-owned units	Private-owned units	Foreign funded units	Other types of ownership
1980										
1985	100								13.87	
1988	100	27.76	61.31	6.30	4.64	79.79			18.13	2.09
1990	100	17.54	64.85	14.66	2.95	63.08			36.01	0.90
1993	100	16.67	57.33	19.55	6.46	48.90	0.93	0.00	48.39	1.78
1995	100	9.80	68.37	14.51	7.33	38.21	1.73	0.00	57.94	2.11
1997	100	11.16	70.11	11.35	7.39	37.55	1.99	0.00	58.95	1.52
1999	100	22.12	67.10	6.71	4.07	41.50	2.91	0.29	54.13	1.18
2000	100	26.67	63.14	6.37	3.82	40.16	3.28	0.71	54.39	1.01
2001	100	28.34	62.23	5.81	3.62	38.38	4.04	1.89	54.59	1.09
2002	100	25.95	63.84	5.57	4.63	34.63	2.96	4.30	57.47	0.65

Notes:
(a)'Export processing trade' includes processing with supplied and imported materials.
(b)'Imports of equipment' includes processing equipment and equipment needed by foreign-funded enterprises.
Source: *Guangdong Statistical Yearbook*, various years

Hong Kong business people engaged in export activity in the Chinese mainland were manufactured all or in part in Guangdong Province.[30] More than 90% of Hong Kong's imports from the Pearl River Delta region were reshipped to a third economy.[31] The main destinations of re-exported commodities were the United States, Japan, the EU, and Canada. In 2002, 70 to 80% of export products from the Pearl River Delta region were sold in international markets via Hong Kong, and about 80% of the imports to the Pearl River Delta region passed through Hong Kong.[32]

TECHNOLOGY

Since China's reform program, Hong Kong has been instrumental in the transfer of technology to the Pearl River Delta region. This transfer has come about largely through the direct transfer accompanying investments by Hong Kong firms, the copying of Hong Kong sourced technology by facilities in the Pearl River Delta region, and by Hong Kong acting as intermediary for technology developed elsewhere.

A substantial amount of technology transfer has been coupled with the investments of Hong Kong firms.[33] In the early years of the reform process, much of the technology that was transferred was embodied in imported capital equipment. After 30 years of a planned and closed economy, China had limited capacity for commercial research and development, or even the direct purchase or absorption of modern technologies. Foreign technology was needed if China were to start to meet domestic demand, as well as to produce for export markets. Technology transfer brought about by Hong Kong investments into the Pearl River Delta region at the time had an enormous impact, in part because the investment brought with it modern product design, production equipment, production management, quality control, packaging expertise, and marketing knowledge.[34] Hong Kong-invested facilities generally exhibited large quality advantages over local firms in the Pearl River Delta region, even in labour-intensive products that could be made on equipment from the Chinese mainland. This form of technology transfer continued into the late 1990s, by which time many facilities in the Pearl River Delta region had developed their own technological capabilities and the ability to absorb or copy foreign technology. By the late 1990s, direct technological transfer from Hong Kong firms to the Pearl River Delta region had diminished in importance.

Almost as soon as Hong Kong companies began to transfer technology into the Pearl River Delta region, there were firms that began to copy the technology and even in some cases the products themselves. A large number of Pearl River

Delta region enterprises participated in outward processing for Hong Kong firms. Some of these companies simply produced beyond the agreed amount and sold the rest on the domestic market. Other firms fulfilled their processing contracts and then kept the equipment. Many other companies in the region reverse engineered the products of Hong Kong-invested outward processing enterprises and started producing similar products for the domestic market. Hong Kong companies usually found it fruitless to try to counteract such behaviour.[35]

Since the mid-1990s, the role of Hong Kong firms in technology transfer to the Pearl River Delta region has shifted from that of direct provider more to that of intermediary, sourcing technology on international markets for this region's facilities. However, more and more companies from the Pearl River Delta region are starting to source technology on world markets themselves without Hong Kong or Hong Kong-based entities acting as intermediaries. Given the trends over the last two decades, it is not surprising that direct technology transfer from Hong Kong companies to the Pearl River Delta region would become one of several modes of technology transfer. Increasingly, the most advanced technology introduced into the Pearl River Delta region comes from Taiwanese, Japanese, Korean, or Western firms that use Hong Kong as a base of operations. Direct investments of leading-edge foreign firms coupled with increasing capabilities in the Pearl River Delta region are creating new dynamics.[36]

MANAGEMENT

Transfer and exchange of management experience often is even more important to a developing region than technology transfer. China entered its reform period severely lacking in experience in modern management of market-oriented enterprises. For example, China started its trial MBA programs at Qinghua University, Beijing University, and the People's University of China only in 1991. At the onset of China's reform program, the Pearl River Delta region was more backward from a managerial standpoint than other regions of the country. At the time, Hong Kong-invested enterprises in the region mainly relied on Hong Kong managers, technicians, and some senior workers to manage a large mainland workforce engaged in relatively simple activities.

In the 1990s, this situation began to change. University education in China improved, and more university students from the Chinese mainland began to seek jobs in the Pearl River Delta region as it emerged as one of China's most prosperous areas. At the same time, people from the Pearl River Delta region began to use their accumulated experience to master modern management methods. This led to a division of labour in Hong Kong-invested enterprises in the Pearl River Delta region, with the Hong Kong investors making policy decisions and taking up senior management posts, and their organisations or management personnel in Hong Kong taking charge of international market development, accepting orders, coordinating transportation, and engaging in international finance. Increasingly, people in internal management, accounting, technology, and quality control were recruited from the Chinese mainland. Hong Kong management personnel gradually withdrew from first-line management and even parts of second-line management. Some Hong Kong-invested enterprises began to recruit university graduates and to give them the appropriate training. Others tended to attract people with practical experience from other areas in China. These people increasingly are populating the middle ranks of management in Hong Kong-invested and foreign-invested enterprises. In addition to managing within Hong Kong-invested enterprises, many of the mainland managers developed or recruited by Hong Kong firms have become the entrepreneurs that are now developing the Pearl River Delta region's own private economy.

For firms from Taiwan, the rest of Asia, and the rest of the world, Hong Kong plays a management intermediary role.[37] Hong Kong is the Asia Pacific headquarters location for numerous multinational corporations. It also serves as a springboard for enterprises in Taiwan and South-east Asian countries to invest in China, especially in South China. These enterprises have employed a large number of Hong Kong people to help manage their Pearl River Delta operations. Several also have expatriate managers who live in Hong Kong and commute to facilities in the Pearl River Delta region. Given the limitations on direct linkages across the Taiwan Straits, the exchange of personnel and goods for Taiwanese enterprises are mostly conducted through Hong Kong. The development of Taiwanese enterprises in Pearl River Delta has, therefore, created many new business and managerial opportunities for Hong Kong.[38] Taiwanese enterprises use not just the physical infrastructure of Hong Kong, but also financial and other support services. Taiwanese enterprises, for example, often prefer to have financial trading in Hong Kong and take delivery on the Chinese mainland, thus effectively avoiding some of the risks associated with transacting on the mainland.

As the non-governmental local sector of the Pearl River Delta region economy has developed, many of these companies have started to recruit management and professional people from Hong Kong, especially those with experience in international marketing, financial services, and human resource management. A number of Pearl River Delta region enterprises have put advertisements in Hong Kong newspapers or have held events in Hong Kong to recruit professional personnel resulting in a new type of managerial interaction between Hong Kong and the Pearl River Delta region.

Table 4.9   Hong Kong residents who had worked in the Chinese mainland in the previous 12 months

	Number	Percentage of Hong Kong workforce
October to December 1998	52,300	1.9
October to December 1999	45,600	1.7
April to June 1992	64,200	2.3
September to October 1995	122,300	4.2
May to June 1998	157,300	5.0
April to June 2001	190,800	5.9
April to June 2002	198,100	6.1
January to March 2003	238,200	7.4

Source: Hong Kong Special Administrative Region Government, Census and Statistics Department 2003d

This combination of forces has resulted in a substantial increase in the number of Hong Kong residents that commute to work in the Pearl River Delta region. Between January and March 2003, an estimated 238,200 Hong Kong residents, or 7.4% of the Hong Kong workforce, had worked regularly in the Chinese mainland in the previous 12 months (see Table 4.9). The vast majority of them had worked as managers, administrators, and professionals. Some 88% of the total worked in Guangdong Province, with Shenzhen and Dongguan as the leading locations. The median number of trips to the Chinese mainland made by these people in the previous 12 months was 30. The survey covered people who actually worked in China rather than those who simply conducted business negotiations or other short-term activities there. It also did not include Hong Kong people who had moved their residence into the Chinese mainland, and therefore understates the interaction.

INTERACTION IN THE SERVICE SECTORS

While the interaction between Hong and the Pearl River Delta region has been most obvious to the outside world in the manufacturing sector, the interaction in the service sector has been critically important as well. The Greater Pearl River Delta region would not have emerged to the same extent on the global stage without the supporting service linkages that exist within the region.

Transportation and travel

Hong Kong enterprises have made substantial investments in land transportation in the Pearl River Delta region.[39] Hong Kong firms have been major participants in some of the major highway projects in the region, including the

Guangzhou–Shenzhen expressway, the most important road link in the eastern Delta (Hopewell Holdings, New World Infrastructure, and Cheung Kong); the Humen Bridge, which links the Guangzhou–Shenzhen and Guangzhou–Zhuhai expressways (Hopewell and Yuexiu); the Guangzhou–Zhaoqing expressway (Tai He Group); and the Meilin–Guanlan expressway (Hui Ji Group).[40] Hong Kong businessman Henry Fok has invested in several bridges, a ferry, and roads in and around Panyu, south of Guangzhou City. Other Hong Kong businesses have also been actively engaged in major infrastructure initiatives within the Pearl River Delta region.[41] Hong Kong investors have brought not only capital, but also new concepts, such as toll highways. The Hong Kong-invested Guangzhou–Foshan expressway, for example, was the first road to levy tolls in China. Since 1992, the inflow of funds from Hong Kong has helped make the Pearl River Delta region the leader in the Chinese mainland in terms of density of expressways, a critical advantage over other parts of China.

Hong Kong firms also have played an important role in the development of port facilities in the Pearl River Delta region.[42] Yantian, the most important container port in this region, was partly developed and is managed by Hong Kong-based Hutchison Port Holdings (HPH), the world's leading port operator. HPH also has collaborated in ports in Nanhai, Zhuhai, and Jiangmen. In most cases, HPH has at least a 50% ownership share and also manages the port.[43] Other Hong Kong-invested port facilities can be found, for example, in Shekou (Swire Pacific), Chiwan (Swire Pacific), and Nansha (Henry Ying Tung Fok). Hong Kong entities have been also active in providing ferry service throughout the Greater Pearl River Delta region. In addition to investment, Hong Kong firms provide management and expertise. This has allowed the ports of the Pearl River Delta region to register impressive gains in efficiency to levels well beyond those found in other developing countries.

Transportation linkages between Hong Kong and the Pearl River Delta region have expanded enormously since 1980. From 1980 to 1999, the GDP of the Pearl River Delta region and Hong Kong increased 15 times and five times, respectively, and the shipment of cargo between the two surged 103 times. According to industry sources, highway transport accounted for 84% of the freight transit from the Pearl River Delta region into Hong Kong in 2001, with waterways accounting for 15% and rail only 1%. In 2002, the three-highway border crossing points between Hong Kong and Shenzhen accounted for the transit of some 360,000 TEUs of cargo each month. By far the busiest crossing point for truck traffic was at Lok Ma Chau, which handled 75% of the overland cargo flows into Hong Kong in 2002.[44]

In 2002, Guangdong dispatched 119,520 cargo vessels and 27,870 passenger ships to Hong Kong, 4,871,899 cargo vehicles with Hong Kong as the destination, and 1,324,894 passenger buses with Hong Kong as the destination. Guangdong received 4,883,177 cargo vehicles and 1,320,447 passenger vehicles from Hong Kong. Direct bus services between Hong Kong and major cities of the Pearl River Delta have greatly improved the land transport linkages. For example, there were 275,131 passenger vehicle trips between Guangdong and Hong Kong in 1992. By 2002, this figure had increased to 2,645,341, or nearly 10 times the figure of 10 years before.[45]

In November 2001, the Hong Kong government performed a survey of cross-boundary travel between Hong Kong and the Chinese mainland at the eight land, air, and sea transit points.[46] The 333,000 cross-boundary passenger trips per day uncovered represented a 17% increase from 1999. Of the trips to the Chinese mainland, 42% were for leisure, 31% for business, 20% to visit friends or relatives, and 4% for travel to work. Of the trips to Hong Kong, 32% involved trips for work, 23% for business, and 21% for leisure. The survey indicated that there were in the order of 31,300 vehicle trips per day, an increase of 9.7% over 1999. The vast majority of the vehicle trips across the border were made by container trucks (40%) or other goods vehicles (39%). Private cars accounted for 17% of the vehicle trips, coaches 3%, and shuttle buses 1%. Empty containers accounted for 23% of the container truck traffic to Hong Kong and 71% of the container truck traffic to the Chinese mainland.

Land transportation between Hong Kong and the Pearl River Delta region has been seriously constrained by delays at the border crossings between Hong Kong and Shenzhen for both passenger and cargo traffic. In 2002, delays in the order of two hours or more were common for passengers crossing the border. Trucks trying to cross the border often waited four hours or more – a wait which virtually doubled the cost of trucking goods from the Pearl River Delta region to Hong Kong, since the trucks generally could make only one trip, rather than two trips per day. As of 2004, though multiple steps were being taken to improve cross-border flows (see Chapter 6), connectivity across the boundary between Hong Kong and Shenzhen remained a major issue.

Tourism

Close geographic, cultural, and family links between Hong Kong and the Pearl River Delta region have provided a solid foundation for tourism. The processes of reform and opening have boosted flows of growth in business and leisure travel in both directions. Hong Kong investors built the first high-grade hotels in the Pearl River Delta region, such as the White Swan Hotel and the Garden Hotel in Guangzhou. This helped establish standards for the hospitality industry in the region, improved the availability of accommodation for business and leisure travellers, and provided support for further economic interaction.

Hong Kong tourists have been a major source of foreign exchange earnings for the Pearl River Delta region. Over 90% of the foreign tourists to the Pearl River Delta region come from Hong Kong.[47] According to the Hong Kong Government Census and Statistics Department and the Hong Kong Retail Management Association, in 2000, Hong Kong residents spent the equivalent of US$2.6 billion in Guangdong Province on personal travel, with 36% of this spent in Shenzhen. Of the total Guangdong expenditure, US$1.36 billion went for lodging and meals, US$730 million for entertainment, transportation, and other services, and US$270 million for shopping.[48]

The rapid growth of the Pearl River Delta region has also contributed to the development of tourism in Hong Kong. Before the outbreak of SARS, in 2002 tourism from the Chinese mainland was one of the bright spots in Hong Kong's otherwise lacklustre economy. In that year, 41.2% of tourist arrivals to Hong Kong were from the Chinese mainland. Around 80% of these came from Guangdong Province.[49] In 2002, tourism receipts from visitors from the Chinese mainland to Hong Kong reached US$3.43 billion, up from US$2.95 billion in 2001.[50] Visitors from the Chinese mainland spent an average of US$723 per trip to Hong Kong, the highest among any visitor group, up from US$663 in 2001.[51] These figures did not reflect the full spending potential of mainland tourists because such tourists to Hong Kong had to travel on approved group tours, which tended to limit the travel frequencies and spending patterns of the participants.

Arrivals from the Chinese mainland fell precipitously during the first half of 2003 as cross-border traffic fell sharply due to SARS. In July 2003, as SARS receded, the Central Government started a process of relaxing restrictions on individual travel to Hong Kong. Before then, mainland travellers to Hong Kong had been required to join group tours. As a first step, the right to visit Hong Kong under individual travel permits was extended to mainland tourists from eight major urban centres in the Pearl River Delta region, as well as Beijing and Shanghai. The result was an immediate rise in the number of mainland visitors to Hong Kong and an associated boost in tourist spending which was welcome to Hong Kong's retail, hotel, and restaurant sectors.[52] In December 2003, approximately 667,000 mainlanders visited Hong Kong on individual visas, most of them from the Pearl River Delta region, and by a leading analyst's estimate their average per capita spending was roughly US$1,026.[53]

Prior to the implementation of the Closer Economic Partnership Arrangement (CEPA) between the People's Republic of China and Hong Kong in 1994, business interaction in tourism services was severely restricted by barriers to market entry in the Pearl River Delta region. Some Hong Kong firms managed to provide foreign tourism services for residents in the Pearl River Delta region by 'receiving orders on the mainland and carrying out operations in Hong Kong'. Some residents of the Pearl River Delta region found it more convenient and less expensive to participate in foreign tours or business tours organised by Hong Kong travel services than by domestic travel services.

Residential real estate

Hong Kong developers have brought Hong Kong capital, Hong Kong designs, and Hong Kong construction techniques into the Pearl River Delta region. They have created entire office complexes and residential estates, including New World Garden in Dongguan and Ersha Island villas in Guangzhou (New World), Haiyi Golf Links and villas in Dongguan (Changjiang Industry), Jincheng Garden in Guangzhou (New Honji Real Estate), and Dongfeng Plaza in Guangzhou (Lixin Group). One early example was Clifford Gardens, a complete residential and vacation home community developed by Hong Kong interests in Panyu that included schools, shopping, a farm, a hotel, a lake, and full-time security staff. In the period 1991 to 1999, Hong Kong interests supplied 43% of the funds (and 90% of the foreign funds) invested in Guangzhou's real estate industry.[54] Hong Kong developers have been participating in the redevelopment of central Guangzhou and have been developing several large residential estates along the new Guangzhou mass transit system, investments that should help transform land usage in and around the city. Hong Kong developers also have been quite active in Shenzhen, Dongguan, and have been increasingly active in Zhuhai and other cities of the region.

The Pearl River Delta region has provided an ample supply of land suitable for residential use at prices affordable to Hong Kong residents. Growing numbers of people from Hong Kong have been buying holiday homes or even primary residences in the region, especially in Shenzhen, Dongguan, Shunde, and Panyu. The Bank of China's Shenzhen branch indicated that Hong Kong people bought 6.1 million square feet of housing worth RMB 2.8 billion in Shenzhen in 2001. The Bank of China launched a mortgage scheme in 2002 to allow Hong Kong people to make their mortgage payments in Hong Kong dollars in Hong Kong.[55] In practice, however, the Pearl River Delta region residential property market has served several distinct, though limited, categories of Hong Kong-based demand. These have included weekend and holiday homes; residences serving dual business and residential purposes, doubling as office premises and short-term overnight accommodation; residences for the elderly, including group retirement housing and nursing homes; and, to a limited extent, primary residences, largely for childless couples commuting to Hong Kong for work.[56]

Residential property prices have tended to vary by geographic location within the Pearl River Delta region – property with easy access to Hong Kong commanding a premium. However, factor price equalisation between the Hong Kong and Shenzhen residential property markets has not occurred due to several factors. The travel time to get to jobs in Hong Kong should not, in and of itself, be insurmountable. A more basic impediment is that for the 31% of Hong Kong residents who live in subsidised public rental housing, it is cheaper to stay in Hong Kong than to move across the border.[57] In addition, Hong Kong purchasers have been willing to pay a premium for the intangibles attached to purchases of property located within the Hong Kong Special Administrative Region. These include secure title to property, political rights, and neighbourhood-specific public services in the areas of security, education, and medical services.

Retail shopping

In June 1992, the Chinese Government decided to open the retail sector to foreign investors gradually, starting with the special economic zones. In 1993, China Resources of Hong Kong opened a supermarket in Shenzhen, the first Hong Kong retailer to enter the region. Hong Kong-invested chain stores and franchised shops, such as ParknShop, Giordano, Theme, Bossini, U2, Baleno, Free Bird, Seven-Eleven, Circle K, Watson's, Jusco, TrustMart, Tianmao Group, Wanja, the Dickson Group, and others entered the region. By 2002, there were more than 500 wholesale, retail sales, and catering enterprises financed by Hong Kong investment in Guangzhou alone.[58] Foreign retailers often use the Pearl River Delta region as their starting point for China and some of these stores are among their very biggest in the world. Restrictions on wholly for- eign-owned enterprises in the retail sector have meant that the Hong Kong investment has entered mostly through joint ventures.[59] Even so, most of the investment has been allowed by local governments using flexible interpretations of Central Government policies or with the tacit consent of Central Government, resulting in a more open playing field than that provided for in China's WTO accession protocol.

Linked with growing travel and tourism between Hong Kong and the Pearl River Delta region has been an increase in cross-border shopping. Spending on retail purchases in Hong Kong by visitors from the Pearl River Delta region has risen along with their incomes. In 2000, visitors from the Chinese mainland spent 65% of their total Hong Kong expenditures on shopping, making their per capita retail shopping expenditures the highest of any visitor group.[60] In the Pearl River Delta region, import duties on luxury consumer goods have been high and distribution inefficient. Even in Guangzhou, the Pearl River Delta's largest city, 'imported' branded goods (real or counterfeit) tend to be sold in high-end shopping centres at prices higher than in Hong Kong. Among visitors from Guangdong Province and elsewhere in the mainland, Hong Kong has become a sought-after shopping destination for foreign name brand products, such Japanese electronics and electrical goods, and luxury goods, such as French perfume, Italian shoes, and European garments.[61] Demand generated by visitors from the Chinese mainland also has become a mainstay of Hong Kong's gold and jewellery industries. Mainland tourists are attracted by Hong Kong's stringent gold purity standards.

As crossing the border has become easier, more and more low and middle-income people from Hong Kong have started to go to Shenzhen and other places in the Pearl River Delta region to shop. The border crossing areas in Shenzhen have filled with shops that cater to cross-border trade. Whereas at one time the traffic across the boundary from Hong Kong had been dominated by business trips and family visits, leisure and shopping trips were the dominant reasons for transit by 2003.

LIMITS TO INTERACTION

Despite the extensiveness of the interaction between Hong Kong and the Pearl River Delta region, there have been a number of limits to the interaction. One has involved mindset and understanding. Many people on both sides have not been sufficiently familiar with the possibilities created by the interaction to pursue opportunities aggressively. Another has involved language and culture. In many instances in the Chinese mainland, it has been necessary to communicate in the local dialect of the customer. This is often different from Putonghua, the national language and also the language of the Beijing area, or Cantonese, the main dialect in Hong Kong and Guangdong Province. Given the long separation between Hong Kong and the Chinese mainland, the fact that Hong Kong has been open to foreign influence while China has been closed to such influence, and the difference in affluence between Hong Kong and the Pearl River Delta region, it is not surprising that cultural gaps have arisen that need to be narrowed before business can take place on a completely fluid basis. If anything, this tendency has been heightened somewhat by the existence of regionalism in China, which stresses local connections and limits dealings with 'outsiders', including those from other provinces or jurisdictions.

There also have been limits to interaction that have resulted from the 'one country, two systems' formula under which Hong Kong was returned to Chinese administration. The most obvious has been the existence of a border (or 'boundary') between Hong Kong and Shenzhen that separates Hong Kong and the Chinese mainland into two customs zones and two zones for immigration purposes. Thus while there has been extensive and increasing travel between Hong Kong and the Pearl River Delta region, that travel has been by no means without its frictions. These have been readily apparent in the need for visas for travel and in the customs inspections (and resulting delays) that goods have gone through in order to cross the boundary. Less obvious, but just as important, have been the high expense to Hong Kong residents of obtaining Pearl River Delta jurisdiction licence plates (as of 2003, only a small number had been issued relative to the size of Hong Kong's driving population) and difficulties in obtaining a driver's licence across the border. Also less visible have been limits on the number of licences granted for cross-boundary trucking that add to the cost of trucking across the boundary, or limits on investments in the Chinese mainland in general, or limits associated with particular types of investments in the Pearl River Delta region, such as export processing rules, which limit the flexibility of some firms to sell into the Chinese mainland from their mainland facilities.

Most service sectors in the Chinese mainland have been restricted to outside companies in one way or another, even under China's WTO accession agreement and the CEPA with Hong Kong. Since Hong Kong has been regarded as a foreign country when it comes to the provision of services in the mainland, Hong Kong service providers have faced a number of government restrictions when doing business in China. For many Hong Kong-based firms in financial and business services, licensing has been the first obstacle. Some interviewees described the various regulations as being 'overwhelming'. They found that restrictions were not always apparent, that there were often differences between different townships and provinces, and that rules were not consistently predictive of outcomes. On its part, Hong Kong also has licensing rules in many professions that are based on a completely different system than that found on the Chinese mainland.

The barriers to outside service firms doing business in the Chinese mainland have differed by sector. When compared to areas such as recruitment, management consultancy, and advertising, where the institutional barriers have not been insurmountable, the legal and accountancy sectors have been much more constrained. In legal services, the foundations of Hong Kong and mainland legal systems are different. Hong Kong operates under the British common law system, whereas the system in the mainland is founded on principles of continental law. This has had repercussions on the range of services that Hong Kong-based lawyers have been able to provide to companies in China. Prior to CEPA, Hong Kong lawyers have been considered 'foreign' service providers and as such have not been allowed to practise Chinese law; these restrictions are being eased somewhat under CEPA (see Chapter 7). They have also been restricted by the 'one office one location' rule, which has limited the geographical coverage of their business on the mainland, and the prohibition on Hong Kong lawyers forming partnerships with mainland lawyers.

Similarly, Hong Kong-based accountancy firms have faced sector-specific restrictions when operating in China. Though there are differences in accounting systems between Hong Kong and the Pearl River Delta region, dual reports have not been allowed, and there has been no mutual recognition of qualifications. The requirement that accountancy firms should have 'international status' and have paid in capital of US$20 million to register a company in China has prevented these firms from expanding Hong Kong offices into the Pearl River Delta region.

There also have been tax and currency implications for Hong Kong-based service firms doing business in the Pearl River Delta region. Local Pearl River Delta region companies have been discouraged from engaging the services of firms from Hong Kong if bills would have to be settled in Hong Kong dollars, given the difficulty of obtaining foreign exchange in many instances. Hong Kong service providers, however, have been reluctant to bill their Pearl River Delta region clients locally in renminbi, in light of a rate of tax payable double that of Hong Kong.[62]

Overcoming limits: Informal market access

Even in sectors that have formal limits on participation by outside firms, some have found ways to operate in the Pearl River Delta region anyway. Official data on the penetration of Hong Kong and other foreign-investment firms in the Pearl River Delta region do not reflect service activities that have developed through a number of informal mechanisms used to bypass official restrictions. Capital of foreign origin has been registered under names of local people or hidden in other ways. Capital that has entered openly and legally has been used beyond a strict service or geographic mandate. Foreign firms have officially entered joint ventures as the non-controlling party, but in fact have controlled the venture, for example, with overseas investors lending money to the domestic partners for their share of investment. Foreign investment has been introduced by local government modifications of Central Government policy or with Central Government consent, either explicit or tacit.[63] Since the Pearl River Delta region is an area approved by the Central Government for experiments in opening up the service sector, local governments have had a certain degree of autonomy and have introduced projects restricted under Central Government policies.

Some informal access mechanisms have fallen outside mainland regulations. Foreign investment in most consumer services has been prohibited by Chinese Government policy, but there have been many enterprises in which foreign capital has funded companies registered under the names of locals. Import and export services in China have been off limits to foreign companies, but foreign investors have been known to register in the name of a domestic company with businesses affiliated to a state-owned specialised foreign trade company, which is paid a management fee. Although foreign insurance providers in the Pearl River Delta region have been subject to tight restrictions, some companies have marketed to customers in the Pearl River Delta region and then signed them up when they travel to Hong Kong or Macao.

In print media, foreign investors have participated by focusing on operations, such as advertising, distribution, and printing, but not by being involved in the editorial aspects of the business. Foreign real estate agencies have formed joint ventures registered as domestic enterprises to enter the industry. Foreign advertising firms have been restricted to serving foreign-invested enterprises, but some have developed local customers by launching joint ventures with domestic firms. In some restricted professions, Hong Kong-based professionals have been invited to provide specialist services or advice by government agencies in the Chinese mainland. Liberalised access to China's service markets under the CEPA should reduce – but not eliminate – pressures for informal access by Hong Kong firms to the Pearl River Delta region, though the effects will vary sector by sector (see Chapter 7).

THE VALUE OF LINKAGES TO HONG KONG

The linkages between Hong Kong and the Pearl River Delta region have been valuable to both. One can get at least a partial picture of the value of this interaction by looking at the development of different parts of the Pearl River Delta region. Hong Kong's interaction with this region is highly location specific. This has been particularly true for Hong Kong's SMEs, which are dependent on service facilities and networks, and so have generally chosen investment locations near to Hong Kong.[64] The vast majority of the interaction has been between Hong Kong and the eastern and central parts of the Delta. This has been true of investment links, trade links, service links, travel links, and passenger links. The result has been a dramatic difference in the development patterns in different parts of the Pearl River Delta region.

The main reason for the differences in the density of links between Hong Kong and various parts of the Pearl River Delta region is connectivity. The vast majority of the Hong Kong-based company owners and senior managers that we interviewed indicated that their firms would invest only in facilities that could be reasonably reached in three hours by automobile from Hong Kong. They wanted to ensure that it was possible to leave Hong Kong in the morning, visit the factory, and then return to Hong Kong the same day. This roughly translates to a trip of three hours or less. For most firms this precluded locations other than the eastern and central portions of the Pearl River Delta from Shenzhen to Guangzhou.[65] The same 'magic three hours' was cited by Hong Kong-based service providers, who indicated that they generally would not try to serve clients more than a three-hour automobile trip from Hong Kong. It also was cited by foreign buyers, who want to be able to visit the factories where their products are made within a three-hour trip of Hong Kong. These owners, managers, service providers, and buyers did not want to be restricted to ferries and ferry timetables.

According to the Hong Kong government's 2001 survey of cross-border travel, the vast majority of passenger trips and vehicle trips that connected Hong Kong with the Chinese mainland actually linked Hong Kong to the eastern or central portion of the Pearl River Delta region.[66] Of the passengers crossing from Hong Kong into the Chinese mainland, 61% had Shenzhen as their destination, 14% had Dongguan as their destination, 8% had Guang-zhou as their destination, and 17% were going to other destinations. The sources or destinations of cross-border passenger car trips between Hong Kong and the Chinese mainland were: Shenzhen 64%, Dongguan 17%, Guangzhou 4%, Huizhou 3%, and 'Other' 12%. Passenger cars are important because they are the preferred means of travel of factory owners, foreign investors, and senior managers. Of the container trucks and goods vehicles crossing the boundary, the sources or destinations in the Chinese mainland were: Shenzhen 52%, Dongguan 34%, Huizhou 5%, and 'Other' 9%. According to industry sources, only one-third of the container throughput for the port of Hong Kong comes from the western part of the Pearl River Delta region, with two-thirds coming from the eastern portion of the Delta. The simple conclusion from these results is that the connectivity between Hong Kong and the eastern portion of the Pearl River Delta region is far greater than that between Hong Kong and the western portion of the Pearl River Delta region.

The value of this connectivity can be seen by tracing the differences in development between the eastern and western portion of the Pearl River Delta region. According to the Guangdong Statistical Bureau, in 1980, for example, Zhuhai and Zhongshan, the two jurisdictions immediately north of Macao on the western side of the Delta had registered populations of 365,000 and 1,010,000. Shenzhen and Dongguan had populations of 321,000 and 1,127,000. The GDP of Zhuhai and Zhongshan were RMB 375 million (US$250.3 million) and RMB 635 million (US$423.8 million), while those of Shenzhen and Dongguan were RMB 270 million (US$180.2 million) and RMB 704 million (US$469.8 million). In other words, in 1980, the combination of Zhuhai and Zhongshan was nearly identical to the combination of Shenzhen and Dongguan in terms of population and economic output. By 1990, the combined Census population of Shenzhen and Dongguan (1.7 million and 1.7 million) had outpaced that of Zhuhai and Zhongshan (635,500 and 1.2 million). The combined GDP of Shenzhen and Dongguan, RMB 13.6 billion (US$2.8 billion) and RMB 6.5 billion (US$1.4 billion), was more than twice that of Zhuhai and Zhongshan, RMB 4.1 billion and RMB 4.4 billion (roughly US$0.9 billion each). By 2000, the Census populations of Shenzhen and Dongguan were seven million and 6.5 million, while those of Zhuhai and Zhongshan were 1.2 million and 2.4 million. In 2002, the combined GDP of Shenzhen and Dongguan, RMB 225.68 billion (US$27.3 billion) and RMB 67.29 billion (US$8.1 billion), were now more than three times that of Zhuhai and Zhongshan, RMB 40.63 billion (US$4.9 billion) and RMB 41.57 billion (US$5.0 billion). From a virtual dead heat in 1980, the combination of Shenzhen and Dongguan had grown to more than three and a half times the economic output of their western counterparts (see Table 4.10).

Why did the two portions of the Pearl River Delta region that started with virtually identical populations and economic outputs diverge so dramatically? Both are in the Pearl River Delta region. Both have a Special Economic Zone (Shenzhen and Zhuhai). Both are just north of Special Administrative Regions of China (Hong Kong and Macao). The main difference has been the connectivity

Table 4.10 Comparisons of the east and west sides of the Pearl River Delta

	1980		1990		2000	2002
	Population (millions)	GDP RMB (billions)	Population (millions)	GDB RMB (billions)	Population (millions)	GDP RMB (billions)
Shenzhen + Dongguan	1.45	0.974	3.400	20.10	13.50	292.97
Zhongshan + Zhuhai	1.38	1.010	1.835	8.50	3.60	82.20

Source: Calculations by Enright, Scott & Associates Ltd, based on *Guangdong Statistical Yearbook*, various years

of the eastern portion of the Delta with Hong Kong. The result has been a huge influx of investment, technology, and management from Hong Kong firms and foreign firms with Hong Kong offices into the eastern portion of the Delta. This investment, in turn, powered the development of an export economy in Shenzhen and Dongguan that allowed those two jurisdictions to leave their western Delta counterparts far behind. As of 2002, the value of connectivity to Hong Kong was in the order of RMB 210 billion (or in excess of US$25 billion) per year in GDP, a figure that had been growing rapidly, for just Shenzhen and Dongguan. This translates to approximately US$1,850 per inhabitant of Shenzhen and Dongguan in a country whose per capita GDP only exceeded US$1,000 in 2003. The differential here is not between the areas adjacent to Hong Kong and areas in China's interior. Nor is the differential between areas adjacent to Hong Kong and outlying areas of Guangdong Province. The differential is between areas adjacent to Hong Kong and areas similarly situated that are less than 30 kilometres away. This makes the value of the direct connectivity with Hong Kong all the more impressive.

THE IMPORTANCE OF THE INTERACTION

The interaction of Hong Kong and the Pearl River Delta region has been crucial to the prosperity that both have enjoyed over the last two decades. In the Pearl River Delta region, Hong Kong firms have helped develop a world-class manufacturing base that has greatly improved their ability to serve world markets. These developments have made the Pearl River Delta region the most dynamic economy in the Chinese mainland since the onset of China's economic reform process, as well as one of the most affluent. They also have allowed Hong Kong to have the world's busiest container port and the world's busiest international cargo airport. They have enhanced Hong Kong's role as a centre for finance, management, coordination, and communication. They increasingly are making the entire Greater Pearl River Delta region an important market for firms from Hong Kong, the Pearl River Delta region, the rest of China, and the rest of the world.[67]

Over the last two decades the economic interaction between Hong Kong and the Pearl River Delta region has grown and deepened to the point where it is impossible to seriously discuss the development of one without also discussing the development of the other. It is the interaction that has fostered the development of a competitive economic system with distinctive inner workings. It is to this system we turn next.

CHAPTER FIVE

Combinations and Competitiveness in the Greater Pearl River Delta Region[1]

T he interaction between Hong Kong and the Pearl River Delta region has created a unique combination of economic systems that has fostered the development of a range of internationally competitive industries and clusters in the Greater Pearl River Delta. The combination builds off a division of labour driven by differences in systems, resources, costs, skills, capabilities, market knowledge, and external linkages. The resulting complementarity has been a great advantage and source of development for Hong Kong and the Pearl River Delta region.[2] At the same time, there is an increasing sense of competition between Hong Kong and the Pearl River Delta region in a range of activities and industries.[3] In order for business people, policymakers, and investors to understand the competitiveness of the Greater Pearl River Delta region, it is necessary to delve into the combinations, complementarity, and competition in the region on an industry-by-industry and activity-by-activity basis.

MANUFACTURING INDUSTRIES

The complementarities between Hong Kong and the Pearl River Delta region in the manufacturing sector have become more pronounced over time. These complementarities can be best seen by tracking the evolution of the activities of Hong Kong-owned or invested manufacturing and related trading companies in the region. In the 1980s, many Hong Kong firms started their migration into the Pearl River Delta region by moving relatively simple assembly activities in a search for lower costs. Over time, more and more extensive manufacturing activities were moved out of Hong Kong or built up for the first time in the Pearl River Delta region. As the Pearl River Delta region continued to grow, Hong Kong firms and firms from Taiwan and elsewhere began to place other activities related to logistics, quality control, sourcing, and packaging into the region. At the same time, many of the highest value-added activities were concentrated in Hong Kong.[4]

The trends can be seen clearly in results of two surveys carried out by the Hong Kong Trade Development Council portrayed in Figures 5.1, 5.2, and 5.3.[5] In these surveys, Hong Kong companies were asked about the future locations of their various activities. In 1997, well over 90% of the firms expected that their trade documentation and finance would be located in Hong Kong in the future. At the other extreme, fewer than 20% expected any of their manufacturing activities to be located in Hong Kong (see Figure 5.1). In general, the higher

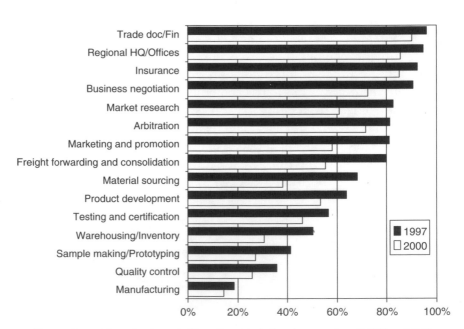

Source: Created from data from the Hong Kong Trade Development Council 1998 and 2002a

Figure 5.1 Hong Kong manufacturing and trading companies' activities expected to be performed there in the future

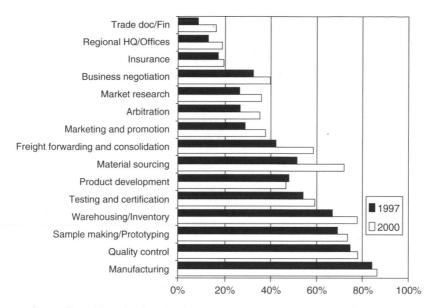

Source: Created from data from the Hong Kong Trade Development Council 1998 and 2002a

Figure 5.2   Hong Kong manufacturing and trading companies' activities expected to be performed in the Chinese mainland in the future

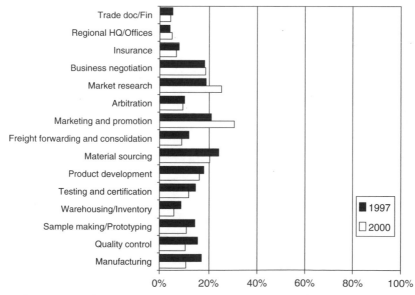

Source: Created from data from the Hong Kong Trade Development Council 1998 and 2002a

Figure 5.3   Hong Kong manufacturing and trading companies' activities expected to be performed in third economies in the future

value added the activity, the greater the expectation that it would be performed in Hong Kong in the future.

In 1997, the same companies exhibited the opposite expectations about the location of their activities in the Chinese mainland (see Figure 5.2). In fact, the two figures show the almost pure complementarity between Hong Kong and the Chinese mainland. Since the vast majority of the activities of the Hong Kong firms in the mainland were in, and were expected to be in, the Pearl River Delta region, the figures show the complementarity between Hong Kong and the Pearl River Delta region for manufacturing and related trading companies. The year 2000 results in Figures 5.1 and 5.2 show the expectation of an almost across the board decrease in activities to be located in Hong Kong and a similar increase in the activities to be performed in the Chinese mainland. Figure 5.3 shows that some activities (such as market research, marketing, and promotion) were expected to be expanded in third economies (neither Hong Kong nor the Chinese mainland) and other activities (mostly linked to manufacturing and logistics) were expected to contract in third economies.

To a certain extent these results are to be expected, given the rapid development of the Pearl River Delta region and the increasing number of activities that can be performed there. The most dramatic movements out of Hong Kong were expected in some areas related to business negotiation, marketing, freight forwarding, and consolidation, material sourcing, and warehousing and inventory. Some of these expected movements out of Hong Kong represented movements of marketing-related activities closer to customers in China and in third economies. Some of the movements represented the further consolidation of manufacturing and closely related activities into the Chinese mainland from both Hong Kong and third economies. Others represented an increased focus on performing logistics and sourcing activities in the Chinese mainland.

Our own interviews indicated a similar pattern. For Hong Kong firms with activities in the Pearl River Delta region, a small number of senior-level staff in Hong Kong generally oversees a much larger staff based in the Pearl River Delta region. Although top management is based in Hong Kong, it is not uncommon for top managers to spend four days per week on site in the Pearl River Delta region.[6] Hong Kong is still the preferred location due to family and lifestyle considerations. Many senior managers would not consider moving away from Hong Kong's housing, schooling, medical facilities, cultural amenities, and other support services. Many Hong Kong-based senior managers have mixed feelings about localising upper-level management in the Pearl River Delta region. While they appreciate the rising skill levels and wage advantages they could obtain in this region, they are less comfortable about the loyalty and specialist expertise of managers from the Chinese mainland. The corporate communications and finance functions for the Hong Kong firms tend to be kept in Hong Kong in close proximity to the seat of senior management.

The managers told us not only that the vast majority of production had moved out of Hong Kong, but that some Hong Kong firms have exited manufacturing altogether to focus on supply chain management. Purchasing departments of Hong Kong firms that purchase inputs primarily from within the Chinese mainland are increasingly moving to the Pearl River Delta region, while Hong Kong remains the dominant location for purchasing offices for Hong Kong firms that purchase inputs from international markets. Technological development is often split, with research, customer-oriented design, and fine-tuning being carried out in Hong Kong and the bulk of the basic application development undertaken by technical staff in the Pearl River Delta region. Quality control is increasingly performed in the Pearl River Delta region, though Hong Kong retains a role. Routine bookkeeping associated with production has often been moved to the Pearl River Delta region (though frequently performed by Hong Kong people), while senior-level accounting remains in Hong Kong.

For many internationally oriented firms, the sales and marketing teams tend to be based in Hong Kong, where the knowledge of international markets is far superior to that found in the Pearl River Delta region. On the other hand, in some industries, notably toys, international buyers already have set up offices in the Pearl River Delta region, forcing Hong Kong-based firms to move their sales teams as well. In general, however, the activities associated with commercialisation of the products for the international markets are performed in Hong Kong to take advantage of the knowledge and expertise of international and individual markets. Although many Hong Kong firms still use Hong Kong as a base for commercialising their products for the Chinese mainland, increasingly they are looking to locations in the Pearl River Delta region to perform this role.

Light manufacturing

The Greater Pearl River Delta region has become perhaps the world's leading centre for a wide range of light-manufactured goods and one of the leading locations for assembly manufacturing of higher technology electronics products. The region is a world leader in the production of garments, textiles, footwear, toys, plastic products, travel goods, handbags, umbrellas, artificial flowers, and imitation jewellery.[7] Competitiveness in these industries has been built largely on the combination and complementarity of Hong Kong and Pearl River Delta region attributes. Increasing competition in recent years has increased the dynamism of the sector.

The region's greatest strengths in these industries include a low-cost and productive workforce, relatively inexpensive land, reasonable infrastructure, improving technical skills, and a supportive policy regime. The industries also benefit from the investment, management, market knowledge, technology, and international connections obtained through Hong Kong. Labour costs for assembly labour have stayed surprisingly low in the Pearl River Delta region (see Table 5.1) because the bulk of the workforce in the manufacturing facilities, at least in the export-oriented industries on the eastern side of the Pearl River Delta region, is made up of migrant workers from the inner provinces. Many of these workers come into the region for one or two years, make some money, and then return to their home provinces. Managers in some industries report that wages for assembly labour have not changed much in real terms for nearly a decade. Despite rising land costs in Shenzhen, the cost of industrial land is still relatively low elsewhere in the Pearl River Delta region.[8] The Greater Pearl River Delta region also benefits from infrastructure that is generally far better than that found in economies at similar levels of development. The combination of Hong Kong and the Pearl River Delta region means that Third World level costs are combined with First World calibre management, infrastructure, and market knowledge. This combination has proven to be virtually unbeatable in any industry in which it can be brought to bear.

In several light manufacturing industries, such as toys, clothing, luggage, and handbags, the competition in the Greater Pearl River Delta region is between Hong Kong producers with Pearl River Delta facilities and Chinese mainland companies with facilities in the Pearl River Delta region. Hong Kong companies that once were virtually unrivalled in the low-priced segments of their industries now face stiff competition from Pearl River Delta region counterparts.[9] Hong Kong firms have retained strong positions in mid-priced segments through the development of strategies that add value via design, technology, systems integration, marketing, novel channels, or specialist capabilities.

Toys

One good example of the combinations and competitiveness of light manufacturing industries in the Greater Pearl River Delta region is the toy industry. China dominates toy production worldwide. According to the International Toy Association, China accounts for approximately 70% of world production in the toy industry, with some 80% of production sold in export markets. The United States-based Toy Industry Association estimated that China accounted for 72% of all toy imports into the United States in 2002. China's position was even more dominant in dolls and accessories (92%) and general toys (84%). The association Toys Industry of Europe estimated that China was the source of 62.5% of

Table 5.1 Factory costs in selected Pearl River Delta Region cities, 2002

	Shenzhen	Dongguan	Huizhou	Guangzhou	Foshan	Jiangmen	Zhongshan	Zhuhai
Monthly salaries and wages (RMB)								
– Middle manager	3,000–5,000	3,000–5,000	2,000–3,000	3,000–5,000	3,000–5,000	3,000–5,000	3,000–5,000	3,000–5,000
– Supervisor	2,000–3,000	2,000–3,000	1,500–2,000	1,500–2,000	1,500–2,000	1,500–2,000	1,500–2,000	1,500–2,000
– Skilled labour	1,500–2,000	800–1,500	1,000–1,500	1,000–1,400	800–1,200	1,000–1,500	1,000–1,500	800–1,500
– Unskilled labour	800–900	500–800	500–700	600–800	400–800	600–800	600–800	400–600
Social charges	18.0–19.0%	15.5–16.5%	15.5–16.5%	31.2–32.2%	21.5%	21.5%	12.0%	19.5%
Factory and running costs								
– Monthly factory rental (RMB/sq. m.)	11–14	8–9	8–10	12–25	8–10	8–10	12–13	6–12
– Electricity (RMB/KW hr)	0.61–0.93	1.08	0.62	0.70	0.69	0.76	0.80	0.68–0.78
– Water (RMB/cu. m.)	1.75	1.16	1.90	1.05	1.05	1.25	1.16	1.18
– Waste discharge fee (RMB/cu. m.)	0.34	0.33	0.30	0.30	0.30	Exempt	Exempt	0.18
Taxation[a]								
– Maximum corporate income tax	15%	33%	33%	33%	24%	24%	24%	15%
– VAT	17%	17%	17%	17%	17%	17%	17%	17%
– Personal income tax	5–45%	5–45%	5–45%	5–45%	5–45%	5–45%	5–45%	5–45%

Note: (a) There are additional taxes and fees, such as inspection taxes and fees, real estate taxes, and others not included in this table.
Source: The Dutch Chamber of Commerce in Guangzhou

the imports of toys into the European Union (excluding intra EU trade) in 2002. Within China, the industry is dominated by Guangdong. The Chinese Toy Association has estimated that between 60 and 70% of China's toy exports come from Guangdong Province.[10] Finally, Guangdong production is dominated by Hong Kong firms that, by our estimation, employed in the order of one million people in the Pearl River Delta region as of 2003.[11]

Worldwide, the toy sector is characterised by a limited number of large companies that outsource production to Hong Kong firms operating in the Pearl River Delta region and elsewhere in China. In the toy sector, different activities are carried out in different places. Manufacturing and much of purchasing are carried out in the Pearl River Delta region, supported by the region's strong cluster of toys, components, and material inputs. The purchasing of imported components is performed in Hong Kong. In R&D, Hong Kong toy manufacturers draw on the advantages of both Hong Kong and the Pearl River Delta region. Research often takes place in Hong Kong with its superior access to overseas markets and information, and development is carried out in the Pearl River Delta region, where the engineering talent is cheaper (see Figure 5.4).[12]

Planning, sales, and marketing activities have tended to be concentrated in Hong Kong. This has been driven in part by the communication links between Hong Kong and the major Western markets for the Hong Kong toy industry.

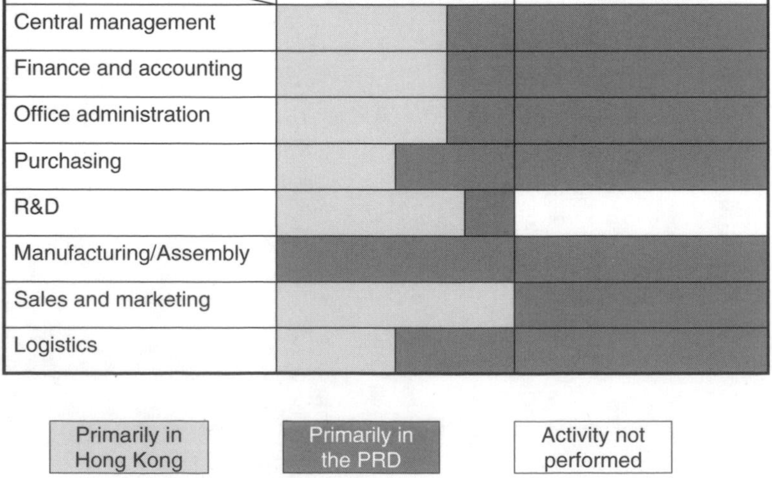

Activity \ Ownership	Hong Kong manufacturers	Mainland manufacturers
Central management		
Finance and accounting		
Office administration		
Purchasing		
R&D		
Manufacturing/Assembly		
Sales and marketing		
Logistics		

Legend: Primarily in Hong Kong | Primarily in the PRD | Activity not performed

Source: Enright, Scott & Associates Ltd research

Figure 5.4   The Hong Kong–Pearl River Delta toy industry value chain

Approximately 80% of Hong Kong toy manufacture is based on OEM production, with one-third of the market being controlled by US giants Hasbro and Mattel. The Hong Kong toy business is, therefore, very much tied to the United States. Because major US buyers such as Toys 'R' Us and Wal-mart have set up their purchasing and consolidation centres in the Pearl River Delta region, activities such as marketing, accounting, and especially shipping are increasingly being carried out there, particularly in Shenzhen. Such a high percentage of the exports of Hong Kong toy companies is shipped out of the Shenzhen port of Yantian, that it has become known in the industry as 'the toy port'.

Different segments of the toy industry use the Hong Kong/Pearl River Delta combination in different ways. Hong Kong toy firms that are engaged in low-cost production typical of the soft toy or low-end electronic toys sectors tend to retain a small office and showroom in Hong Kong, but have already migrated production and a fair degree of back-office activities to the Pearl River Delta region. These firms continue to look for ways to cut costs by, for example, moving their Hong Kong Island office to lower cost locations in Hong Kong. It is common for the owners of these firms to spend four days a week in the Pearl River Delta region and maintain a Hong Kong office solely for the purpose of coordinating overseas sales and shipments. All other activities are carried out in the Pearl River Delta region.

In another segment, Hong Kong toy firms that produce low-volume, premium items for Western markets tend to have a full Hong Kong office, which serves as the company's headquarters and sales centre, as well as their own manufacturing facilities in the Pearl River Delta region. The emphasis on precision has led such firms to become highly vertically integrated so as to maintain high quality control standards. These firms do not envisage wholesale mass migration of activities into the Pearl River Delta region and, in particular, value the Hong Kong office for its future role in sales and marketing, planning, and logistics.

Some Hong Kong toy firms are essentially marketing firms that subcontract production in the Pearl River Delta region. These firms do not own production facilities and often have a small staff of five to 20 people in Hong Kong. Essentially, the key strengths of these firms lie in the sourcing, packaging, and understanding of Western markets. As major Western buyers move into the Pearl River Delta region, these companies are increasingly carrying out their activities there. Other Hong Kong toy firms operate as design firms that either directly or indirectly subcontract manufacturing. This type of firm will often use a Hong Kong-owned toy manufacturer to organise production, as close geographical proximity makes it easier to communicate the designs. Companies within the Pearl River Delta region are increasingly being used for prototyping and model-making.

In the toy sector, Hong Kong-owned firms and Chinese mainland-owned firms are competing head-to-head in the lower end of the market. The mainland firms tend to sell to the developing markets and to European nations where distribution is still relatively fragmented. They tend to reverse engineer products developed by Hong Kong firms, and their cost structures are lower because they do not spend on Hong Kong marketing offices or on research and development (R&D). In the middle tier of the market, Hong Kong firms stay ahead by constantly developing new products in a segment where the shelf life of a new product often is six months. Mainland-owned firms are not as strong competitors in the OEM, ODM, and branded market segments, where Hong Kong firms tend to prevail. The Hong Kong firms in these segments take advantage of their reputation, design capabilities, financial strength, logistics capabilities, and knowledge of international markets. Even if they are not direct competitors, mainland-owned firms still exert a negative influence on price in these segments due to their presence in lower priced segments.

Garments

The Greater Pearl River Delta region plays a major role in global production and trade in garments. China is the world's leading exporter of textiles and clothing, accounting for 16% of the world total in 2001. Its share would be larger were it not limited by the global quota system governing trade in apparel. China is also the world's largest producer. According to a US industry source, 'the breadth and variety' of China's apparel production is unmatched in the world'.[13] Within China, Guangdong Province was the largest producer of garments for export, accounting for about one-third of the national total. More than two-thirds of the garment firms in Guangdong produce for export, with total exports of approximately US$10 billion in 2001.[14]

China's competitive advantages in apparel include low labour costs, high labour productivity, and the presence of related and supporting industries. Hong Kong also has been a key source of advantage for China's garment industry, managing and funding much of its export output, and structuring and coordinating the supply chains linking China with the world's leading markets. The vast majority of Hong Kong's garment exports have consisted of re-exports, mostly from China. In 2002, Hong Kong's garment re-exports from China were US$12.6 billion out of total garment re-exports of nearly US$14.1 billion, and its domestic exports of garments were just under US$4.2 billion.[15] Macy's, JC Penney, Federated, Karstadt Quelle, Sears, Target, Carrefour, Gap, and

The Limited are examples of leading department stores, discount stores, and speciality chains that source from Hong Kong.

The export-oriented segment of Guangdong's garment industry was pioneered by Hong Kong capital and management, and Hong Kong firms retain a prominent role. In 2002, Hong Kong garment firms had 4,200 factory facilities in Guangdong Province, employing 715,000 workers.[16] Approximately 60% of the materials used in garment production in Guangdong Province are imported, mostly through Hong Kong, while the rest are sourced from well-developed clusters of related and supporting industries in the Pearl River Delta region. Most production takes place in the Pearl River Delta region, where the wages of an entry-level worker are a small fraction of the comparable cost in Hong Kong (see Figure 5.5). Some piece work and finishing work is performed in Hong Kong in order for products to be considered to have Hong Kong origin for purposes of the international garment trade. Design and marketing activities for international markets are largely carried out in Hong Kong, while activities of this sort for mainland markets are conducted there. Logistics activities, traditionally centred in Hong Kong, are shifting towards the Pearl River Delta region, Shenzhen in particular, drawn by the growth of the Shenzhen seaports and the concentration of consolidation and buying activities of some of the world's leading merchandisers in Shenzhen.

The Pearl River Delta region's garment industry is a leader within China in many garment lines. The city of Dongguan is a nationwide centre for women's

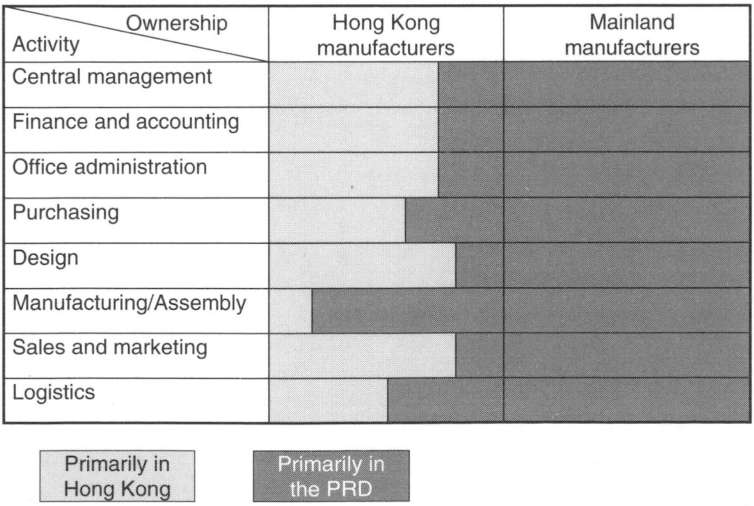

Activity \ Ownership	Hong Kong manufacturers	Mainland manufacturers
Central management	Primarily in Hong Kong	Primarily in the PRD
Finance and accounting	Primarily in Hong Kong	Primarily in the PRD
Office administration	Primarily in Hong Kong	Primarily in the PRD
Purchasing	Primarily in Hong Kong	Primarily in the PRD
Design	Primarily in Hong Kong	Primarily in the PRD
Manufacturing/Assembly	Primarily in Hong Kong / Primarily in the PRD	Primarily in the PRD
Sales and marketing	Primarily in Hong Kong	Primarily in the PRD
Logistics	Primarily in Hong Kong	Primarily in the PRD

Legend: Primarily in Hong Kong — Primarily in the PRD

Source: Enright, Scott & Associates Ltd research

Figure 5.5 The Hong Kong–Pearl River Delta garment industry value chain

wear and woollen sweaters, Zhongshan for leisure wear, and Nanhai for fabrics and lingerie, while Zhengcheng is China's largest jean distribution centre.[17] Foshan is home to 31% of China's children's garment manufacturing firms (2,300 firms) and is a major knitting centre.[18] The town of Zhangcha, in Foshan city, has become a key production base and distribution centre for knit products in China.[19] In Zhencheng, the town of Xintang alone has 2,600 denim producers and employs 80,000 line workers in denim products, making it one of China's four leading denim producing locations.[20]

Hong Kong's garment industry includes well-known manufacturing retailers with their own brands, including Baleno, Bossini, Crocodile, Episode, Esprit, G-2000, Giordano, Hang-Ten, Jean West, Moiselle, and U-2. Many of these have been expanding into the mainland markets, where they face competition from local and imported brands. In international markets, mainland-owned firms are gaining in design, international marketing, and logistics capabilities. Head-to-head competition between mainland-owned and Hong Kong firms is particularly fierce in less affluent overseas markets including Africa, the Caribbean, India, and some parts of the Middle East.

Electrical and electronics industries

The Greater Pearl River Delta region has become a world leader in the production of a range of electrical and electronics products, including a wide range of electrical goods, home appliances, telephones, facsimile machines, computers, computer peripherals, watches, and communications products. By 2002, electrical and electronics products had become the largest component of China's exports and China also had become one of the world's leading exporters of electronics products, with exports of electronic and electrical products exceeding US$100 billion. In that year, 25 out of the 30 leading trans-national exporters from China were electronics or telecommunications companies.[21] The electronics sector in China got its start with the investment of Hong Kong firms in the mid-1980s. These were followed by Taiwanese firms, and then firms from Japan and Korea. In addition, electronics contract manufacturing firms from all over the world also have set up major facilities in China. Virtually all major companies in several product segments either produce electronics goods in China or outsource production to China facilities of contract manufacturers.

Consumer Electronics and Home Appliances

China's position was particularly strong in consumer electronics and home appliances (see Table 5.2). In 2002, China accounted for roughly 40% of world exports in consumer electronics.[22] In some products, China is completely

Table 5.2   China's world production share in selected electrical and electronic industries, 2001

Product	World market (million units)	China's production share %
Colour TVs	39	29
Air-conditioners	18	30
Refrigerators	13	16
Washing machines	14	24
Monitors	46	42
Cameras	55	50
Telephones	96	50
Microwave ovens	13	30
VCD/DVD players	20	70
Radio-recorders	240	70

Source: Nasa Hsiung Tsai 2002

dominant. In 2003, for example, China produced roughly 90% of the world's output of DVD players.[23] China accounted for 70% of the unit volume and 47% of the value of Japan's imports in home appliances and 60% by volume and 33% in value of Japan's imports of audio equipment in 2002. China accounts for between 50 and 90% of US unit volume imports in goods ranging from video recording and reproducing apparatus to electric shavers, food processors, microwave ovens, and hair dryers.[24] China's position as a production platform in many electronics and electrical products was expected to improve substantially in the early 2000s. The main reasons for this expected growth were the continued globalisation of the electronics production chain, an abundance of labour, much lower salaries (in the order of 10% of those in developed nations), and a reasonable pool of technically qualified workers.[25] According to a manager from Flextronics, the world's largest electronics contract manufacturer, 'Most [of] everything in the electronics industry is coming to China in the next four to five years'.[26]

As seen in a previous chapter, Guangdong dominates Chinese production in a wide range of electrical and electronics products. It should be noted that the region is a leader in terms of production, not in terms of technology development. While many of the world's leading technology-based companies manufacture in the Pearl River Delta region, and many are placing increasingly challenging activities in the region, they still do the vast majority of their technology development elsewhere. The region's local technology-based companies are improving, but still cannot compare with leading companies from the United States, Europe, Japan, Korea, or Taiwan in technology development capabilities. On the other hand, the Pearl River Delta region compares quite well to other locations in the Chinese mainland across a range of technology-based activities.

The region's advantages as a production base mirror those listed above. Although the production process for electronics goods requires greater precision in order to meet tolerances, in general assembly, manufacturing is still a relatively labour-intensive activity that benefits from low-cost, productive labour, relatively well-organised and managed facilities, and access to the infrastructure required to ship components and finished goods quickly and accurately. Again, it has been the combination of the land, labour, and regulations found in the Pearl River Delta with technology and commercialisation skills imported from other places through Hong Kong that has proven to be extremely strong. The region also has benefited from the relative openness of places like Shenzhen, which has attracted technological workers from all over the Chinese mainland.

Weaknesses in the Greater Pearl River Delta region have included a lack of local technological development capabilities, a lack of leading universities to train technology-based workers, and the fact that foreign companies have been increasingly going to other places in the Chinese mainland. The region also suffers from intellectual property protection that is considered not only well behind international standards, but behind other areas in the Chinese mainland as well.[27]

Hong Kong firms in the sector include companies like Starlight, Ngai Lik, Alco, Raymond, Orient Power, Grande Holdings, and Vtech. These companies are known for leading positions in particular fields, such as Starlight in DVD players and Vtech in cordless telephones. Most of these companies produce for OEM suppliers, such as the major international brands. Grande Holdings, which holds the Kawai, Akai, Sansui, and Nakamichi brands, and Vtech, are exceptions in that they produce for their own brands as well as others. Hong Kong companies employed approximately 1.6 million people in the Pearl River Delta region in the electronics and electrical appliance sectors in 2002.[28]

In the electronics sector, the head offices of Hong Kong-owned electronics producers are generally located in Hong Kong, though management is tending to spend an increasing amount of time in the Pearl River Delta region. Accounting is done in both Hong Kong and the Pearl River Delta region, while finance remains in Hong Kong. Office administration functions exist both in Hong Kong and in the Pearl River Delta region to support factory operations there. Sales, marketing, corporate communications, and customer support activities are generally carried out in Hong Kong, though some sales support for China markets takes place in the Pearl River Delta region (see Figure 5.6). Some companies that sell their products in China also repackage their products in the

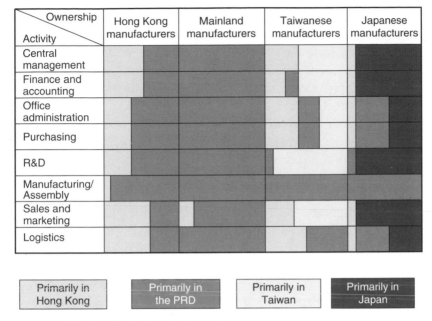

Ownership / Activity	Hong Kong manufacturers	Mainland manufacturers	Taiwanese manufacturers	Japanese manufacturers
Central management				
Finance and accounting				
Office administration				
Purchasing				
R&D				
Manufacturing/ Assembly				
Sales and marketing				
Logistics				

Primarily in Hong Kong   Primarily in the PRD   Primarily in Taiwan   Primarily in Japan

Source: Enright, Scott & Associates Ltd research

Figure 5.6   The Hong Kong–Pearl River Delta electronics industry value chain

Pearl River Delta region to ensure that they will appeal to mainland tastes.[29] Similar patterns can be seen in many foreign electronics companies that have their management offices in Hong Kong handling liaison with corporate parents, finance, logistics, and other support activities in Hong Kong, and their manufacturing and related activities in the Pearl River Delta region.

Hong Kong electronics firms generally do their manufacturing in the Pearl River Delta region, though some high-quality, zero-defect assembly still takes place in Hong Kong (see Figure 5.6). Interviewees maintained that they could not guarantee zero defects from their production facilities in the Pearl River Delta region. Research and development activities are split. Information collection takes place in Hong Kong, as does high-end R&D and prototyping work. Routine development is carried out in the Pearl River Delta region, while engineering is done on both sides of the border.[30] Purchasing is carried out in both Hong Kong and the Pearl River Delta region, depending on requirements. High-precision machinery and components are sourced from Taiwan, Japan, the United States, and Germany via Hong Kong, while basic components are purchased in the Pearl River Delta region. Under current mainland regulations, Hong Kong companies have to import some machinery, even when it is being produced in the Pearl River Delta region by foreign machine manufacturers with production facilities there, because the latter operate under export-only licences. This is expected to change under WTO so that they can directly deliver their products to firms in the Pearl River Delta region.[31]

Taiwanese electronics firms that carry out production in the Pearl River Delta rely extensively upon Hong Kong for the rest of the value chain, except R&D performed in Taiwan. They procure many components and materials locally, drawing upon the region's intensively concentrated cluster of electronics-related firms. Within 40 square kilometres of Dongguan, it is possible to source 95% of the components required for computer assembly, which is 'very attractive to Taiwanese investors', according to city officials.[32] World-class technology available only from global leaders tends to be sourced and imported through Hong Kong. Taiwanese electronics firms with offices in Hong Kong use those offices to perform 'corporate management, fund transfer, and the front-end and back-end functions of the supply chain including purchasing, sales, market development, import and export, [and] transport and distribution'.[33] Taiwanese electronics firms based in Shenzhen or Dongguan rely heavily on Hong Kong for transit travel between China and Taiwan, cargo trans-shipment and the re-export of goods, and banking and financial services. The presence of Taiwanese financial and other professional service providers in Hong Kong helps to cement this function. For these Taiwanese firms, Hong Kong also plays a substantial role in sales and market development, purchasing, and accounting and audits.[34]

Starting in the late 1990s, Taiwan's major electronics firms including Delta Electronics, Foxconn, Quanta, and Yageo Corp., began to place large new investments into Shanghai and the Yangtze River Delta, attracted by the presence of international procurement offices of personal computer firms such as Dell, IBM, and Compaq, the availability of R&D expertise, and the desire for a central geographic location in the mainland market.[35] What has emerged since the late 1990s is a situation where many Taiwanese electronics firms are present in both the Pearl River Delta and Yangtze River Delta regions, pursuing dual north/south strategies in China. Large Taiwanese electronics firms that have made or announced new investments in the Pearl River Delta region during the five-year period 1999–2004 include Acer Inc., Asia Optical, Elite Computer System (ECS), Gold Peak, Primax Electronics, and Wistron Corp.

Most of the major multinational consumer electronics companies, including firms like Sony, NEC, Toshiba, Hitachi, Canon, Ricoh, Matsushita, Samsung, LG, Nokia, and Ericsson are active in the Pearl River Delta region (see Figure 5.6). These multinational firms tend to do their R&D at their home locations or other facilities in the advanced economies. They carry out production in several locations around the world, with China in general, and the Pearl River Delta region in particular, increasing in prominence. These firms carry out sourcing through their home locations, Hong Kong, and the Pearl River Delta region for their Pearl River Delta-based production. They carry out the bulk of their marketing and sales in the major consumer markets of North America, Europe, and Japan, though China is becoming increasingly important.

In the electronics sector, many firms have found that today's partner from the Pearl River Delta region is tomorrow's competitor, particularly in low-end consumer electronics. In this sector, a partnership of two years can provide enough technology transfer for the recipient to set up as a direct competitor. At that point, the Pearl River Delta competitor will typically look to compete in both domestic and international markets. This is particularly a threat to Hong Kong companies and Taiwanese companies that compete as suppliers to OEMs.

Many Pearl River Delta firms are able to make incremental upgrades on the products of foreign firms. At the higher end, firms like Huawei and TCL are capable of competing with the leading Hong Kong and international firms. They are rapidly assimilating advanced business concepts and are starting to rely on subcontracting networks themselves. Many managers in the electronics sector believe that companies from the Chinese mainland are better equipped to sell into the mainland markets than the outside firms. This is confirmed by the large share of the domestic market in electrical and electronic goods that is taken up by Chinese firms. After making rapid gains at the expense of foreign brands in the 1990s, by 2000 China's top three domestic brands of air-conditioners, washing machines, and refrigerators controlled over 80% of their respective domestic markets, while China's top nine television makers had a market share of around 90%.[36] By 2003, a similar phenomenon was under way in mobile phone handsets, with domestic brands controlling a market share of above 50% in 'second tier/inland markets' accounting for most new handset sales.[37] Several of the mainland firms have the financial and market-ing backing of local or national government, and have developed distribution systems throughout the Chinese mainland.

Watches

According to the Federation of the Swiss Watch Industry, there were approxi-mately 700 million watches produced worldwide in 2000. Hong Kong and China accounted for 80% of the unit production, or roughly 560 million. In comparison, Switzerland and Japan produced 31 million and 16 million units, respectively. In terms of value, Swiss production accounted for more than half of global production value. The average unit value of exports of Swiss watches was Sfr. 312 (US$ 193.70), while the average unit value of Hong Kong exports was Sfr. 10 (US$ 6.20). In 2003, the average unit value of Swiss exports was Sfr. 362

(US$448.20), while that of Hong Kong was Sfr. 7 (US$8.70).[38] Hong Kong was the world's second leading exporter of watches in value (after Switzerland) and unit volume (after the Chinese mainland) in 2001. Hong Kong was the world's leading exporter of clocks by value and the second largest (after the Chinese mainland) by value. The vast majority of Hong Kong's exports in these categories consisted of re-exports. For example, in 2003, Hong Kong's domestic exports of watches and clocks were US$109.5 million, while its re-exports from China were US$2.74 billion and its total re-exports were US$5.29 billion.[39]

Within China, the Pearl River Delta region was the only main manufacturing region for watches and Hong Kong firms have dominated Pearl River Delta production. For these firms, the majority of activities are carried out in Hong Kong. These activities include central management and support functions, as well as purchasing, marketing and sales, and distribution. Design is carried out mostly in Hong Kong, while some engineering-related research occurs in the Pearl River Delta region. Hong Kong watch companies sell mostly to the United States or Europe, and typically produce OEM designs for their customers. Manufacturing is heavily concentrated in the Pearl River Delta region, where they employed an estimated 510,000 workers in 2002.[40] Some purchasing is carried out in the Pearl River Delta region given the clustering of component producers there. Some routine administrative work also takes place there to support the manufacturing operations, though the bulk is done in Hong Kong. Some Hong Kong watch companies have their own production facilities, while others choose to subcontract production to local factories, some on a very large scale. As one Hong Kong manager put it, 'Our strategy is to treat the entire Pearl River basin as our own factory' (see Figure 5.7).

Shipping has traditionally been done through the Hong Kong ports, partly due to mainland export licensing requirements. Larger, bulkier clocks may be shipped out of Yantian, Shenzhen's leading seaport. Watches, in contrast, tend to be dispatched by air from Hong Kong, air transport being more appropriate for items that are high fashion, seasonal, and lightweight.

Firms from the Chinese mainland, often run by former employees of Hong Kong firms, have become strong competitors in the low end of the global watch market. They reverse engineer Hong Kong products and offer their goods to foreign buyers at steep discounts, often 50% or more. In 2002, industry sources estimated that mainland firms had obtained 10% of the market. On the other hand, Hong Kong firms continue to dominate the OEM, ODM, and premium (watches used as premiums, not premium-priced watches) segments. Here their abilities in design, ability to deliver large quantities with short lead times, knowledge of international markets, reputation for reliability, and financial strength are key advantages.

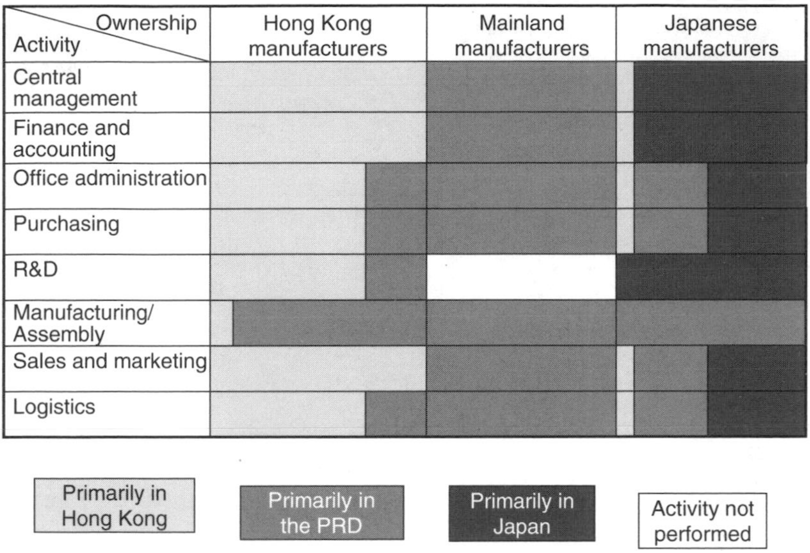

Ownership / Activity	Hong Kong manufacturers	Mainland manufacturers	Japanese manufacturers
Central management			
Finance and accounting			
Office administration			
Purchasing			
R&D			
Manufacturing/ Assembly			
Sales and marketing			
Logistics			

Primarily in Hong Kong	Primarily in the PRD	Primarily in Japan	Activity not performed

Source: Enright, Scott & Associates Ltd research

Figure 5.7   The Hong Kong–Pearl River Delta watch industry value chain

Heavy manufacturing

The Greater Pearl River Delta region has generally not been strong in heavy manufacturing in international or national terms. The Pearl River Delta region is far from China's traditional industrial heartland in the north and the east. It did not benefit from policies to decentralise industrial development into the interior in the 1950s and 1960s. It lacked easy access to the natural resources necessary for heavy industry, as the region was largely cut off from trade and the internal transportation system left much to be desired. Proximity to Hong Kong did not help the Pearl River Delta region much in this regard, given Hong Kong's own lack of a heavy industrial base. Heavy industry also has been less open to foreign investment and, given the large, long-term investments involved, historically had been less favoured by foreign investors in China.

China's international position in heavy industry is somewhat mixed. Although China is the world's leading producer in industries like steel cement, and several chemical products, it is far behind other nations in terms of its efficiency and sophistication in these industries. As a result, China is a substantial net importer of most heavy industrial products, including steel, machinery of all types, electrical generating equipment, and other heavy industrial goods. An exception is shipbuilding, in which China is already the world's third-leading producer and has an improving international position. Within China,

Table 5.3   Guangdong's share of Chinese mainland output in selected goods, 2001

Industry	Guangdong's share %
Steel	2.35
Steel sheet	3.97
Steel rail	1.53
Steel pipe (seamless)	0.35
Steel pipe (welded)	3.39
Sulphuric acid	5.06
Synthetic ammonia	0.17
Chemical fertilisers	0.66
Plastics	12.23
Chemical fibres	5.68
Tires	3.18
Motor vehicles excluding cars	2.38
Cars	7.26
Internal combustion engines	0.23
Industrial boilers	1.77
Power-generating equipment	1.40
Metal-cutting machine tools	5.94
Plain glass	2.73
Cement	9.10

Source: Calculated from data in China State Statistical Bureau 2003

heavy industries, such as steel, chemicals, shipbuilding, and most machinery industries have been centred in the north-east, the Bohai region, and the Yangtze River Delta region. The north-east became a heavy industrial centre under Japanese occupation in the 1930s, while the Bohai and Yangtze River Delta areas received subsequent investments after the founding of the People's Republic of China in 1949. In the 1960s and 1970s, some heavy industrial facilities were placed in the western part of the country in order to disperse development, and in order to make them less vulnerable to outside attack.

The Pearl River Delta region's position, or lack of position, in heavy industries can be seen in Table 5.3. The table shows that Guangdong lagged well behind its share of GDP in many heavy industrial products, such as steel, most chemical products, automobiles and related products, equipment for industries and utilities, and materials. Among the goods listed, only plastics, linked to the plastic products industry found in the region, and cement, which is usually produced locally for local markets, either exceeded or equalled Guangdong's share of the Chinese mainland GDP. However, there are signs that this situation of heavy industries in the Pearl River Delta region is evolving and potentially becoming much stronger (see Chapter 8).

Transportation services

Transportation services in the Greater Pearl River Delta region are driven by international trade. Given the growing prominence of the Greater Pearl River Delta region as one of the world's great manufacturing and export bases, it is not surprising that the region also is one of the largest markets for sea and air cargo services in the world. As a result, Hong Kong has the world's busiest container port and the world's busiest airport for international airfreight.[41] In addition, the ports of neighbouring Shenzhen are rapidly assuming a leadership position, not just in the Chinese mainland, but in international terms as well.[42] While Hong Kong was once the only choice for international sea and air cargo in the region, developments in the Pearl River Delta region have been providing shippers with additional capacity and additional choice. The result has again been a unique combination of complementarity and competition within the Greater Pearl River Delta region.

Sea Cargo

Hong Kong remains the busiest container port in the world and the leading port for the trade of the Greater Pearl River Delta region. Hong Kong owed its initial development to the presence of its excellent natural deepwater harbour. As China began to open up in the 1970s and 1980s, the port of Hong Kong was the natural choice for trade into and out of South China, as well as much of the rest of the country.[43] By 2002, Hong Kong was the world's busiest and most efficient maritime container port, visited by more than 36,000 vessels each year. Hong Kong handled approximately 40% of China's exports, compared to 10% through Shanghai. An estimated 80% of the exports and imports of Guangdong Province passed through Hong Kong in that year. In terms of volume, Hong Kong's total container traffic was 19.1 million TEUs in 2002, 7.4% above the previous year.[44] Hong Kong's sea transport role is supported by world-class capabilities container handling; customs administration; communications; logistics and freight forwarding; trade documentation; and trade-related services; as well as Hong Kong's status as a free port and its highly developed judicial, legal, and regulatory regimes. It also offers the highest frequency of shipping line visits and the densest route network of any seaport handling China trade.[45]

Shenzhen's container ports, which have become major players in their own right, handled approximately 20% of the exports and imports of Guangdong Province in 2002. Shenzhen's leading container ports, Yantian, Shekou, and Chiwan, are all partially owned and mostly operated by Hong Kong firms. Buoyed by the Pearl River Delta's rapid export growth, Shenzhen's overall

Table 5.4 Comparative statistics on container throughput of Hong Kong and Shenzhen, 1997–2002

Period	HK terminals at Kwai Chung		HK overall ports		Shenzhen overall ports	
	000 TEUs	Growth %	000 TEUs	Growth %	000 TEUs	Growth %
1997	9,564	9.3	14,386	8.2	1,146	–
1998	9,555	–0.1	14,582	1.4	19,52	70.4
1999	10, 295	7.7	16,211	11.2	2,984	52.9
2000	11,603	12.7	18,098	11.6	3,959	32.7
2001	11,285	–2.7	17,826	–1.5	5,043	27.4
2002	11,892	5.4	19,144	7.4	7,614	51.0

Sources: Hong Kong Shippers' Council, citing Hong Kong Special Administrative Region Government, Census and Statistics Department and Marine Department; Hong Kong Port and Maritime Board; Shenzhen Municipal Transport Bureau; and the Shenzhen Municipal Port Authority

container throughput grew by 827.5% between 1997 and 2002.[46] In 2002, the Shenzhen ports overall handled 7.6 million container TEUs (see Table 5.4), a figure that surpassed official city estimates for that year and represented an annual growth of 51%.[47] Among the principal Shenzhen ports, Yantian, located 23 nautical miles north-east of Hong Kong, is favoured for shipments from throughout the Pearl River Delta region heading to the United States, and Shekou for freight coming from the western portion of the Pearl River Delta and heading for Europe. Outside of Shenzhen, Guangzhou has a river port at Huangpu and is planning a new port complex to be located at Nansha.[48]

  The Shenzhen seaports provide a lower priced alternative to Hong Kong's container port due to lower land-haulage costs and port handling charges. As of November 2002, the cost of trucking from factories in the Pearl River Delta region to the Shenzhen ports was reported to be half that of trucking to Hong Kong. This was due in large part to delays crossing the Shenzhen–Hong Kong border, which often meant a truck could make one trip a day from a Pearl River Delta factory to Hong Kong, but two trips to Shenzhen ports. In addition, terminal handling charges in Shenzhen were between 21 and 49% lower than in Hong Kong, depending on the destination and container size.[49] However, potential savings in trucking and terminal handling were often offset by higher ocean freight costs out of Shenzhen, resulting in a net savings of 20 to 33% for many shippers that used Shenzhen ports. Cost calculations vary case by case and are influenced by the precise location of the factory, and whether the load is a whole or partial container load. For example, exporters claim that it is generally better to transport less than full container loads to Hong Kong for consolidation, due to minimum customer charges, delays in filling up containers, and delays in customs clearance caused by unrelated merchandise sharing a container in Shenzhen.[50]

In addition to costs, the choice of port within the Greater Pearl River Delta region is influenced by frequency of sailings, licence terms, buyer practices and preferences, customs clearances, and quality of support services.[51] Hong Kong generally has more frequent sailings than Shenzhen ports, meaning that a container could stay at the port for three days to two weeks longer in Shenzhen than Hong Kong. However, the frequency of sailings continues to improve at the Shenzhen ports, and for some destinations actually is superior to Hong Kong. Some companies operate with licences that require them to ship from one port or another. While in the past most other customers that specified a port would specify Hong Kong, increasingly buyers in some categories are specifying Shenzhen ports. This is particularly true of some large United States distributors, like Wal-Mart, that have set up their own consolidation centres in Shenzhen. Others may have their own cost or business reasons.

Hong Kong Customs provide world-class efficiency, transparency, and predictability, at 'international standards'. Cargo passes through Hong Kong Customs faster and with far more certainty and security, reflecting superior systems, procedures, and technical know-how than in other ports in the region. Cargo shipped out through the Shenzhen ports must undergo China Customs clearance, which has traditionally entailed extensive paperwork and the presentation of physical accounting records on a shipment-specific basis.[52] Transition to an electronic system is currently under way, but exporters still report onerous information requirements, lack of predictability, unanticipated cargo detentions, and lengthy sampling procedures.

Our interviews suggest that low-price cargoes, like toys and rattan furniture, are increasingly routing through the Shenzhen ports due to the paramount importance of cost considerations in their supply chain equation. In the case of toys, the presence of consolidation centres of large United States retailers in Shenzhen also favours the Shenzhen ports. One shipping executive estimated that as much as 90% of the toys produced for export in the Pearl River Delta region now ship out of the Shenzhen ports, with Yantian being the main port. An exception is toys with high 'cut-and-sewn' content, which are subject to quota.

On the other hand, Hong Kong remains the port of choice for high-value products where a premium is placed on security, speed, or reliability.[53] High-end electronics, like computer peripherals and mobile phones, where shipment time is critical, are usually shipped out of Hong Kong. Watches are a highly seasonal fashion item and are quite time-sensitive in terms of shipping speed to the end customer. For these reasons, watches produced in the Pearl River Delta region often ship out of Hong Kong. In interviews, exporters also noted the superiority of supporting services in Hong Kong, including export finance, trade documentation, and logistics. They claimed that routing cargo through Hong Kong meant higher prices for higher efficiency. Some are willing to pay this price, while others as one exporter told us were 'willing to lose sleep the night before shipment from Yantian, in order to save the money'.

Air Cargo

Of total export cargo shipped from the Greater Pearl River Delta region, 99% (by volume) ships via maritime container transport, with 1% travelling via air-freight. Nevertheless, airfreight represents more than a quarter of the value of goods shipped.[54] There are five principal airports within a 50-kilometre radius in the Greater Pearl River Delta region: in Guangzhou, Hong Kong, Macao, Shenzhen, and Zhuhai. The international air cargo segment has been domi-nated by Hong Kong, but the emergence of airports in Guangzhou and Shenzhen is starting to provide alternatives for shippers. While the planning for the individual airports has proceeded almost completely independently of each other, in recent years, discussions among the airport managers has allowed them to start thinking more in terms of complementarity and combinations.

The Hong Kong International Airport is one of the world's foremost airports and the busiest in the world in terms of international air cargo throughput in 2003. It far outstrips the Pearl River Delta region airports on all parameters, including international passenger flows, freight tonnage, and passenger and freight destinations. The Hong Kong International Airport handled 33.5 million passengers and 2.5 million tonnes of cargo in 2002.[55] In 2003, it offered services to 135 cities worldwide (95 international destinations and 40 in China), with normally about 3,300 passenger flights and nearly 400 cargo flights weekly. Two air cargo terminals are in operation at the airport. Hong Kong Air Cargo Terminals Limited (HACTL) operates the Super Terminal 1 Building, which is the world's largest stand-alone air cargo facility with an initial capacity of up to 2.6 million tonnes of freight per year. Asia Airfreight Terminal Company Limited (AAT) operates the second air cargo terminal, with an annual handling capacity of 0.4 million tonnes.[56]

Guangzhou's Baiyun Airport, China Southern Airline's hub, has been oriented primarily towards destinations on the Chinese mainland, and acts as a centre for air transportation in southern China. In 2002, the airport served approximately 77 domestic and 21 international destinations, handling 16 million passengers and 592,560 tonnes of cargo.[57] Guangzhou's new airport,

Baiyun International Airport, which has cost an estimated US$2.4 billion, began operation in June 2004 (see Chapter 7). Shenzhen's Bao'an International Airport is growing in importance as a feeder for mainland domestic passengers and for freight. Bao'an International Airport had around 60 domestic routes to other destinations in the Chinese mainland in 2003. In 2002, it handled 9.35 million passengers and 334,100 tonnes of cargo.[58] Shenzhen draws passengers from the mainland that use Hong Kong via Shenzhen to connect to international destinations, and diverts some passengers from Hong Kong to Shenzhen for destinations within China who wish to take advantage of lower fares. Federal Express started to run flights from Shenzhen to Europe and to North America in November 1999.[59] Macao International Airport is a player of some substance, particularly for traffic connecting Taiwan with the Chinese mainland. In 2001, there were around 142 flights per week between Macao and 13 cities in the mainland, and 248 flights per week between Macao and Taiwan. In 2002, the Macao Airport handled 4.2 million passengers and 111.3 tonnes of cargo.[60] The Zhuhai Airport is not a significant player in the region. The Civil Aviation Administration of China (CAAC) disapproved of its construction, and it was subsequently excluded from official Chinese air route planning. In 2002, Zhuhai handled only 750,000 passengers despite a capacity of 12 million passengers.[61]

Trade-related services

The Greater Pearl River Delta region is a world leader in terms of trade-related services. The massive export surge of the Greater Pearl River Delta region over the last two decades also has created enormous demand for trading, sourcing, freight-forwarding, logistics, trade finance, legal, and other related services in the region. The Pearl River Delta region, as China's leading trading region, also leads in terms of trade-related services in the Chinese mainland.

The Greater Pearl River Delta region's tradition of trading and the large local trading community have clearly contributed to its competitiveness, as has the international market know-how and access provided by Hong Kong. Hong Kong's separate legal, financial, and administrative system has proven a magnet to the buying and sourcing offices of multinational companies, as well as to the logistical, information, and other services related to trade. Increasingly, these are being linked to similar services that are developing in the Pearl River Delta region.

Despite its strengths, the Greater Pearl River Delta region has some disadvantages when it comes to trade-related services. The existence of a border, with the accompanying customs checks and transportation bottlenecks, is a clear disadvantage compared to other regions in which goods and people can flow more freely. In addition, the existence of multiple jurisdictions in the Greater Pearl River Delta region, each with its own development plans, has resulted in duplicative investments that can reduce the potential for the sort of hub and spoke systems that would maximise efficiency.

Trading Services

Hong Kong plays a major role in providing access to foreign markets for production originating in the Pearl River Delta region. Hong Kong's import and export trade sector employed 499,735 people in 103,383 establishments as of December 2002. Its exports of trade-related services reached US$13.6 billion in 2001, or 34.6% of Hong Kong's service exports.[62] Hong Kong's trading role is supported by the city's strengths as a centre for trading and commercial activities, and by the strategic strengths of Hong Kong-based traders and suppliers. Hong Kong offers a critical mass of sales representatives conveniently located within a small area that allows foreign buyers to meet with large numbers of sales representatives without having to travel to the factories.[63] For those who do wish to visit the factories, the dense concentration in the Pearl River Delta region facilitates the visits. Hong Kong offers world-class hard and soft infrastructure, including airport facilities and air flight connections, communications, ports and logistics, and professional support services.[64]

At the high-end, Hong Kong traders and suppliers mastermind the supply chain linking the Pearl River Delta region's manufacturing base with the world's largest consumer markets.[65] These firms have become active in the OEM, ODM, 'branded', and 'premium' lines of business by building up a respected profile, building a position of trust with the world's largest buyers, and delivering goods to customer shelves via a process that is 'trouble free'. Compared to mainland counterparts, Hong Kong traders and suppliers are viewed as having superior knowledge of foreign markets, deeper understanding of customer needs, a higher degree of responsiveness to customers, and greater attention to detail. Hong Kong traders and suppliers also play a pivotal role in translating the requirements of foreign customers into precise technical specifications for relay to manufacturing teams in the Pearl River Delta region. Hong Kong firms can martial the production capabilities of thousands of factories in the Pearl River Delta and oversee the completion of mega-orders. They provide selective screening of those production facilities in the Pearl River Delta region capable of performing to specification. Avoidance of product defects that could cause a recall is a major concern to foreign buyers. As a result, the factories that are chosen for meeting large orders tend to be Hong Kong-owned, not mainland-owned.

In addition to trade mediated by trading companies, an increasing portion of the trade of the Greater Pearl River Delta region involves the backward integration of major retailers into sourcing and the forward integration of Chinese factories approaching customers directly. Some of the Chinese firms have set up marketing offices in Hong Kong, while others use the Canton Fair (which tends to attract buyers from third world markets, as well as buyers operating in cut-rate segments), foreign trade fairs overseas, or even marketing offices overseas. Some foreign buyers in price-sensitive markets and segments are seeking direct contact with Pearl River Delta firms to access lower priced products, through trade fairs, including the Canton Fair, Hong Kong-based buying offices, or direct visits to the Pearl River Delta region. In addition, major Western buyers are setting up sourcing centres in Shenzhen, supported by Shenzhen-based freight consolidation warehouses to permit export direct from Shenzhen ports. However, they have not shifted entirely to sourcing directly from mainland-owned factories. Interviews suggest that major buyers now based in Shenzhen are still relying on large Hong Kong trading firms to manage design and production activities in Hong Kong and the Pearl River Delta region.

While small- and medium-sized Hong Kong traders voiced the opinion that forward integration, backward integration, and the Internet, which in some cases provides direct access between source and buyer, were potential threats to their businesses, the larger Hong Kong firms had taken measures to strengthen their direct contacts with foreign buyers through their own overseas marketing and sales offices, and by using the new technologies to improve the efficiency of their own operations. In any case, the multiple sourcing options that were becoming available actually improved the flexibility of the interaction between the Greater Pearl River Delta region and the rest of the world. The ability to use experienced Hong Kong-based trading companies, or to set up offices readily in either Hong Kong or the Pearl River Delta region, is making the Greater Pearl River Delta region an even easier place from which to source goods for international markets.

Logistics Services

Logistics encompasses several activities associated with managing the transportation and distribution of goods. As firms focus more and more on developing efficient supply chains, logistics activities are viewed as important potential sources of advantage and disadvantage. In addition to the physical flows, today many logistics firms are equally concerned about the flows of information related to the goods. Numerous specialist suppliers have emerged to serve customers in the Greater Pearl River Delta region and elsewhere. Hong Kong historically has been a logistics centre for China and the rest of Asia. Increasingly, however, Shenzhen is emerging as a centre for logistics for the export industries of the Pearl River Delta region. In addition, as the economies of the Greater Pearl River Delta region become more intertwined, the role of Guangzhou, the traditional centre for logistics for South China, is becoming more important.

Hong Kong is a leading logistics hub for the Asia-Pacific region. Local and international companies use Hong Kong as a location to coordinate product flows encompassing China, Japan, South Korea, Taiwan, and even Singapore. Logistics services provided in Hong Kong include a variety of value-adding services, such as assembly, mix and match, and packaging. Hong Kong is also home to providers of supporting services to the logistics industry, including operating software and strategic input. Hong Kong's logistics industry is viewed as a 'high-end, low-end business'. At the high end, the world's leading multinational logistics firms are present in Hong Kong. These firms often use Hong Kong as headquarters for managing all of Greater China or South China. They tend to view Hong Kong and the Pearl River Delta as a single region, with large flows into and out of Hong Kong. At the low end, many smaller, Hong Kong-owned logistics providers serve Hong Kong's small- and medium-sized export traders.

Hong Kong's advantages as a logistics provider include its world-class transportation, financial, and legal infrastructure, plus a much broader base of experience and technological expertise. In addition, Hong Kong's free flows of merchandise make it a highly convenient location for receiving products from different factories in the Pearl River Delta region or elsewhere, mixing them, and re-packing them as a single item for export prior to shipping.

Historically, China has not offered a level playing field for foreign investors in logistics. Prior to China's concessions under the Closer Economic Partnership Arrangement (CEPA), foreign shareholders generally could not have more than 49% equity ownership in mainland-based logistics operations.[66] Forging a successful relationship with a mainland partner has been a major challenge for many Hong Kong firms trying to expand into the Pearl River Delta region. Hong Kong logistics firms with minority stakes in Pearl River Delta operations try to maintain their headquarters in Hong Kong. However, the exigencies of this location-dependent business are forcing many logistics providers to spend more and more time in the Pearl River Delta region. Figure 5.8 shows the distribution of the value chain between Hong Kong and the Pearl River Delta region for Hong Kong-based logistics providers.

While Hong Kong has remained dominant as a location for managing international logistics activities for the Greater Pearl River Delta region,

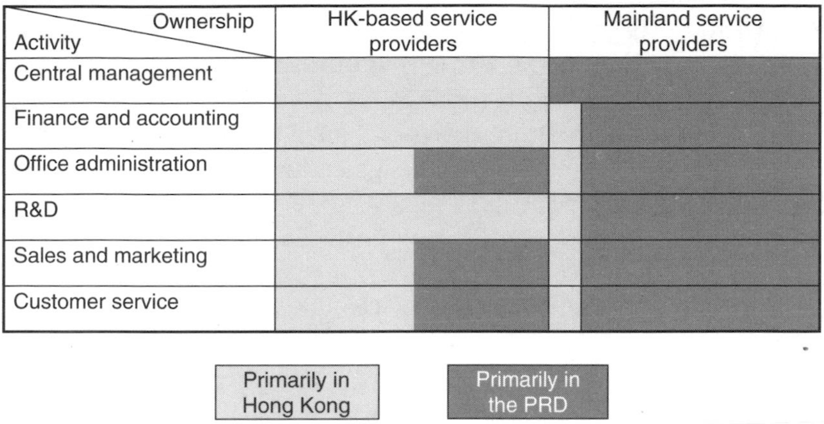

Activity \ Ownership	HK-based service providers	Mainland service providers
Central management		
Finance and accounting		
Office administration		
R&D		
Sales and marketing		
Customer service		

Primarily in Hong Kong   Primarily in the PRD

Source: Enright, Scott & Associates Ltd research

Figure 5.8 The Hong Kong–Pearl River Delta logistics industry value chain

Shenzhen and Guangzhou also play important logistics roles. Shenzhen has emerged as a secondary centre for logistics for export-oriented industries based in the Pearl River Delta region. Shenzhen provides a low-cost location for consolidators close to the Shenzhen ports. As the Shenzhen ports have grown and the number of foreign buying offices in Shenzhen has increased, more and more logistics companies are setting up to meet the demand. Guangzhou has been the traditional logistics centre for domestic cargo in the Pearl River Delta region. Guangzhou is at the heart of the region's transportation systems and provides the main links between the Pearl River Delta region and China's national road, rail, and air networks. Guangzhou and its surrounding communities are also home to literally hundreds of markets for goods ranging from building materials, to light consumer goods, to consumer durables, to industrial inputs, and to machinery. In a region where distribution has historically been limited, these markets play a crucial role in the distribution system for all of South China. In some products, the clientele of the markets is even national in scope.[67]

Many logistics firms, ranging from large multinationals to the smallest of firms, have moved from Hong Kong into the Pearl River Delta region, mostly into Guangzhou and Shenzhen. Some consolidators, for example, have relocated their centres to Shenzhen, mostly near Yantian. A wide range of labour-intensive activities are performed in these consolidation centres, including packing, mix and matching, labelling, and the affixing of bar codes to help direct product to its destination.[68] Cost is a critical issue and wage rates for logistics staff in Shenzhen have been much lower than in Hong Kong. For example, in 2003, clerical staff could be hired in Shenzhen for the equivalent of US$154 per month, or as little as one-tenth the salary of someone doing the same job in Hong Kong. Pearl River Delta warehouse workers were reported to offer the same set of skills as their counterparts in Hong Kong, at substantially lower wages and higher levels of motivation, given the fact that such jobs were viewed as undesirable by many in Hong Kong.

In any case, as in many industries, high-end logistics management tends to be run out of Hong Kong, while lower value activities are increasingly moving into the Pearl River Delta region. The emerging mix of companies and locations has provided greater variety and greater choice, allowing companies to determine which price and performance combinations they desire, and ultimately contributing to the competitiveness of the entire region.

Financial and business services

Due to restrictions on the operations of foreign service providers on the Chinese mainland, the business service sectors of the Greater Pearl River Delta region are less integrated than many other sectors of the economy. Thus, the competitiveness of Hong Kong and of the Pearl River Delta region in business services for the most part has to be treated separately. Hong Kong is an international business service centre of regional and international importance. This can be seen by Hong Kong's position as the leading centre for the regional headquarters of multinational firms in Asia, its position as a leading financial centre in Asia, and the breadth and depth of Hong Kong's professional and business service sectors. The main cities in the Pearl River Delta region, Guangzhou and Shenzhen, in comparison, lag behind both Shanghai and Beijing in terms of their prominence as business service centres.

Hong Kong has benefited from its years as an international centre and its legal, financial, and administrative systems. Hong Kong's free flows of capital, light-handed but international calibre regulatory system, and skilled professionals from all over the world have greatly contributed to its position as a business service centre. This has been accentuated by its trading roles. On the Chinese mainland, on the other hand, Shanghai and Beijing have respectively been the traditional centres for commerce and government relations. As a result, a denser set of business services has grown in these cities to serve both domestic and international clients. The lead of these cities has been influenced by restrictions on foreign firms that allow them to have only one or a few offices in the Chinese mainland. Of the 96 representative offices of foreign law firms in the Chinese mainland, in 2002, for example, only three were in Guangzhou. Of the 37 representative offices of Hong Kong law firms in the Chinese mainland, nine had offices in Guangzhou and three in Shenzhen. In both cases, the vast majority of offices were in Shanghai and Beijing.[69]

Economic interaction between Hong Kong and the Pearl River Delta region has brought about a steady increase in the demand for business services on both sides of the border. This demand has been driven on three levels. The movement of manufacturers from Hong Kong into the Pearl River Delta region has fostered demand for cross-border support services, while the growth in multinational concerns in the region has fuelled demand for high-quality services, particularly in the legal and financial sectors. The emergence of the Pearl River Delta region as a manufacturing powerhouse has also increased the demand for services from local producers in the Pearl River Delta region who seek to upgrade their systems and processes in order to compete on a global scale.

Financial Services

In financial services, Hong Kong is by far the major international financial centre in the Greater Pearl River Delta region. For those Pearl River Delta-based companies that gain clearance from the Central Government to list in Hong Kong, Hong Kong provides access to international capital flows. The main investment banking, fundraising, project finance, and other 'big ticket' financial services are provided out of Hong Kong. Guangzhou and Shenzhen provide the retail and corporate banking activities for consumers and businesses in the Pearl River Delta region. As of late 2003, a small number of Hong Kong banks were entering the Pearl River Delta region, in particular Shenzhen, to provide a limited range of services (see Chapter 7). In general, management, finance, and accounting functions are carried out in Hong Kong. Some large Hong Kong financial service providers, notably HSBC, have relocated back-end support operations from Hong Kong into the Pearl River Delta to take advantage of salary differentials between the two locations (see Figure 5.9). Foreign banks with operations in Shenzhen also attempted to support those operations from Hong Kong.

Business Services

The ability to combine complementary activities in Hong Kong and the Pearl River Delta region in business services is influenced by restrictions on the activities of foreign firms in the Chinese mainland, the ownership of the companies involved in the service transactions, and the source of investment flows into the Pearl River Delta region. While Hong Kong and multinational service providers have had a great deal of interaction in Hong Kong, in the Pearl River Delta region, Hong Kong companies, Pearl River Delta region-based suppliers, and

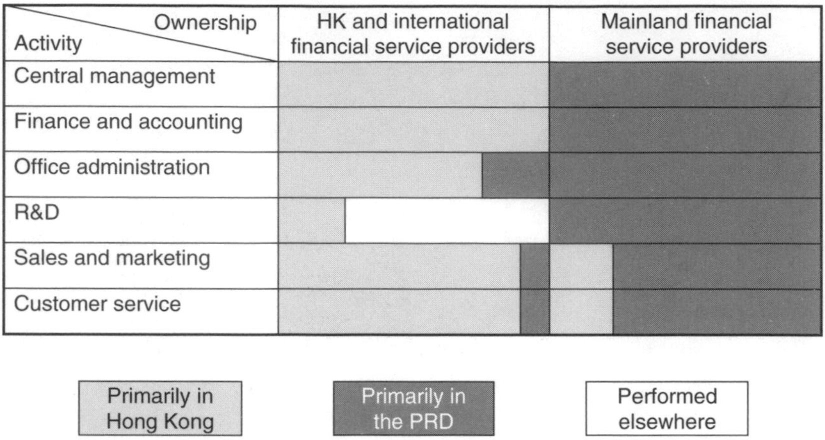

Activity \ Ownership	HK and international financial service providers	Mainland financial service providers
Central management		
Finance and accounting		
Office administration		
R&D		
Sales and marketing		
Customer service		

Primarily in Hong Kong	Primarily in the PRD	Performed elsewhere

Source: Enright, Scott & Associates Ltd research

Figure 5.9   The Hong Kong–Pearl River Delta financial sector value chain

multinational service companies have served distinct market segments and performed different functions. The result has been less interaction, cross-fertilisation, and direct competition than in many manufacturing industries.

For business services not covered by market-entry restrictions, Hong Kong business service companies have tended to be the providers of choice for Hong Kong-invested companies in the Pearl River Delta region. Smaller foreign-invested companies also have tended to use Hong Kong service providers. Large multinationals have tended to have global agreements with international service firms with branches in Hong Kong and elsewhere in China. Large mainland firms aiming at overseas expansion have tended to draw on the experience of multinational service firms, whereas local, mainland-focused businesses have tended to source their service providers from within the Pearl River Delta region. Many of the international companies will tend to have in-house service expertise imported from their respective countries. Smaller Hong Kong and Pearl River Delta region companies tend to outsource service functions to small-scale operators with just a handful of clients. Relationships and trust have figured strongly in such service provision.

Depending on the ownership of the service firm, providers have displayed different market orientations. For Hong Kong-owned service firms, the majority of their business has been firmly rooted in Hong Kong, or with Hong Kong-owned firms in the Pearl River Delta region. An emerging area for such companies is in meeting the requirements of foreign small- and medium-sized companies with operations in the Pearl River Delta region. The existence of

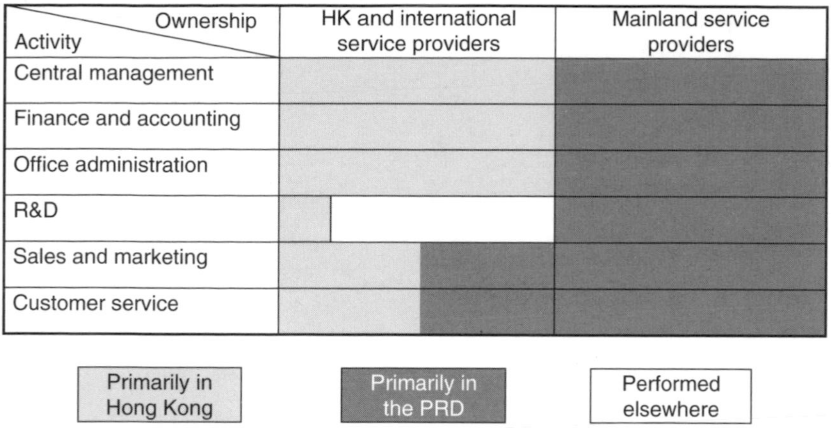

Ownership \ Activity	HK and international service providers	Mainland service providers
Central management		
Finance and accounting		
Office administration		
R&D		
Sales and marketing		
Customer service		

Primarily in Hong Kong	Primarily in the PRD	Performed elsewhere

Source: Enright, Scott & Associates Ltd research

Figure 5.10   The Hong Kong–Pearl River Delta professional services value chain

a large number of Hong Kong-owned companies in the light-manufacturing sector, for example, has created an abundance of work for these small service firms, though again, most of the clients are serviced from Hong Kong. In general, the management, finance, and accounting functions of Hong Kong professional services firms are carried out in Hong Kong. Some sales and marketing and customer service activities are conducted in the Pearl River Delta region, in proximity to clients, but the formal and informal restrictions discussed above have resulted in most activities locating in Hong Kong (see Figure 5.10).

Local service providers in the Pearl River Delta region are generally of such small scale that they do not pursue business much beyond their immediate locality. Pearl River Delta firms, in general, do not provide services to firms in Hong Kong, unless they are Hong Kong companies with a physical presence in the Pearl River Delta region. Even then, the services provided are for clients requiring low-cost basic services, or a high degree of local knowledge. For top-tier services requiring Western applications, Hong Kong-based service providers have an absolute advantage over their mainland counterparts. Their superior international exposure, professional standards, and management practices mean that clients tend to have confidence in their services. For the time being at least, local service firms in the Pearl River Delta region do not generally reach these standards.

For multinational firms, their main business in the Greater Pearl River Delta region remains in Hong Kong, with a strong focus on Beijing and Shanghai for their China expansion strategy, both due to market development

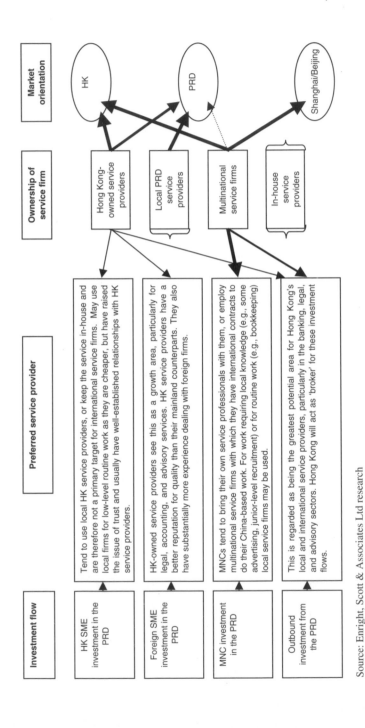

Source: Enright, Scott & Associates Ltd research

Figure 5.11   Service demand derived from inward and outbound investment flows to and from the Pearl River Delta region

and, in some fields, to 'one office, one location' restrictions. It has been quite common for such firms, particularly in the financial, legal, and accounting sectors, not to consider the Pearl River Delta region a significant market.[70] These firms may also draw on their mainland or Hong Kong offices to service large-scale projects for international clients in the Pearl River Delta region.

EMERGENCE OF AN INTEGRATED ECONOMIC REGION

The above discussions indicate that the Greater Pearl River Delta region is becoming a single integrated economic region for some industries and remains as separate sub-regions for other industries. The ability of the Hong Kong and Pearl River Delta region economies to create combinations that enhance competitiveness has been the subject of a survey carried out by Michael Enright and James Newton of the University of Hong Kong in conjunction with the Hong Kong Trade Development Council in 2002. In the survey, Hong Kong-based industry participants were asked to assess the competitiveness of the Hong Kong industry compared to Guangdong, and to Hong Kong and Guangdong in combination for a broad range of sectors.

In the vast majority of cases, the respondents reported that the Hong Kong–Guangdong combination was more competitive than either entity on its own. The industries that fell into this category, mostly light manufacturing and services related to manufacturing or logistics, are the industries in which the respondents believed that combinations and complementarities have enhanced competitiveness.

Hong Kong was rated as more competitive in a handful of sectors than the Hong Kong–Guangdong combination. These sectors, including real estate, insurance, accounting and legal services, education and training, business management and consulting services, and other professional services, reflect Hong Kong's strengths as a world-class international services platform, as well as the stiff barriers to entry that have limited the participation of foreign and Hong Kong firms in the Chinese mainland. In essence, this meant that in these sectors, since the combination is not allowed to operate, there is no mutual reinforcement between Hong Kong and Guangdong. Thus the combination is seen as actually less competitive than the Hong Kong industry alone.

Guangdong was rated more competitive than both the Hong Kong–Guangdong combination and Hong Kong in a few sectors, most of which involve the processing of raw materials sourced in Guangdong. It rated the most competitive of the three options for chemicals, textiles, plastic products, and other manufacturing. Guangdong was rated as the equal of the

Hong Kong–Guangdong combination in packaging materials, travel goods and handbags, garments, and jewellery. In these latter industries, the participants apparently felt that Hong Kong did not necessarily add sufficiently to the mix to merit the Hong Kong–Guangdong combination being the most competitive.

The striking result of the survey is that in most of the industries and sectors covered, the combination of Hong Kong and the Pearl River Delta region is viewed by industry participants as more competitive than either Hong Kong or the Pearl River Delta separately. The complementarities and competition have fostered more competitive combinations indicative of an increasingly integrated economic region, the Greater Pearl River Delta region.

COMPETITIVENESS AND THE GREATER PEARL RIVER DELTA REGION

The Greater Pearl River Delta region has become an economic powerhouse over the last several years, with strong positions in a variety of industries. In light manufacturing, trade-related services, transportation, and logistics, the region is a world leader. The region also has a strong and growing position as a manufacturing centre for electronics and related technology-based products. On the other hand, the region has not been very competitive in heavy industry, such as chemicals, steel, or heavy machinery. Its competitiveness in business services is uneven, with some world-class services available in Hong Kong, but less extensive offerings available in the Pearl River Delta region.

The competitiveness of the region's economy is due in large part to the economic interaction that has fostered a deep division of labour. This division has allowed the different jurisdictions to specialise in activities in which they have had comparative advantages, while linking with activities that were better performed in other places in the Greater Pearl River Delta region. The result has been a complementarity that has contributed to the competitiveness, not just of Hong Kong and not just of the Pearl River Delta region, but of the Greater Pearl River Delta region as a whole, a region that is more competitive than its constituent parts could hope to be.

In many industries in which the combination of Hong Kong and the Pearl River Delta region can be brought to bear, it can be very difficult for other parts of the world to compete. However, there are industries in which the combination of Hong Kong and the Pearl River Delta region has not substantially enhanced competitiveness. These industries tend to be industries in which neither has much of a history, such as heavy manufacturing, or industries in which regulation and other barriers prevent effective interaction, such as several service sectors. This would suggest that greater interaction and the reduction of barriers might provide a further impetus to the Greater Pearl River Delta region's economy, a theme we will return to later in the book.

As the economy of the Pearl River Delta region has grown in size and sophistication, it has been able to take on more and more activities. This is to be expected from an economy that had been isolated for so long and has been opened gradually in only the last two and a half decades. It also is to be expected that some activities would decentralise out of Hong Kong, a city with some of the world's highest costs, as soon as this was feasible. As a result, it is not surprising that there is increasing competition among firms and locations in different activities and industries. While this competition might be inconvenient to some in the region and a threat to others, it is this competition that is likely to force greater efficiency in both Hong Kong and the Pearl River Delta region, efficiency that is likely to benefit the region as a whole. At the same time, by providing more choices for customers and for foreign investors, it actually makes the region more attractive as a sourcing and investment location.

CHAPTER SIX

Forces Shaping the Greater Pearl River Delta Region

T here are several forces that will shape the economic future of the Greater Pearl River Delta region. Many of these are national in nature, influencing the entire Chinese economy, while others are local. The former include the liberalisation and greater openness in the Chinese economy, the extension of accessible markets in China, and increasing linkages both within and outside of China. The latter include the economic plans found in the Greater Pearl River Delta region, the producer services gap, the mix of costs and capabilities, improvements to physical linkages, and changing mindsets and strategies found in the region.

LIBERALISATION AND OPENNESS IN CHINA

China's continuing process of economic liberalisation and opening will have an important influence on the economies of the Greater Pearl Delta region. The two main features of this process are China's accession into the World Trade Organization (WTO) and the Closer Economic Partnership Arrangement (CEPA) between China and Hong Kong. Both are best understood as steps in a reform process that started in 1979 and will continue well into the future. Given the international orientation of the Greater Pearl River Delta region, and the fact that the region has been operating at world quality and cost standards for years, it is not far-fetched to conclude that the region will receive a strong boost from greater liberalisation and openness in China's economy. In addition, WTO accession, CEPA, and China's general opening should stimulate substantial growth in trade and investment in the Pearl River Delta region. Much of this trade and investment will involve Hong Kong. Hong Kong will start to provide far more of the services to the Pearl River Delta region that major economic cities around the world provide to their surrounding areas than has been the case to date.[1]

China's accession to the World Trade Organization

China joined the WTO in 2001. In order to enter, China reached an accession agreement with member states that went well beyond the commitments of most other members of the organisation. In its protocol of accession, China committed to undertake far-reaching reforms to implement WTO standards in the areas of market access, national treatment, regulatory transparency, and intellectual property protection, among others. China's market liberalisation commitments include the reduction of tariff rates for agricultural products and industrial goods; the elimination of tariffs on IT equipment, computers, and other IT products; the elimination of nearly all non-tariff quantitative barriers (such as quotas and licences); the granting of trading and distribution rights; and a range of sector-specific measures to liberalise a wide range of services, including wholesale and retail trade, telecommunications, and financial services.

Tariff reduction is an area where China has made rapid and significant progress under WTO, with China's overall average tariff rate falling from over 15% in 2001 to 12% in 2002. In January 2004, China circulated a draft Foreign Trade Law to introduce an automatic trading rights system intended to bring China into compliance with its commitments on trading rights for foreign-invested enterprises. Progress also has been made in the issuing of intellectual property rules: new trademark and copyright regulations were issued in 2002; and new patent, trademark, and copyright rules in 2003. However, the phasing-in of trading rights remained at the top of the list of concerns tabled by the United States in 2004, while the enforcement of intellectual property rights continued to be of concern to both the United States and European Union.[2] The limited progress in market access in agriculture and services was also of concern.

Over time, entry into the WTO will have different impacts on different industries. In garments and textiles, entry will allow China access to larger quotas in foreign markets and will allow it to participate when the quota regime is phased out in the future. In electronics goods, Chinese producers have had relatively free access to international markets. For producers active in China, China's membership in the WTO provides a framework for extending market access and for combating protectionism in other markets. In heavy industries, like steel and chemicals, WTO membership is likely to open China up to much tougher competition from imports than has been the case in the past. In other industries, such as automobiles, WTO entry has provided a stimulus for foreign firms to invest into an industry in which domestic producers were mostly inefficient. In parts of agriculture, WTO entry could create tremendous difficulties as China struggles to improve productivity in order to keep pace with imported goods. Entry into the WTO also will have far-reaching implications for the service sector in China, benefiting the parts of China that are best able to attract foreign investment in the service sector and are best able to use this investment to help develop the local economies.

China's accession to the WTO will substantially increase the openness of the Pearl River Delta region's economy. Given its proximity to Hong Kong, and what that implies in terms of access to international trade and spill-over of tastes, one would expect that imports would rise in the Pearl River Delta region faster than in most other regions of the Chinese mainland. Many companies will find it worthwhile to extend their sales and distribution networks from Hong Kong into the region and many Hong Kong firms are already entering the region. In general, in goods markets, WTO entry will allow the export-oriented firms of the Pearl River Delta region to expand their markets, while the industries that will be hardest hit are not generally found in the Pearl River Delta region. In fact, by making it easier to import intermediate goods and capital equipment, greater openness should allow Pearl River Delta region production facilities greater scope to leverage their competitive advantages. The Pearl River Delta region, with its proximity to world-class service providers based in Hong Kong, should be a strong beneficiary of opening in the service sector as well. The question will be how far and how fast the various sectors will open and how creative Hong Kong, the Pearl River Delta region, and foreign firms will be in developing the opportunities and serving customers that they have never been able to serve before.[3]

Closer Economic Partnership Arrangement

The Closer Economic Partnership Arrangement (CEPA) signed in 2003 between the Chinese mainland and Hong Kong governments grants preferential access to China's markets from Hong Kong. CEPA goes further than China's WTO commitments with respect to trade in goods, as well as market access in services.[4] Under CEPA, Hong Kong manufactured goods under 374 mainland tariff codes can enter the Chinese mainland duty free, with more categories to be added in 2006. CEPA grants preferential market access to Hong Kong service providers in 18 service sectors. Sectors that have received concessions under CEPA include real estate services, distribution and retail, banking, logistics, legal services, convention and exhibition services, management consulting, construction, medical and dental services, freight forwarding, storage and warehousing, and land and maritime transport, among others.

China's liberalisation commitments under CEPA in services include the early liberalisation of market openings already committed to under the WTO, in effect giving Hong Kong a time advantage over other economies. This time advantage ranges from one to four years, depending on the sector. Another type of preference under CEPA is the lowering of thresholds, facilitating the entry of small and medium-sized firms into the mainland in sectors including banking. CEPA also commits China to some preferential regulatory changes such as mutual recognition and an easing of pre-existing restrictions on Hong Kong professionals. CEPA also includes some new liberalisation provisions that do not have counterparts in China's WTO Protocol of Accession; for example, in the exhibition services and audio-visual sectors.[5]

To qualify as a 'Hong Kong company' under CEPA, a company must be incorporated and registered in Hong Kong under the Hong Kong Companies Ordinance (or set up under Hong Kong ordinances by private bill, which in practice has occurred only rarely).[6] If these criteria are met, the company qualifies as a 'Hong Kong company' regardless of the nationality of its shareholders. In contrast, companies that are incorporated under laws of other jurisdictions do not qualify as Hong Kong companies under CEPA. This is true even if the company has a registered branch there. In addition, the company must engage in substantive business operations in Hong Kong. The relevant criteria are the nature and scope of business, the number of years in operation (three to five years are required), payment of Hong Kong profits tax in accordance with the law, ownership or rental of business premises in Hong Kong, and employment of local staff (at least 50%).[7] A special provision applies to Hong Kong service suppliers that are acquired by or merged with overseas service suppliers on or after CEPA's effective date, resulting in the acquisition by the overseas service suppliers of more than 50% of equity interest. Such companies will be regarded as a Hong Kong service supplier for purposes of CEPA one year after the date of the acquisition or merger.[8]

With CEPA, the Greater Pearl River Delta region is integrating even faster than was previously the case. CEPA will allow the type of integration already present in manufacturing to be extended to many services sectors, a move towards a seamless Greater Pearl River Delta market. Qualifying companies will be able to extend their informal networks to address wider business opportunities. While CEPA covers the entire Chinese mainland, and is not limited to the Pearl River Delta region on the mainland side, the largest impact will be on the Pearl River Delta region given the proximity and existing business relationships. Meanwhile, representatives of dozens of mainland jurisdictions from all over China have also been seeking out opportunities to benefit from CEPA. These trends are already resulting in new businesses, greater efficiencies, and a much broader portfolio of choice for customers.

CEPA can be expected to benefit the Greater Pearl River Delta region relative to other regions in China for the foreseeable future. In addition to providing opportunities for Hong Kong entities, our research has shown that one of the major constraints on the further upgrading of the Pearl River Delta region's manufacturing base is a systemic shortage of world-class producer services. Hong Kong's world-class services platform is ideally positioned to address this deficit and give the Pearl River Delta region a powerful boost along its development trajectory. Within the Pearl River Delta region, officials of the different localities are positively disposed towards CEPA and in general recognise that their localities stand to benefit from its implementation.

CEPA also can be expected to create new opportunities for foreign firms based in Hong Kong. Since CEPA came into effect, three of the first sectors to see strategic moves by foreign companies have been logistics, distribution, and financial services. There have been moves by Hong Kong-based multinational logistics firms such as BAX Global and Mitex International (a Mitsui Soko subsidiary) to set up wholly owned logistics operations in the Chinese mainland.[9] Multinational firms based in Hong Kong have begun to use CEPA to leverage their distribution of international brands in the Chinese mainland. For example, in the timepiece and jewellery sectors, multinational firms with value-adding operations in Hong Kong can ship Hong Kong-origin product into the mainland exempt of import duties ranging from 14 to 23% and 26.7 to 35%, respectively.[10] In finance, Standard Chartered Bank and Citibank have applied for authorisation to set up Hong Kong-incorporated subsidiaries. This is an indication that under CEPA and WTO, Hong Kong is likely to play an expanding role as an 'integral part' of their China strategies, in particular with respect to mainland-related business in Hong Kong.[11]

THE EXTENSION OF ACCESSIBLE MARKETS IN CHINA

One of the dreams for companies around the world has been the ability to serve China's 1.3 billion population. There have been a number of features of the Chinese market that have rendered much of this potential market inaccessible. The relative poverty of the nation has meant that most of China's people have limited purchasing power. The vast majority of China's population, in the order of 800 million, has been in a rural setting and difficult to reach. The infrastructure to reach people all over China has been lacking. Support for local companies and inter-regional protectionism has limited the development of national markets in China. The combination of growing purchasing power, urbanisation, enhanced infrastructure development, and greater market orientation is likely to result in a major expansion in the accessible market in China. In each case, the Greater Pearl River Delta region is likely to obtain disproportionate benefits.

Growth in purchasing power

Rising purchasing power has become one of the major attractions of the Chinese mainland. According to the International Monetary Fund (IMF), China's GDP based on purchasing power parity (PPP) was US$6,137.3 billion in 2002, larger than that of Japan and second only to the United States.[12] The World Bank's World Development Indicators show that when correction for purchasing power parity is made, China's gross national income per capita in 2002 was US$4,390,[13] close to the US$5,000 per person usually thought of as representing substantial purchasing power. While such adjustments must be made with caution, the conclusion is that China already is an enormous market for many types of firms.

Even without the PPP correction, the number of people in the Chinese mainland with earnings of at least US$5,000 per year is forecast to rise from around 60 million in 2002 to 160 million in 2010.[14] Their spending power will be bolstered by higher paying urban jobs, increasingly in the private sector, while the one child policy will boost per capita spending. As China's economy progresses, China's savings rates of roughly 40% of household income[15] are likely to come down, unlocking additional purchasing power. Young adults are adopting the income profiles of older adults to an increasing extent, and they are displaying a new consumer culture that is increasingly brand conscious and trend driven.[16] It is not uncommon for a young mainland professional to spend the equivalent of one month's salary on the latest model of mobile phone.[17]

The Pearl River Delta region has had one of the world's fastest growing regional economies for over two decades. This growth has allowed the region to support levels of development and living standards that are well beyond those found in most of China. In 2002, Shenzhen had the highest official GDP per capita of any city in the mainland, with a per capita GDP of RMB 46,388 (US$ 5,602).[18] In 2003, Shenzhen was expected to overtake Beijing and Shanghai as the biggest vehicle market in the Chinese mainland within two years.[19] The Pearl River Delta accounted for almost one out of every three cars sold in the Chinese mainland, and car ownership within Guangdong Province was predicted to grow at 40% per year.[20] Retail sales for Guangdong Province reached RMB 501.4 billion (US$ 60.6 billion) in 2002, the highest of any province on the Chinese mainland. Consumer spending in the Pearl River Delta is strongly influenced by Hong Kong consumer trends and spending patterns, as a result of close interaction between the two populations, as well as the reach into the Pearl River Delta of Hong Kong broadcast television, including entertainment and advertising. Youths in the Pearl River Delta are among the most brand-conscious in the Chinese mainland, and tend to prefer brands with an international, trend-setting image such as Coca-Cola, Nike, and Budweiser.[21] The upshot is that the Pearl River Delta region is likely to be a much more important market in the future than it has been to date.

Urbanisation

Urbanisation is a strong trend in China as a whole. Mainland planners anticipate that between 300 million and 500 million people will come off the farm and into urban settings by 2020.[22] Many of these people will naturally gravitate towards the most economically dynamic regions in the country. While the Yangtze River Delta and Bohai regions have their own large indigenous populations, to a great extent, the Pearl River Delta region, particularly on the west side of the Delta, is relatively under-populated. It is not farfetched to conclude that the Greater Pearl River Delta region's population could increase dramatically in the not too distant future. When combined with the urban development and infrastructure being built in the region, this population is likely to make the region that much more powerful in economic terms.

Guangdong Province has the highest percentage of urban dwellers of all the provinces of the Chinese mainland (50.5% in 2000), with the exception of the provincial-level cities Beijing, Shanghai, and Tianjin. At the same time, the urban populations in Shenzhen (92.4%), Zhuhai (85.5%), Guangzhou (83.8%), Foshan (75.1%), Zhongshan (60.1%), and Dongguan (60.0%) all exceeded the provincial average.[23] In the 2001 to 2005 period, Guangdong officials believe that urbanisation in the province will increase by 40%.[24] The expectation is that eventually there will be a virtual urban continuum that runs from Hong Kong up through Guangzhou and around to Macao. This would represent a vast expansion of the urban population from 50 million to perhaps 70 million or more. It would also represent huge potential demand for goods and services required by cities and city dwellers.

Some cities in the Pearl River Delta region will see extensive development or redevelopment. Guangzhou, for instance, is developing a completely new urban system by creating industrial locations and residential communities outside the traditional city centre and then rebuilding the centre as a modern commercial metropolis. The total area under development or redevelopment is equal to roughly half the size of Tokyo's 23 wards. Between 2003 and 2013, Guangzhou plans to spend roughly as much on urban redevelopment as Shanghai spent in the 1990s. It will undertake projects that will result in the transformation of the city, much in the way that Shanghai has been transformed. Shenzhen is building a new city centre and undergoing dramatic development and redevelopment as well. Other cities all around the Pearl River Delta region are doing the same. The result will be modern cities with the sort of highly developed city centres, manufacturing outskirts, mass transport, and residential communities seen in cities elsewhere in the world. There will be enormous gains in terms of ability to provide high-level services, efficiency of transportation, and specialisation of urban districts. All should add substantially to the region's development potential.

National transportation infrastructure

The national transportation system will have an important influence on business throughout China. China was able to become a major trading power without an effective national transportation system. The coastal regions that dominate China's trade and inward investment require efficient transportation for just a few hundred kilometres inland from major ports. Initially, the focus was on building this infrastructure to link local hinterlands to the major export ports. However, the development of the national highway, railway, and inland waterway systems should substantially improve transportation throughout China.

China is in the process of building a vast national highway system that will connect all of the cities in the mainland with populations greater than 500,000 people (around 100 cities). This 35,000 kilometre system, more than three-quarters completed by 2002, will include a total of 12 inter-provincial expressways, five running north–south and seven east–west across China.[25]

The principal north–south axis is the 2,310 km Beijing–Zhuhai Expressway connecting Beijing to the city of Zhuhai in the Pearl River Delta region.[26] As of 2004, the Beijing–Zhuhai Expressway had cut the road transport time from Wuhan to Guangzhou from three days to around 12 hours.[27] An additional highway in this system will extend from the Pearl River Delta to China's northeast, another from the Pearl River Delta westward to Chengdu in Sichuan, and another to Kunming in Yunnan. The latter will connect to an international highway from Kunming through Indo-China to Singapore. These highways will situate the Greater Pearl River Delta region at the hub of a modern road transport system radiating across China and beyond.

Although the national railway system in China was initially designed to transport coal, still the dominant source of energy and heating in the country, increasingly, the Railway Ministry is focusing on moving people and goods. The Tenth Five-year Plan focuses on accelerating railway construction in western China and adding capacity along China's main corridors, including the Beijing–Shanghai corridor. The Central Government also aims to make the national railway system 'more responsive to market needs' in view of the railways' decline in share of the national freight transport market from 71% in 1980 to 51% in 2002.[28] The Tenth Five-year Plan includes a high-speed passenger rail network based around four north–south and two east–west lines, and will significantly cut journey times between the major cities.

Guangdong Province, with the support of China's Railway Ministry, is taking steps to position itself as one of the mainland's four largest railway passenger transport hubs, along with Shanghai, Beijing, and Wuhan, by 2020. At the heart of the plan is a new Guangzhou railway station, envisioned as 'Asia's largest railway station complex', that would serve as the terminus of a future high-speed Beijing–Guangzhou passenger express.[29] This express train would cut the 24-hour train journey between the two cities to an estimated 10 or 12 hours. Travel times between Guangzhou and Wuhan would be cut from 10 hours to four hours when a new Wuhan–Guangzhou high-speed line comes into operation in 2010.[30] Further in the future, there is the prospect of Guangzhou linking to a Pan-Asia Railway running from Kunming in Yunnan Province to Singapore.

The impact of the further development of China's national transportation system will be substantial. It will allow the interior regions better access to coastal markets and coastal regions better access to interior markets. It should dramatically expand the efficient catchment area for China's ports, expand the use of multi-modal transportation, and contribute to the eventual creation of a single national market. In addition, such developments could foster the emergence of a small number of cities that develop as the logistics and transportation centres for the entire Chinese mainland. The Pearl River Delta region, with its advanced logistics capabilities and international linkages, is likely to play a strong role in the future as a centre for South and West China, and as a link between China and the rest of the world. This, in turn, will benefit Hong Kong and Macao by expanding the scope of their connectivity into the Chinese mainland.

Greater market orientation

Greater market orientation in China has shown itself in many ways. WTO entry, CEPA, decentralisation of responsibility for finances and for state enterprises, and prohibitions of barriers to trade between provinces are all examples. Discriminating against a Chinese company from another province is one thing, discriminating against a foreign company producing in another province in China is a WTO dispute in the making. The foreign logistics and distribution companies that will be able to operate in the Chinese mainland under the WTO agreement will prove far better at setting up efficient national distribution systems than have been in place in China to date. As market orientation progresses, it will be more and more difficult for local governments to support or subsidise money-losing enterprises. These pressures identified above enhance the push towards a market economy in which underlying competitiveness and efficiency will become increasingly important in determining business outcomes. Each of these features should further the trend towards a national market.[31]

Movements towards a single national market will mean that the competitiveness of different regions will determine where most production takes place. China's regions vary enormously in terms of their competitiveness. The Pearl River Delta region has literally tens of thousands of firms and facilities that have been operating at world quality and cost standards for a long time. As China becomes more of a single national market, producers from the region should have an easier time selling throughout the Chinese mainland.

The Greater Pearl River Delta region has been a leader in terms of private sector and market-oriented development in China. Hong Kong is perhaps the most market-oriented economy in the world. Within the Chinese mainland, the Pearl River Delta region has been in the vanguard of private-sector and market-oriented development. The export-oriented industries of the region have had to operate in tough international markets at world quality and cost levels. Given the state of reform and of market-oriented development, it is probably in the Greater Pearl River Delta region's best interest for the Chinese mainland to develop a single national market as soon as possible.

LINKAGES INSIDE AND OUTSIDE OF CHINA

In addition to the linkages that might be fostered by better transportation and communication, there are other linkages that are being explored both within China and between China and other parts of Asia. Most notable have been moves to link up the provinces of South and South-west China and moves to link China to ASEAN countries as well as to Japan and Korea.

Linkages within China

As of early 2004, efforts were under way to form a coalition to bring Hong Kong, Macao, and nine mainland provinces in South and South-west China into a single, integrated economic region, to be known as the '9+2 Pan-Pearl Delta Region'. The nine mainland provinces – Guangdong, Fujian, Jiangxi, Guangxi, Hainan, Hunan, Sichuan, Yunnan, and Guizhou – accounted for 34% of the 2000 population of the Chinese mainland, and 33% of GDP, 45% of exports, and 36% of utilised foreign direct investment in 2002. Guangdong was easily the largest economy among the nine provinces, accounting for 11% of GDP, 36% of exports, and 22% of utilised foreign investment.

Proponents of the initiative, looking ahead to a China increasingly charac-terised by competition among regions, envisaged a vast new economic region.[32] In this vision, Hong Kong and Guangdong Province would be complementary parts of the Pan-Pearl River Delta's 'dragon's head', attracting foreign investment and serving as the 'engine for development' for a vastly expanded catchment area encompassing much of South and South-west China. In the words of Guangdong Governor Huang Huahua, 'we hope to build a Pan Pearl River Delta that is a regional economic system in which there is a complementary sharing of resources, a big market and benefits for all parties'.[33]

The region would be powered by much closer planning and economic relationships facilitated by transportation links between Hong Kong, Macao, Guangdong, and the eight other provinces. These eight provinces lack a major seaport, as well as international linkages. Improvements in the transportation system were likely to bring much of the larger region into the catchment area of the ports and airports of the Greater Pearl River Delta region. Proponents of the Pan-Pearl River Delta announced in June 2004 plans for a regional railway system, with Guangzhou at its hub, that would bring cities in western provinces such as Sichuan, Yunnan, and Guizhou within a day trip of Guangzhou by passenger train by 2020 (current travel times can be 40 hours or more).[34] Better access will allow the interior regions to serve the richer coastal areas, which in turn are likely to be sources of capital and entrepreneurs that will help develop the interior. In a sense, the '9+2' arrangement is the natural extension of the process through which Hong Kong and Macao have aided the development of the Pearl River Delta region. At the same time, it will be hard for the influence of other major Chinese cities, such as Shanghai, to reach the expanded region. The advantages of the highly externally oriented Hong Kong and the Pearl River Delta region economies could therefore be brought into full play.

Wider Asian linkages

China has been exploring wider linkages as well, particularly with its Asian neighbours. Starting with the Asian Financial Crisis in 1997, the 10 member countries of the Association of South East Asian Nations (ASEAN) have fostered closer relations with China, Japan, and Korea. Of the three countries, China has acted the fastest to enter into a Free Trade Agreement (FTA) with ASEAN. In November 2001, leaders of ASEAN and China endorsed the setting up of an ASEAN–China Free Trade Area (ASEAN+1) by 2010. In October 2003, China took the initial step of signing the ASEAN Treaty of Amity and Cooperation and since then its leadership has signalled its commitment to enter into the China–ASEAN Free Trade Agreement on schedule. In December 2003, China and ASEAN agreed to a special round of tariff cuts in advance of the FTA, on a wide range of agricultural and manufactured goods. China aims to achieve bilateral trade with ASEAN in excess of US$100 billion by 2005.[35]

The ASEAN–China Free Trade Area is forecast to contain 1.7 billion consumers, making it the world's most populous trading bloc. It will have a GDP of about US$2 trillion and its total trade will amount to an estimated US$1.23 trillion. An ASEAN–China FTA is projected to increase ASEAN's exports to China by 48% and China's exports to ASEAN by 55.1%. It is projected to increase ASEAN's GDP by 0.9% (US$5.4 billion) and China's GDP by 0.3% (US$2.2 billion) in absolute terms. The three sectors of China's exports that will benefit the most from the ASEAN–China FTA are expected to be textiles and apparel, electrical appliances and machinery, and other manufactures.[36]

An ASEAN–China FTA may eventually be extended to include Japan and possibly Korea. The leaders of ASEAN and Japan have agreed to start talks on a 'comprehensive economic partnership' by 2005, with the aim of concluding a pact, 'including elements of a free trade area', by 2012. Korea has adopted a more cautious approach to an FTA with ASEAN. It has been studying the possibility of individual, bilateral free trade agreements with Singapore and Japan, on the assumption that such efforts would 'eventually serve as building blocks' for an ASEAN–Korea FTA'.[37] There also is the possibility, though not in the near future, of an East Asian Free Trade Area (EAFTA), a trilateral FTA linking China, Japan, and Korea.

If the linkages between China and ASEAN pan out, the Greater Pearl River Delta region in general, and Hong Kong and Guangzhou in particular, could benefit from a wide range of activities linking China with South-east Asia. As an internationally oriented economy with close links to South-east Asia, the Greater Pearl River Delta region is positioned to become the bridgehead for investors from the Chinese mainland to invest in South-east Asia. Historically, Hong Kong has been the place from which companies from South-east Asia have accessed the Chinese mainland. In many cases, they have set up their international arms in Hong Kong and use Hong Kong to make and manage their investments, not just in China, but the rest of the region as well. Thus an ASEAN+1 agreement could disproportionately benefit the Greater Pearl River Delta region.

CORPORATE STRATEGIC SHIFTS IN CHINA

The last few years have seen several strategic shifts on the part of local and foreign companies in China. For the world's major multinational companies, China has moved right to the top of the list. For many companies, such as computer-maker Hewlett Packard (HP), 'the name of new opportunity is China'.[38] For Alcatel, China 'is the most important communications market in the world'.[39] For Intel, according to its CEO, 'probably this year [2004] or next, China will surpass Japan as our largest customer'.[40] For China's domestic companies, however, the nation's reform process has been a two-edged sword. On the one hand, it has made life much more difficult for money-losing state-owned enterprises by forcing tens of thousands of firms to find their own way without the benefit of ongoing state support. On the other hand, the reform process has opened up the possibilities for the private and collective sectors to become much more active.

Shifts in strategies of foreign multinationals

Foreign companies in China have reached a watershed in their development. In many cases, they are moving from being outsiders, new to China and unfamiliar with its workings, to insiders, much more astute and aware of the advantages and pitfalls found there. They have become better at educating the local customers about the potential value of their offerings and better at educating themselves to the ins and outs of the market. Many foreign firms have moved well beyond 'entry mode' to 'positioning mode'. Instead of trying to establish a foothold, they are now trying to establish strong, sustainable competitive positions. In many cases, this involves moving beyond the initial region in which they made their first investments, to multi-regional or national strategies. In the process, many companies are moving to wholly owned foreign enterprise (WOFE) status, or renegotiating joint venture arrangements with local partners in order to expand their footprint in China.

With the changes in strategic emphasis has come a focus on profitable operations. Only a few years ago, most foreign multinationals lost money on their China operations. This is no longer the case. Roughly 10% of the respondents to surveys by the American Chambers of Commerce in Shanghai and Beijing indicated that they were 'very profitable' in China in 2002 and another 65% were 'profitable'. Of the unprofitable firms, 91% expected to be profitable within a three-year time frame. Some 42% of respondents indicated that their margins in China exceeded their global average, while 29% reported margins in China on par with their global average, and 29% reported margins lower than their global average.[41]

For many foreign companies, the main issue in China today is how to scale their operations from a single region, to multiple regions, to national coverage. Many have found that they could succeed in a single region by relying on a limited number of key individuals, but that multi-regional or national success requires systems that can be replicated and scaled to wider and wider geographic areas. This has created substantial challenges in terms of attraction and retention of key personnel, the creation of management systems and controls, and the creation and instilling of strong corporate cultures.

The shifts in corporate strategies in China bode well for China as a whole and for the Greater Pearl River Delta region in particular. Increasing attention on China by multinational companies is bound to result in greater investment and trade commitments for the region. At the same time, many of the foreign companies that invested first to serve markets in other locations in China are starting to extend their investments to southern China as well. As these investments become more balanced around the country, it is likely that the management structures will also become more balanced, with South China operations managed out of Guangzhou, Hong Kong, or Shenzhen, rather than Shanghai or Beijing. On the other hand, for companies that invested first in the Pearl River Delta region, we would expect a further balancing of their investments and management structures. This will not be a zero sum game of one region winning at the expense of others, but rather a positive sum game in which all the main economic regions in China will receive greater investments and managerial attention.

Chinese companies

For many Chinese companies, the challenges have been even greater. State enterprises have had to try to retool to become market-oriented, profit-driven entities. Private firms have faced the challenge of developing new markets without the formal recognition of the Chinese legal system and without access to most forms of finance. In both cases, the legacies of the past have weighed heavily on present operations and future opportunities.

When Zhu Rongji became prime minister in 1998, he made reforming the state-owned sector a high priority. Over the next five years, the Central Government cut most state-owned enterprises loose to fend for themselves without the state support to which they were accustomed. In essence, many state-owned enterprises at the national and provincial levels were turned over to municipalities and other local governments and closed down or restructured. The number of state-owned enterprises fell from 262,000 in 1997 to 174,000 in 2001, which in turn resulted in massive layoffs nationwide.[42] Tens of millions of workers have been cut from the ranks of the former state-owned enterprises, giving rise to occasional social unrest in some parts of the country.

Under the policy of 'grasp the big, let go the small', a limited number of state-owned firms were selected for preferential treatment by the Central Government. The State-Owned Assets Supervision and Administration Commission has the mandate to turn a group of 30 to 50 state-owned enterprises into 'national champions' by 2010. Of these, the three leading oil companies, PetroChina, Sinopec, and CNOOC, as well as Baosteel, Haier, and TCL appear to be relatively well positioned.[43] Many others have floundered despite state support. In aerospace, for example, Avic has had difficulty developing its own aircraft despite efforts dating back to the early 1980s, while Sanjiu, the pharmaceuticals firm, has lost ground to foreign competition due in part to failure to develop adequate R&D capabilities.[44] Challenges faced by the 'national champions' include inconsistent Central Government policies, protectionism at the provincial level that impedes the acquisition of competitors, and state pressure to maintain employment at uncompetitive levels.[45]

China's private sector, in contrast, has developed into the most dynamic part of the mainland economy. Growing at an annual rate of around 20%, it accounts for as much as 60% of fixed capital investment, and most of China's new jobs. According to the IMF, China's private firms generated 17.5 million jobs between 1995 and 2001.[46] While 90% of China's private firms are small, with fewer than eight employees, the number of large private firms is on the rise.[47] Private firms face numerous challenges in China, starting with the uncertain status of private property rights which makes it difficult for private-sector firms to access credit and raise capital.

Some Chinese firms themselves are moving to compete in international markets. While the international moves of China's oil companies are best viewed as attempts to ensure China's energy security, moves by companies like Haier, TCL, and Huawei are classic internationalisation moves by companies that have become relatively strong in the domestic market. Haier has expanded into international markets from a large home base in refrigerators and other white goods, achieving overseas sales of US$1 billion in 2003 and capturing around 30% of the United States market for small refrigerators.[48] TCL started out in 1980 as a state-owned enterprise producing fixed-line phones. It went on to become a leading consumer electronics brand name in China, and launched an ambitious drive in overseas markets. In 2002, TCL realised US$1.1 billion in international sales, mostly in Asia. Mainland telecommunications equipment supplier Huawei has a market presence in some 40 countries world-wide and has entered into an agreement with 3Com to build an international brand.[49]

Similarly, as indigenous Chinese companies grow and develop, many such firms have been seeking out locations in the Greater Pearl River Delta region from which to make and manage major investments. As of 2004, CNOOC together with Shell was constructing a vast petrochemical complex in Huizhou, north-east of Shenzhen, to use liquefied natural gas imported from Australia and Indonesia.[50] The Zhongji Group, the largest producer of semi-trailers in China and a major exporter, had begun production in the suburbs of Shenzhen.[51] China Huaneng Group, one of the five largest power companies in China, had acquired stakes in Shenzhen Energy Group. Several mainland auto-makers had accessed or were seeking to access the Hong Kong capital market, recognising the Hong Kong stock market 'as a good platform for automakers on the mainland to woo overseas investment'.[52] These were just a few examples of the mainland firms that were entering the Greater Pearl River Delta region in large numbers.

Hong Kong companies

Among many Hong Kong companies, we see a strategic shift towards the markets of the Pearl River Delta region and the mainland as a whole. In the five years following 1997, during the Asian Crisis, many Hong Kong firms drew back from activities in the Asia Pacific outside of China while pursuing opportunities on the mainland. Their focus there has strengthened since 2002, bolstered by China's market liberalisation measures under WTO and CEPA.

CEPA's liberalisation of a range of service sectors has motivated many Hong Kong firms to expand or refine their mainland presence, or to enter it for the first time. In logistics, for example, CEPA has allowed Hong Kong firms to formalise and rationalise pre-existing operations in the Pearl River Delta and elsewhere, providing a firmer foundation for future growth. In activities such as trading, distribution, importing, and exporting, setting up a CEPA wholly owned foreign enterprise in the mainland can offer advantages over using a foreign or bonded zone company.[53] These provisions have attracted the attention of a number of Hong Kong firms, including LiFung Distribution. Medium-sized Hong Kong banks such as Wing Lung Bank and Dah Sing Bank have been setting up operations in Shenzhen, in particular, attracted by the city's liberalised financial services regime. In other sectors, CEPA's influence has been indirect. The favourable impact of mainland tourist spending on Hong Kong retail sales, brought about by CEPA's liberalisation of tourist flows into Hong Kong, has encouraged a variety of Hong Kong firms to venture into the mainland. Hong Kong's leading cosmetics retailer, Sa Sa International Holdings Ltd, has focused on market prospects on the mainland following success at home in selling its cosmetics to mainland tourists.

Another force shaping the strategies of many Hong Kong companies is growing competition from mainland firms, especially in trading and light manufacturing. Faced with fierce price competition, some Hong Kong traders and light manufacturers have chosen to close down their family businesses when the outgoing director reaches retirement, while others have tried to cut costs by relocating production activities to more distant areas in Guangdong Province and beyond. Other Hong Kong trading firms have responded by going higher-end, transforming themselves into marketing and design firms, developing their own brands, and pursuing a range of value-adding strategies designed to keep them systematically at the forefront of consumer markets in ways that are difficult to replicate.[54]

CAPABILITIES AND COSTS

The future evolution of the economies of the Greater Pearl River Delta region also will be shaped by the capabilities and costs found in the region. The growth of skills and capabilities in the Pearl River Delta region combined with the steep cost gradient between Hong Kong and the Pearl River Delta region are causing a shift of activities into the Pearl River Delta region. The producer services gap between the Pearl River Delta region and Hong Kong, largely the result of barriers to entry in the mainland, will increasingly act as a gravitational force pulling producer services into the Pearl River Delta region as China opens under CEPA and the WTO. Together, these forces will create the impetus to move activities across the border into the Pearl River Delta region, resulting in further development of that region and a refocusing of the Hong Kong economy on high-end activities.

Growing capabilities in the Pearl River Delta region

The Pearl River Delta region is becoming increasingly self-sufficient in economic matters as the skills and capabilities in the region grow. To an increasing extent, skills and capabilities are available locally across the length of the corporate value chain, in both manufacturing and services. Capabilities in manufacturing and related activities, including production, R&D, and design, are available from within the PRD region and from elsewhere on the mainland. Managerial talent is also available locally and domestically. Marketing and sales capabilities are developing rapidly, according to international customers. Administrative support personnel and other office staff with suitable Chinese and English language skills are available across the Pearl River Delta region. Skills and capabilities are also developing among supporting industries that provide inputs, components, and capital goods to local light manufacturers, and in value-adding services provision, allowing the Pearl River Delta region to deepen and to become more diversified.

A broader, more diversified Pearl River Delta region economy provides substantial additional potential for interaction with the Hong Kong economy. The development of the Pearl River Delta region is still dependent on Hong Kong, but not as dependent as it was in the past. At the same time, there is concern in the Pearl River Delta region that it might be losing out to other areas in China, notably the Yangtze River Delta region, for some types of development. Thus, the different jurisdictions within the Pearl River Delta region are trying to redefine their economic roles in the national and global economies. Many in the region look to further interaction with Hong Kong to help them in this endeavour.

Costs

A high cost base will serve to limit the range of corporate activities and employment opportunities in Hong Kong. Hong Kong is showing a tendency towards developing a 'high–low' economy in which high value-added activities, and the lower level maintenance and support activities required to keep a large city running, are found in Hong Kong. Middle-level activities of the sort that employ middle or lower middle class employment may be increasingly located outside of the city. Hong Kong-based managers in manufacturing firms and trade-related services firms interviewed for this study indicated that their

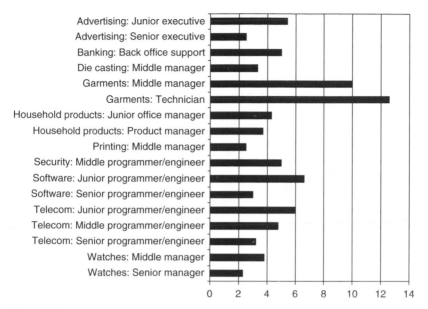

Note: Salaries in the Pearl River Delta region = 1.
Source: Enright, Scott & Associates Ltd research

Figure 6.1   Ratio of salaries in Hong Kong compared to the Pearl River Delta

firms continue to seek to relocate jobs into the Pearl River Delta region due to cost considerations. Other service providers predict that they will move many back office jobs into the region.

Our interviewees indicated that there was a substantial gap in the salaries paid to office staff and low- and middle-level managers from Hong Kong and those from the Pearl River Delta region, with the Hong Kong person earning four to six times what their Pearl River Delta counterpart would earn (see Figure 6.1). While many managers claimed that their Hong Kong staff was more efficient, many also indicated that the difference in efficiency did not make up for that type of salary differential. Higher up the ladder, the salary differential for top managerial positions narrowed to two or three to one.[55] This reflects the fact that individuals with top senior management skills are in short supply in the Pearl River Delta region and therefore command salaries more comparable to their Hong Kong counterparts.

The steep wage differentials shown in Figure 6.1 are underpinned by corresponding differentials in residential property prices between Hong Kong and the Pearl River Delta region. In 2003, the asking price of new, mid-priced residential properties in Guangzhou was in the range of US$482 to US$723 per square metre gross, a small fraction of prices for mid-range flats in

Hong Kong.[56] The wage levels of Hong Kong office workers and managers reflect the much higher prices they have to pay to live in Hong Kong. This process has accelerated the flow of jobs across the border into the Pearl River Delta region, where workers at salary levels four to six times lower than those in Hong Kong can afford housing that is one-sixth the price.

Over the medium term, it is unlikely that the salary and property price differentials will remain at 2003 levels. As skills, capabilities, infrastructure, and the administrative environment improve in the Pearl River Delta region, we would expect the differentials to be reduced. However, given the fact that Hong Kong is increasingly attracting high-value activities from Hong Kong, foreign, and Chinese firms, it is likely that significant differentials will remain for quite some time, as in the case of cities like New York, London, and Tokyo.

The producer services gap

Another force that will influence the development of the economies of the Greater Pearl River Delta region is the producer service gap between the Pearl River Delta region and Hong Kong. Historically, the service sector has been viewed as unproductive or even parasitic in some quarters in the Chinese main-land. Although these attitudes have changed since China began its reform pro-gram, a focus on engineering and production has left the nation ill-equipped to provide high-level services. Historically, the Pearl River Delta region was even more backward than many other parts of the Chinese mainland when it came to the service sector. The growth of the region's manufacturing base and the subsequent diversification of the economy have given rise to tremendous demand for producer services of all kinds. At the same time, the rise in consu-mer incomes and the withdrawal of state enterprises from providing many social services, such as housing, education, healthcare, and social security, has dramatically increased demand for consumer services.

Despite this rise in demand, the development of the service sector in the Pearl River Delta region remains limited. In 2002, the service sector accounted for 40.8% of Guangdong's GDP, 44.4% of Shenzhen's GDP, and 55.7% of Guangzhou's GDP,[57] each far below the services share of the typical advanced national economy (70 or 75% of GDP) or advanced commercial cities (80 or 85% of GDP). In Hong Kong, for example, the service sector accounts for 86% of GDP. Overall, producer services equal roughly three-fifths of Hong Kong's GDP and only around one-quarter of Guangzhou's GDP. When we realise that Guangzhou has the most producer service-intensive economy in the Pearl River Delta region, we can see the magnitude of the gap.[58]

Ironically, the types of producer services that are needed most in the Pearl River Delta region – transportation services, trade-related services, accounting, advertising, consulting, and financial services – are precisely those in which Hong Kong specialises. Historically, restrictions on foreign companies prevented Hong Kong firms and the Hong Kong offices of multinationals from providing many of these services. This is why China's WTO entry and CEPA are potentially so important for the entire region. If greater interaction between Hong Kong and the Pearl River Delta region – perhaps through an easing of restrictions on Hong Kong-based service providers – increases the portion of the Pearl River Delta region's GDP in the service sector by 5%, it could result in an additional RMB 35 billion to RMB 40 billion (approximately US$4–5 billion) in GDP per year.

CONNECTIVITY WITHIN THE GREATER PEARL RIVER DELTA REGION

As was seen earlier in this volume, the value of connectivity between Hong Kong and parts of the Pearl River Delta region has been enormous. Limitations in connectivity have held back what would have even more impressive development. In recent years, however, a number of steps have been taken to improve connectivity between Hong Kong and other parts of the Greater Pearl River Delta region. These include infrastructure and policy developments regarding connections between Hong Kong and Shenzhen, as well as developments regarding the connections between Hong Kong and the western part of the Pearl River Delta region.

Connectivity between Hong Kong and Shenzhen

Significant progress has been made in strengthening the cross-boundary connectivity between Hong Kong and Shenzhen. For vehicle crossings, infrastructure will be greatly expanded when the 'Western Corridor' highway linking Hong Kong with western Shenzhen enters into operation at the end of 2005. The three existing vehicle crossings between Hong Kong and Shenzhen can handle a daily total of 42,000 vehicles, while the Western Corridor will be able to accommodate an additional 80,000 vehicles per day.[59]

As for railway passenger traffic, which accounts for 76% of cross-boundary travellers, the Hong Kong government plans to alleviate congestion at the existing passenger railway crossing with a spur line to Lok Ma Chau–Huanggang. The daily cross-boundary flow is expected to increase by 150,000 people when this railway extension enters into operation in 2007. Guangdong and Hong Kong authorities have announced plans to study a High Speed Rail (HSR) link between Guangzhou and Hong Kong, which according to some estimates could cut travel times between the two cities to as little as 40 minutes.

Steps also have been taken to streamline immigration procedures on both sides of the Hong Kong–Shenzhen boundary and to extend the hours of operation of the border crossings in the face of growing demand. In January 2003, when the Lok Ma Cha–Huanggang crossing commenced 24-hour operations, the passenger traffic flowing through the checkpoint from midnight until dawn was almost 75% higher than projected by Hong Kong's Immigration Department. Guangdong Governor Huang Huahua has announced that the Western Corridor will operate on a 24-hour basis and that extending the hours of operation of other checkpoints could be considered as well.[60]

Additional improvements will need to be made to enhance connectivity for both passengers and freight transport. Issues that officials on both sides are addressing include reducing the driving time between Hong Kong, Shenzhen, and the rest of the Pearl River Delta region, and speeding up the customs-clearance processes on both sides.[61] Connectivity across the boundary between Hong Kong and Shenzhen was the number one issue identified by Hong Kong interviewees for the present project. In fact, many stated that if this problem were solved, many of the other issues regarding further economic interaction between Hong Kong and the Pearl River Delta region could more or less solve themselves.

Connectivity between Hong Kong and the Western Pearl River Delta

Efforts are under way to link Hong Kong and the western Pearl River Delta by bridge. China's State Council agreed in August 2003 that the Hong Kong–Zhuhai–Macau Bridge Advance Work Co-ordination Group should be established with Hong Kong as convenor. Priority is being given to a Y-shaped bridge linking Zhuhai and Macao with Hong Kong's Lantau Island.[62] As of late 2004, the link was expected to take the form of a road bridge, rather than a road–rail combination bridge, and it was hoped that work on the bridge could start by year-end 2005 or early 2006. The bridge should take three to four years to complete once construction begins.[63]

As was indicated in Chapter 4, in 1980, Shenzhen and Dongguan (the two jurisdictions just north of Hong Kong on the eastern side of the Pearl River Delta) had a combined GDP that was nearly identical to the combined GDP of Zhuhai and Zhongshan (the two jurisdictions just north of Macao on the western side of the Pearl River Delta). By 2002, the combined GDP of Shenzhen and Dongguan, RMB 292.97 billion (US$35.4 billion), was more than 3.5 times that of Zhuhai and Zhongshan, at RMB 82.2 billion (US$9.9 billion). Much of this difference could be ascribed to the difference in exports and foreign investment. In 2002, the combined exports of Shenzhen and Dongguan, US$70.3 billion, were nearly 6.5 times those of Zhuhai and Zhongshan, at US$10.93 billion. The combined utilised inward investment of Shenzhen and Dongguan in 2002, US$4.65 billion, was nearly 3.5 times that of Zhuhai and Zhongshan, at US$1.34 billion. Much of the difference in performance could be attributed to the eastern side's better linkages with Hong Kong and the capital, management, technology, services, and other benefits resulting from those linkages.

If a direct link between Hong Kong and the western part of the Delta allowed Zhuhai and Zhongshan to close the development gap with Shenzhen and Dongguan by even a fraction, the result could be a benefit to the western part of the Delta of hundreds of billions of renminbi in GDP, tens of billions of US dollars in exports, and billions of US dollars in foreign investment per year. It should be noted that in this regard a link between the western part of the Delta and Shenzhen is not nearly a good substitute for a link with Hong Kong. After all, it was not capital and expertise from Shenzhen or Guangzhou that helped develop Dongguan, it was capital and expertise from Hong Kong. While a link to Shenzhen would facilitate cargo flows to Shenzhen's ports and maybe to the port of Hong Kong, it would be less likely to foster as direct links for owners, investors, service providers, and buyers.

For Hong Kong, a bridge would bring much of the western Delta area into easy contact for all types of businesses, investments, and services. If a bridge were to allow the Hong Kong SAR to expand its exports of trade-related services and transportation services by just 10%, it could mean more than 57,000 jobs and US$2.56 billion in additional service exports per year (using year 2001 figures for employment and trade in services). When we realise that a bridge would be a long-lived investment, with a life of 30 to 40 years or more, we see that the value of a bridge to the region is likely to dwarf all the figures that have been estimated as the costs of such an undertaking (which have ranged from US$2.1 billion to US$3.7 billion, depending on the source and route).[64]

ECONOMIC DEVELOPMENT PLANS

Last, but certainly not least, the economic development of the Greater Pearl River Delta region will be influenced by economic plans made at the national and local levels. Although the economy of the Chinese mainland has become much more market-oriented in recent years, there is still a strong planning component to China's development. Development plans set forth overall goals, identify key government infrastructure and development investments, and provide an overall framework within which both state and non-state enterprises operate. In many localities within the region, local government officials remain very influential, regardless of whether the dominant forms of ownership are private or collective. Although Hong Kong has a different economic system and technically does not fall under the national five-year economic plans, economic planning both in Hong Kong and on the Chinese mainland will clearly influence the SAR going forward.

National Plans

China's Tenth Five-year Plan (2001 to 2005) calls for the implementation of the nation's World Trade Organization (WTO) accession agreement, a further modernisation of the economy, a greater role for private enterprise, and enhanced development of the central and western provinces. The more developed areas along the coast, particularly the Bohai Rim region, the Yangtze River Delta region, and the Pearl River Delta region, in the face of greater market competition at home and abroad, are to speed up technological development and innovation, and develop their high-tech and export-oriented industries. These regions are supposed to lead China's economic development and work to strengthen cooperation with, and the development of, less economically advanced regions. The Pearl River Delta region is supposed to upgrade its manufacturing industries, expand its technology-based industries, and develop a more modern service sector. The goals are to improve the region's ability to succeed in international competition and to provide space for lesser developed areas to take on lower value-added activities. At the time of writing, work is starting on China's Eleventh Five-year Plan, which will reflect the policy priorities of the new national leadership. These priorities include greater focus on sustainable development and balancing growth between the coastal regions and China's interior. Particular emphasis is placed on fostering the development of China's less economically advanced regions, such as the north-east, and improving conditions for China's 800 million rural population.[65]

Guangdong's provincial plan

The Tenth Five-year Plan of Guangdong Province (2001 to 2005) calls for provincial GDP to increase by 9% per year to reach RMB 1,630 billion (US$196.9 billion) by 2005. The province hopes to upgrade traditional industries, such as garments and textiles, food and beverages, and construction materials; expand the newer 'pillar industries' of electronics and IT equipment, electrical appliances and machinery, and petrochemicals; and develop new strengths in the automobile, pharmaceutical, paper product, and environmental industries. In the service sector, the province plans to improve the conditions for market access, break down industry monopolies, and actively develop a modern service sector in order to meet the conditions of the WTO accession agreement. The plan indicates that the Pearl River Delta region is to lead the further modernisation of the provincial economy by linking the urban and rural economies, modernising infrastructure, becoming a high-technology zone, promoting the region as an important base for international trade, and pioneering a sustainable market-oriented economic system.[66]

Local and municipality plans

Each local and municipal government in the Pearl River Delta region also develops its own economic plan. These plans are supposed to be consistent with the national and provincial plans. In recent years, as decision-making in economic affairs and government finance has become more and more decentralised, the local plans have taken on increased importance. In addition, these plans can change substantially when new local leaders take office. The plans of Guangzhou and Shenzhen, in particular, are likely to influence the development of the region in coming years.

Guangzhou's Tenth Five-year Plan targets an average growth rate of 12% per year in GDP and 10% per year in per capita income. The plan prioritises the development of the 'pillar industries' of information technology, automotives, and petrochemicals in several technology and industrial parks. In the service sector, priority has been given to developing Guangzhou into the leading service centre for the Pearl River Delta region, into an international transport and logistics centre, and into a distribution centre for South China. The idea is to build the financial, commercial, transportation, information, science and technology, human resources, and education and training systems necessary to attract large firms from China and from abroad to set up factories, research and development centres, headquarters, and offices in Guangzhou.[67]

In November 2001, after the promulgation of Guangzhou's Tenth Five-year Plan, the city announced plans to develop Nansha, an area south of Guangzhou proper, into a heavy industrial and logistics centre, with steel, chemical, and heavy industrial facilities, and of the bulk port required for industrial materials. The idea was to give South China the heavy industrial base that it has traditionally lacked to support the automotive and machinery industries developing in Guangzhou, and to supply the growing South China market with heavy industrial products. Other components of the Nansha development plan include container port facilities, a logistics centre, and a high-technology zone. Manufacturing is expected to migrate from Guangzhou to Nansha, freeing up land in Guangzhou proper for the development of a modern commercial city and creating an economy in Nansha equal in size to that of Guangzhou proper.

Guangzhou shows every intention of attempting to regain the economic primacy in the Greater Pearl River Delta region that some people believe has been temporarily usurped by Hong Kong and Shenzhen due to historical circumstances.[68] Resources from the province and the provincial capital provide Guangzhou with ample funds to carry out its plans, without too much regard to neighbouring jurisdictions.

Shenzhen's Tenth Five-year Plan calls for GDP growth of 12% a year from 2001 to 2005. Priority is being given to a range of high-technology industries, including computers, integrated circuits, telecommunications equipment, digitally controlled appliances, and biomedical products. Shenzhen also aims to become a leading international logistics centre, leveraging its location at the heart of one of the world's leading manufacturing regions.[69] The Plan called for Shenzhen's seaports to have a cargo handling capacity of 70 million tonnes, to reach 6.5 million TEUs in container capacity, and to operate more than 100 international shipping routes by 2005.[70] It is likely, however, that these expectations will be surpassed as container capacity had already approached the 2005 target by the end of 2002. Shenzhen also hopes to improve customs and administrative systems in order to streamline the passage of cargo into and out of the city. In order to enhance its position as a logistics and commercial hub, Shenzhen has approached numerous major multinational companies to see if the firms would place buying or sourcing offices in Shenzhen.

Shenzhen plans to push for substantial economic integration with Hong Kong, with particular regard to cooperation in science, technology, ports, infrastructure, tourism, and environmental protection. Shenzhen wishes to continue to capture manufacturing and service industries from Hong Kong, as well as to become a place for Hong Kong people to live, work, and shop. Shenzhen plans to enhance its service sector through the early liberalisation of certain sectors in order to attract increased service activities and persuade multinational headquarters and offices to relocate to Shenzhen from Hong Kong.[71] The city also plans to help other parts of the Pearl River Delta region develop through use of its financial, logistics, technology, and infrastructure.[72]

Dongguan's Tenth Five-year Plan calls for an average annual GDP growth of 12% and a doubling of most economic aggregates from 2001 to 2005. Dongguan is to be built into an international industrial, trade, and port city based on its manufacturing capabilities, high-technology R&D, and foreign trade. The city's plan emphasises cooperation with Hong Kong and Taiwan in finance, trade, technology, and manufacturing.[73] The goal is to deepen and upgrade traditional industries, to expand in high-technology industries, and to attract suitable foreign investments. The electronics and information technology equipment industries are slated to be the focal points of development.[74] To support this development, the Dongguan city government is setting up a 72-hectare science, technology, and industrial park at Songshan Lake. The park will focus on knowledge-intensive industries and is planned to become a centre for innovation, technology, education, and culture.[75] The lakeside setting is designed to be an attractive place for professionals to live and work.

Elsewhere in the Pearl River Delta region, Foshan plans to focus on electronics, industrial and home appliances, plastic products, food and beverages, ceramics and building materials, garments, and Chinese medicine.[76] Huizhou plans to develop opportunities in the petrochemical field arising from the joint venture by CNOOC and Royal Dutch Shell, and to build on the strengths of its consumer electronics and information technology equipment industries. Zhuhai plans to focus on electronics, information technology equipment, R&D, and education.[77] Jiangmen will continue to develop itself as a regional manufacturing centre, especially in the production of motorcycles, home electrical appliances, chemical fibres and textiles, batteries, pharmaceuticals, and light chemical products. Zhongshan intends to strengthen its packaging and printing sector, as well as encourage the areas of information and communications technology, refined petrochemicals, and sustainable energy sources. Zhaoqing is targeting electronics manufacturing, biotechnology related to agricultural production, new materials, machinery and equipment such as motor parts and control systems, garments and fashion, forestry for the production of pulp and paper, and beverages such as distilled water and soft drinks.

Development plans in Hong Kong

Historically, the Hong Kong government focused on creating an environment within which the private sector could prosper, setting and enforcing clear rules of the economic game, making sure that the administrative and regulatory system was simple and conducive to business, limiting taxation and government expenditures, and allowing the private sector to take on economic activities, such as tunnels and other infrastructure, that would be taken on by the government in many other places. Direct government intervention and involvement in the economy tended to be limited to infrastructure, education, some public utilities, and other support activities.[78]

Housing was the main sector in which the government intervened directly, a result of the entry of millions of refugees in the 1950s and 1960s. By 2003, the Hong Kong government provided housing for approximately one-third of Hong Kong's population.[79]

Since 1997, the Hong Kong government has become more active in economic affairs, increasing its promotion activities through the Hong Kong Trade Development Council and the Invest Hong Kong investment promotion agency, creating support programs for small businesses, and even investing in projects like Hong Kong Disneyland (to open in 2005) and the Cyberport development. The Hong Kong government has supported a number of initiatives that it hopes will improve Hong Kong's position as a technology centre, providing heavily subsidised land in the cases of a new Science Park and Cyberport (focused on IT development), funding a mid-stream research institute modelled on Taiwan's ITRI (ASTRI), and creating a venture capital fund to be administered by private-sector firms. Hong Kong does not have formal development plans as found in the Chinese mainland. As a result, its plans tend to represent areas in which government chooses to invest in infrastructure, education, and support programs. The government's control of zoning and land supply, however, gives it a tool with which it can try to micromanage development. The government claims that it does not grant subsidies, but this is true only in a narrow sense. Instead of cash subsidies, the Hong Kong government has provided subsidised land for selected projects.

In 2000, the Hong Kong Chief Executive's Commission on Strategic Development put forth the notion of Hong Kong becoming 'Asia's World City', an international city that could eventually perform for Asia roles similar to those performed by New York and London for North America and Europe respectively. The Commission focused on four principal themes: strengthening links with the Chinese mainland, enhancing competitiveness, improving quality of life, and reinforcing identity and image. Several specific sectors were identified as crucial to Hong Kong's development. These included financial and business services; tourism; regional headquarters for multinational companies; information services and technology; and trade, transportation, and logistics.[80]

Since 2002, however, one of the major driving forces of Hong Kong's policy has been to promote improved interaction with Macao and the Pearl River Delta region. The approach has been to identify and attempt to reduce the constraints that businesses face in doing business across the boundary. This can be seen in the government's territorial development blueprint through 2030, released in November 2003, that focuses on improving the living environment and economic competitiveness, and fostering stronger links with the mainland. It underscores the need for additional investments in airport, seaport, and road and rail infrastructure. The blueprint proposes an additional cross-border checkpoint to accommodate projected increases in land crossings between Hong Kong and Shenzhen. These proposals will be reviewed by Hong Kong's Legislative Council and undergo a process of public consultation.[81]

DRIVING FORCES

The forces identified in this chapter point towards continued growth and even greater prosperity in China. China is continuing to open, its markets are becoming more attractive, and its internal and external linkages are improving. As a result, companies of all sorts are focusing more attention on the country. Given the traditional position of the Greater Pearl River Delta region, all of these developments should benefit the region disproportionately. After all, the Greater Pearl River Delta region has had to operate at world quality and cost standards for more than two decades, something no other place in the Chinese mainland can claim.

Within the Greater Pearl River Delta region itself, capabilities and costs will cause an evolution of the division of labour that has developed in the region. Greater openness, combined with the producer services gap, will provide substantial opportunities for Hong Kong firms and the Hong Kong offices of multinational firms to help raise the level of the Pearl River Delta region's economy. Improved connectivity within the region will enhance the interaction by bringing the western side of the Delta into closer contact with Hong Kong and by reducing the inefficiencies that exist at present. The development plans and policies found in the region are likely to enhance this interaction further. The result could be an economically integrated region in which development anywhere in the region will feed off of, and benefit, development elsewhere in the region. We next turn to the likely future economic interaction within the region.

CHAPTER SEVEN

Future Interaction between Hong Kong and the Pearl River Delta Region

T he economic interaction between Hong Kong and the Pearl River Delta region will have a crucial impact on the development of both economies in the future, just as it has in the past. The forces identified in the previous chapter will have an important impact on several dimensions of the economic interaction, including investment, trade, technology, and management, among others. Given the extensive interaction that already exists in the manufacturing sector and the new openings of China's service sector, the main changes in the interaction are likely to involve the service sector. This is particularly important given the differential in service sector capabilities identified in the previous chapter, as well as the importance of service sector interaction for multinational firms.

INVESTMENT

Hong Kong has been the dominant source of international investment into the Pearl River Delta region since the region began to open in the late 1970s. Official estimates indicate that roughly 70,000 Hong Kong firms had invested nearly US$80 billion in Guangdong Province through 2001.[1] In recent years, however, Hong Kong's share of inward investment into the region has been declining. As firms from Taiwan, Japan, and the West have become more familiar and comfortable with operating in the Pearl River Delta region, they make up an increasing portion of the companies investing there. In addition, these companies tend to make much larger investments on average than their Hong Kong counterparts. There will be greater openness to investment from overseas as China implements its WTO undertakings and as investments are sought in the Pearl River Delta region in the automotive sector, in heavy industries associated with the Nansha development program, and in other industries that favour Western and Japanese firms. Foreign service firms will also take advantage of their size and international status to extend their positions in retailing and business services. For these reasons, the share of Hong Kong investment into the Pearl River Delta region is likely to decrease.

Even with a decline in share, however, Hong Kong investment should retain a leading share well into the foreseeable future and the absolute value of Hong Kong investment into the region will continue to grow. Many investments are already on the drawing board. According to the Hong Kong Chinese Manufacturers' Association, members have invested only around half of the amount that they have contracted to invest in the Chinese mainland. Greater openness is attracting additional Hong Kong investment. A study carried out by the Hong Kong Centre for Economic Research found that the number of Hong Kong manufacturing and trading firms entering Guangdong Province for the first time more than doubled in 2001 over 2000, an indication that China's liberalisation under the WTO and CEPA should continue to drive new investment.[2]

Hong Kong firms are also likely to be major participants in the infrastructure, real estate, and retail development opportunities that are rapidly expanding in the Pearl River Delta region. Some of the industries that will be opened under China's WTO accession agreement – such as telecommunications, banking, transportation, wholesaling, and distribution – are industries in which Hong Kong firms are likely to take on major positions in the Pearl River Delta region. Preferential access to a variety of service sectors under CEPA should allow many Hong Kong firms to formalise and expand their existing investments in the Pearl River Delta region and should allow other Hong Kong firms to enter the region for the first time on an accelerated timetable compared to WTO.[3]

Hong Kong's position as a base for foreign multinationals to make and manage investments in the Pearl River Delta region also should grow substantially. As indicated above, the thousands of firms that use Hong Kong as a base for the Pearl River Delta region will grow in number. Increasing openness and economic development will bring greater investment in a wider range of industries than has been the case before. In addition, as foreign firms develop their businesses in the Chinese mainland, firms that chose to place their first operations in the eastern or northern part of the Chinese mainland eventually will place operations in the south as well. Hong Kong retains its advantages as a location for foreign firms to place their management, financial, logistics, and international market-related activities linked to South China. Improved transportation within the Greater Pearl River Delta region and improved border-crossing efficiency will make it easier to travel from Hong Kong to facilities or operations in the Pearl River Delta region.

The most significant change, however, is likely to be a dramatic increase in the number of firms from the Pearl River Delta region that invest in offices in Hong Kong. According to a survey carried out by the Hong Kong Trade Development Council in 2002 among private-sector firms in the Chinese mainland, 19.7% of the responding firms from the Pearl River Delta region already had an office in Hong Kong, 14.5% already had plans to place an office in Hong Kong, and 49.3% indicated that they might place an office in Hong Kong in the future. Only 16.6% indicated that they had no plans to place an office in Hong Kong.[4] Responding managers indicated that no other city could replace Hong Kong as an international commercial and financial centre. Some 81% of the Pearl River Delta-based managers indicated that it was easy to manage regional business activities from Hong Kong. The managers also viewed Hong Kong as superior to cities in the Chinese mainland and elsewhere on a variety of attributes (see Table 7.1). All of this promises a substantial increase in the number of Pearl River Delta region companies investing in Hong Kong.

Table 7.1 PRD-based private-sector managers' comparisons of Hong Kong with the Chinese mainland and other cities, 2002

Attribute	Percentage of PRD respondents claiming Hong Kong is superior to Chinese mainland and other cities
Concentration of foreign business associations and multinational companies	85.5
Ready access to market intelligence	82.6
Easy to locate agents and do sourcing	66.0
Base for developing world markets	65.9
Platform for seeking foreign capital and business partners	52.6
Human resources	58.0

Source: Hong Kong Trade Development Council 2002b

TRADE

Most of the present trade between Hong Kong and the Pearl River Delta region, some 80% by some estimates, relates to export processing by facilities in the Pearl River Delta region.[5] Since these types of exports are expected to increase substantially over time, the volume of this trade is expected to grow as well. One feature that will influence this trade is the nature of export processing regulations, which are relatively restrictive in terms of requiring single-step processing, in which only companies performing a single production step are able to take advantage of the tax and duty breaks associated with export processing.

Although there is little doubt that the volume of trade and trade interaction between Hong Kong and the Pearl River Delta region will grow, one major influence on the future trade relations between Hong Kong and the Pearl River Delta region is whether Hong Kong-funded enterprises in the Pearl River Delta region will still use Hong Kong for trade-related services and as a transit point for goods. According to the Hong Kong Trade Development Council, offshore trade (trade that is transhipped through Hong Kong without even entering its customs statistics or shipped directly to third markets without ever touching Hong Kong) of Hong Kong-invested or Hong Kong-controlled enterprises has been growing dramatically. Although re-exports are still the dominant mode of exports for Hong Kong firms from the Chinese mainland, transhipments and direct shipments represented a total of 32.9% of the exports of Hong Kong-related firms from the mainland in 2000, up from 28.2% in 1997.[6]

The exports of the Pearl River Delta region are still largely tied to foreign-invested or contracted firms. While many local firms in the Pearl River Delta region have begun to export, for the most part they still focus on the domestic market. Many firms located on the western side of the Pearl River Delta region that produce international quality products have found it too difficult or expensive to set up their own international marketing and sales channels. Ironically, these are precisely functions that Hong Kong-based firms and offices excel at providing. In the future, it is expected that many Pearl River Delta firms would seek out Hong Kong partners or set up Hong Kong offices in order to access international markets. At the same time, more and more Hong Kong firms will seek out Pearl River Delta sources of supply for an expanding range of international markets. This should result in an additional trade flow involving Hong Kong and the Pearl River Delta region.

China's opening under its protocol of accession to the WTO should result in substantial increases in imports of all types into the Pearl River Delta region. Hong Kong and Hong Kong firms are well positioned to act in an intermediary role for much of this trade, linking the Pearl River Delta region to international sources of industrial and consumer goods on a large scale. This implies that Hong Kong import traders will be able to expand their businesses in the future just as the Hong Kong export traders have done in the past.[7] Hong Kong import traders also will be expanding operations into the Chinese mainland. CEPA allows Hong Kong companies, effective 1 January 2004, to set up wholly owned foreign trading companies in the mainland.[8]

Hong Kong exports into the Chinese mainland, including the Pearl River Delta region, will also benefit from duty free treatment under CEPA. The agreement allows Hong Kong-manufactured goods under 374 mainland tariff codes to enter the Chinese mainland free of import tariffs, with additional items to qualify by 2006. CEPA is not expected to result in a dramatic, overall increase in exports of goods made in Hong Kong into the Chinese mainland due to costs in Hong Kong.[9] Nevertheless, CEPA is expected to boost Hong Kong's exports into China of specific types of products including high-end fashion garments, jewellery, branded watches, and products with advanced technology and high intellectual property content.[10]

Interaction in convention and exhibition services is also positioned for growth, driven by the strong performance of the region's light industrial base, the emergence of mainland-owned firms looking to forge direct relations with overseas customers, and growing interest among overseas retailers and distributors in sourcing direct from within the region. As of late 2003, Shenzhen city officials were hoping for experienced exhibition organisers from Hong Kong to help develop the potential of the city's convention and exhibition centre scheduled to open in 2004.[11] CEPA allows Hong Kong firms to supply convention and exhibition services in the Chinese mainland, on a wholly owned basis.[12] This is expected to formalise the presence of Hong Kong exhibition firms in the Pearl River Delta region, many of whom have already been active there, and to facilitate some new entry from Hong Kong as well.[13]

TECHNOLOGY

The Pearl River Delta region already is a leader in terms of production of technology-intensive products in the Chinese mainland. By 2002, Guangdong accounted for more than 30% of China's electronics output, 50% of biomedical output, 50% of advanced ceramic components, and 68% of China's medical electronics output.[14] According to the plans of the Guangdong Provincial Government, the Pearl River Delta will focus on six high-technology industries, electronics, biotechnology, new materials, opto-mechanical-electronic devises, environmental technologies, and oceanic technologies. The technology base of the Pearl River Delta region is expected to expand substantially, particularly given the large investments that local governments and foreign companies are expected to make in the region.

The interaction between Hong Kong and the Pearl River Delta region in technology is likely to change substantially in the future. When China began its reform process, it was behind in virtually all areas of technology and the Pearl River Delta region was behind several other places in the Chinese mainland. Hong Kong firms initially brought in the technologies associated with the production of light-manufactured goods and later shifted from being suppliers of technology to technology intermediaries, bringing in advanced technology developed elsewhere into the region.

Hong Kong firms are expected to continue to perform design and development activities in Hong Kong and then transfer ideas into production facilities in the Pearl River Delta region. Hong Kong will continue to operate as a technological intermediary given its superior knowledge and access to international information networks. This role includes the ability to forecast trends in consumer demand and end-products in the world's leading markets, identify pertinent, cutting-edge technologies, and translate them into new applications.[15] Prospects for this role are good, as technological change driven by consumer demand is predicted to continue into the foreseeable future. As the Pearl River Delta region's high-tech production base develops, locally owned firms will become more sophisticated customers and innovators in their own right, giving rise to prospects for mutually beneficial collaboration.

For Hong Kong high-tech firms with activities on both sides of the border, Hong Kong will continue to play a central strategy-setting and marketing role for day-to-day activities and a central role for overall company direction. It will remain the location for customer-related activities directed at overseas markets, and for defining new products aimed at those markets. Hong Kong also will remain the lead location for collecting new technology and information related to overseas consumer requirements.[16] In this respect, Hong Kong's 'free flows' of people and ideas will be an enduring source of advantage. Technology will continue to flow into Hong Kong through person-to-person relationships that are contact-based. According to Enright, Scott & Associates Ltd research, one Hong Kong executive explained, 'As a systems integrator, we don't own the technology, we just buy it, so we are talking about the relationship. It's not likely that companies in the PRD can make such close relationships'.

While Hong Kong firms will continue to be active in developing and transferring technology into the Pearl River Delta region, the bulk of the most advanced technological development in the region is likely to come from the research and development facilities that are being set up in the Pearl River

Delta region by foreign multinational firms and by firms from the Chinese mainland. The most advanced technology in the Pearl River Delta region already comes from Western, Japanese, and Taiwanese firms active in the region. The combination of cutting-edge science and technology from the multinational companies with the burgeoning technical workforce of the Chinese mainland is likely to prove to be a very difficult combination to beat.[17]

Several jurisdictions in the Pearl River Delta region plan to improve their university bases. As of 2004, Shenzhen, Dongguan, and Zhuhai were all planning or building university towns and developments to attract major universities to set up educational and research facilities. The idea is to overcome the traditional shortages in locally produced scientists, engineers, and technicians that have required firms to bring people with the appropriate skills in from other places in the Chinese mainland. Several Hong Kong universities are also involved in research and programs in the Pearl River Delta region with an eye towards providing technological capabilities to the region. In addition, several local jurisdictions in the Pearl River Delta region have come to agreements for the Hong Kong Productivity Council to provide services in the Pearl River Delta region. The Productivity Council has been setting up industrial development centres in conjunction with Pearl River Delta region jurisdictions to introduce business support and commercialisation activities.

Hong Kong has the potential to play an important role in the financing and commercialisation of breakthroughs made in the Pearl River Delta region. Hong Kong has a critical mass of venture capitalists and links to the international capital markets that can aid in the identification and financing of technology based start-up companies and eventually list these companies on the Hong Kong Stock Exchange. Proximity to Hong Kong already has caused a number of firms from elsewhere in the Chinese mainland to set up operations in the Pearl River Delta region. The idea is to get access to the market knowledge, information flows, and experience available in Hong Kong and the Pearl River Delta region.

Significant corporate research and development facilities are far more likely to locate in Shenzhen or Guangzhou than in Hong Kong in the future. In most major cities around the world, the main types of research and development (R&D) that are performed inside the cities are university research and medical research linked to teaching hospitals. Most corporate R&D is priced out of the cities and into the surrounding areas. Thus corporate R&D takes place in Silicon Valley, not in San Francisco; along the M4, not in London; in the crescents around Paris, not in Paris; along Routes 128 and 495, not in Boston. Hong Kong, with fewer scientific and technological resources, and with a much greater cost differential with the surrounding areas, is actually less promising than these other cities. It simply is not cost effective for most corporations to perform significant corporate R&D in Hong Kong.

The R&D activities most likely to take place in Hong Kong are those that do not require large amounts of land or large numbers of people and where the intellectual property is particularly important and portable, the latter being features that might discourage investments in the Chinese mainland.[18] In this respect, the pharmaceutical, medical, software, and information technology sectors are areas where Hong Kong and overseas firms alike tend to prefer, or express interest in, locating their most sensitive R&D activities within Hong Kong, and this will continue to be the case for the foreseeable future.

MANAGEMENT

The interaction between Hong Kong and the Pearl River Delta region in terms of management should become much more fluid over the next several years. The source of managerial talent in a given firm will depend a great deal on the home nation or region of the firm involved and their managerial requirements. For Hong Kong firms, one important question is the extent to which they will localise the management of their activities. The vast majority of these companies will keep their head office in Hong Kong, and so the key decision-makers will continue to be based in Hong Kong. Hong Kong managers also will continue to play a lead role in the Pearl River Delta region activities of Hong Kong firms.

The consensus from the Hong Kong managers we interviewed was that they will command lead roles at senior-most levels and in specialised roles involving supply chain management, finance, and accounting. Hong Kong managers will keep on leveraging their years of experience in dealing with the local production base, overseas consumer markets, multinational firms, international logistics, and international trade regimes. Managerial positions that can be filled by local Pearl River Delta managers, or managers from other parts of the Chinese mainland, will be general management-type positions at the junior to mid-level. The trend towards localisation will continue, particularly in more mature companies, and there will be an increasing pool of local talent available as access to education and opportunities increases for mainland managers both within China and abroad. However, a number of factors stand in the way of localisation, including perceptions that Hong Kong managers will be more trustworthy and loyal than managers from the Chinese mainland.

One strong driver of localisation, particularly at the low and middle management levels, is cost. As indicated in the previous chapter, interviewees indicated that there was a substantial gap in the salaries paid to low and middle-level managers from Hong Kong and those from the Pearl River Delta region, with the Hong Kong person earning four to six times what their Pearl River Delta counterpart would earn. While many managers claimed that their Hong Kong staff was more efficient, many also indicated that the difference in efficiency did not make up for that type of salary differential. In fact, many Hong Kong-based firms that we interviewed indicated that they would move entry to mid-level managerial and white-collar positions from Hong Kong to the Pearl River Delta region. Higher up the ladder, the narrower salary differential meant less pressure for movement of managerial jobs.[19]

Most of the managers that we interviewed, both in Hong Kong and the Pearl River Delta region, indicated that while management talent is converging between Hong Kong and the Pearl River Delta region, this convergence would take time. The Pearl River Delta region has been developing a market-oriented economy for a much shorter time than Hong Kong and the business and market sense that comes with this development is very hard to obtain overnight. Several interviewees expected it to be 2015 or later before management capabilities in the Pearl River Delta region would be what they were in Hong Kong in 2003, and Hong Kong will be a moving target going forward.[20]

FUTURE INTERACTION IN THE SERVICE SECTORS

The interaction between Hong Kong and the Pearl River Delta region in the manufacturing sector already is quite extensive. Although it will continue to develop over time, the course of further decentralisation of manufacturing from Hong Kong and further deepening and broadening of manufacturing in the Pearl River Delta region seems clear. China's WTO accession agreement promises to open a range of service industries to foreign investors and competitors, while CEPA will extend in many cases preferential access to Hong Kong firms across a range of financial and professional service sectors. Both CEPA and China's WTO entry will represent substantial new opportunities for Hong Kong firms and the Hong Kong offices of foreign multinationals. At the same time, enhanced interaction in services will benefit Pearl River Delta region producers and consumers by introducing a wider range of high value services into the Pearl River Delta region.[21]

As Hong Kong manufacturers moved production to the Pearl River Delta region, it was natural for some services to migrate as well. However, due to restrictions on the Chinese mainland, Hong Kong's service sector has not been able to move into the Pearl River Delta region nearly as easily as its manufacturing did. A survey on producer services required by enterprises in Dongguan

Table 7.2   Sources of producer services used by surveyed enterprises, per cent

	Hong Kong	PRD	Mainland China	Asia	Others
Professional services	11.3	13.5	27.8	2.3	3.4
Information and intermediary services	4.5	6.9	17.4	3.1	4.3
Financial services	7.8	11.2	23.7	1.8	2.6
Trade and trade-related services	19.6	9.7	15.1	2.9	3.5

Source: The Centre for Urban and Regional Studies 2002a, p. 37

by Guangzhou's Zhongshan University has indicated that Hong Kong was a substantial source of productive services for Dongguan facilities, particularly trade and trade-related services (see Table 7.2). What was also striking, however, was the scope for additional service provision for Hong Kong service providers, should the markets be opened. In particular, the share of Hong Kong providers in professional, information, intermediary, and financial services was far lower than that in trade and trade-related services, and far lower than might be expected given the skills and capabilities that can be found in Hong Kong in these sectors.

In a survey by the Hong Kong Trade Development Council of private-sector firms in the Chinese mainland (see Table 7.3), a far higher percentage of Pearl River Delta respondents indicated that Hong Kong-based services meet the needs of mainland enterprises. The mismatch indicates that there should be a greater opportunity for Hong Kong and Hong Kong firms to service Pearl River Delta firms in the future than was the case in the early 2000s.

Expanding Hong Kong investments into the Pearl River Delta region should result in additional demand for related services. This demand will flow in large measure to Hong Kong-owned firms. Multinational investment in the

Table 7.3   Hong Kong services that meet mainland enterprises' needs, 2002, %

Service	Percentage of Pearl River Delta private sector respondents
Banking	50.1
Accounting and finance	46.2
Business consultancy	41.6
Logistics and transportation	52.3
Legal and administration	36.9

Source: Hong Kong Trade Development Council 2002b

Pearl River Delta region is also projected to grow at a healthy rate post-WTO, again generating demand for services. Hong Kong's status as the regional headquarters' capital in the Asia Pacific for Western multinationals ensures that Hong Kong-based multinational service providers will capture a significant portion of the demand for services generated by Western multinational activities in the Pearl River Delta region. Though some multinational firms view opportunities for service-oriented work inside the Pearl River Delta region to be relatively small scale compared to areas such as Beijing and Shanghai, others see the Pearl River Delta region, with its large number of private enterprises and its affluent urban consumers, as a region meriting focused attention. The Chinese mainland's market opening concessions in services under CEPA apply to Hong Kong companies regardless of the nationality of shareholders, enhancing Hong Kong's potential as a platform for multinational service providers to enter the Chinese mainland.

Firms from the Chinese mainland with activities in the Pearl River Delta region are focusing to an increasing extent on accessing foreign capital and international markets. This outward push may well prove a strong new opportunity for Hong Kong-based service providers. This demand will probably be serviced by a combination of local providers, Pearl River Delta region offices of Hong Kong and multinational service providers, and Hong Kong offices of Hong Kong and multinational service providers. The high-end work is likely to be done in or through Hong Kong.[22] At the same time, more and more Pearl River Delta region enterprises will set up offices in Hong Kong to access the information flows and service providers located in Hong Kong. As a result, Hong Kong will play a pivotal role in the mediation of outbound investments from the Pearl River Delta region, just as it has for inbound investments into the Pearl River Delta region. Mainland firms will also come to Hong Kong to form joint ventures, register companies, raise capital, and tap into Hong Kong's base of world-class service provision, a trend that will be accelerated by CEPA. Overseas firms looking to gain a foothold in the China market will continue to engage the services of Hong Kong-based companies.

Though China's liberalisation under the WTO and CEPA has great potential for Hong Kong and foreign service providers, it remains to be seen how fast the restrictions that are limiting growth in services will be lifted in practice. Nevertheless, by 2004, Hong Kong-based firms that had been adopting a 'wait and see' attitude with respect to service sector reform in China just a few years before were actively exploring opportunities under CEPA across the boundary in the Pearl River Delta region and elsewhere in the Chinese mainland. In the following section we describe the likely future interaction in a variety of service sectors.

Transportation and travel

The interaction between Hong Kong and the Pearl River Delta region in transportation and travel will be critical to the future of the entire Greater Pearl River Delta region. Many efforts are now in process to handle what is expected to be a surge in cross-boundary transportation and travel involving all means of transport.

Land Transport by Road and Rail

Passenger and passenger vehicle flows between Hong Kong and the Pearl River Delta region are likely to grow strongly in coming years. Passenger traffic across the Hong Kong–Shenzhen boundary has been growing at double-digit rates and is likely to continue to do so. According to the Hong Kong Immigration Department, for example, in 2003 on average around 233,000 passenger crossings were recorded daily, with the daily average on weekends and holidays at about 254,000 crossings. The number of crossings made by private cars and coaches surged by 19.4% and 21.3% in 2002 and 2003, respectively. As for cross-border cargo flows, crossings by goods vehicles grew by 4.2% in 2003 over 2002, while container crossings fell by 1.9%. These figures suggest a slowing of growth in cross-border cargo flows destined for the Hong Kong port and reflect the rising share of cargo flows to the Shenzhen ports.[23] Cross-border flows of freight transport should receive a boost from CEPA, which allows Hong Kong companies to form wholly owned operations to provide road freight transport services, including direct non-stop road freight transport services between Hong Kong and cities in the Pearl River Delta region and beyond.[24]

Passenger and cargo-related demand have already resulted in numerous efforts to improve the infrastructure and procedures necessary to facilitate cross-border movements and transportation around the Greater Pearl River Delta region. The 'Western Corridor', linking Yuen Long in Hong Kong to Shekou in Shenzhen by bridge, due for completion in 2005–06, is expected to accommodate 2.5 times the number of present border crossings between Hong Kong and Shenzhen.[25] New expressways or highways are being built or planned between Guangzhou and Zhuhai, between Guangzhou and Shenzhen, from Guangzhou to Boluo and Huizhou, between Huizhou and the Shenzhen–Hong Kong border, and between Zhuhai and Yangjiang. As of 2004, preliminary design work was under way for a bridge link between the western and eastern sides of the Pearl River Delta region, with priority being given to a Y-shaped bridge linking Zhuhai and Macao with Hong Kong's Lantau Island.[26]

Railway passenger flows, which account for 76% of cross-border travellers, are predicted to grow substantially when a spur line to the Lok Ma

Chau–Huanggang crossing is completed in 2007 (see Chapter 6). Further into the future, a high-speed passenger rail could reduce travel times between Hong Kong and Guangzhou from around two hours to 40 minutes. With respect to rail freight, KCRC has undertaken feasibility studies on a Port Rail Line to provide container shuttle services between Hong Kong's container port at Kwai Chung and a rail freight centre in Shenzhen. The freight distribution centre, already the largest marshalling yard in South China, would provide back-up consolidation and distribution capacity for Hong Kong's port. Also envisioned is on-site mainland customs to facilitate cargo runs and trucking flows.[27]

Maritime Transport and Sea Links

There already are numerous sea links between Hong Kong and the Pearl River Delta region. Several of the region's ports, particularly those on the western side of the Pearl River Delta region, are feeder ports to Hong Kong. As trade into and out of the Greater Pearl River Delta region grows, this interaction should continue to expand. The Marine Cargo Terminal at the Hong Kong International Airport, which handles barge traffic, will continue to facilitate intermodal freight transportation. As with the land transport routes, Hong Kong and Pearl River Delta region authorities have been taking initiatives to drastically reduce the customs procedures for container ships between the two jurisdictions. Passenger flows will benefit from high-speed ferry links between the Hong Kong International Airport and major destinations in the Pearl River Delta region, introduced in 2003. Investment by Hong Kong firms in the ports of the Pearl River Delta region is also expected to grow. Hong Kong firms also are likely to expand activities in the Pearl River Delta region in maritime transport services, pursuant to China's opening up of this sector. Under CEPA, effective 1 January 2004, Hong Kong companies can form wholly owned operations to provide maritime transport services in areas including international ship management and storage and warehousing for international maritime freight.[28]

Air Transport

There will be increasing interaction among the airports in the Greater Pearl River Delta region. The Hong Kong Planning Department anticipates annual passenger and cargo growth at the Hong Kong International Airport of around 6% until 2020 and has flagged the possible need for an additional runway by that time.[29] The recently established A 5 group, a cooperative group of representatives from the Greater Pearl River Delta Region's five main airports, has also started to undertake joint studies with the aim of easing passenger and cargo flows and attracting more business into the region (see Chapter 8).[30] Interaction among airlines is also increasing. In November 2003, Hong Kong Dragon Airlines ('Dragonair') announced it would start code-share services with China Southern Airlines on the latter's twice-daily service between Hong Kong and Guangzhou.[31]

Another possible source of future interaction between Hong Kong and the Pearl River Delta region might be in the provision of helicopter commuter flights between Hong Kong and locations in the Pearl River Delta region. In March 2002, permission was granted to Hong Kong's first helicopter service to the Pearl River Delta region. Such a service can shorten the journey time between Hong Kong and Zhuhai, for example, to 17 minutes,[32] as compared to over an hour by ferry and more than four hours by car. Whether helicopter service providers can overcome licensing restrictions and extend their services to beyond Zhuhai and Macao to locations in the Pearl River Delta region remains to be seen.

Logistics

Interaction in logistics and related services will continue to grow, driven by strong and growing cargo flows to and from the region's manufacturing facilities. Sourcing and consolidation activities will continue to concentrate in Shenzhen. As of 2004, leading multinational retailers with sourcing operations in Shenzhen included Wal-Mart and Toys 'R' Us. OBI had announced the relocation of its Asian sourcing centre from Hong Kong to Shenzhen, while Target was reportedly considering setting up a procurement centre in Shenzhen.[33] Shenzhen's continued evolution as a sourcing and export hub will create demand for a wide assortment of logistics activities offered by Hong Kong firms. Under CEPA, effective 1 January 2004, Hong Kong companies are allowed to set up wholly owned operations to provide a variety of logistics services including road transport, storage and warehousing, loading and unloading, value-adding processing, packaging, delivery and related information, and consultancy services.[34]

With the closer economic relations between Hong Kong and the Pearl River Delta region, improved cargo transportation efficiency across the boundary between Hong Kong and Shenzhen has become a major issue. One focal point has been customs procedures. Hong Kong and Pearl River Delta region authorities are working on plans for the co-location of customs facilities at the border crossing, so that goods vehicles need only pass through one set of procedures. As of 2004, several measures were under way to improve customs facilities and reduce border congestion, including the use of automatic vehicle registration systems and scanner checks for individuals using smart ID cards.[35]

In addition, the opening of all border checkpoints on a 24-hour basis was under consideration. Under CEPA, Hong Kong and China have undertaken to facilitate customs clearance through ongoing collaboration.[36]

Bonded service has been put in place for shipments between Hong Kong's Air Cargo Terminal (HACTL) and three main air cargo destinations in the Pearl River Delta region: Guangzhou's Baiyun Airport, bonded warehouse facilities in Dongguan, and Bao'an Airport in Shenzhen.[37] To expedite cargo flows in the opposite direction, HACTL announced in October 2003 the opening of a consolidation centre in Shenzhen's Futian Free Trade Zone. Products will be pre-cleared for customs at the centre and trucked directly to the Hong Kong International Airport by Hactl's wholly owned bonded trucking service. The aim is to reduce the transit time for a shipment from Dongguan to Hong Kong's airport from about nine hours to five hours and 'realise cost savings for exporters and their agents'.[38] Pre-clearance arrangements also will be put in place for cargo transported by truck or barge to Hong Kong's port.

Tourism

Tourism linkages within the Greater Pearl River Delta region are likely to expand dramatically in the future. In 2004, the Pearl River Delta region was Hong Kong's largest source of tourists. The Hong Kong Planning Department has projected that inbound tourist flows into Hong Kong from the Chinese mainland as a whole will reach 24 million annually by 2011, 31 million by 2016, and 46 million by 2030.[39] These flows will include a very significant movement of increasingly affluent visitors from the Pearl River Delta region. While it used to be necessary to join a tour group, the Chinese mainland has been progressively extending the right to visit Hong Kong on individual travel permits to residents across Guangdong Province and other areas of China.[40] This will mean much larger numbers of mainland visitors will enter Hong Kong to attend meetings, sponsor exhibitions, go shopping, and engage business activities. Inflows of tourists from the mainland into Macao will also grow rapidly with the mainland's relaxation of restrictions on individual travel.

Major new attractions will boost tourist interaction. Hong Kong Disneyland is slated to open in 2005. Shenzhen's theme parks are a major destination for tourists from the Chinese mainland and they are likely to try to tap into tourist flows attracted by Disneyland. In Macao, earlier foreign investment projects have been dwarfed by the commitment made by Las Vegas Sands, the Galaxy Group and Wynn Resorts to develop the gaming, hotels, and conventions sector. As of 2004, the combined investment of these companies alone was expected to exceed US$1.5 billion. When the Sands Macao Casino opened in

May 2004, it attracted 15,000 visitors on its opening day, including many people from the Pearl River Delta region eager to experience Las Vegas-style gaming. At least four additional casinos expected to open within a few years. This massive expansion in capacity will primarily target visitors from the Chinese mainland and elsewhere in Asia.

China's liberalisation under WTO and CEPA is expected to bring more foreign business people and investors into the region. It also is expected to have a positive impact on flows of Hong Kong tourists into the Pearl River Delta region and Pearl River Delta region people into Hong Kong. Under CEPA, Hong Kong travel agencies may form joint venture travel agencies in the mainland, with mainland agencies as majority shareholders.[41] Many Hong Kong travel agencies have expressed their intentions of entering the tourism market in the Pearl River Delta region in the form of joint ventures. Guangdong officials claim that they will allow Hong Kong travel agencies to compete with state travel agencies in the province.[42]

Real estate

An increasing number of Hong Kong people will be buying real estate in the Pearl River Delta region and more people from the Pearl River Delta region will be buying real estate in Hong Kong. Although the property markets of Hong Kong and the Pearl River Delta region will be more closely coupled than they were in the past, the property markets in Hong Kong and in the Pearl River Delta region are not expected to converge completely in the foreseeable future. The 'two systems' part of 'one country, two systems' means that Hong Kong will remain a distinct region with its own system until at least 2047. The different systems imply different attributes for real estate in the different jurisdictions. Thus we would expect that the coupling of the Hong Kong and Pearl River Delta real estate markets would be weaker than that found in most major cities and their surroundings elsewhere in the world. Hong Kong should be able to support a significant gradient in residential real estate due to its affluence and social amenities, and in commercial real estate by its distinct positioning as one of the world's leading business cities.[43]

Greater fluidity of movement between Hong Kong and the Pearl River Delta region is expected to have a larger impact on property prices in the Pearl River Delta region than in Hong Kong. A survey released in January 2002 by the Business and Professionals Federation of Hong Kong shows that travelling time between home and work is a minor factor to Hong Kong people in deciding where to live.[44] Efforts now under way to facilitate cross-border flows at

Shenzhen, including the Western Crossing and the rail spur line to Lok Ma Chau, will not induce Hong Kong people to relocate across the border in substantial numbers. Hong Kong residency entails entitlements to state-funded educational, medical, and social benefits that are not transferable across the Shenzhen boundary. Shenzhen is not likely to reach a comparable level of social benefits for quite some time if ever. Similarly, a bridge connecting Hong Kong to Zhuhai or Macao is expected to result in significant increases in residential land prices in Zhuhai and Macao, but not a precipitous drop in Hong Kong. The prime residential areas in Hong Kong, such as the Peak, Mid-Levels, and the South Side, may well develop into the 'Grosse Pointe' of the entire Greater Pearl River Delta region, catering to the most affluent on both sides of the border. Demand for high-end residences for the families of multinational executives is also expected to remain concentrated in those areas.

In commercial real estate, convergence between Hong Kong and Shenzhen is not expected to occur beyond 2015 if then. As a general rule, in developed countries around the world, the truly premium sites are located in the prime business areas in the key cities. Hong Kong's high-end financial service providers are expected to remain in Central, including financiers, bankers, lawyers, accountants, and management consultants, along with the high-end retail establishments that cater to them. Multinational firms basing regional headquarters in Hong Kong are seen as another source of future demand that is unlikely to migrate *en masse* across the border. At the same time, as of 2004, the relatively small supply of Grade A office properties in Guangzhou was expected to see growing demand from multinational firms setting up in the city.

A number of Hong Kong property developers and real estate agencies already have a well-established presence in localities across the Pearl River Delta region, and are looking to expand their presence post CEPA. CEPA allows Hong Kong service providers to provide real estate services in the mainland through wholly owned operations.[45] Hong Kong firms are hoping that this enhanced access under CEPA will generate substantial opportunities. CEPA's liberalisation of the real estate services sector is likely to generate increased interaction in the construction and surveying sectors as well. Much of the work done by Hong Kong construction and surveying firms in the Pearl River Delta region has been generated by Hong Kong developers and clients. CEPA grants concessions to Hong Kong firms in construction and surveying, which should make it easier to operate in the mainland. For example, CEPA allows Hong Kong firms to wholly acquire mainland construction enterprises, and provides that such wholly owned enterprises will be exempted from foreign investment restrictions when undertaking Chinese-foreign joint construction projects.[46]

Retail shopping

The interaction between Hong Kong and the Pearl River Delta region in retail shopping is also slated to increase substantially in the future. This is in part a natural consequence of easier cross-border travel, in part a natural division of labour in terms of the retailing sectors of different parts of the region, and in part due to relatively high costs in Hong Kong. Easier cross-border travel means that more and more people will travel to shop, and more and more people will shop in new locations because they travel. In terms of a division of labour, we would expect that luxury goods retailing would tend to concentrate in Hong Kong due to its affluence, intellectual property safeguards, and position in the international distribution network of luxury goods companies. Large super-stores will tend to be located in Pearl River Delta jurisdictions where land costs are cheap enough to support that form of mass retailing.

In terms of cross-boundary shopping, Hong Kong is likely to attract grow-ing numbers of tourist shoppers from the Pearl River Delta region and other areas in the Chinese mainland. Hong Kong's products and services are differen-tiated by high-quality, high business standards, and an overall reputation for fair dealing. These 'soft' aspects will be difficult for retailers inside the Pearl River Delta region to replicate in the near future. Pearl River Delta shoppers are also attracted to Hong Kong because of Hong Kong's leadership in setting consumer trends and tastes for the region, and because shopping in Hong Kong is per-ceived as a 'fun, international experience'. Hong Kong's affluence means that it is likely to remain a trendsetter for the foreseeable future, while rising tourist flows will bring a larger number of Pearl River Delta region-based shoppers into Hong Kong.

Hong Kong people will continue to shop in the Pearl River Delta region, in particular Shenzhen, attracted by low-priced goods and services in general, and the rise of modern-scale 'hypermarkets' and suburban shopping centres. Improvements in border crossing points and supporting infrastructure will greatly reduce the travel time from Hong Kong to Shenzhen. Nevertheless, the Guangzhou–Hong Kong–Shenzhen corridor is unlikely to become a unified retail shopping area by 2015. At a minimum, motor vehicle regulations would have to change to allow the Hong Kong population to drive their cars across the border. In urban areas around the world, daily shopping tends to be located in close proximity to place of residence. The development of retail 'hyperstores', already evident along the highways of Shenzhen, is likely to accelerate with the Pearl River Delta region, while smaller urban supermarkets and other retail outlets will prevail within Hong Kong. Similar differentiation has occurred between downtown urban areas and their suburban counterparts across the United States. At the high end, Hong Kong will continue its hold on the luxury segment catering to the most affluent spenders, including Hong Kong locals and expatriates, because of the enduring gap in consumer spending power between Hong Kong and the Pearl River Delta region.

The future holds strong growth prospects for retailing in the Pearl River Delta region, driven by rising incomes, population growth, and ongoing urbanisation. The ability of Hong Kong-based firms to tap into future opportunities in retail will depend largely upon the pace and scope of market opening. Under the WTO, China has committed to opening its retail sector, through wholly owned retail commercial enterprises, to overseas firms with a minimum turnover of US$2 billion, among other requirements. According to the Hong Kong General Chamber of Commerce, no Hong Kong company would have been able to meet this threshold.[47] Under CEPA, China set a lower entry threshold of US$100 million in annual turnover, bringing some Hong Kong firms within its reach.[48] At the other end of the scale, under CEPA, Guangdong Province has been opened to small-scale Hong Kong retailers operating a single shop of not more than 300 square metres.[49] This playing field effectively excludes medium-sized Hong Kong retailers except through measures such as mergers and acquisitions, or informal mechanisms, pending further liberalisation.[50]

Telecommunications

Interaction in telecommunications is positioned for strong growth. As of 2004, Guangdong Province, a leader in information and communications technology (ICT) development in China, intended to accelerate the construction of ICT infrastructure by completing a broadband optical fibre trunk network between district-level cities and above, enhancing the local networks at the city level, fostering development of public and private networks, and gradually extending the information network to all sectors of the economy. Targets included expanding the number of Internet users to over 10 million, and raising business e-readiness to 60% by 2005.[51] For their part, Hong Kong telecommunications firms are ideally situated to help drive this process forward. Hong Kong has one of the world's most sophisticated telecom services platforms and has witnessed intense competition as several world-class telecommunications providers service a relatively small population. Hong Kong ICT firms have a long history of understanding transnational business processes and have a wealth of experience in commercialising ICT solutions to match operational needs. With respect to the Pearl River Delta region, Hong Kong's telecommunications firms can offer commercialising experience that comes from many years of experience operating in an open market environment. The key factor will be the pace and scope at which China opens its telecommunications market to Hong Kong providers.

CEPA has resulted in considerable activity among Hong Kong telecommunications providers interested in entering or expanding their presence in mainland markets, including the Pearl River Delta region. For example, City Telecom, which already operates a call centre in Guangzhou, was reported to be planning expansion into the mainland.[52] The time advantage granted to Hong Kong providers under CEPA potentially sets precedent for future time advantage concessions for Hong Kong service providers as China makes further progress in its liberalisation of this sector.[53] As of 2004, in future negotiations, Hong Kong hoped to continue to press for Hong Kong operators to be permitted to run majority-owned operations and for inclusion of more 'value-added services' under CEPA, and for extension of CEPA to computer services and e-business.[54]

Finance, banking, and insurance

Given China's closed capital account and Hong Kong's open economic system, financial sector expertise, legal system, and regulatory environment, Hong Kong will continue to expand as an international financial centre for China overall, as well as the Pearl River Delta region.[55] As of 2004, a new stream of mainland initial public offerings (IPOs) was anticipated in Hong Kong, involving state-owned enterprises in the energy, financial, and insurance sectors, among others.[56] Industry insiders report that the Central Government recognises listing in Hong Kong as a useful vehicle for fostering improved corporate governance standards among mainland firms, due to Hong Kong's more rigorous listing rules. The Hong Kong financial sector has the knowledge, facilities, human resources, and global reputations to handle such deals. However, growth in this area is limited by mainland controls on foreign listings and the willingness of the Central Government to allow Chinese citizens to invest in Hong Kong-listed companies.[57]

Venture capitalists accounted for only around US$500 million of the total US$40 billion in foreign investment in the Chinese mainland in 2001.[58] This too is seen as an area of potential growth in interaction between Hong Kong and the Pearl River Delta region. Part of the reason is that investment opportunities in Hong Kong alone are regarded as limited, as many potential high-value sectors, such as telecommunications, are already saturated. However, professionals in the field claim that the lack of a unified code of practice to regulate the venture capital industry in China is a major barrier to entry for the Hong Kong venture capital sector.

Moves to allow mainland investors access to the Hong Kong stock market have tremendous potential for Hong Kong investment houses and related service providers, such as lawyers and electronic trading systems support firms, to manage these investment flows. Hong Kong's well-developed expertise in management and capital markets operations means that it is ideally positioned to act as a bridge between the Chinese mainland and the world's capital markets. At the same time, Hong Kong financial firms have a leading role to play in helping the mainland to upgrade its financial systems.[59]

While some Hong Kong banks have been reported to take strategic stakes in banks from the Chinese mainland, prior to CEPA the Hong Kong banking community generally took a cautious approach to expansion in the mainland. The signing of CEPA commitments on liberalisation of trade in services in September 2003 is resulting in new entry into the mainland. Under CEPA, Hong Kong banks are allowed to set up branches or body corporates in the mainland, subject to a total asset requirement of US$6 billion. This threshold is significantly lower than the US$10 billion asset requirement set by China under the WTO, opening the way for medium-sized Hong Kong banks to enter mainland markets. CEPA is expected to enable Hong Kong's 'smaller local banks' to extend their business beyond Hong Kong, in particular to Hong Kong-based producers in the Pearl River Delta region. [60]

Mainland branches of Hong Kong banks are allowed to apply to conduct RMB business if they have been operating on the mainland for more than two years (rather than three years under China's WTO commitments), subject to a profitability assessment by the relevant mainland authorities on all branches.[61] This provision is expected to give Hong Kong banks an advantage in conducting renminbi business.[62] Under China's WTO accession agreement, current restrictions on the commercial banking sector are due to be dismantled by 2005. Thereafter, fierce competition is predicted between banks from the Chinese mainland and their foreign counterparts. Again, Hong Kong has a pivotal roleto play in this process. The Hong Kong–Pearl River Delta combination, in particular, has great potential as a testing ground for China's future reform of the banking sector.

In November 2003, China's State Council approved a scheme to enable Hong Kong banks to provide yuan-denominated credit card remittance, exchange, and deposit services.[63] This policy initiative should foster heightened economic interaction between Hong Kong and the Pearl River Delta region. It will greatly facilitate trips by Hong Kong residents into the Pearl River Delta region for both business and leisure. Hong Kong residents who travel frequently across the border will be able to open yuan bank accounts and take out yuan-denominated credit cards in Hong Kong. The scheme also will boost tourist spending by Guangdong residents on visits to Hong Kong, in particular by enabling visitors from the Chinese mainland to make purchases at Hong Kong retail outlets using yuan-denominated credit cards.[64]

Shenzhen leads most mainland cities in many aspects of finance and banking, having more foreign and overseas banks than any other Chinese mainland city apart from Shanghai. Guangzhou and Shenzhen together had around 10 million Jetco cardholders and around 900 ATMs by 2003.[65] The growth of these ATM networks is seen as providing opportunities for payment system operators. However, the lack of a unified credit rating system in China is making it very difficult for potential customers to obtain credit cards and also provides an obstacle to credit card operators in developing business in China, as it is difficult for them to manage the risk effectively. Shenzhen-based China Merchants Bank has used Hong Kong as a base for international activities, targeting customer requirements for cross-border banking. This represents only one example of an increasing trend of financial institutions from the Chinese mainland setting up offices in Hong Kong to make and manage their international banking investments.

China's insurance sector is set to liberalise, albeit slowly, under China's WTO accession agreement. Under CEPA, groups formed by Hong Kong insurance firms may enter the mainland insurance market subject to 'market access conditions' that set a threshold of US$ 5 billion in terms of total group assets and more than 30 years of experience.[66] While the US$ 5 billion asset requirement is the same in China's WTO commitment, permission for Hong Kong insurance firms to meet this and other threshold requirements on a joint basis through re-grouping and strategic merger goes beyond China's WTO commitment. In addition, while the maximum limit on capital participation in a mainland insurance company in China's WTO commitment is 10%, CEPA allows capital participation by a Hong Kong firm in a mainland insurance company of up to 24.9%.[67] CEPA also liberalises access to mainland markets for individual practitioners including agents and actuaries.

If CEPA's stringent market access conditions are an indication, it is likely to take some time before Hong Kong-based insurance companies or the Hong Kong offices of foreign insurance companies are able to profit on a large scale from developments in the Pearl River Delta region. However, given the fact that over 100 foreign insurance companies operate in Hong Kong, it is likely that they will try to use Hong Kong as a base from which to access the Pearl River Delta region's insurance market. As in many other areas, the likely result is that the Pearl River Delta region will be ahead of most of the rest of China in the reform and opening process. Given the vast insurance needs in a country where many types of insurance typically found in market economies did not exist just a few years ago, the potential for Hong Kong and foreign insurance companies to provide services in the Pearl River Delta region is substantial.

Law, accounting, and other business services

Interaction between Hong Kong and the Pearl River Delta region in legal services should grow substantially. As more firms use Hong Kong to access the Pearl River Delta region, there will be substantial additional demand for legal services geared to the Chinese mainland. Inside the Pearl River Delta region, the development of Hong Kong-based legal services will remain tied to the pace at which China's restrictions on the scope of practice for foreign lawyers are eased. CEPA provides a framework for Hong Kong lawyers to sit the national lawyers' exams (though successful candidates may not practise litigation), mainland law firms to hire Hong Kong lawyers (though not to handle matters of mainland law), and for Hong Kong law firms' representative offices in the mainland to operate 'in association' with mainland law firms, but not to permit Hong Kong law firms to enter partnerships with mainland firms on the mainland.[68]

A key driver of future demand for Hong Kong's legal sector is the projected inflow of firms from the Chinese mainland into Hong Kong. Many of these firms, a significant portion of which will be from the Pearl River Delta region, will use Hong Kong as a platform for accessing international capital and foreign markets. Thus, they will need legal services from those knowledgeable in Hong Kong and international law. Future growth is expected in work related to Hong Kong IPOs, anti-dumping, shipping and banking law, and arbitration.

China's entry into the WTO and an increasing number of mainland firms seeking external investment should increase the interaction between Hong Kong and the Pearl River Delta region in accounting. International audit firms from Hong Kong have been used to audit major state-owned enterprises in Shenzhen in readiness for company sell-offs, and mainland authorities increasingly demand that international firms audit corporate statements. At the same time, Hong Kong-owned accounting firms plan to target small- and medium-sized enterprises in the Pearl River Delta region.[69] However, China's concessions in accounting were limited in nature. For example, under CEPA, Hong Kong accounting firms may provide temporary auditing services in the mainland under a 'Temporary Auditing Business Permit' with one-year validity, increased from six months' validity, which somewhat eases the regulatory burden on Hong Kong CPAs two visit mainland locations for due diligence audits.[70] In addition, a number of Hong Kong accountants interviewed saw potential in diversifying into consultancy services for Pearl River Delta firms wishing to target overseas markets, and for small foreign-owned companies wishing to set up operations in the Pearl River Delta region.

The advertising industry is positioned to feel the effects of China's WTO membership, as foreign advertising firms will be able to have a majority stake in joint ventures in 2004, and in 2006 they will be able to set up wholly foreign-owned enterprises. Under CEPA, Hong Kong advertising service providers are allowed to set up wholly owned advertising firms in the mainland.[71] A significant increase in work is expected, as brand equity becomes an increasingly important competitive weapon in China and as firms from the mainland aim to promote their products abroad and at home on a national scale. Urbanisation in the Pearl River Delta region also will drive interaction in advertising. For Hong Kong's small- and medium-sized enterprises in advertising, prospects in the Pearl River Delta region will be focused on specialised areas, such as film production, post-production services, and packaging design for export markets. Meanwhile, a new generation of locally owned mainland firms has become skilled in advertising, promotion sampling, and on-ground support. They know their market, charge lower fees than Hong Kong firms, and their quality of service is improving.

There may also be an increase in firms from the Pearl River Delta region coming to Hong Kong to promote their products as a test-bed for further expansion overseas. For example, Huizhou-based TCL committed US$1.9 million in 2002 to advertising its household electronics products in Hong Kong.[72] This trend is likely to increase as more Pearl River Delta region firms target Hong Kong for their products. Given the fact that Hong Kong television programs are received in Guangdong Province, people from the region are likely to have a good idea of the lifestyles, tastes, and fashions of Hong Kong consumers. Coupled with linguistic and cultural similarities, this should help Pearl River Delta firms penetrate Hong Kong markets in the future.

Demand should continue to be strong for business consultancy services in the Greater Pearl River Delta region. China through CEPA gives Hong Kong management consultants access to mainland markets four years before consultants from other countries under its WTO commitments. Under CEPA, Hong Kong service providers are allowed to provide via wholly owned operations on the mainland a range of management consulting services including financial management consulting (except business tax), marketing management, human resources management, production management, and public relations services.[73] Hong Kong's consulting firms, which range from global consultancies to high-end 'boutique' firms, with deep expertise in China markets, will continue to assist foreign companies in gaining access to the Chinese mainland

and are well positioned to help mainland companies commercialise their products for global markets.

Consumer and medical services

Developments in the Pearl River Delta region are fuelling demand for consumer services. Already there is a substantial amount of informal interaction through the operations of Hong Kong-based firms in some parts of the Pearl River Delta region. In the future, we would expect to see far more interaction in education, training, and perhaps elderly care. Hong Kong universities have already set up research and training centres in the Pearl River Delta region and are increasingly involved in joint research projects and exchanges. The flow of students is starting to go in both directions, with some Pearl River Delta region students coming to Hong Kong and a small, but growing number of Hong Kong students electing to go to university in the Pearl River Delta region. One of the most common reasons that both Hong Kong and foreign business people cite for not relocating their families to the Pearl River Delta region is the lack of adequate schooling for their children. As larger numbers of Hong Kong and expatriate staff find work in the Pearl River Delta region, opportunities for providers of private schools and day-care facilities should increase.

The proportion of Hong Kong's population aged 65 and over is projected to rise from 11% in 2001 to 24% in 2031.[74] Hong Kong retirees are increasingly looking to settle in the Pearl River Delta region, attracted by its lower costs and attractive and roomier housing stock.[75] This trend may well continue, driving up demand inside the Pearl River Delta region for private housing, nursing, and medical services. On the other hand, the population of the Pearl River Delta region is skewed towards younger people of employment age. Thus, to the extent that elderly-related personal services develop in the Pearl River Delta region in the near future, much of this may be driven by Hong Kong demand.

Future interaction in the medical services sector will be fostered by CEPA, which opens up the mainland to individual medical practitioners from Hong Kong. Under CEPA, Hong Kong medical practitioners may practise in the mainland under a renewable, three-year licence. In addition, Hong Kong-qualified medical practitioners are allowed to sit the mainland's medical qualification examinations in clinical medicine, Chinese medicine, and dental medicine.[76] This new access opens the possibility for Hong Kong doctors to set up private practices in the Pearl River Delta region and elsewhere in China. Private hospitals and other healthcare service providers in the Pearl River Delta region will be able to offer the services of Hong Kong medical practitioners. These developments bode well for the growth of medical and health care businesses in the Pearl River Delta region aimed at the region's increasingly affluent consumers, at Hong Kong people residing in the region, and, in particular, Hong Kong retirees.[77]

THE FUTURE ECONOMIC INTERACTION

Developments in Hong Kong and the Pearl River Delta region are generally regarded as advantageous for increased interaction in both manufacturing and services. The manufacturing sector already is tightly integrated and promises to be more so going forward. In the service sector, the nature of China's economic opening under its WTO accession agreement and CEPA, and China's own efforts to develop and stimulate its economy should enhance the interaction as well. The precise nature of the interaction, particularly in the service sector, is uncertain in that it depends greatly on the extent and timing of regulatory changes and the ability of firms from Hong Kong, the rest of China, and the rest of the world to deal with these changes.

As the economic interaction between the Hong Kong and the Pearl River Delta region increases, there should be ample opportunities for Hong Kong firms, for Pearl River Delta region firms, and for foreign multinationals to benefit. The interaction, however, will take on different forms as the economies develop. The future interaction will create new dynamics involving new divisions of labour and new competition between Hong Kong and the Pearl River Delta region. These, in turn, will be influenced by the relative strengths and weaknesses of the economies in question and the opportunities that companies of all types see in the future, subjects that will be taken up in the next chapter.

CHAPTER EIGHT

Future Combinations and Competitiveness in the Greater Pearl River Delta Region

T he competitiveness of the Greater Pearl River Delta region continues to be closely linked to the economic interaction among the jurisdictions in the region. As we have seen, this interaction is likely to develop in interesting ways in response to a number of driving forces. Deeper and more complex interaction is likely to influence the competitiveness of the region in the future. Understanding the likely evolution of the competitiveness and development potential of different types of industries in the Greater Pearl River Delta region will be essential for companies that are considering to use China as a production platform or who are considering to serve the China market. It also will be essential for firms that face or will be facing competition from companies that invest in the region. It will be essential as well for governments interested in how the rise of China might influence the development prospects of their own nations or regions.

MANUFACTURING INDUSTRIES

The initial economic interaction between Hong Kong and the Pearl River Delta region was based on the decentralisation of Hong Kong's manufacturing activities to the Pearl River Delta region. Over time, however, this interaction has taken on many new facets. Today, the range of activities of manufacturing companies performed in the Pearl River Delta region is expanding. The interaction today involves not just Hong Kong-owned enterprises, but also enterprises owned or operated by Taiwanese, Japanese, Korean, and Western companies. The interaction also involves a much wider range of industries than those involved in the initial shifts into the Pearl River Delta region. Manufacturing operations into this region will continue to grow in size, in the quest to achieve greater scale economies. More activities directly related to manufacturing, such as sourcing, packaging, quality control, and warehousing, will be moved from Hong Kong to the Pearl River Delta region. Procurement offices will migrate into this region, as it becomes a more and more important source of components and inputs. As this division of labour evolves and the economy continues to deepen, we can expect to see the Greater Pearl River Delta region become an even more competitive base for light manufactures. There is also potential for the emergence of a competitive heavy industrial base in autos, steel, and petrochemicals.

Light manufacturing

The Greater Pearl River Delta region is poised to expand its position in light-manufactured goods. Despite increases in land costs within the Pearl River Delta region, most experts interviewed for this project indicated that the region would retain and expand its position as a light-manufacturing base. The region will continue to benefit from relatively low assembly manufacturing wages, high-quality infrastructure, improving capabilities, access to international markets through Hong Kong and direct from the Pearl River Delta region, and the presence of a wide range of supplier and supporting industries. At the same time, China's WTO accession, CEPA, and China's growing importance as an investment location will further enhance the Pearl River Delta's position.

Wage rates for assembly manufacturing will continue to be low in parts of the Pearl River Delta region since most of this labour comes from China's inner provinces, such as Hunan, Guizhou, Jiangxi, Sichuan, Hubei, Henan, and Anhui. In essence, the wage rates will remain low until the hundreds of millions of people expected to come out of the rural setting have already moved to the cities. The opening of the Beijing–Kowloon Railway has made it far easier for migrant workers from Central China to come to Guangdong. The result has been a situation in which real wages in assembly manufacturing have been remarkably stable and low in the Pearl River Delta region. Some managers indicate that these wages are lower than can be found in the Yangtze River Delta region or in Northern China. Access to labour from all over China allows the Pearl River Delta region to keep wages relatively low. Only in the garment sector did managers indicate that lower wages might give other parts of China an advantage over the Pearl River Delta region.

The eastern part of the Pearl River Delta region and Hong Kong have infrastructure that is better than elsewhere in China. This is particularly true of the highway and port systems. Planned investments in the region should make transportation around the Pearl River Delta region far better than is the case today. In the ports of Shenzhen and Hong Kong, the Greater Pearl River Delta region has ports that are more efficient than elsewhere in China and less subject to silting and other difficulties than new ports in Shanghai. New investments in the region's ports are likely to continue to enhance the Greater Pearl River Delta's relative position. The region has more international air cargo and air transport capacity than anywhere else in China. The combination of Hong Kong's international routes and Guangzhou's domestic network is likely to continue to be an advantage well into the future. The new airport in Guangzhou and Hong Kong's new air service agreements with the United States and Europe should enhance the region's position further.

All of these developments combined with an increasing importance of short cycle times for supply chain management means that the Pearl River Delta's light-manufacturing base is not likely to move far from its ports and airports. This is particularly true since the unwritten rule for foreign invested facilities engaging in labour intensive production is that the factories should be no more than a three-hour drive from a major transportation hub. Any further and the goods risk not being able to get to the port within one day, therefore involving storage and uncertainty in getting on board the appropriate ship. Locations beyond the three-hour travel time, such as those in the western part of the Pearl River Delta region, have been less favourable.[1] The expansion of the transportation infrastructure will expand the three-hour catchment area, which should make the manufacturing base centred on the Greater Pearl River Delta region much larger in the future.

China's accession to the WTO and its increasing exports might provide a further impetus to the Pearl River Delta's light-manufacturing base. China's share of world trade in garments, for example, is projected to grow following the phasing out of garment and textile quotas. WTO entry also has ended the need to renew China's Normal Trade Relations status in the United States and other industrial economies. As a result, investors can be more confident that their Chinese facilities will continue to have access to important markets. China's growth as an export base also is fuelling additional investment in light manufacturing at the expense of other countries, mostly in South-east Asia.

Toys

China is set to continue as the world's largest toy manufacturer. There is no country rising on the horizon to dethrone it from the number one position. The Greater Pearl River Delta region, with its distinctive combinations and complementarities, is increasingly dominating China's production and trade in toys. Global industry trends are increasingly favouring the Greater Pearl River Delta region. Larger, more powerful US distributors are continuing to rely upon the Greater Pearl River Delta region because of its unmatched capabilities in low-cost contract manufacturing for mass production, as well as logistics and shipping. Large retailers are tending to rely more heavily on direct sourcing, in the Greater Pearl River Delta region. Another trend is to reduce inventory costs by reducing lead times, which plays into the strength of Hong Kong firms that can organise large production runs very quickly. Our research indicates that the region's unmatched supplier base of inputs and components for toy production will continue to deepen and expand. These factors, combined with the strengths of Hong Kong's supply chain management and Shenzhen's ports, should anchor China's toy production in the Greater Pearl River Delta region for the foreseeable future.

Among Hong Kong firms, we expect to see further consolidation with the winners moving up the value chain. Hong Kong firms will increasingly move into ODM, branded manufacturing, or specialised segments. To an increasing extent, strategies will focus on technological changes driven by consumer electronics, and new product applications. Reductions in toy product life-cycles and competition from mainland producers will exert pressure on Hong Kong-owned firms to move quickly in identifying trends, to invest in continuous improvements, and to focus on higher end products and rapid turnaround orders.

Mainland firms will further develop their manufacturing and marketing capabilities and make inroads into second and third-tier markets worldwide. Mainland firms generally have lower overhead costs than their counterparts from Hong Kong or overseas, and by virtue of connections or shared ownership they can often source locally produced components at lower prices and on better terms. Within the Pearl River Delta region, they operate free of the regulatory constraints and duties imposed on foreign firms with export processing licenses. Given the advantages that mainland firms enjoy in the domestic arena, 'cooperation' or 'partnership' between overseas firms, Hong Kong firms, and mainland firms in mainland markets is likely to become more widespread.

Japanese, Taiwanese, and Western multinationals will continue to be important brand and license holders doing business in the Greater Pearl River Delta region. They will continue to source in the region and to enhance their sourcing offices and related quality control and logistics activities. A recent

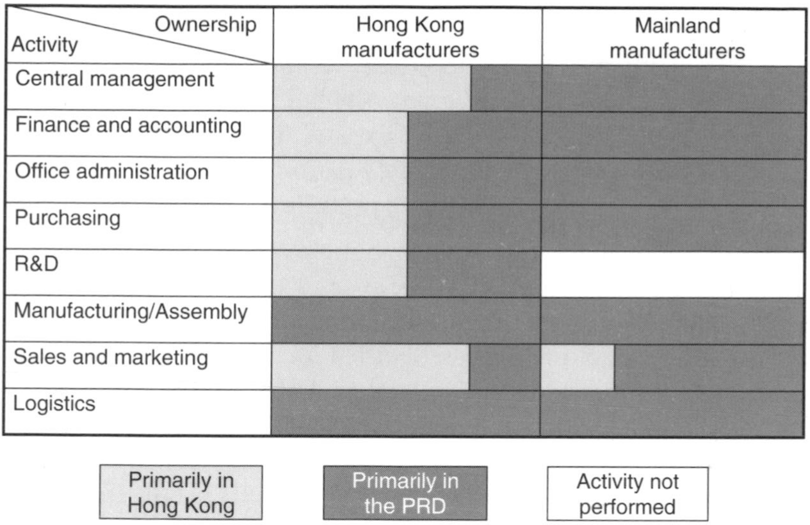

Activity \ Ownership	Hong Kong manufacturers	Mainland manufacturers
Central management	Primarily in Hong Kong / Primarily in the PRD	Primarily in the PRD
Finance and accounting	Primarily in Hong Kong / Primarily in the PRD	Primarily in the PRD
Office administration	Primarily in Hong Kong / Primarily in the PRD	Primarily in the PRD
Purchasing	Primarily in Hong Kong / Primarily in the PRD	Primarily in the PRD
R&D	Primarily in Hong Kong / Primarily in the PRD	Activity not performed
Manufacturing/Assembly	Primarily in the PRD	Primarily in the PRD
Sales and marketing	Primarily in Hong Kong / Primarily in the PRD	Primarily in Hong Kong / Primarily in the PRD
Logistics	Primarily in the PRD	Primarily in the PRD

Legend: Primarily in Hong Kong | Primarily in the PRD | Activity not performed

Source: Enright, Scott & Associates Ltd research

Figure 8.1   The future Hong Kong–Pearl River Delta toy industry value chain

development in the world's leading markets has been increasing concern with respect to the labour practices of subcontractor facilities. The International Council of Toy Industries (ICTI) has set up a body of standards. Increasingly, the major toy companies worldwide are hiring independent firms to audit the companies from which they source.

Among most Hong Kong toy exporters, central management will remain mostly in Hong Kong, which will remain their headquarters hub (see Figure 8.1). More routine work in accounting and office administration will locate into the Pearl River Delta region, attracted by improving capabilities and lower costs. Similar movement is expected in R&D, as mainland engineers move up the ranks. Marketing and sales activities for overseas markets will remain primarily in Hong Kong. Some firms will move their marketing activities directed at overseas customers into the Pearl River Delta region, making use of e-mail, the Internet, and video e-conferencing.[2] This movement will be driven by the relocation of major international customers out of Hong Kong into Shenzhen. The presence of giant distributors such as Wal-Mart and Toys 'R' Us in Shenzhen is likely to continue to induce their suppliers in Hong Kong to relocate customer-specific sales and service activities across the border. At the same time, we expect to see an influx of the international sales and marketing activities of mainland firms into Hong Kong seeking to tap its strengths as a global hub for the toy trade.

The coordination of shipping, logistics, and other export-related activities will continue to shift into the Pearl River Delta region to take advantage of the low-cost shipping and logistics base in Shenzhen. This trend will strengthen as the world's major distributors further expand their flows of goods outwards from Shenzhen and its consolidation centres, and as the Shenzhen ports continue to upgrade their Customs clearance procedures.

Garments

The major development in world garment markets going forward is the elimination of the global quota regime, scheduled for 2005. If garment quotas are eliminated, more garment manufacturing will shift into China. The phasing out of quotas plus China's accession to the WTO should mean that China has much more access to world markets. The Guangdong Government Development Research Centre has estimated that these developments should increase China's share of world trade in garments from under 30% to around 50% or more over the next several years.[3] In the United States, the US International Trade Commission has estimated that China is likely to become 'the supplier of choice for most U.S. importers' following quota elimination in 2005.[4]

The Greater Pearl River Delta region is likely to benefit disproportionately from these developments. Guangdong Province, especially the Pearl River Delta region, is very competitive in garment exports already. The firms that have set up the garment industry around much of Asia are Hong Kong firms that set up operations across Asia and beyond to get around quota restrictions. Hong Kong companies are among the leading producers of garments in South-east Asia, the Caribbean, and as far away as Mauritius. However, the mainland is by far the preferred location for Hong Kong manufacturers because of its low costs, cultural similarities, and geographical proximity, as well as its domestic consumer market.[5] For the majority of these Hong Kong firms, the phasing out of quotas will allow them to bring more production home to South China. The elimination of quotas will allow them to consolidate production closer to their Hong Kong headquarters and thereby simplify logistics while substantially reducing cost.

In the meantime, mainland garment firms are increasingly getting into the act. This business has been dominated by Hong Kong manufacturers and trading companies and to a certain extent by the Hong Kong sourcing operations of multinationals. The Hong Kong firms are now viewing firms from Guangdong Province as their main competitors. Local companies are starting to access international markets direct, and to deal with overseas buying offices in Hong Kong and Shenzhen. This is an industry in which the Yangtze River Delta region is also developing – in particular, in textiles, silks, and men's

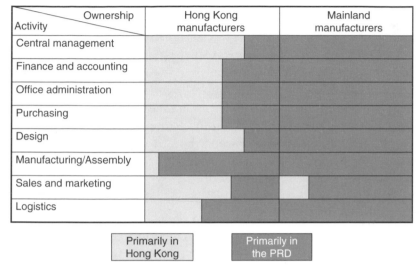

Activity \ Ownership	Hong Kong manufacturers	Mainland manufacturers
Central management		
Finance and accounting		
Office administration		
Purchasing		
Design		
Manufacturing/Assembly		
Sales and marketing		
Logistics		

Primarily in Hong Kong	Primarily in the PRD

Source: Enright, Scott & Associates Ltd research

Figure 8.2   The future Hong Kong–Pearl River Delta garment industry value chain

wear – with Shanghai and its environs becoming more of a force in the international garment market. While some experts believe that the Pearl River Delta region may lose some share to other regions in China, the overall growth of China's position in the garment industry is likely to ensure that the sales volume of Pearl River Delta region factories will increase substantially. The Greater Pearl River Delta region will not be the only region to benefit, but China's global share is set for such growth that there will be plenty of business for both Hong Kong and Shanghai, and their respective hinterlands.

For Hong Kong garment exporters, central management will remain mostly in Hong Kong, which will remain their headquarters hub (see Figure 8.2), and accounting and office administration will locate increasingly into the Pearl River Delta region. Fashion design, in contrast, will tend to stay in Hong Kong because of the importance of continuous exposure to international fashions and trends. Some value-adding manufacturing activities in the higher end segments may remain in or relocate to Hong Kong, so that product may qualify as being of Hong Kong origin under CEPA and enter the mainland free of import tariffs. The sales and marketing activities for overseas markets will be divided. Firms focusing on buyers located overseas will tend to stay in Hong Kong, while firms focusing on major international retailers with buying offices in Shenzhen will move more of their marketing activities across the boundary.[6] In addition, some multinational firms are considering relocating their sales and marketing functions from Hong Kong into Shanghai, as that city and its adjacent areas emerge as centres for garment production and distribution. An increasing number of Hong Kong fashion firms in the branded segment are placing sales and marketing activities in Guangzhou and Shenzhen directed at Pearl River Delta consumers. At the same time, more mainland firms targeting overseas customers will place international sales and marketing activities in Hong Kong.

A significant portion of garments by value will continue to ship by air out of Hong Kong International Airport because retailers are willing to pay a premium to keep inventories at a minimum and fashion seasons are becoming compressed.

Other Industries

As the Greater Pearl River Delta region's existing light manufacturing base expands, it is developing strong or dominant positions in new industries as well. Furniture, for example, has traditionally been a local industry in most places of the world. With the exception of design-intensive and do-it-yourself, knock-down furniture (like Ikea's), logistics costs have meant that furniture was usually produced in the same country as consumption. After all, shipping furniture essentially involves shipping air wrapped in wood or metal. However, in recent years, Dongguan has emerged as a furniture producer of major importance. As a result, furniture employment in the United States, which had been relatively stable for a number of years, fell by roughly a third in less than three years.[7] This shows that the Greater Pearl River Delta region continues to have the ability to fundamentally alter production patterns around the world.

Electronics and other technology-based industries

China's position in electronics and other technology-based industries is also growing. In the Pearl River Delta region, simple, one-step assembly is rapidly giving way to multiple-step processing and component production as well as assembly. Other activities are starting to be performed in the region as well, potentially resulting in a substantial increase in local value-added and technology content.

Electrical and Electronics Industries

With output of approximately US$200 billion per year, China accounts for more than 40% of world exports in consumer electronics. Its electronics sector has attracted more than US$70 billion in foreign capital and 40,000 foreign-invested enterprises, and has grown at 33% annually for the last decade. China is expected to remain 'the strategic place to be for electronics manufacturing' worldwide, and the movement of electronics manufacturing into China from other locations is accelerating.[8]

For a wide range of handheld consumer electronics, home consumer electronics, and PC components and peripherals, the Pearl River Delta is very well positioned to remain in the lead within China. Global trends in this industry include contract manufacturing, vertical integration, and mass production to achieve growing economies of scale. All of these trends play into the strengths of the Greater Pearl River Delta region. According to industry sources, Guangdong Province has the biggest component-supply base in the world, and it is growing, with thousands of producers supplying a broad range of components and inputs. Industry leaders in EMS and ODM manufacture, such as Flextronics and Hong Hai, are increasingly using this supplier base to 'rationalise' their operations by 'incorporating' the supply chain and integrating vertically.[9]

While electronics production in the Yangtze River Delta region has been growing rapidly as well, it has generally not been at the expense of the Pearl River Delta region, where the electronics sector has been growing at 30% per year. A pattern of specialisation is emerging between the Pearl River Delta and Yangtze River Delta regions. The Pearl River Delta region is likely to continue to predominate in many types of handheld consumer electronics and home consumer electronics. The Yangtze River Delta has emerged as dominant in chip production and is attracting a massive influx in investment in notebook computers, in particular from Taiwanese firms. In integrated circuits, the Pearl River Delta is more focused on final assembly while the Yangtze River Delta does more IC design and research, as well as chip manufacturing. However, the Pearl River Delta region will see additional investment going into integrated circuit manufacture, in particular in chips that meet the fast-evolving requirements of a variety of final consumer products. Industry experts predict that the Pearl River Delta region will be attracting additional facilities to produce semiconductors and other advanced components for the production base in the region.[10]

The major multinational electronics firms, like other big multinationals, are locating in multiple areas of China. Leading Asian electronics companies, such as Canon and LG, and European companies such as Nokia and Ericsson, have major production facilities in the Pearl River Delta region, as well as elsewhere in China. IBM's wholly owned enterprise in Shenzhen represents an investment of over US$880 million. Dongguan's continuing position of global leadership in computers and peripherals is largely due to Taiwanese investments. While many multinational firms were opening up major new facilities in Shanghai and the Yangtze River Delta during 2002–04, large investments continued to flow into the Pearl River Delta region as well. In 2003, Taiwan-based mainboard producer Elite Computer System (ECS) launched a US$600 million, 780,000 square metre production base in Shenzhen. In early 2004, while Flextronics was preparing to open a 65,000 square metre facility in Shanghai, it also was significantly expanding its 200,000-plus square metre footprint in Zhuhai[11] in the Pearl River Delta region.

A survey conducted in 2002 revealed that within the Pearl River Delta region, Taiwanese firms in general (including electronics firms) tend to think in terms of 'northern expansion' rather than 'northern relocation'.[12] In that survey, more than half of the Taiwanese respondents operating in the Pearl River Delta indicated that the Pearl River Delta region would be the location of future investments. The Pearl River Delta region is also the home of an increasing number of Chinese technology-based firms. More than half of the 'high-technology' products (usually defined as electronics, information technology equipment, electrical appliances, and electrical machinery) produced in Shenzhen in 2001 were based on indigenous intellectual property.[13]

Hong Kong-based firms that source technology from the United States, Europe, and other foreign markets report that Hong Kong will continue to play a valuable role as a 'window' open to overseas technology. In addition to technology 'sourcing', high-tech firms will continue to use Hong Kong as corporate headquarters, as well as the location of overseas sales and customer service activities and banking. Hong Kong is also expected to remain an important market for software and other high-tech services provision within the Asia Pacific region, due to its high, and growing, concentration of the regional headquarters and offices of multinational firms (see Figure 8.3). As discussed earlier, intellectual property-related concerns keep many Hong Kong-based firms, especially small- and medium-sized firms, from relocating technology-related activities, including production activities, across the border. CEPA may reinforce this trend. The Hong Kong firms whom we interviewed generally do not foresee significant improvements in the mainland's intellectual property regime under WTO.

For many Hong Kong firms, the coordination of shipping and related activities is likely to remain in Hong Kong. Sophisticated and high-value electronics will continue to ship by air out of Hong Kong International Airport. Other factors include fuller service provision by Hong Kong banks, shipping companies, and a wide variety of trade-related service providers, Hong Kong's world-class air freight platform, and advanced customs support for exports incorporating sophisticated technology. In addition, Hong Kong's free flow of merchandise

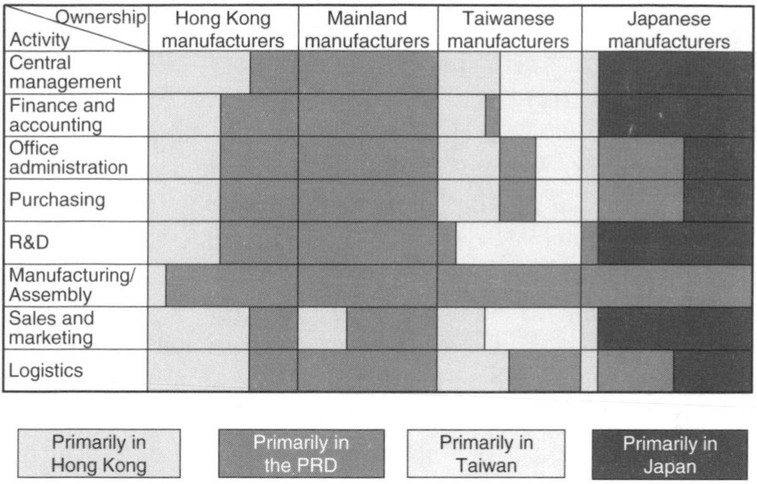

Ownership / Activity	Hong Kong manufacturers	Mainland manufacturers	Taiwanese manufacturers	Japanese manufacturers
Central management				
Finance and accounting				
Office administration				
Purchasing				
R&D				
Manufacturing/ Assembly				
Sales and marketing				
Logistics				

Primarily in Hong Kong   Primarily in the PRD   Primarily in Taiwan   Primarily in Japan

Source: Enright, Scott & Associates Ltd research

Figure 8.3   The future Hong Kong–Pearl River Delta electronics industry value chain

facilitate logistical operations integrating inputs shipped in from multiple locations across Asia, supporting the dispersed Asian electronics production systems of many multinational firms, and Hong Kong will retain this function vis-à-vis the Pearl River Delta region.

Marketing and sales activities for the markets of the Chinese mainland will continue to move from Hong Kong into the Pearl River Delta region, with measures to 'safeguard' sensitive company information in the mainland business environment. One electronics firm, for example, is relocating a trusted Hong Kong employee into the Pearl River Delta region for exclusive access to the firm's own pricing structures, disclosure of which to the mainland staff would 'give away the game'. Another firm reported that a past effort to set up a sales office in the Pearl River Delta region backfired when the mainland sales staff took away the firm's clients. Fears of this type of behaviour will serve to limit the activities that Hong Kong firms and foreign multinationals place in the Pearl River Delta region for a considerable period. Over time, a portion of the overall sales and marketing activities currently in Hong Kong will migrate to the Pearl River Delta, with Hong Kong retaining a robust function for international markets, including high-end trade fairs and exhibitions.

Watches

Managers in the watch industry believe that the Greater Pearl River Delta region will remain one of the world's leading manufacturing locations in the industry. Outside of Switzerland, the major competitors in the watch industry, from

Hong Kong, the Chinese mainland, South Korea, and Japan, are all doing much if not all of their manufacturing in the Pearl River Delta region. The presence of a dense supply base, market knowledge largely based in Hong Kong, easy access to buyers through Hong Kong, and rapid air cargo shipments through Hong Kong are viewed as likely to keep watch manufacturing in the region.[14]

Mainland firms will become increasingly dominant in the low-end watch segment. Similar to the case of the toy industry, discussed above, mainland producers enjoy low-cost sourcing from local supporting industries, and incur little or no R&D costs, enabling them to offer the lowest prices. Hong Kong firms will focus increasingly on ODM business while taking greater care to protect their patent rights, and will make more intensive use of computer-aided design (CAD) and other modern production technology. Die-casting, mould making, plastic manufacturing, metal stamping, surface finishing and plating are all areas where Hong Kong firms will be drivers of change. Hong Kong exporters will increasingly be required to handle larger numbers of orders in smaller quantities and to meet shorter delivery lead times. The end result of this confluence of competitive and market pressures means that the Greater Pearl River Delta region will in the future provide international customers with an even broader 'portfolio of choice'.[15]

Among Hong Kong firms, most central management functions will remain in Hong Kong, though managers will continue to commute on a regular basis between it and the Pearl River Delta region (see Figure 8.4). Office administration and purchasing will increasingly gravitate into the Pearl River Delta region.

Ownership / Activity	Hong Kong manufacturers	Mainland manufacturers	Japanese manufacturers
Central management			
Finance and accounting			
Office administration			
Purchasing			
R&D			
Manufacturing/ Assembly			
Sales and marketing			
Logistics			

Primarily in Hong Kong | Primarily in the PRD | Primarily in Japan | Activity not performed

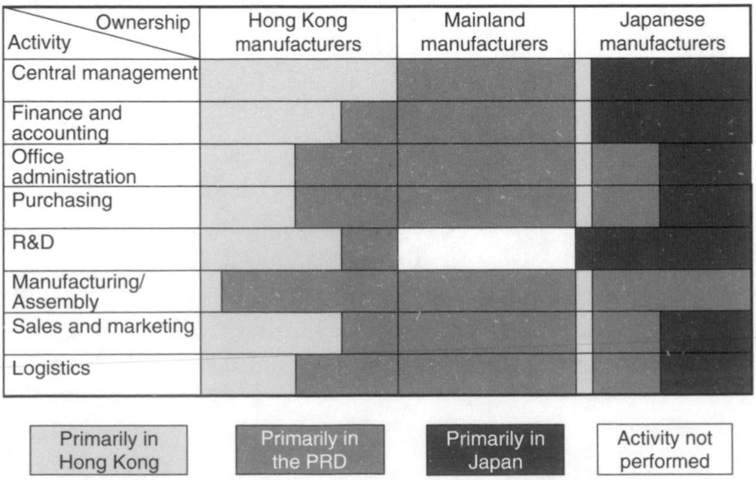

Source: Enright, Scott & Associates Ltd research

Figure 8.4   The future Hong Kong–Pearl River Delta watch industry value chain

The vast majority of manufacturing and assembly will take place in the Pearl River Delta region. Some activities in branded and fashion watches will locate in Hong Kong to allow fast response times to overseas orders and also in order for products to qualify for Hong Kong origin under CEPA. Most sales and marketing activities will remain in Hong Kong while shipping will increasingly shift into the Pearl River Delta region except for time-sensitive fashion pieces, which will ship by air out of Hong Kong. Mainland firms will increasingly shift sales and marketing activities aimed at international markets into Hong Kong.

Heavy industry

South China has historically lacked the natural and human resources considered necessary to compete in heavy industry, and there is not much experience in heavy industry in the Pearl River Delta region. Over the last two decades, the growth of industry, urban centres, and purchases of consumer durables has created substantial demand for autos, steel, chemicals, building materials, heavy machinery, and other heavy industrial products, as well as renewed interest in heavier industry. Guangdong authorities believe that the province should have a fully diversified economy that can meet most of its heavy industrial and materials needs. Towards that end, they have planned a heavy industrial zone for Nansha, south of the centre of Guangzhou. The main thrust of the Nansha development is to bring heavy industry to South China.

Hong Kong, with an economy based on services, light industry, and electronics, has never had much of a position in heavier industries. Hong Kong's contribution is likely to be much more focused on making the Pearl River Delta region more accessible to international firms, linking Pearl River Delta region production to international markets, linking foreign suppliers of inputs and capital goods to the region, and investing in new entities that might arise.

Autos

By 2004, China overtook Germany to become the world's third-largest auto market, and is expected to overtake Japan as the world's second-largest auto market by 2009.[16] Domestic capacity is growing fast and consolidation may be in the offing. Production of passenger cars in November 2003 grew by nearly 72% over the same month in 2002.[17] General Motor's profits in China more than tripled in 2003.[18] Companies such as General Motors and Ford are now looking to source billions of US dollars of auto parts in China. These developments indicate that the pundits who predicted the end of the auto industry for China post-WTO were wrong.

Guangzhou is poised to become a major production centre for the automotive industry, encompassing auto production, as well as production of engines, parts, components, and related inputs and materials. In the late 1990s, Honda took over the failed Peugeot venture and began to turn it around. This facility, which produced 60,000 cars in 2002 and 112,000 in 2003, is expected to increase capacity to more than 200,000 cars in 2004. Honda's export-oriented second plant in Guangzhou, a joint venture with Guangzhou Automobile Industry Group and Dongfeng Motors, will produce 300,000 units per year. Fengshen, a joint venture between Nissan, Dongfeng, and Yulon produced 35,000 units in 2002, and is expected to have capacity for 240,000 units by 2007. Toyota's future plant will have a capacity of 500,000 Camry sedans per year.[19] Bao Long is expected to produce 50,000 vehicles by 2005. In 2004, according to city officials, Guangzhou's motor industry ranked third in China after Shanghai and Jilin.[20] Total auto production in Guangzhou is expected to increase from 100,000 units in 2002 to between 400,000 and 500,000 in 2005, and eventually to 800,000 or more.

Honda, whose new plant will be geared towards export markets, obviously believes that China in general and Guangzhou in particular, will be able to build to world quality and cost standards. It bears to note that the Pearl River Delta region is the first region in China to be chosen for what is essentially the export processing of automobiles. Clearly, Honda has examined Guangzhou and seen the potential for exports around the world. This bodes well for the future.

The attraction of foreign auto parts suppliers will dramatically improve the sophistication of these businesses as well. Hundreds of suppliers to the auto firms already have located in Guangzhou and many more are expected. As discussed in Chapter 3, Denso, Japan's biggest car parts maker has set up a joint venture in Guangzhou to make auto air-conditioners and other car parts, to serve Honda as well as local bus producers – its third air-conditioner factory near Guangzhou.[21] Toyota's new engine joint venture with Guangzhou Automobile Group will have an initial capacity of 300,000 engines, 200,000 of which will be for export, with capacity expanding to more than 500,000 car engines per year.[22]

Steel

China produces twice as much steel as the United States and will soon displace Japan as the world's biggest importer of iron ore.[23] Though China is the largest steel producer in the world, it still imports much of its high-quality steel and that is where demand is emerging. At the national level, the Chinese steel industry will undergo consolidation and movement towards matching of supply and demand. Foreign steel producers are increasingly approaching the Chinese market by linking with local producers either in joint ventures or technology tie-ups. We should expect to see further growth in domestic steel capacity, growth in demand, and additional consolidation of the Chinese steel industry as some of the large Chinese players continue to take over smaller Chinese firms.

To date, mainland steel producers, centred in China's northern and eastern regions, have not been successful in producing high-quality galvanised sheet steel, which is imported from Japan and South Korea. In January 2004, JFE Steel Corp., a Japanese steel group, entered into a joint venture with Guangzhou Iron & Steel Enterprise Holdings Ltd. to produce 400,000 tons of hot-dip galvanised sheet steel per year at Nansha starting in early 2006.[24] The output will be used primarily in auto production, and to a lesser extent in electric appliances and construction. JFE Steel Corp. also aspires to use the Nansha facility as a base from which to export steel to other Asian markets. If the venture is successful, Guangzhou will become the first location in the mainland to export high-quality galvanised sheet steel.

While historically, South China did not have a strong steel industry, the growth of the auto, appliance, electronics, machinery, construction, transportation, and infrastructure sectors in the Pearl River Delta region will generate sufficient demand to justify local production. The key question is what will happen when South China demand is coupled with imported raw materials, foreign investment and technology, and a Chinese workforce. Much of the technology and know-how in the steel industry is embodied in equipment. The Nansha development could try to do what Korea's POSCO did two decades ago: invest in modern equipment and bypass many traditional players. Certainly, South China is not encumbered by the inefficient and outdated facilities that are endemic in the more traditional heavy industrial zones of China's north. The lack of a history in heavy industry could ultimately turn into a benefit for the Greater Pearl River Delta region. If so, it will likely be land and labour from China, capital and technology from other countries, and Hong Kong mediation that will prove a winning combination.

Chemicals

China's chemicals sector is as large as Germany's and is projected to equal Europe's in size by 2010.[25] In chemicals, China is experiencing massive new investments nationwide, huge demand, and high levels of imports. BASF, Bayer, BP, DuPont, and Exxon Mobil have all made large investments in the mainland attracted by China's strong growth potential.[26] Globally, the chemical industry is its own largest customer; once large investments start to flow into a location, complete production chains take shape quickly. Thus we expect the production capacity going into China will soon be part of complete production chains of much larger scope.

In the Pearl River Delta region, the chemical sector is seeing substantial development east, west, and centre. To the region's east, the Shell–CNOOC joint venture in Huizhou will create an international scale petrochemical complex. At more than US$5 billion, it represents the largest single foreign investment ever made in China. To the region's west, BP opened a world-scale purified terephthalic acid (PTA) facility in Zhuhai in 2003. As of 2004, Zhuhai was making efforts to attract Taiwanese investment in ethylene and related products. In the centre, at Nansha, an area of 32.8 square kilometres, has been set aside to develop products along the entire petrochemical industry chain, including refined oil, ethylene, and fine chemicals. These investments are logical first steps in creating three complete production complexes in the Pearl River Delta region: one in the east (Huizhou), one in the west (Zhuhai) and one in the centre (Nansha).

The emergence of local industrial bases in the Pearl River Delta region should create ready demand for chemicals and related products in autos (paints and coatings), in garments and textiles (synthetic fibres, dyes), in urban construction (paints, coatings, plastics), in electronics (plastics), in consumer goods (household chemicals, plastics), and in paper (process chemicals). All of these together will generate demand for the three emerging production complexes. The coastal location also makes exports possible. In chemicals, the question will be exactly where these large investments place the Pearl River Delta region on the national and international stage. Certainly, there is ample evidence in this industry around the world of large investments bringing in world-class technology that allows plants to compete effectively.

Services

China's service sector is underdeveloped relative to the rest of the economy. Services accounted for slightly over 32% of China's GDP in 2003, which is half or slightly more than half of the percentage share of service sectors in most advanced economies. Prior to China's opening, private-sector services were considered unnecessary. This was the legacy of a system in which the state-owned enterprises were vertically integrated and most services were provided by the State. The skills and capabilities in services traditionally lagged behind those in manufacturing. However, China is becoming a very big market for service companies. The major multinational services providers have located in the mainland and standards are gradually improving.

Historically, the Pearl River Delta region lagged behind locations such as Beijing and Shanghai with respect to services. In contrast, Hong Kong has been a leader, locally, regionally, and globally, in a broad range of business and trade-related services. As manufacturing evolves in the Pearl River Delta region, services related directly to manufacturing are at least partially gravitating into the Pearl River Delta region from Hong Kong. Going forward, China's accession to the WTO and the Closer Economic Partnership Arrangement (CEPA) should provide substantial opportunities for the development of the services sector in the Greater Pearl River Delta region overall.

The liberalisation that will result from these agreements will create the potential for Hong Kong to serve as a high-end services base for South China. With the emergence of a consumer economy in the Pearl River Delta region, we expect to see high-end, international services provided from Hòng Kong, domestic services provided from Guangzhou, and local services provided from Shenzhen. As east–west connectivity evolves within the Greater Pearl River Delta, it is likely that Macao and Zhuhai will increasingly provide services for their growing manufacturing hinterlands as well.

From the perspective of multinational service providers, this dynamic means that overseas firms which already have a presence in Hong Kong will be able to enhance that presence to serve South China. For South China, it means that the demand for services will be better met as the interaction within the Greater Pearl River Delta region becomes more fluid, improving efficiency throughout the economy. One would expect the Pearl River Delta region in particular to become more service oriented than many other places in China.

Transportation services

Sea Cargo

In sea cargo, the Greater Pearl River Delta region is uniquely positioned worldwide. Hong Kong is the world's largest port in terms of container throughput, and Shenzhen, which has the fastest growing ports in China,[27] may become the world's third-leading container port city by the end of 2004. That the Greater Pearl River Delta, with its small geographic area, generates sufficient cargo throughput to support the world's first and soon-to-be third-largest port demonstrates the extraordinary dynamism of South China's manufacturing base.

Overall demand projections for the Greater Pearl River Delta region are exploding as the region's export base continues to expand and as China's accession into the WTO results in increased imports and exports.[28] In the first two months of 2004, volumes at the Shenzhen port were up 30% over the previous year.[29] Within the Greater Pearl River Delta region, efficiency is high and the infrastructure is first rate. Overland haulage between factory gate and the ports will become more efficient with further streamlining of the boundary crossing between Shenzhen and Hong Kong and the opening of the Western Corridor. The future bridge linking Hong Kong to the west side of the Pearl River Delta will mean a substantial increase in investment to the west, increased cargo output, and substantial additional demand for logistics.

In March 2004, a strategy report commissioned by the Hong Kong government predicted that Hong Kong would continue to handle most of the region's cargo for another 10 years.[30] Hong Kong should retain a strong position for high value and rapid turnaround cargo due to its efficiency, advanced customs procedures, and dense shipping network. In addition, Hong Kong with its superior deep-water draft, should play an important role for the next generation of container ships. Upon completion in 2005, Hong Kong's Container Terminal 9 will increase Hong Kong's handling capacity by more than 2.6 million TEUs. The Hong Kong Government has voiced its support for Container Terminal 10, a US$1.15 billion facility that is under consideration.[31] However, unless Hong Kong improves its price competitiveness vis-à-vis Shenzhen's ports, Hong Kong's share of South China's outbound cargo is forecast to fall below 50% by 2014, though the volumes will be higher than at present because of a rapidly expanding pie. Hong Kong port's total throughput (including mid-stream operations, river trade, and other operations, which account for about 40% of the total) grew by 8.3% in the first eight months of 2003 over the same period in 2002.[32]

In Shenzhen, an additional nine berths with a total capacity of 3.3 million TEUs should be completed at Yantian by year-end 2004, and as of March 2004, additional expansion plans were before China's State Planning Commission for approval. Also, before the State Planning Commission were a Phase III expansion at Shekou and plans for a US$724.6 million project at Dachan Bay that would add five berths by 2008 and as many as 20 berths by 2014.[33] Modern Terminals Ltd (MTL), a subsidiary of Hong Kong-based Wharf Group, has committed to provide half of the capital for the Dachan Bay project. According to industry observers, on the basis of booming throughput at Shenzhen's ports, 'it is conceivable all three projects will be needed in their entirety'.[34] Shenzhen's ports will benefit from their strategic positions close to the cargo base of Shenzhen and Dongguan and their proximity to consolidation centres serving Wal-Mart and other leading merchandisers. Shenzhen is projected to overtake Hong Kong by 2005 in terms of number of berths with over 50% more than Hong Kong by 2010. According to forecasts by Merrill Lynch, Shenzhen container throughput will grow at an annual rate of 13% between 2002 and 2015.[35]

Competition among ports in the Greater Pearl River Delta region will continue to be driven by costs and capacity investments. As of 2004, the biggest single cost advantage of the Shenzhen ports over Hong Kong continued to be the lower cost of trucking. It cost around US$200 less per 20-foot box to haul cargo by truck from factories in the Pearl River Delta region to the port terminal in Shenzhen than to the Hong Kong port.[36] Container handling charges will also continue to drive the competition between Hong Kong and Shenzhen in sea transport. As of 2004, container handling charges in Shenzhen continued to be substantially lower than those in Hong Kong, depending on the size and destination of the shipment. CLSA claimed that Hong Kong-based operators, which operate the container ports in both Hong Kong and Shenzhen, use an oligopolistic pricing structure to maximise profits across the ports in both Hong Kong and Shenzhen.[37]

In order to streamline cargo flows and reduce costs, the Hong Kong government is considering more extensive provision of 24-hour border checkpoints. Other possible measures include new pre-clearance arrangements for cargo, an Automated Vehicle Clearance system, additional clearance depots, and working with Guangdong to liberalise the licensing regime for truck drivers. This could lead to greater coordination between the Hong Kong government and governments within the Pearl River Delta region and, ultimately, result in substantial productivity gains for the larger Greater Pearl River Delta region. While the pricing of container handling charges is primarily a commercial matter between the shipping lines and the shippers, we expect to see continued action by the Hong Kong government to facilitate communication and cooperation among the relevant parties.[38]

Port competition is likely to take place through capacity investments as well. If investors in port facilities operate on a commercial basis, they will take the capacity of other competing locations into account before making their own investments. In particular, if there is overcapacity in nearby jurisdictions, commercial investors could be deterred from new investments. At the 2004 National People's Congress, Minister of Communications Zhang Chunxian expressed the Central Government's intention to reign in duplicate investments around the Greater Pearl River Delta region and to ensure that future investments are demand driven. This should temper the ambitions of Dongguan and several smaller jurisdictions within the region to build duplicative port facilities. The big question mark is Guangzhou's plan to develop a container port with 10 to 12 berths and capacity of more than 1.5 million TEUs annually by 2010, with much larger operations in place by 2020 in Nansha.[39] Industry observers doubt the commercial viability of a Nansha container port, given the site's shallow-water constraints; the planned bridge link between Hong Kong, Zhuhai, and

Macao; and the fact that the heavy industry base which Nansha would serve is still in its infancy. In some quarters there are fears that an investment of the magnitude of the Nansha port, made on a non-commercial basis, could discourage other new investment made on a commercial basis within the Greater Pearl River Delta region. At the time this book goes to press, however, dredging is speeding ahead at Nansha 'like there is no tomorrow'.[40]

Air Transport

The World Tourism Organization has predicted that China will be the world's number one tourism destination by 2020. Increased air passenger traffic in and out of the mainland and Hong Kong will be driven by the mainland's increased openness, expanding freedom to travel, and the rise in international business. The Greater Pearl River Delta region's air cargo and passenger flows are set to develop and expand in coming years as China continues to liberalise, cargo output continues to expand, and mainland residents take advantage of new affluence and freedom to travel. Macao's vast expansion of its recreation and casino sector will also boost air passenger flows, in particular between Macao, the mainland, and leading Asian cities. Growth of the economies of the Mekong Delta will bolster international air flows between South-east Asia and South China. International passenger traffic into and out of all the airports in Hong Kong, Guangdong Province, and Macao is projected to grow from approximately 58 million in 2001 to 240 million by 2010.[41] Within the Greater Pearl River Delta region as a whole, we should see a more extensive portfolio of choices in the air transport sector, burgeoning demand, the emergence of new businesses in a variety of sectors, and new air routes connecting the region to mainland and international destinations.

The Hong Kong International Airport is likely to remain the principal access point for international passenger and freight traffic into and out of the region well into the future. Cargo flows at the airport are growing fast, propelled by exports of electronics and time-sensitive consumer goods from the Pearl River Delta region. In the first two months of 2004, Hong Kong's air cargo traffic grew over 17% on a year-on-year basis.[42] Hong Kong Airport Authority plans anticipate passenger and cargo throughput in Hong Kong to grow at an average annual rate of around 6% through 2020.[43] The ultimate design capacity of the Hong Kong International Airport, which handled 33.5 million passengers and 2.48 million tonnes of cargo in 2002, is 87 million passengers and nine million tonnes of cargo.[44]

The Hong Kong International Airport's dense network of international flights is unlikely to be matched any time soon by any other airport in the region, especially given the strength of local carriers, Cathay Pacific and

Dragonair, and the liberalised air services agreement reached with the United States in 2002. Hong Kong has the potential to be a major hub for air passenger travel between the Chinese mainland and major overseas destinations. It already offers superior connections and pricing. For passengers wishing to fly from the city of Wuhan in the Yangtze River Basin to London, as of May 2004, there were two flights each day from Wuhan to Hong Kong International Airport, and six flights daily from Hong Kong to London. For passengers flying into Shenzhen and transferring to Hong Kong International Airport, there were seven flights each day from Wuhan into Shenzhen and six flights daily from Hong Kong to London. In comparison, there were eight flights each day from Wuhan to Beijing, but only two flights daily from Beijing to London. Passengers making the trip through Shanghai had the choice of 10 flights daily from Wuhan to Hongqiao Airport in Shanghai, but then would have to transfer across the city to Pudong International Airport for the single daily flight from Shanghai to London.[45] Of these options, the routing from Wuhan to Shenzhen to Hong Kong to London was the least expensive. Hong Kong and Chinese mainland carriers are actively seeking to serve more destinations in the Chinese mainland from Hong Kong, which should further boost Hong Kong's role as hub for the mainland's international air traffic.

Guangzhou will increasingly serve as a hub for domestic, mainland traffic and as a second, lower cost option for international traffic, in particular between China and South-east Asian destinations. The new Guangzhou Baiyun International Airport, scheduled to open in June 2004, is projected to handle over 25 million passengers annually by 2010, as well as more than one million tonnes of cargo.[46] Its ultimate design capacity is reported to be 80 million passengers and 2.5 million tonnes of cargo.[47] Guangzhou has been designated as one of the top three domestic hubs and international airports in the Chinese mainland (the others are in Beijing and Shanghai). As such, it is expected to dominate domestic air transportation between the Pearl River Delta region and the rest of the Chinese mainland, particularly with smaller cities in the mainland, which are emerging as new tourist and business destinations. These 'cross-province' flights are anticipated to supplement Hong Kong's mainland routes and vastly expand the menu of connections from the Greater Pearl River Delta region to destinations across the mainland.[48] In the international sphere, Guangzhou is seeking to extend fifth freedoms to foreign carriers in an effort to become a major international hub connecting South China to South-east Asia and beyond. In January 2004, Federal Express signed an agreement in principle to move the transport and distribution hub for its Asia Pacific operations from Subic Bay in the Philippines to Guangzhou's new airport.[49] Three months later, Philippine airport authorities announced the imminent signing of a

25-year lease with Federal Express for a 42-hectare site at the former Clark air force base, on the opposite side of the airport from United Parcel Services (UPS). A spokesman for Federal Express explained that Guangzhou and the former Clark air force base were the 'front runners' in selecting its future hub.[50] DHL, on the other hand, ran its Asia Pacific hub out of Hong Kong.

Shenzhen's Bao'an Airport is expected to handle 15 million passengers in 2005, which will put it at full capacity, and it has plans for future expansion.[51] The Shenzhen airport would seem to be well situated to become a major airport for air cargo, given its position in the heart of the Pearl River Delta's export base. Some industry analysts, for example, once believed that the presence of Federal Express could eventually make Shenzhen a major cargo airport, though that seems to have been superseded by discussions with Guangzhou. Shenzhen is likely to expand its position as a hub for domestic travel within China, though this will depend on its ability to obtain permission to fly to more domestic destinations. It is not clear that such permission will be forthcoming given the hub status of Guangzhou and the plans of domestic airlines.

Macao International Airport is well positioned to serve the burgeoning tourist flows from the mainland and elsewhere in Asia to be attracted by Macao's vast new recreation and casino developments. While many of its mainland visitors will travel to Macao by land, and others will cross over from Hong Kong, air flows will be fed by new traffic from cities in the mainland, with which it has strong links, and elsewhere in Asia. Macao's air passenger traffic of 4.17 million passengers in 2002 was up by 9.6% over the previous year, following strong growth in 2000 (22.7%) and 2001 (17.5%).[52] Though passenger traffic was hit hard by the SARS outbreak in 2003, it was rebounding in 2004. Macao International Airport has excess capacity to accommodate future growth. In 2004, under its 'open skies policy', Macao was pursuing new air services agreements with destinations in the Asia Pacific region as well as in Europe, America, and elsewhere,[53] and had started to attract discount airline carriers.

In contrast to the other international airports within the Greater Pearl River Delta region, it is not clear that Zhuhai Airport has a niche. As of March 2004, the Zhuhai Airport reportedly owed at least 13 billion RMB (US$1.57 billion) to creditors and was losing around 20 million RMB (US$2.42 million) per month.[54] Some observers have suggested that the relative emptiness of Zhuhai Airport could make it suitable for aircraft maintenance, or as a satellite cargo facility affiliated with the Hong Kong Airport. However, this appears to be a plan to bail out Zhuhai Airport rather than a commercially based proposal. Zhuhai is on the opposite side of the Pearl River Delta from the Delta's main export base, and does not have sufficient flight frequency to justify the costs associated with operating a major airport.[55]

Overall, we expect to see more of both competition and cooperation within the Greater Pearl River Delta region's air transport sector. In the short term, competition within the region will not re-direct air cargo flows to the same extent as sea cargo flows. Compared to demand for sea shipment, demand for air shipment is less sensitive to differentials in land haulage costs from factory gate to port terminal. Demand for the airfreight of high-value consumer goods is being driven by external trends. International distributors are reducing risk by minimising the time that goods spend in inventory and show willingness to pay a premium for the 'just in time' air shipment offered by Hong Kong. Nevertheless, over the longer term, as the airports at Guangzhou and Shenzhen develop their air networks and cargo handling capabilities, we are likely to see heightened competition among the region's leading airports.

There are signs of growing cooperation in the Greater Pearl River Delta region. While multiple airports in the Greater Pearl River Delta region provide choice for travellers and shippers, there are challenges associated with so many airports so close together, yet in separate jurisdictions. Divisions of airspace, air traffic control responsibilities, and communications requirements can sometimes result in inefficient flight patterns and delays in takeoffs and landings. The region's airports have created the PRD A5 Forum in order to foster cooperation in emergency support, smooth passenger and cargo processing, joint promotion, safety and security, training and development, and future planning. The Forum also sought to identify and promote the complementary strengths of the different airports, possibly in preparation for closer cooperation. In February 2004, Shenzhen officials announced that they had invited the Airport Authority of Hong Kong to be a strategic investor in the Shenzhen Airport and in March 2004, *Financial Times* reported that the Hong Kong Airport Authority was in talks to buy a stake in the Zhuhai Airport as well.[56] Such steps would foster more cooperation within the Greater Pearl River Delta region, including the possible linking of schedules among the airports in question, the decentralisation of activities like maintenance and some cargo operations, the entry into the region of budget carriers, and more private aviation. The end result should be a substantially expanded portfolio of choice in air transport services for the region as a whole.

The potential for air transportation in the region, as well as competition between airports, will be strongly influenced by air service rights. As China opens up its skies more international flights are becoming available from Beijing and Shanghai. Hong Kong's air freedoms regime is viewed as less open than those of other places in the region such as Bangkok and Singapore. Because Hong Kong historically has had a less open air services regime than other airports in Asia, it has lost some of the hubbing activities of companies like Federal

Express and UPS. The air services agreement that Hong Kong reached with the United States in October 2002, which enhanced fifth freedom rights for US carriers in Hong Kong and allowed Cathay Pacific to serve additional cities in the United States and to code share with American Airlines, appears to show that the Hong Kong Government was becoming concerned about the potential loss of Hong Kong's hub status. At the same time, Hong Kong carriers are seeking expanded landing rights in the Chinese mainland, something that would naturally extend Hong Kong's position as a regional hub. The gradual erosion of the 'one-route, one-airline' policy in Hong Kong indicates that Hong Kong also is starting to take competition in air services more seriously.

Trade-related services

The Greater Pearl River Delta region shows every indication of extending its position in trade-related services. The deepening and broadening of its industrial base will create substantial new demand for trade-related services in the region. Investments in ports, airports, highways, and railways will bring the region closer together and will enhance its efficiency. This will be combined with the expertise found in Hong Kong and increasingly in the Pearl River Delta region. As the Pearl River Delta region expands its role in manufacturing and deepens its production base, the demand for trade-related services will expand further. Its skills and capabilities in trade-related services should benefit significantly by greater interaction with Hong Kong service providers made possible by the CEPA between China and Hong Kong. In addition, as China's economy opens under its WTO accession agreement, there will be an entire new dynamic, in which import trading will rise to take its place alongside export trading as critical activities for the Greater Pearl River Delta region.

Trading Services

Trading services are set to grow and develop very substantially in the Greater Pearl River Delta region. Buying offices and traders will continue to benefit from the dense network of support services found in Hong Kong. The Greater Pearl River Delta region will continue to benefit as the home of China's two most important trade fairs, the traditional and the High Technology Fair in Shenzhen. It also will benefit from the large number of leading international trade fairs held each year in Hong Kong.

Hong Kong should continue to play the lead role in providing overseas market access for the Greater Pearl River Delta region. Hong Kong's strengths as a region-wide hub for trading and commercial activities rest on powerful hard and soft infrastructure advantages and 'service cluster strengths' that will not be replicated by any city in the Pearl River Delta region anytime soon. Shenzhen and Guangzhou lack the critical mass and overall systems. Shanghai is too far away to act as a hub for the Pearl River Delta region. Soft infrastructure advantages, including free flows of capital, goods, people, and information, lie firmly with Hong Kong. Hong Kong's soft infrastructure advantages, including the rule of law, first-world judicial and legal system, enforceability of contracts, level playing field, political stability, security, transparency, and intellectual property protection, are of great value to the foreign market access function and will prove difficult for mainland cities to replicate.

Guangzhou should continue to develop strongly as South China's leading commercial hub for domestic trade and distribution. Guangzhou will also build up its profile as an international trading hub for South China, especially for low- to middle-end light manufactures in second- and third-tier markets around the world. Shenzhen should become increasingly important as a location for purchasing centres. The movement by some of the world's major distribution chains, such as Levis and Wal-Mart, of their buying operations for South China into the Pearl River Delta region, is gaining in momentum.[57] These very large firms increasingly have the financial clout to subcontract the setting up of dedicated consolidation centres convenient to the maritime port facilities in Shenzhen, which in turn are sufficiently developed to accommodate their shipping requirements. In February 2002, Wal-Mart moved its global sourcing centre from Hong Kong to Shenzhen, where it manages the purchase of an estimated US$15 billion of goods annually from the Chinese mainland. Other major retailers, such as Target from the United States and Tesco from the United Kingdom, plan to base their largest mainland sourcing operations in Shenzhen. Computer and electronics manufacturers Sony and IBM each spend an estimated US$4 billion to US$5 billion per annum buying components from their Shenzhen purchasing centres.[58]

China's liberalisation under WTO is likely to encourage the growth of mainland-based traders within the Pearl River Delta region, and the development of their skills and capabilities. China's WTO accession will make it easier for overseas firms to set up in the mainland, where they will be able to work directly with mainland traders and agents. It also will make selling direct into the mainland easier. CEPA makes it much easier for Hong Kong service suppliers to engage in trading, wholesale, distribution, and retail activities in the mainland. Liberalisation under CEPA is accelerating the pre-existing trend of Hong Kong firms in these sectors expanding into the Pearl River Delta region, attracted by the growth potential of fast-growing urban areas and purchasing power.

Mainland traders will compete by making direct contact with foreign buyers, through the Internet, the Canton Trade Fair or trade fairs overseas, the backward engineering of commodity products, and improved English language and marketing skills. They are targeting buyers in third world markets and mid-tier markets in Europe, for example, where numerous actors still prevail in distribution. The Indian trading community in Hong Kong, for example, is increasingly encountering mainland traders in third world markets for basic commodity goods, such as footwear, where the mainland traders are competing very aggressively on price, and this trend is set to continue.

Hong Kong traders will compete by drawing upon their distinctive strengths, including the ability to deliver on time, to meet stringent quality requirements, to communicate with foreign buyers, to understand overseas markets, and to coordinate complex commercial practices. In the ODM and 'branded' segments, the control of Hong Kong firms over production and supply chain management should continue strong across a wide spectrum of light manufactures. Many interviewees from small- and medium-sized Hong Kong firms voiced concern that their strategic advantages in 'foreign market access' over mainland traders would last only three to five years. Others indicate that this logic is flawed and that any catching up would take far longer. It also assumes that Hong Kong firms stand still.

The most innovative of Hong Kong's trading companies continue to develop strategies to keep them ahead of the competition. An example is the 'as seen on TV' merchandising strategy, where products sourced by Hong Kong traders from the Pearl River Delta region and elsewhere in the mainland are advertised directly to consumers through TV commercials that air in North America.[59] Transforming product 'from engineered product to fashion item, at the best quality for the lowest price' will continue to be a strategy in watches and clocks.[60] Other Hong Kong traders will find systematic means to transform their experience base into formidable barriers to entry. One trader, for example, has built up over time a cumulative computer database of 100,000 specific colour matches for a specific item of fabric. Others will continue to invest heavily in client relationships. Marketing, design, and branding will also receive more attention as sources of future competitive strength.

Under CEPA, many Hong Kong firms will be locating more sales and marketing activities targeting the South China market within the Pearl River Delta region. As mainland markets are highly localised, and are expected to remain so for some time, Hong Kong firms will increasingly field marketing and sales staff in multiple mainland locations. They expect to continue to hire sales personnel locally in the Pearl River Delta region. Activities that are expected to remain in Hong Kong include overall formulation and coordination of sales strategy, and the drafting of training manuals for mainland sales personnel. At the same time, there will be movement in the other direction, from the mainland into Hong Kong, as mainland firms set up operations in Hong Kong to draw upon the services and expertise of Hong Kong's international trading platform.

In terms of import flows, China under WTO is expected to become more open, and more shipments will flow direct to their destinations on the mainland. The pace of change will depend in large part on the ability of mainland locations to resolve internal disputes over jurisdiction and streamline their customs procedures. Meaningful progress on this front may well require another five to 10 years. In terms of upside for the Greater Pearl River Delta region, China's WTO membership and CEPA should provide Hong Kong firms with a more level playing field inside the mainland, while lower import tariffs should boost overall trade flows and yield a larger pie for everyone.

Logistics Services

Logistics is increasingly becoming a focus of companies and of regions. Companies are realising that managing their supply chains well is critical to competitive success in the marketplace. Regions are realising that logistics is rapidly becoming an attractive, high value-added industry that can add substantially to local wealth. Advances in information and communication technology are revolutionising the logistics business, allowing the companies and centres that are able to handle vast information and product flows to have substantial advantages over competitors. The rise of third-party and even fourth-party logistics providers has increased specialisation and levels of expertise in the industry. It also has made customers increasingly more demanding of the logistics companies and the logistics centres that they employ. The future competitiveness of logistics services in the Greater Pearl River Delta region will be driven in large part by competition and cooperation among its leading jurisdictions. Key factors will include the networks of each of the major hubs, the availability and quality of advanced services, the information handling capability of the hubs, costs, and the ability to provide integrated management for flows of information and goods.

Hong Kong and Shenzhen will serve as the Greater Pearl River Delta region's hubs for international logistics activities. Hong Kong will remain an important regional hub for managing and coordinating multi-directional flows of products and components within the Asia Pacific region and between the Asia Pacific and the rest of the world. Its world-class hard and soft infrastructure, and supporting services, are without par in the Chinese mainland. Hong Kong will attract and retain regional and sub-regional operations of multinational logistics firms.[61] Shenzhen will provide a low-cost alternative to Hong Kong for logistics provision proximate to the Pearl River Delta region's export processing base and the Shenzhen ports. It will continue to attract and retain consolidation centres serving export flows to the ports. Shenzhen's cost advantage relative to Hong Kong will lessen somewhat over time, because rental costs of warehouse space in Shenzhen are rising. Wage differentials, on the other hand, are expected to remain significant for at least another 10 years.

Hong Kong and Shenzhen may be on the way to becoming almost a single hub with warehousing and consolidation activities taking place in Shenzhen for physical flows through Hong Kong and Shenzhen. Within this hub, logistics companies would set up a single management structure to manage the flows of goods through Hong Kong and Shenzhen in an integrated manner. The various options for physical goods flow through Hong Kong or Shenzhen would become a portfolio of choices managed in an integrated fashion by logistics companies. In all likelihood, this integrated management for many companies would be based in Hong Kong to take advantage of Hong Kong's network of key decision-makers and access to international market information. Such an integration of hubs would require significant improvements in the cross-border transport of goods. In order to truly operate as a single hub, there must be flexibility in terms of moving goods back and forth, depending on what is optimal at the moment. Failing such flexibility, Hong Kong and Shenzhen still could be viewed by logistics companies as linked, but without such immediate flexibility.[62]

Guangzhou, on the other hand, will continue to be a hub for domestically oriented logistics activities. Guangzhou has been the historical centre of logistics for domestic flows of goods in the region. As China opens its distribution and transportation industries under its WTO accession agreement and CEPA, it is likely that Hong Kong and foreign companies that wish to be active in the Pearl River Delta region, and South China in general, will place significant activities into Guangzhou. This is likely to be the best place to deal with customers and to deal with the myriad of transportation, warehousing, and consolidation activities geared towards the domestic mainland market. Here the Hong Kong and foreign providers will meet indigenous companies that will provide support services and competition. The new Baiyun International Airport will give Guangzhou a strengthened role as an air hub for domestically oriented logistics as well. The new airport, coupled with plans for port development at Nansha, could also put Guangzhou on the map as a centre for internationally oriented logistics activities, though these are still likely to be dominated by Hong Kong and Shenzhen.[63]

Competition in domestically oriented logistics services for the Pearl River Delta region and South China markets will be heavily influenced by cost, geographic position, and connections to the rest of the region. It is hard to imagine that either Hong Kong or Shenzhen could compete successfully with Guangzhou along these dimensions. Even with a bridge link between Hong Kong and the western part of the Pearl River Delta region, Guangzhou's location with respect to the population centres in the Pearl River Delta region and the regional transportation network should ensure its position. The only competition could come from a combination of Hong Kong and Shenzhen, should the international portion of the logistics industry become so prominent that it absorbs the domestic system into a single hub. Given the disparate nature of the goods that are involved in the export trade and those involved in domestic shipments in the Pearl River Delta region, this is unlikely to take place.

There will be more intense competition in logistics services between the various jurisdictions in the Greater Pearl River Delta region in the future. Hong Kong, Guangzhou, and Shenzhen all have made logistics services a cornerstone of their future development plans.[64] The question is whether this competition will be direct head-to-head competition or more differentiated competition, with the different jurisdictions performing mostly different functions and thus limiting direct competition to a limited range of activities in which there is direct overlap. In addition, in the context of the expected growth of trade and distribution in the region, the competition will be for pieces of a much larger pie than is available at present. This limits the potential for destructive competition between jurisdictions going forward.

One main dimension of the future competition will involve the existing networks and systems of the different centres. Hong Kong's linkages with the rest of the world through its port and airport should enable its logistics providers to maintain a strong if not dominant position in high-end logistics services, particularly those associated with goods moving by air. Even so, in the future, shippers looking at air shipment into China will 'cost compare' entering through Hong Kong or going direct to their mainland destination. The final result will be dictated by the frequency, cost, and reliability of the various air cargo platforms. The systems developed by Hong Kong providers and the Hong Kong offices of foreign providers to manage complete supply chains should also hold Hong Kong in good stead for supply chain management activities, not just with respect to the Greater Pearl River Delta region, but also for trade in and around Asia, and between Asia and the rest of the world. The legal, financial, communications, and business systems in Hong Kong should also leave it in a good position for providing services associated with logistics, including real time tracking, financing, settlement, and advisory services.

In the future, the trend will be for the logistics hubs of Guangzhou and Hong Kong–Shenzhen to become more tightly linked. For goods imported

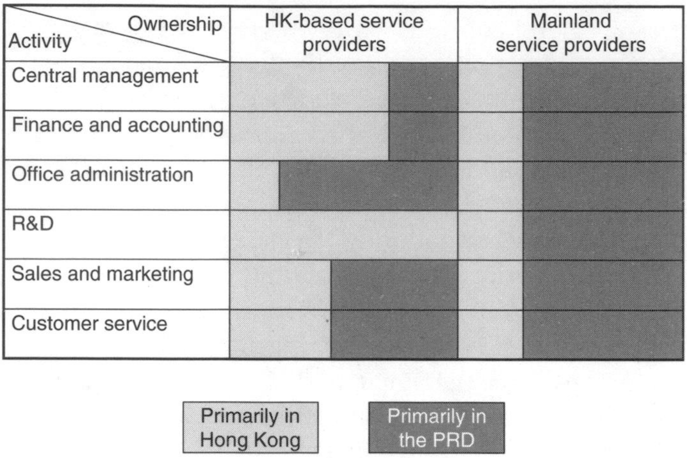

Ownership / Activity	HK-based service providers	Mainland service providers
Central management		
Finance and accounting		
Office administration		
R&D		
Sales and marketing		
Customer service		

Primarily in Hong Kong   Primarily in the PRD

Source: Enright, Scott & Associates Ltd research

Figure 8.5 The future Hong Kong–Pearl River Delta logistics industry value chain

into the Pearl River Delta region, the tendency will be for smoother transit from the international logistics hub to the domestic logistics hub, and then on into the domestic distribution system. In addition, export cargo originating from Guangzhou and surrounding areas will be funnelled into the domestic hub and then linked to the international hub for export. Such a division of labour will help to optimise the entire logistics system for the Greater Pearl River Delta region. The future logistics industry value chain will reflect this increasing integration (see Figure 8.5).

Financial and business services

China is emerging as a large market for financial and business services, but is still dramatically under-served because of its history, regulations, and penchant for state control. There is a growing realisation of the important roles that the financial and business service sectors play in a modern, advanced economy. Nevertheless, services overall as a percentage of GDP are low; in particular, financial and business services. The historical role of the financial service sector in the Chinese mainland has been as an instrument of policy funding state enterprises. The role of the financial sector as an efficient allocator of capital to maximise economic development potential is just starting to emerge in China, and it conflicts with history. Because of this, business services as discrete, separate industries with discrete, separate companies have lagged well behind what one might have expected in an economy the size of China. In both the financial and business service sectors, limited openness is a hold-over from the past. Hong Kong, on the other hand, has one of the most advanced and open financial and business service sectors in the world. Hong Kong has long been a home for international finance for the offices of multinational service companies, and a source of high-quality services for the Asia Pacific region.

In the Greater Pearl River Delta region, demand for financial and business services should grow substantially. Services are already the main driving force of Hong Kong's economy, and the demand for these services in the Pearl River Delta region is growing. The division of labour and nature of competition between Hong Kong and the Pearl River Delta region in financial and business services will influence the development of the Greater Pearl River Delta region. Going forward, in the Greater Pearl River Delta region as a whole, we would expect to see more of a critical mass in terms of markets, more access, and greater ability to set up service operations all over the region. A hierarchy of service sectors is likely to emerge, with Hong Kong as the international hub, Shenzhen as a secondary international hub, Guangzhou and Shenzhen both playing important roles for South China, and Macao and Zhuhai playing important roles for what will be a burgeoning manufacturing base on the western side of the Pearl River Delta region. This will make the Pearl River Delta region more comparable in the range and sophistication of services on offer to Shanghai and Beijing. For Hong Kong companies and for the Hong Kong-based businesses of overseas firms in a variety of service sectors, this will substantially improve the region as an investment location.

Hong Kong will retain a very strong position in internationally related services, such as international finance, and as a hub location for professional services, such as accounting, advertising, consulting, and legal services. As indicated above, Hong Kong's position as a regional headquarters for multinational firms is improving, as is its position as a management and coordination centre for business into and out of China. All of these generate substantial demand for high-level professional services. Hong Kong's role as a regional hub also has meant that many international professional service firms use Hong Kong as a base to serve the rest of the region. Hong Kong's advantages in terms of legal and administrative systems, communications network, history as a cosmopolitan city, and international linkages continue to make it the city of choice for the regional activities of professional service firms.

Financial Services

We would expect an increasingly integrated Greater Pearl River Delta region to become one of the best served areas in China for financial services. With the liberalisation of China's economy, listings of Chinese companies on international bourses should proliferate, expanding Hong Kong's financial sector in the process. As of early 2004, Hong Kong's financial sector was on the upswing buoyed by a surge in very large IPOs by mainland firms. The initial public offering in Hong Kong of PICC Property & Casualty Co., part of People's Insurance Co. of China, raised US$800 million in Hong Kong during the third quarter of 2003, while that of China Life Insurance Co. in Hong Kong and New York, raised US$3.46 billion and was the world's largest IPO.[65] As mentioned in Chapter 6, the Central Government is likely to keep the floodgates into Hong Kong open, partly in the hope that Hong Kong listings will have a positive influence on the corporate governance of mainland firms. As Chinese restrictions on mainland companies listing in Hong Kong are eased, we should expect that many Pearl River Delta-based companies will prefer to list in Hong Kong to obtain access to international capital flows.[66]

The resumption of IPOs on the Shenzhen Stock Exchange, which may occur in 2004 or 2005, would widen the options open to Chinese firms seeking to raise capital within the region. While this would benefit firms from all over China, it may benefit firms from the Pearl River Delta region more than others, and may boost the entire region's fundraising and services capabilities. In addition, it will be natural for the hundreds of overseas banks and insurance firms already set up in Hong Kong to use their Hong Kong base to expand incrementally out into the Pearl River Delta region, especially to Shenzhen, which is making efforts to stay at the forefront of China's opening in the banking sector. Movement into Shenzhen and other Pearl River Delta cities will be facilitated by CEPA s liberalisation of threshold requirements for market entry into the mainland by Hong Kong financial service suppliers. Multinational banks and financial institutions will increasingly set up South China operations, as Standard Chartered is already doing.

The main investment banking, fundraising, project finance, and other 'big ticket' financial services will largely be provided out of Hong Kong, which will remain the major international financial centre. Guangzhou and Shenzhen will provide much of the retail and corporate banking activities for consumers and businesses in the Pearl River Delta region. The movement by large service providers of back-end support operations from Hong Kong into the Pearl River Delta region is expected to continue and perhaps accelerate (see Figure 8.6). The salary differentials between clerical and support workers in Hong Kong and the Pearl River Delta region are projected to continue for at least another 15 years. As a result, data processing, customer call centres, bill processing, and other backroom activities of Hong Kong-based financial institutions increasingly will be moved to centres across the boundary in the Pearl River Delta region including Shenzhen and Zhuhai.

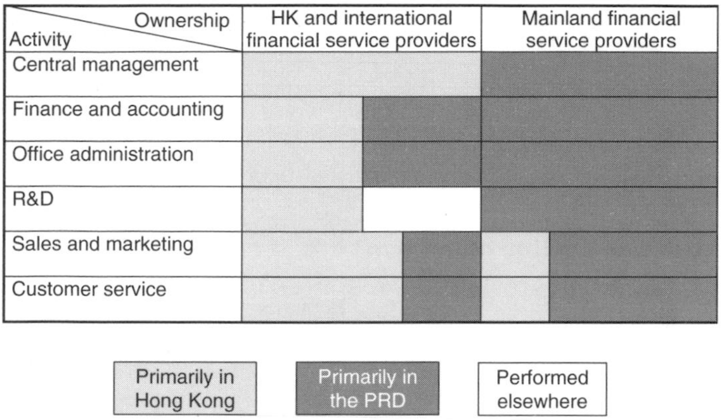

Ownership / Activity	HK and international financial service providers	Mainland financial service providers
Central management		
Finance and accounting		
Office administration		
R&D		
Sales and marketing		
Customer service		

Primarily in Hong Kong	Primarily in the PRD	Performed elsewhere

Source: Enright, Scott & Associates Ltd research

Figure 8.6   The future Hong Kong–Pearl River Delta financial sector value chain

Business and Professional Services

With China's entry into WTO and CEPA, we should see in the Greater Pearl River Delta region a dramatic opening of the services sector, huge new market opportunities for foreign companies, and the development of local service firms. While the local firms are unlikely to serve international markets any time soon, they will support and facilitate the Pearl River Delta region's own development. For the Pearl River Delta region, the greater opening should allow places like Guangzhou and Shenzhen to attract service activities from multinational and Hong Kong companies that have not been feasible before. As in other sectors, this will help stimulate improvement in the quantity and quality of locally provided services. For Hong Kong, the greater openness will provide a much larger scope for it to expand its position as a service centre for China, enormously improve its ability to be a high-end service centre for the Greater Pearl River Delta region, and in the process also expand its role as an Asia Pacific centre.

In the Greater Pearl River Delta region, the market for business and professional services is likely to become much more integrated (see Figure 8.7). The main reasons will be the opening of the Chinese market under the WTO accession agreement and CEPA, greater development in the Pearl River Delta region, and greater knowledge of the Pearl River Delta region's market on the part of Hong Kong firms. There is a clear trend towards the service activities most closely linked to manufacturing processes shifting from Hong Kong into the Pearl River Delta region. The end result should be an expansion of the high-end service sectors in business and professional services in Hong Kong, an increasing sophistication of service offerings in the Pearl River Delta region by both Hong Kong and Pearl River Delta firms and offices, and a shift of

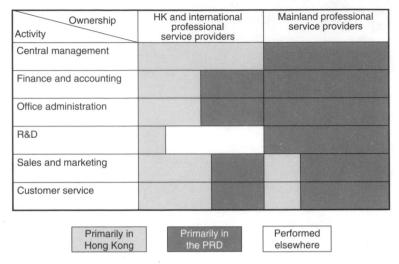

Activity ＼ Ownership	HK and international professional service providers	Mainland professional service providers
Central management		
Finance and accounting		
Office administration		
R&D		
Sales and marketing		
Customer service		

Primarily in Hong Kong	Primarily in the PRD	Performed elsewhere

Source: Enright, Scott & Associates Ltd research

Figure 8.7   The future Hong Kong–Pearl River Delta professional services value chain

backroom-type activities out of Hong Kong and into the Pearl River Delta region. On the latter point, companies like the telecommunications services provider PCCW have moved significant portions of their back office and supporting activities to the Pearl River Delta region in search of lower costs. In some service areas, such as high-end financial services, consulting, accounting, and engineering experts based in Hong Kong are likely to be called in to deal with particular projects or large-scale undertakings in the Greater Pearl River Delta region. This is already happening in the development of Macao's new recreation and casino complexes, with investors drawing upon a broad range of multinational service providers based in Hong Kong. Going forward, Hong Kong will increasingly serve as an entry point for international talents that then can be leveraged locally.

There will be keener competition in business and professional services among the jurisdictions of the Greater Pearl River Delta region in the future. The development plans of Shenzhen and Guangzhou are directly targeting the service sector as a means to move into higher value activities and as a means to improve performance of the local manufacturing sectors. The past view of the service sector as 'unproductive' or 'parasitic' is falling away faster in the Pearl River Delta region than anywhere else in the Chinese mainland. While some of the plans in local jurisdictions in the Pearl River Delta region call for cooperation with Hong Kong and Hong Kong service providers to upgrade the capabilities of the local service sector, other plans, such as Shenzhen's plan to attract multinational regional headquarters away from Hong Kong, are less cooperative in nature. At the same time, greater openness under China's WTO accession agreement and CEPA will allow Hong Kong firms to compete in sectors that once were closed, placing further pressure on Pearl River Delta-based firms and offices.

Tourism

Tourism in the Greater Pearl River Delta region is also expected to grow substantially. Hong Kong is a major international tourist destination, as well as an increasingly popular location for visitors from the Chinese mainland. The Disneyland theme park to open on Hong Kong's Lantau Island in 2005 or 2006 is projected to attract more than five million visitors in its first year of operation, rising to 10 million visitors per year by 2020. Hong Kong also will continue to attract many visitors interested in a modern, metropolitan, East-meets-West setting. Macao builds off its history and its European links. It has also received substantial new investments that could make it a tourism and gaming centre for the entire Asian region (see Chapter 7).[67] The Pearl River Delta region has numerous attractions that make it alluring to a Chinese mainland clientele, though not yet to the international tourism market. Attractions include a variety of theme parks, numerous golf resorts, nature parks, and aesthetic natural locations. Should the jurisdictions in the Greater Pearl River Delta region make further efforts to pool their marketing and link their attractions, they could offer combined tours and promotions that might enhance their overall positions.

The western side of the Pearl River Delta region, in particular, is viewed as an area with significant underdeveloped potential in tourism. With its low-cost land, golf facilities, and natural hot spring resources, the western side has the potential to help meet the region's growing demand for an open-area recreation belt within reach of the main urban centres. Better linkages between Hong Kong and the western side of the Delta, including the bridge link planned between Hong Kong, Macao, and Zhuhai, could help realise this potential.

FUTURE COMBINATIONS AND COMPETITIVENESS

The nature of the combinations and competitiveness within the Greater Pearl River Delta region will evolve considerably in the future. The evolving division of labour among jurisdictions in the region is creating more variety and more choice for investors, sourcing agents, and other firms. The overall picture is a region likely to retain its present advantages while adding new advantages and overcoming traditional obstacles. Thus we would expect the complementarity and combinations to enhance the competitiveness of the region in its existing industries and to allow it to become far more competitive in new industries than has been the case. However, there are a number of issues that the region will have to face if it is to take full advantage of its potential. These issues are the subject of the next chapter.

CHAPTER NINE

Issues for the Greater Pearl River Delta Region

T he previous chapter indicates that there is enormous potential for the Greater Pearl River Delta region to extend its position as one of the world's most dynamic economic regions. However, there are a number of issues that the region faces that could influence its future development. These stem from its rapid growth, its political administration, obstacles to economic interaction, competition from other regions in China, and aspects of China's geopolitical relations. While none of these issues is likely to fundamentally alter a bright economic future, each has the potential to slow the region's rate of growth and affect the ultimate levels of wealth that it will generate.

CHALLENGES OF RAPID GROWTH

The Greater Pearl River Delta region faces many challenges arising from the rapid growth of the region. The pace of development has placed strains on the infrastructure, the environment, and public services in Guangdong Province.

Some of these issues, particularly the environment, have become a concern in Macao and Hong Kong as well.

Electrical power

One vital area of infrastructure that has shown signs of strain in the Pearl River Delta region is electrical power. In 1999, China put an end to guaranteed fixed returns that had attracted foreign investors into the energy sector, which given the long-term nature of the investments involved, placed a damper on flows of foreign capital into the sector. Meanwhile, low estimates of demand for power resulted in insufficient indigenous investment in new projects nationwide. As the economy of the Pearl River Delta region took off, its power infrastructure simply did not keep up.[1]

Guangdong Province's power requirement for 2004 was forecast at 232.5 billion kilowatt hours, a 15% increase from 2003.[2] Export-oriented manufacturing is an important driver of demand. In 2003, Dongguan, with a population in the order of 6.5 million, but with vast export-oriented production, consumed more power than Guangzhou, with a population of around 10 million. Shenzhen's electricity consumption was up 27.8% in the first quarter of 2004 over the same period in 2003, again driven by expanding factory output.[3] The gap between local demand and local supply was expected to be at least 29.5 billion kilowatt hours in 2004 and was widening.[4] In the first three months of 2004, there were as many instances where power shortages forced firms to alter production schedules as occurred in all of 2003.[5] In February 2004, Guangzhou Honda was the first multinational firm to confirm that its local operations were being affected by power shortages.[6] By spring 2004, other foreign investors in the Pearl River Delta region were reporting that power shortages were placing their 24/7 operations at risk.[7] By one estimate, about 30% of Guangdong Province was experiencing power cuts of one or two days per week.[8]

In the short run, Guangdong is expected to buy power from other mainland provinces and Hong Kong to fill the gap.[9] In the longer run, Guangdong is planning to build China's largest nuclear power plant in Yangjiang, an eight million kilowatt–US$8 billion facility to come on stream starting in 2006, and two additional nuclear reactors at Daya Bay.[10] Guangdong is also building two large hydroelectric power plants and has asked the Central Government for a larger share of electricity from the Three Gorges Dam.[11] In addition, there are signs that private investment from Hong Kong may be picking up, both Cheung Kong Infrastructure and Hopewell Holdings indicating interest in new investments in the sector in Guangdong.[12] In any case, Guangdong will face the challenge of ensuring sufficient power for its future development.

The environment

Environmental degradation in the Pearl River Delta region has been a product of very rapid development. This area now has far more people and business activity than it has ever had in the past, and growth has been very rapid.[13] Fragmented jurisdictions, low levels of development (in Guangdong), and differing priorities have hindered efforts to improve the environment. Recognising the importance of environmental issues, the Hong Kong/Guangdong Joint Working Group on Sustainable Development and Environmental Protection, established in 1999, has set up expert groups and special panels to consider specific issues of environmental protection and sustainable development requiring cooperation between Hong Kong and Guangdong.

Air pollution is a serious issue affecting health and business throughout the Greater Pearl River Delta region. Air pollution from the heart of the manufacturing areas of the Pearl River Delta region, the source of 80% of the region's air pollution, affects Hong Kong and Macao as well.[14] Major polluters include power plants, cement plants, factories, and vehicles. While the Nan Ling Mountains to the north of the Pearl River Delta shield the region from air pollution from further north in China, they also serve to trap local emissions inside the region, especially during the winter months.[15] In 2003, the number of hours during which air pollution was classed as 'very high' in Hong Kong hit a record of 602 hours, more than double the number of hours in 2002.[16] A joint study by Hong Kong and Guangdong predicted in 2002 that as a result of growing economic activity, unless action is taken, by 2010 sulphur dioxide emissions would increase by 53%, nitrogen oxide and respirable suspended particles each by 34%, and volatile organic compounds by 25%.[17]

In 2002, a joint Hong Kong–Guangdong study set targets for the reduction of major air pollutants from 1997 levels, by between 20% and 55% by 2010.[18] To achieve these targets, the two governments are drawing up a regional air quality management plan that will specify measures to be implemented by either side.[19] Regional cooperation also is under way on a pilot air emissions trading scheme for power plants, to be launched in 2006 or later.[20] In 2004, officials in Guangzhou announced targets for ecological improvement and have stipulated that all projects will be tested for their impact on the environment. Specific targets include: using LNG and LPG rather than coal, curbing increasing population numbers, developing a transport network in the city area, which will include new expressways, but with focus on rail transport.[21] Guangdong is making progress in reducing sulphur dioxide emissions from large, coal-burning power plants. In Hong Kong, locally generated particulates have been reduced since measures were introduced in 1999 to encourage taxi drivers to switch to cleaner fuel, though as of 2004 efforts to bring about similar change in its minibus fleet have encountered resistance.

The growth of heavy industry in the Pearl River Delta – including large investments in steel, petrochemicals, and auto-making around Guangzhou – is likely to result in new emissions even as emissions from Guangdong's larger power plants are reduced. As a result of power shortages, older, smaller power plants that had been shut down because of environmental concerns were back in operation in 2004 with a detrimental impact on air quality. The region's expanding highway infrastructure and rapid growth in the number of vehicles point to a future increase in vehicular emissions. As of 2004, there were mounting calls in the Greater Pearl River Delta region to hasten the pace of cross-border cooperation to help control future emissions.

Water resources and pollution in the Greater Pearl River Delta region also are pressing issues. Hong Kong, Shenzhen, Dongguan, and Huizhou all draw fresh water from the upper reaches of the Dongjiang River, a Pearl River tributary.[22] The Pearl River and its tributaries are subject to pollution from industrial, human, and animal waste. While the Pearl River Delta region represents less than 6.7% of the greater Pearl River water system, which extends across the provinces of Yunnan, Guizhou, Guangxi, and Guangdong, it discharges nearly 55% of the system's total sewage.[23] In 2001, Guangzhou treated only 23% of its sewage output into the Pearl River, Foshan 24%, and Shenzhen 50 per cent.[24] In a study conducted in 2001, one-quarter of the drinking water sources in Guangdong Province tested at levels suitable only for industrial use.[25] The entire region, including Hong Kong, may face a fresh water shortage by 2012 unless effective action is taken.[26]

In October 2002, Guangdong announced plans to spend US$5.3 billion over eight years to clean up the Pearl River, to build more than 160 waste-water processing plants, and to raise the portion of urban sewage receiving treatment to 60%.[27] In March 2004, Guangdong Province announced that it would implement 120 projects in the areas of water supply and treatment, waste treatment, pollution prevention, and the protection of the rural environment.[28] Local jurisdictions such as Guangzhou, Shenzhen, and Dongguan have devoted funds to tackling the problem as well.[29] Guangzhou has ordered several polluting plants to close and instituted strict rules in place for other enterprises that discharge waste.[30] Dongguan will spend US$700 million on sewage treatment projects by 2010.[31] Hong Kong faces significant challenges of its own. As of 2004, Hong Kong processed about 70% of its wastewater, and completion of the city's controversial water treatment system was expected within 10 to 15 years.[32]

Despite the steps that have been taken, the Greater Pearl River Delta region will continue to face environmental challenges. Further economic growth is likely to result in more factories, more people, and more sources of pollution in the region. Even if individual factories, plants, or vehicles become cleaner, an expansion in their numbers may result in worse pollution than has been the case to date. This makes education about the detrimental impact of environmental degradation and enforcement of environmental legislation even more important than it might be otherwise.

Public services

The growth of the Pearl River Delta has created challenges across a broad range of public services, including public safety, traffic control, health care, mass transit, and education. Urbanisation is continuing at a rapid pace. In 2004, Guangdong Province announced plans to bring more than eight million people from the countryside into the cities by 2010.[33] Under this plan, the urban population of the province would rise from 55% in 2004 to 65% in 2010, while the urban population of the Pearl River Delta region would rise to 80%. The plan intends to expand Guangdong's social security and medical insurance networks to cover more than 60% and 50% of the province's population, respectively. The government also plans to improve urban infrastructure and utilities.

Investment in public services has lagged behind population growth in several of the Pearl River Delta's leading cities. For some budget items, like police and water supply, resources from the Central Government have been allocated on the basis of registered population rather than actual population. In Shenzhen, for example, the city's population expanded from 321,000 people in 1980 to more than seven million people in 2003. This expanding population has been placing pressure on public services including transportation, infrastructure, education, and public safety.[34] In Shenzhen, only 1.4 million persons out of Shenzhen's total population were registered residents in 2003. The result, as one local party leader has described it, has been policemen for 1.4 million people trying to keep order for more than seven million.[35] Dongguan has faced similar issues.

Historically, mass transit in the Pearl River Delta region lagged behind economic growth. However, as of 2004 mass transit was receiving a series of ambitious investments. The 600-kilometre Pearl River Delta high-speed rail network will extend from Shenzhen to Guangzhou to Zhuhai, linking most of the region's major cities, dramatically improving mass transit, and bringing the region much closer together. The high-speed rail line, which may start operation as early as 2007, will reduce travel time from Guangzhou to Zhuhai from 2.5 hours to 48 minutes.[36] Other lines will be completed in phases, with the entire network scheduled for completion by 2020. In addition, the Guangdong Railway

Group Corp. in consultation with the Hong Kong government is planning a high-speed Guangzhou–Hong Kong railway, which should reduce the two-hour journey to less than one hour.[37] At the city level, Guangzhou hopes to add five subway lines to the existing two subway lines in operation as of 2004 before 2010. The Shenzhen subway under construction in 2004 will eventually have 18 stations and will link to Hong Kong at two Shenzhen–Hong Kong border checkpoints.[38]

Education

If the Greater Pearl River Delta region is going to step up its level of development, it will have to improve its various education systems. The Pearl River Delta's ability to attract highly educated people from elsewhere in China will be critical to the further development of its technology-based industries. Shenzhen's Tenth Five-year Plan (2001–05) calls for attracting 300,000 skilled professionals from China and abroad. However, Shenzhen, realising that it must also further develop tertiary education, is doing so through collaboration with some of China's top universities, including Beijing University, Harbin Institute of Technology, and Qinghua University.[39] More than 30 universities have set up R&D activities in Shenzhen in order to take advantage of the city's technical workforce and access to commercialisation capabilities and finance from Hong Kong. Zhuhai has set up a university city to which it plans to attract branch facilities from leading Chinese and foreign universities. Hong Kong universities also have set up research operations in the Pearl River Delta region, and increasingly are cooperating with Pearl River Delta-based universities. Even so, the universities of the Pearl River Delta region are not considered on par with those in eastern or northern China when it comes to research capabilities or in the training of a technological workforce.

Hong Kong faces its own challenges. Only around a quarter of the relevant age cohort in its territory attends any form of tertiary education, less than half the level of places like Taiwan and South Korea, and behind less affluent economies like Thailand and Malaysia. It is hard to imagine that Hong Kong will be able to reach its full potential in a knowledge-based economy without a substantial expansion of tertiary education. However, in the face of government budget deficits, Hong Kong's tertiary education has been subject to steep funding cuts.

Quality of life

One of the major attractions for the mobile professionals that are becoming increasingly important to the Greater Pearl River Delta region is quality of life.

Relatively little attention has been focused on quality of life in the rush to develop. This is starting to change. Nowhere is this more apparent than in Guangzhou, which is trying to improve its image as it bids to host the 2010 Asian Games. As of April 2004, Guangzhou is launching an ambitious plan to improve the city's quality of life and living environment. More than US$3 billion in public spending will be allocated to 'key projects' to include water and waste treatment, a garbage incineration plant, three new medical service facilities, an opera house, a city library, and extensive urban green areas.[40] More than US$400 million will be spent on landscaping alone in an urban beautification program aimed to impress visitors 'from the very moment they set foot in Guangzhou'.[41] If its bid for the 2010 Asian Games is successful, Guangzhou would invest another US$725 million in developing sports facilities, including construction of 10 new competition venues and an Asian Games Village.[42]

Dongguan's Songshan Lake development project is designed to combine high-technology investment with a setting that will be attractive to mobile professionals. Zhuhai is trying to promote itself as a 'garden city' that will have many of the amenities, and fewer of the drawbacks of other cities. Macao is trying to develop into a family-oriented destination and is trying to build on its Chinese and European heritages to provide a unique lifestyle in the region. Hong Kong plans a large cultural centre to be housed in West Kowloon near existing museums and concert halls. Hong Kong also has reduced restrictions on al fresco dining to try to add to the dining experiences available in the Special Administrative region (SAR).

Growing pains

The Greater Pearl River Delta region has exhibited growing pains. The resulting challenges in terms of power, the environment, public services, education, and quality of life will require change and progress throughout the region. In many ways, this is a matter of playing catch up with rapid growth and preparing for future development. However, given the growing affluence of the region, the resources necessary to undertake several of the challenges are available, as can be seen in the massive investments taking place in the power and transportation sectors. The question is what priorities the jurisdictions in the regions decide to focus upon in the coming years.

POLITICAL ADMINISTRATION

The political administration of the Greater Pearl River Delta region is among the most complex found anywhere in the world. The Greater Pearl River Delta region contains one province, one provincial capital, two special administrative regions, two special economic zones, many cities, and multiple development areas. The multiple jurisdictions create substantial complexity in coordination around the region. At the same time, the 'one country, two systems' framework that govern Hong Kong and Macao provide distinctive and perhaps unique challenges for China. Finally, the multiple jurisdictions create informational challenges that were highlighted in the SARS crisis in 2003.

Multiple jurisdictions and complex decision-making

To the uninitiated, the multiple jurisdictions present in the Greater Pearl River Delta region can make identifying the right potential partner or even regulator difficult. There are several other manifestations of the complexity. One is the duplication of investments and infrastructure.[43] The region has five major airports, in Guangzhou, Hong Kong, Macao, Shenzhen, and Zhuhai. The result has been dramatically unused capacity, particularly at Zhuhai airport. Another manifestation has been the potential conflicting development of multiple ports around the region, and the multiple ports already operating around the region in Chiwan, Gaolan, Guangzhou, Hong Kong, Shekou, and Yantian. Another manifestation is duplicative investments in science and technology parks in nearly every major jurisdiction in the Greater Pearl River Delta region.[44] The concern is that jurisdictions will over-invest in competing projects that will eventually lead to destructive competition.

Multiple jurisdictions make coordinating planning around the Greater Pearl River Delta region extremely difficult.[45] There have been a number of meetings between officials from the region and China's National Development and Reform Commission (NDRC) on coordinating infrastructure development in order to reduce duplication of investments. The goal is to take full advantage of existing infrastructure. The NDRC also has committees studying coordination among the ports, airports, and other infrastructure development. Despite the involvement of the NDRC, it remains difficult to coordinate activities in the Greater Pearl River Delta region. Although in theory the NDRC must approve large projects that involve the Chinese mainland, in reality the decentralisation program has moved much infrastructure planning to provincial or local governments. The NDRC does act as a gatekeeper, but one that hesitates to intervene too heavily in local plans.[46]

Multiple jurisdictions make coordination in areas such as the environment, law enforcement, and financial regulation potentially problematic. Law enforcement agencies have found it challenging to mount effective responses to the rising tide of cross-border crime in Hong Kong and Macao that has been facilitated by the freer movement of people across the border, including vice syndicate activities, drug trafficking, and economic crimes. As of 2003, police authorities from the Guangdong, Hong Kong, and Macao were pursuing greater coordination in response to cross-border crime.[47] In terms of financial regulation, Chinese companies that are listed on the Hong Kong Stock Exchange are subject to the discipline of Hong Kong securities laws and regulations, but it can be difficult to enforce judgements against firms in the mainland, or in some cases, to even obtain adequate information on the activities of mainland companies. In one well-publicised case, a Hong Kong investigative team engaged by a multinational firm seeking a partner in China checked out a US$12.5 million highway construction firm in Guangdong Province to find that the firm existed only on paper.[48]

Obstacles associated with multiple systems

The political circumstances in the Greater Pearl River Delta region also create obstacles to closer economic interaction. The 'one country, two systems' formula under which Hong Kong and Macao were returned to Chinese administration was designed as a practical solution, given the different states of development of Hong Kong and Macao on the one hand, and the Chinese mainland on the other. However, the 'two systems' aspect does create some obstacles to closer interaction, including border crossings, customs checks, and the inconvenience involved in dealing with both. Hong Kong and Macao firms are treated as foreign firms in the Chinese mainland, reducing their ability to participate in some sectors of the Pearl River Delta region economy, particularly making it difficult for Hong Kong or Macao-based firms or offices to provide services to the surrounding area the way most major commercial cities elsewhere in the world do. Tourists from the Chinese mainland still face restrictions when going to Hong Kong or Macao.

In addition, the 'two systems' formula historically made it difficult for highly skilled or qualified people from the Chinese mainland to work in Hong Kong or Macao. This has limited the two cities' ability to attract the senior management activities of firms from the Pearl River Delta region and makes it difficult, though not impossible, for Pearl River Delta firms to use Hong Kong or Macao as platforms for international operations. The 'two systems' formula has also made it less likely that people from Hong Kong or Macao will move to the Pearl River Delta region to take up jobs that might be appropriate to their skill levels. Although in recent years there has been much more flexibility in this regard, the different systems result in a far less fluid situation than is the case in most cities.

Substantial progress is being made on reducing the obstacles to interaction due to the separate systems in place in Hong Kong, Macao, and the Pearl River Delta region. China's WTO accession and CEPA are fostering much greater inter- action as are reduced restrictions on tourists from the Chinese mainland to Hong Kong. Finally, reforms of Hong Kong's immigration scheme have allowed talented individuals from the Chinese mainland to work in Hong Kong under provisions similar to those that had been in place for people from elsewhere in the world.

Political challenges of 'One Country, Two Systems'

The 'one country, two systems' formulas have created political and administra- tive problems as well, particularly in Hong Kong. Under this arrangement, Hong Kong is to be administered according to the principles set out in the Sino–British Joint Declaration of 1984 and the 'Basic Law of the Hong Kong Special Adminis- trative Region of the People's Republic of China'. Aside from foreign affairs and defence, the provisions of the Basic Law give Hong Kong substantial autonomy over its own affairs.[49] It provides a framework, within the 'one country, two systems' parameters, for the protection of individual rights and freedoms, as well as for increasing democratisation and moving towards direct elections. While the Basic Law indicates that the ultimate goal is for Hong Kong's Chief Executive and Legislative Council to be elected by universal suffrage, it contains no provisions as to the timetable for this to occur.

In 1997, the Chief Executive was chosen by a 400-person Selection Committee nominated by a 150-member Preparatory Committee picked by Beijing. The Selection Committee also selected the members of the Provisional Legislative Council. In 1998, an expanded electoral committee of 800 persons was selected by a variety of organisations, associations, and business groups. In 1998, 20 members of the Legislative Council (Legco) were chosen by direct election in geographic constituencies with a multiple representative propor- tional system designed, according to many, to limit the number of seats that would be won by pro-democracy forces. Thirty members were returned by 'func- tional constituencies', electorates representing different business or occupa- tional groups. These included, among others, accountancy; agriculture and fisheries; architectural, surveying and planning; commercial; education; engi- neering; finance; financial services; health services; import and export; indus- trial; information technology; insurance; labour; legal; medical; real estate and construction; textiles and garment; tourism; and wholesale and retail sectors, as well as the Urban and Regional Councils. Ten members were chosen by the 800-member Election Committee. In 2000, 24 members of Legco were returned from geographic constituencies, 30 from functional constituencies, and six by the 800-member Election Committee.[50] In 2002, the Election Committee named Tung Chee-hwa for a second term as Chief Executive.

The Basic Law leaves most political power in Hong Kong in the hands of the Chief Executive. While the Hong Kong government can introduce Bills, individual legislators cannot introduce Bills without the permission of the Chief Executive. Although it is not stipulated in the Basic Law, the Legislative Council, under urging from the Hong Kong Government, has adopted a rule that resolutions can only pass if they are supported by a majority of two groups of legislators, one group encompassing those returned from geographical constituencies and the other encompassing those returned from the functional constituencies and by the Electoral Committee. The only real power of Legco is the ability to reject the budget. But then the Chief Executive can dissolve the Legislative Council and call for new elections.

In 2003, the Hong Kong Government attempted to force through an unpopular national security law. According to Article 23 of the Basic Law, 'the Hong Kong Special Administrative Region shall enact laws on its own to prohibit any act of treason, secession, sedition, subversion against the Central People's Government, or theft of state secrets, to prohibit foreign political organisations or bodies from conducting political activities in the Region, and to prohibit political organisations or bodies of the Region from establishing ties with foreign political organisations or bodies.'[51] While there was widespread acknowledgement of this requirement in Hong Kong, the version introduced by the Hong Kong Government was viewed as a potential threat to civil liberties by a significant portion of the population. On 1 July 2003, more than 500,000 people took to the streets in Hong Kong to protest against the proposed legislation. The protest was peaceful, and the legislation was shelved after key political parties indicated that they would not support the Bill. The demonstrations shocked the Hong Kong Government and the Central Government in Beijing. Both tried to shift attention away from political issues by focusing on economic issues, such as CEPA, to improve economic conditions in Hong Kong and lend support to the government under Chief Executive Tung Chee-hwa.

However, calls for direct election of the Chief Executive and the Legislative Council by universal suffrage, and fears that pro-Hong Kong government and pro-Beijing political parties would lose ground in the 2004 Legco elections, prompted the Central Government to step in. In April 2004, the Standing Committee of the National People's Congress, which has the ultimate power to interpret the Basic Law, made the decision that Hong Kong's Chief Executive would not be returned by universal suffrage in 2007. It further decided that, in electing the Legislative Council in 2008, universal suffrage shall not apply to the election of all Council members and that 'the half by half ratio for members of the council from functional groups and from constituency election shall remain unchanged.' It further decided that specific methods for selecting the Chief Executive in 2007 and forming the Legislative Council in 2008 could be modified within the principles of 'gradual and orderly progress' and in accordance with the Basic Law.[52]

Public opinion in Hong Kong appeared to split into two separate groups, one of which termed the Standing Committee's intervention as unnecessary and outside of the Basic Law, the other termed the intervention as necessary for Hong Kong's stability and within the Basic Law. It was clear that the relatively hands-off approach of the Central Government that had characterised relations with Hong Kong from 1997 to 2004 had been replaced by more active intervention. As of mid-2004, it was unclear what form the political discussion in Hong Kong would take and how it would influence relations between Hong Kong and Beijing, as well as the economies of the Greater Pearl River Delta region. Should governments around the world conclude that the autonomy of Hong Kong or Macao had been eroded, they could start treating Hong Kong and Macao as just parts of the Chinese mainland. This could have a severe impact on trade, investment, visa conditions, and other linkages between Hong Kong, Macao, and the rest of the world.

Information flows and public health

Southern China has had a substantial impact on global public health. For example, the region is the point of origin for many of the influenza strains that affect humans. Influenza strains usually originate in wild fowl whose migratory pathways bring them in close proximity to domesticated fowl and poultry on South China farms. Avian influenza strains usually cannot be passed on directly to humans, but often can be transmitted to pigs. In some cases, these strains can mutate and be passed on to humans. South China, with its unique co-location and dense populations of wild fowl, domesticated fowl and poultry, pigs (often raised on the same farms as domesticated fowl and poultry), and humans living in close proximity to the animals, is a unique source of influenza strains.

In 2002 and 2003, South China became known for another virus. Severe Acute Respiratory Syndrome (SARS) emerged in Guangdong Province in late

2002. The disease did not achieve global attention until after it reached Hong Kong in February 2003. A mainland doctor who had been treating SARS patients at a Guangzhou hospital became infected and carried the disease to Hong Kong's Metropole Hotel, where it spread to unsuspecting hotel guests and visitors via corridors and lift lobbies. Within days, the disease had been transmitted to Vietnam, Canada, Singapore, and Taiwan. A woman who unwittingly contracted the disease on 21 February 2003 at the Metropole Hotel travelled from Hong Kong to Toronto, Canada, two days later, starting a chain of infections that would make Toronto the epicentre of the largest outbreak of SARS outside Asia, resulting in some 43 deaths in Canada.[53] Before the disease ran its course in 2003, SARS had spread to 29 countries around the world, infecting nearly 8,100 individuals and resulting in 774 deaths.[54] Locations with the highest numbers of cases were the Chinese mainland (5,327 cases), Hong Kong (1,755 cases), Taiwan (346), Canada (251), Singapore (248), and Vietnam (63).

International travel to Asia fell dramatically, affecting the tourism, airline, and hotel industries. In late April 2003, at the height of the outbreak, tourist arrivals in Hong Kong were down by 70%. Cathay Pacific, Hong Kong's flag airline carrier, had suspended 45% of its services.[55] Hong Kong hotel occupancy rates were only 10% to 20% overall, with some of Hong Kong's best known five-star hotels at or near zero occupancy. Singapore registered a 71% drop in tourist arrivals in May 2003, while Singapore Airlines' passenger numbers fell by 30%.[56] In Beijing, overseas tourist arrivals were down by 47% for the first half of 2003 on a year-on-year basis, for US$650 million in losses over a six-month period.[57] Taiwan, also hard hit, lost an estimated US$350 million in revenues from overseas visitors in April and May 2003.[58] Thailand, with nine cases of SARS, saw international visitor arrivals fall by around 40% at the height of the outbreak.

As SARS showed, the same flows of people and goods that create opportunities also bring new risk of disease transmission.[59] SARS brought under the spotlight numerous challenges that will have to be faced in an effective public health response to infectious diseases in the region. In Guangdong Province, these include a historical lack of resources and manpower, the need to develop electronic information systems in public health administration, and the uneven development of the public health care system between large cities, towns, and rural areas. In Hong Kong, challenges include improving lines of authority and communication within government, ensuring greater accountability for infectious disease control, and the upgrading of medical facilities and equipment. In addition, there is the ongoing issue of differences between Hong Kong and the mainland on free information flows and the role of the media.[60]

Finally, the SARS crisis pointed out the shortcomings of information flows within the Greater Pearl River Delta region. According to an expert review panel on SARS, neither the Hong Kong Department of Health nor international bodies could get access to accurate and timely information from the Chinese mainland during the early stages of the outbreak in late 2002 and early 2003, before SARS spread into Hong Kong from Guangdong Province. The release of accurate and timely information might have 'ameliorated' the spread of the disease.[61] Only after the Hong Kong Department of Health raised the matter with the Ministry of Health in Beijing did the Guangzhou Health Bureau conduct its first press conference. As the outbreak worsened, health authorities of the Greater Pearl River Delta region stepped up communication, cooperation, and exchanges on infectious disease control. By August 2003, there had been pledges of improved cooperation and a team of Guangdong health officials had visited Hong Kong to study the use of information technology systems. Health authorities from Guangdong, Hong Kong, and Macao agreed to expand the scope of information exchange to 'all notifiable diseases within their own jurisdictions' and to report to each other immediately in case of emergency. In September 2003, health authorities from Guangdong, Hong Kong, and Macao set up a monthly exchange of information on infectious diseases in an effort to expand cross-border cooperation. The following month, a Guangdong health official announced that Guangdong was 'ready to work with Hong Kong' and that a new, cross-border infectious diseases surveillance system had been set up to enable Guangdong health officials 'to talk to Hong Kong officials quickly' in the event that the disease returns.[62]

Despite this progress, cross-border exchange of health data continues to pose challenges. In January 2004, an outbreak of SARS occurred in Guangdong Province with four confirmed patients. According to the WHO, the Chinese Ministry of Health did not report the first of these SARS cases until the day after the first patient was discharged from hospital.[63] Hong Kong authorities and the public were not informed about the last case until six days after the case was confirmed as SARS, despite several inquiries from Hong Kong health officials.[64] In February 2004, China's Ministry of Health announced that it will issue regular bulletins on a number of infectious diseases, including SARS, 'as it seeks to allay concerns about a lack of transparency'.[65] However, Hong Kong officials reportedly were told by counterparts in Guangdong not to discuss reports of infectious disease in Guangdong Province 'without official approval.'[66] When an outbreak of H56N1 avian flu occurred in early 2004, Guangdong requested Hong Kong's help in training health workers to deal with the disease in humans, Hong Kong hospitals having experience with several human cases of avian flu in 1997.[67] Attitudes towards the media, however, continued to lag. A senior

Guangdong official threatened to prosecute Hong Kong reporters under mainland laws for allegedly spreading unfounded reports about avian flu in the province.[68]

Within the Greater Pearl River Delta region, in addition to the initiatives already mentioned, efforts are being made to set up working links and networks between Hong Kong public health professionals and their colleagues in Guangdong, and to set up exchanges of professional, hospital, and technical staff within the Pearl River Delta region, and health monitoring efforts are being stepped up at cross-border check points.[69] It is hoped that greater cooperation on matters such as disease surveillance and information exchange will promote overall cooperation going forward.[70] While significant progress has been made, even more will be needed, especially in cross-border communication and information flows.

Complexity in a multi-jurisdictional region

The mixture of systems that exist in the Greater Pearl River Delta region is unique worldwide. While this mixture has been an important source of strength, particularly as China gradually opens to the rest of the world, it creates a variety of administrative and practical problems. The process of political, administrative, and planning interaction among the different jurisdictions, in some cases with widely divergent systems and histories, and between the individual jurisdictions and the Central Government in Beijing, will take time to work out. Different parts of the region will have to learn how to best position themselves to optimise their own position, as well as that of the region. Issues of coordination and information flows have become complex, particularly in a region characterised by very open information flows in some jurisdictions and limited information flows in others.

COMPETITION AMONG REGIONS IN CHINA

The Greater Pearl River Delta region is not the only region in China. While the Greater Pearl River Delta region benefited from its position in the vanguard of China's reform program, other regions have emerged as well. The success of the Pearl River Delta region inspired further change and reform that spread to Shanghai and the Yangtze River Delta in the 1990s, the western provinces in the late 1990s, and Beijing and the north-east in the early 2000s.[71] The result has been an inevitable decline in the share of the Pearl River Delta region in some of China's economic aggregates over the last few years, while its absolute position remains very strong.[72]

Competition with the Yangtze River Delta region

The region most frequently compared to the Pearl River Delta Economic Zone is the Yangtze River Delta region. Unfortunately, most of the comparisons of the two regions are inappropriate. Despite the fact that there is an official definition of a 'Yangtze River Delta Economic Zone' that consisted of Shanghai plus seven Zhejiang cities and seven Jiangsu cities in 2002, and then added another Jiangsu city in 2003, nearly all of the comparisons made by academics, economists, and analysts take Shanghai plus the entire provinces of Zhejiang and Jiangsu as the 'Yangtze River Delta', largely due to the fact that it is more difficult to put together the data for the proper definition than to just take provincial statistics. At the same time, the comparisons between regions tend to ignore Hong Kong and Macao, since they are not found in the 'Pearl River Delta Economic Zone' of Guangdong. The intensive interaction among Hong Kong, Macao, and the Pearl River Delta region means that not including Hong Kong and Macao along with the Pearl River Delta region would be like excluding Shanghai from the Yangtze River Delta region. As a result, most comparisons fail to give an accurate picture (see Tables 9.1 and 9.2).

Table 9.1 Defined Yangtze River Delta versus sum of Shanghai Municipality, Jiangsu Province, and Zhejiang Province

	Yangtze River Delta region	Sum of Shanghai Municipality, Jiangsu Province, and Zhejiang Province	YRD % of sum of city and two provinces
Land area (square kilometres)	100,200	210,741	47.55
Census population 2000 (million)	82.28	135.38	60.77
Registered population 2002 (million)	75.71	129.98	58.25
Total GDP (RMB billion)	1,912.50	2,383.65	80.23
Gross industrial output from enterprises with over 5 million RMB in sales (RMB billion)	2,688.83	3,138.55	85.67
Total trade (US$ billion)	175.22	184.93	94.75
Imports (US$ billion)	82.82	84.98	97.46
Exports (US$ billion)	92.40	99.95	92.44
Utilised FDI (US$ billion)	17.85	18.56	96.19
Retail sales of consumer goods (RMB billion)	624.69	812.86	76.85

Source: Enright and Scott June 2004
Data sources: Calculated from *Shanghai Statistical Yearbook 2003*, *Jiangsu Statistical Yearbook 2003*, *Zhejiang Statistical Yearbook 2003*, and statistical yearbooks 2003 of the respective jurisdictions using the China Statistical Bureau definition of Yangtze River Delta region

When more direct apples to apples comparisons are used, it is readily shown that the Greater Pearl River Delta region has a substantially larger GDP than the Yangtze River Delta, and that when the effects of trade and investment within Hong Kong, Macao, and the Chinese mainland are removed to get a clearer picture of trade and investment with the outside world, the Greater Pearl River Delta far outstrips the Yangtze River Delta. The point is that both regions are extremely important and that both need to be considered by major companies and by governments when they think about China.

According to analysts, the Yangtze River Delta region has a number of advantages over the Pearl River Delta region, including the size of population and economy, location, linkages between the region's main economic city and its hinterland, workforce capabilities, economic diversification, government support, image and profile, and the region's apparently unified development.[73]

While some of these perceptions are accurate, others are not. The population of the Greater Pearl River Delta region has been growing faster than the Yangtze River Delta region and the gap will close further once the western part of the Pearl River Delta region is linked better to the eastern part. The GDP of the Greater Pearl River Delta region was 22% greater than that of the Yangtze River Delta region in 2002. The location of the Yangtze River Delta region is favourable for serving the east–central portion of China, but the Pearl River Delta region is increasingly seen as a favourable location to serve China's southern and south-western provinces. The capabilities of the indigenous workforce in the Greater Pearl River Delta region may lag behind those found in the Yangtze River Delta region, but are supplemented by those attracted from all over China. The city with the most PhDs per capita in the Chinese mainland is not Shanghai, or Beijing, but Shenzhen. The image and reputation of Shanghai as a business centre exceeds that of Shenzhen or Guangzhou, both of which have higher per capita incomes than Shanghai according to official Chinese government statistics, but Hong Kong is still a city of strong international business standing.

At the same time, the Pearl River Delta region has several advantages of its own. These include its links with Hong Kong, its position in international trade and investment, its earlier experience with reform and development, its relatively flexible business environment and local government administration, the ability to attract skills and resources from around China, and the presence of embedded clusters of internationally successful industries.[74] All of these are likely to hold the Greater Pearl River Delta region in good stead as China continues to open and develop.

Although a large portion of the economies of the Greater Pearl River Delta region and the Yangtze River Delta region do not compete directly, in recent years there has emerged increasing competition between the two regions.

Table 9.2 Selected indicators, selected Chinese jurisdictions, 2002 (unless otherwise designated)

	PRD	Guangdong	Yangtze River Delta	China	Hong Kong	Macao	Greater PRD (PRD + HK + MA)
Land area (square kilometres)	40,165[a]	179,757	100,200	9,597,000	1,102	26.8	41,294[a]
Registered population 2002 (million persons)	23.65	76.49	75.71	1,284.53	6.79	0.44	30.88
Census (PRC) or actual (HK, Macao) population 2000 (million persons)[b]	40.77	85.23	82.28	1,265.83	6.73	0.44	47.94
GDP (US$ billion)	113.75	142.15	230.98	1,265.59	161.51	6.73	281.99
– Primary industry (%)	4.9%	8.8%	5.8%	15.4%	0.1%	–	2.0%
– Secondary industry (%)	49.8%	50.4%	51.9%	51.1%	12.4%	12.6%	27.5%
– Tertiary industry (%)	45.3%	40.8%	42.3%	33.5%	87.5%	87.4%[c]	70.6%
GDP per capita (US$)							
– Official 2002 (2001 for YRD)	4,142	1,815	2,722	988	23,797	15,356	–
– GDP 2002/registered population 2002	4,810	1,858	3,051	985	23,800	15,242	–
– GDP 2002/census population 2000	2,790	1,668	2,807	1,000	23,998	15,466	5,883
Real GDP growth rate 1980–2002	16.1%[d]	13.4%	12.5%[e]	9.5%	5.2%	4.9%	12.6%[d, e]
Real GDP growth rate 1990–2002	17.4%[d]	14.0%	13.5%[e]	9.7%	4.0%	3.1%	11.1%[d, e]
Retail sales of consumer goods (US$ billion)	42.05	60.55	75.45	494.09	22.67	0.65	65.37
Gross industrial output (US$ billion)[f]	170.6[a]	197.8	324.7	1,337.9	22.1	2.0	194.7[a]
Value added of gross industrial output (%)	26.30%	26.63%	25.62%	29.78%	31.00%	23.67%	26.80%[a, g]
Imports (US$ billion)	98.39[a]	102.63	82.81[h, i]	295.17	207.62	2.53	308.52[a, g]
Estimated imports from economies other than Hong Kong, Macao, China (US$ billion)			79.45[h, i]				151.83[i]
Exports (US$ billion)	111.55[a]	118.46	92.40	325.60	200.10	2.36	314.01[a, g]
Estimated exports to economies other than Hong Kong, Macao, China (US$ billion)			84.83[k, l]				160.13[m]
Utilised FDI (US$ billion)	11.62[n]	13.11	17.85	52.74	9.68	0.38	21.68[n, g]
Estimated utilised FDI from sources other than Hong Kong, Macao, China 2002 (US$ billion)			13.03[o]				11.39[n, p]

Notes:

(a) Calculated from base sources eliminating the portions of Huizhou and Zhaoqing not part of the official definition of the Pearl River Delta Economic Zone.

(b) The Fifth National Census for the Chinese mainland was carried out in 2000.

(c) Calculated from percentage of production-based GDP at current prices for 2002, less adjustment for financial intermediation services indirectly measured for the tertiary sector. Official figures for Macao's total GDP follow the expenditure approach.

(d) Real GDP for 1980, 1990, and 2002 for the PRD are derived from implicit deflators for Guangdong Province.

(e) Real GDP for 1980, 1990, and 2002 for YRD are derived from implicit deflators for Shanghai.

(f) The Chinese mainland jurisdiction's figures are for firms with > 5 million RMB in sales.

(g) Simple summation of figures from Hong Kong, Macao, and the PRD are used for the Greater Pearl River Delta region. Note that these figures include intra-regional trade and investment, so should be adjusted.

(h) YRD imports with imports from Hong Kong subtracted out for better comparability with (j). No YRD import figures from Macao available.

(i) YRD imports from Hong Kong with estimates for missing 2002 figures for Zhenjiang, Yangzhou, Taizhou, and Hangzhou.

(j) Greater PRD imports from economies other than Hong Kong, Macao, and China calculated for better comparability with (h). Total was calculated as (PRD total imports + HK total imports + Macao total imports) – (HK imports from China + 80% of HK exports to China + HK imports from Macao + Macao imports from HK + Macao imports from China + 80% of Macao exports to China). The 80% of HK's and Macao's exports to China was designed to estimate the imports into the Pearl River Delta region of the Chinese mainland from Hong Kong and Macao.

(k) YRD exports with exports to Hong Kong subtracted out for better comparability with (m). No YRD export figures from Macao available.

(l) YRD exports to Hong Kong with estimates for missing 2002 figures for Zhenjiang, Yangzhou, Taizhou, and Hangzhou.

(m) Greater PRD exports to economies other than Hong Kong, Macao, and China calculated for better comparability with (k). Total was calculated as (PRD total exports + HK total exports + Macao total exports) – (HK exports to China + 80% of HK imports from China + HK exports to Macao + Macao exports to HK + Macao exports to China + 80% of Macao imports from China). The 80% of HK's and Macao's imports from China was designed to estimate the exports of the Pearl River Delta region of the Chinese mainland to Hong Kong and Macao.

(n) The figure includes all of Zhaoqing and Huizhou, since data did not allow for a separation of the portions inside and outside the official definition of the Pearl River Delta Economic Zone.

(o) The Hong Kong and Macao portion of FDI into YRD was estimated from their respective portions of FDI into Shanghai, Jiangsu, and Zhejiang.

(p) Estimated by subtracting the Hong Kong and Macao source FDI into the PRD and the estimated Chinese portion of FDI into Hong Kong and Macao.

The exchange rates used in the table are 2002: US$1 = HK$7.8 = RMB 8.28 = MOP 8.033; 1990: US$1 = HK$7.8 = RMB 4.7832 = MOP 8.02; 1980: US$1 = HK$5.14 = RMB 1.5435 = MOP 6.27.

Source: Enright and Scott 2004

Data sources: Statistical Yearbooks of China, Guangdong, Shanghai, Zhejiang, Jiangsu, and local jurisdictions in Guangdong, Zhejiang, and Jiangsu; China Statistics Bureau, Jiangsu Statistics Bureau, Census and Statistics of Hong Kong, Statistics and Census of Macao, Hong Kong Trade Development Council. Estimates by M. J. Enright and E. E. Scott.

There are several aspects to this competition. One is competition for foreign direct investment. The Yangtze River Delta region is competing with the Greater Pearl River Delta region for foreign investment in light manufacturing, heavier manufacturing, technology-based businesses, and in parts of the service sector. The two regions also are competing in export markets and in the domestic market. To date, producers in the Greater Pearl River Delta region have obtained strong positions in the major advanced country markets. In contrast, the Yangtze River Delta region has been building up exports to developing nations. Increasingly, the two regions are beginning to compete in export markets. The two regions also have become the major producers for many manufactured goods for the entire Chinese mainland. As a result, they face increasing competition in the burgeoning local market as well. Hong Kong and Shanghai may see additional competition over the location of China management centres, as well as buying offices and logistics activities.

Complementarity

There is also a great deal of complementarity between the Greater Pearl River Delta region and the Yangtze River Delta region. In some instances, the two regions serve different market segments. In others, they serve different geographies. Given China's size and potential, there is clearly room for at least two major economic regions, if not several more. Investment by Hong Kong-based firms has been and continues to be an important driver of modernisation of the Chinese mainland's economy, including the Yangtze River Delta region. As of year-end 2002, Hong Kong was the leading source of foreign investment in Shanghai with US$16.2 billion in cumulative contracted foreign capital.[75] A growing Shanghai is good news for Hong Kong and vice versa.

While some analysts seem to believe that development in one part of China comes at the expense of other parts of China, nothing could be further from the truth. China's regions are major markets and major sources of investment for each other. Improvements in the prosperity of China's coastal regions has been a stimulus to the development of China's interior regions and China's coastal regions also have stimulated each other. In this way, the different regions in China will tend to bring each other along. In this context, shifts in attention of the Central Government to different regions over time is best understood as attempts to bring along the regions one by one, paying attention to those that need the most help and can benefit most at any particular time rather than favouring one region or a small set of regions at the expense of others. Given the issues that China still faces in developing its economy, any other way would have been very difficult at best.

Competition as an impetus to improvement

Competition among regions should provide a strong impetus for the different jurisdictions and interests in the Greater Pearl River Delta region to find ways of identifying and developing joint gains and of jointly facing future competition. It is far more likely that the Greater Pearl River Delta region will prosper if it finds ways to coordinate sufficient activities in order to meet the competition from the Yangtze River Delta region. This could include joint promotion, cooperation on infrastructure and the environment, the development of collaborative organisations across the Greater Pearl River Delta region, and a greater sense of regional identity. This dynamic is already in process.

In February 2004, the Greater Pearl River Delta Business Council was formed in Hong Kong, a council of heads of business and professionals directed at fostering closer economic cooperation within the Greater Pearl River Delta region. The Council is expected to complement the Hong Kong–Guangdong Co-operation Joint Conference.[76] In a separate development, the 'Pan–PRD region' initiative announced in February 2004 aims to merge nine mainland provinces in China's south and south–west along with the special administrative regions of Hong Kong and Macao into an integrated and competitive economic region. A forum and a trade fair will be jointly held later in 2004 to promote the region's cooperation and development.[77] Both initiatives have been inspired by the perceived need to strengthen the ability of the Greater Pearl River Delta to compete on a regional basis with other areas of China, in particular the Yangtze River Delta region. It is not necessarily clear that steps of this sort would have been taken without an external stimulus.

POTENTIAL OBSTACLES TO CHINA'S INTERNATIONAL ECONOMY

As the most internationally oriented part of China's economy, the Greater Pearl River Delta region would suffer if circumstances were to limit China's economic interaction with the rest of the world. The three areas with the highest likelihood of creating such limits are relations across the Taiwan Straits, the potential for protectionism against Chinese exports, and potential foreign attempts to impose particular labour and environmental standards on China.

Cross-straits relations

Relations across the Taiwan Straits have been the focus of innumerable analyses, which we do not plan to recount here.[78] Suffice it to say, that relations across the

Straits remain uncertain. The circumstances surrounding the Taiwanese presidential election in 2004 highlighted the salience of the 'Taiwan issue' to the PRC, to Taiwan, and to the international community. Much of the campaign revolved around cross-Straits relations. As the election approached, the KMT-led coalition of Lien Chen and James Soong, moved away from what was seen as a more pro-unification platform to one of emphasising the distinctiveness of Taiwan and the desirability of preserving Taiwan's separate system. Even so, there was no doubt that the leadership in Beijing preferred the KMT-led ticket to the DPP incumbent Chen Shui-bien, whose position in the polls was enhanced by an assassination attempt on the eve of the election. The closeness of the election, in which Chen was declared the winner by just 0.2% of the vote, the refusal of the KMT to accept the result, a recount, and the deep divisions within Taiwan over the whole affair reflected the overall sense of instability. When combined with the hundreds of missiles based on the Chinese mainland aimed at Taiwan, the fact that Beijing has not renounced the use of force to effect reunification, and the discussion of the enactment of a law that would call for an invasion of Taiwan if the latter declared independence, the election outcome heightened tensions. These tensions, in turn, have implications for China's relations with the United States and other countries.

On the other hand, there is some concern in the Greater Pearl River Delta region that should direct links between Taiwan and the Chinese mainland be instituted, Hong Kong and Macao might lose out as transit points for people and goods between Taiwan and the mainland. It has been estimated that direct air links could result in a reduction of Hong Kong's incoming visitors by 5% and a reduction of Hong Kong's total cargo throughput by 2%.[79] For Macao, direct links could result in loss of its role as an air transit point between Taiwan and the Chinese mainland, an important component of its air services. In reality, should direct links be instituted, they would probably be indicative of improved relations between Taiwan and the Chinese mainland that could only help enhance trade and investment throughout all parts of China.

Protectionism

China's growing success in export markets has created a potential backlash. Nowhere has this been more apparent than in the garments and textiles sector, where China's ability to capture market share in a limited number of product categories following its entry into the WTO has sparked a wide range of protectionist initiatives. In November 2003, the US Trade Representative (USTR) imposed a 'safeguard' quota on imports from China of brassieres, night gowns, and knit fabrics, in order to cap rising imports. As of early 2004, the European Commission was considering its own quotas on Chinese textile imports.

In the run-up to the 2004 US presidential elections, debates over the loss of US manufacturing jobs fostered growing protectionist sentiment in the United States. In 2004, the United States lodged its first complaint against China before the WTO over China's value-added tax on semiconductors. In early 2004, a coalition of US manufacturers, including textile producers, was preparing to petition the US Trade Representative to bring a challenge of China's exchange rate policy before the WTO. Though the US government appeared unlikely to do so, the initiative was indicative of the strength of protectionist sentiment among certain sectors of the US public.

During the period 2002–2004, numerous US antidumping actions were brought against Chinese imports on products including colour television receivers, ironing boards, wooden bedroom furniture, hand trucks, carbazole violet pigment, frozen and canned shrimp and prawns, tissue paper and crepe paper products, alloy magnesium, and circular welded line pipe. Under its WTO accession agreement, and at the insistence of the United States, China is considered a 'non-market' economy for purposes of anti-dumping investigations. That means that for purposes of determining an anti-dumping margin, US sales prices are not compared to sales prices in China, but instead to production costs in 'comparable market economies' in the Third World plus a presumed profit margin. The resulting costs of production determined in these cases often result in unfavourably high margins for the Chinese producers and exporters.

In one investigation into frozen crawfish tail meat from China, the US Department of Commerce selected India as the basis for calculating Chinese mainland production costs, despite the fact that India lacks a crawfish industry, and determined a dumping margin of more than 200%.[80] While a 'safeguard quota' on imports by the US Trade Representative, such as the cap on certain textiles and garments from China in November 2003, serves to limit the growth of imports, antidumping duty orders can effectively cut off import flows from China, depending on the case.[81] An antidumping duty order on imports from China of steel concrete reinforcing bars had the effect of reducing imports into the United States by 99.9% in the year following imposition of the order.[82] Following a preliminary finding of dumping by the US Department of Commerce in November 2003 that once again used India as a third country surrogate, Guangdong Province's monthly exports of colour television receivers fell from around 450,000 sets to 210,000 sets.[83]

Although protectionism in the United States is more widely publicised, the European Union has also been very active in restricting imports from China under antidumping and other measures. As of early 2004, EU antidumping cases involved a wide range of products from China, including colour television receivers, bicycles and bicycle parts, non-malleable cast iron, hand pallet trucks, and polyethylene terephthalate. Oxfam has found EU trade policies towards developing countries to be more protectionist than those of the United States, Canada, and Japan, a finding the European Commission disputes.[84]

Labour and environmental standards

Labour conditions within the Pearl River Delta are another by-product of very rapid economic growth. In rural areas across China, millions of unemployed or under-employed workers are willing to leave their homes and move to the Pearl River Delta region in search of employment. For many, their option is to remain on farms that barely provide subsistence or worse. For firms in the Pearl River Delta region, wages just above subsistence are sufficient to draw workers off the farm. The typical migrant is female, in her teens or early twenties, and aims to work in the Pearl River Delta region for a few years before returning to her place of origin. Working conditions vary greatly from firm to firm. Workers who are fortunate in finding placement with a socially responsible employer can achieve their savings goals within a few years. Less fortunate workers can find it difficult or impossible to get ahead. These factors have given rise to working conditions that are increasingly attracting the attention of international watchdog organisations. Issues run the gamut from wages to working hours, occupational safety and health, and the right to organise.

In electronics, firms in the Pearl River Delta region find it easy to meet their needs for unskilled or semi-skilled labour by relying on employment agencies to provide migrant workers. In Dongguan, the legal minimum wage is around US$54 per month and many migrant workers earn considerably less. A report issued in early 2004 by CAFOD found that in Dongguan many electronics workers on the production line earn about US$37 as a basic monthly wage. (In contrast, in early 2004, production line workers in Guadalajara, Mexico were earning about US$176 per month.[85]) In many instances, earning US$54 per month is possible only during peak season and requires massive amounts of overtime. During the peak season, work days of 15 or 16 hours, seven days per week, are common.[86] Factory workers reported low or non-existent levels of participation in factory decision-making and little or no awareness of Chinese labour laws or of their rights to organise.[87]

In toys, in 2001 an investigation of toy companies in Guangdong Province producing for major US distributors reported that work weeks of 90 hours or more were routine; the average production wage ranged between US$0.14 and US$0.19 per hour; and workers were denied as much as 75% of the wages owed under Chinese labour laws. Workers complained of health problems related to the handling of chemicals and other materials, in particular with respect to spray painting, but lacked access to basic information on the substances they were handling. They were not aware of the corporate Codes of Conduct of the major US toy companies where their output was destined.[88] Another series of reports has found 'persistent violations of Chinese Labor Law, the ILO (International Labor Organization) core labor standards as well as the ICTI Code of Business Practice' among mainland toy factories doing contract manufacturing for the world's leading toy labels.[89]

The protection of core labour standards in developing countries, including rights to a minimum wage, to organise, to bargain collectively, and to a limit on working hours, is increasingly emerging as a fair trade issue. In March 2004, the AFL–CIO filed a petition requesting the US Trade Representative to investigate China's labour practices and to impose special duties of up to 77% on imports from China. While the Bush Administration chose not to accept the petition, the world's attention is increasingly focused on labour conditions in China and in the Pearl River Delta. The coopting by management of a factory worker's efforts to organise a representative union in a foreign-owned sportswear factory in Shenzhen received detailed coverage in the *New York Times* in December 2003.[90] The growth of the international movement to strengthen the rights of workers in developing countries means that greater external pressure will be exerted on working conditions in China, including the Pearl River Delta region.

Issues in perspective

The Greater Pearl River Delta region faces many challenges. Rapid growth has created a need to catch up in many areas if the region's development is to be consolidated and extended. The region's unique combination of jurisdictions, with a variety of systems under a single sovereign creates many pressures that will have to be resolved over time. A lack of understanding across the region has the potential to exacerbate the challenges. What is striking, however, is that the region has progressed in the past and continues to progress despite these challenges. If anything, the issues identified in this chapter are better understood than they have been in the past. In addition, concrete steps are being taken in many of the areas. In many ways, the challenges and issues that the Greater Pearl River Delta region faces are forcing the different parts of the region to work together to a much greater extent than had been the case. It is these issues and challenges that may well forge a more unified region in the future.

CHAPTER TEN

The Greater Pearl River Delta Region in Perspective

Although managers, policymakers, and analysts all over the world have noted China's economic emergence, many of the features of this emergence remain largely uninvestigated. How, for example, did China, an economy cut off from the rest of the world for three decades, become such an economic power so quickly? How did Chinese firms understand the tastes and trends in markets so much more advanced than their own? How did Chinese firms understand and then reach world quality and cost standards? How did China develop the managerial, marketing, and technological capabilities to penetrate global markets? The answer is that when one looks at China as a whole, for the most part, China did not. Instead, it has been the Greater Pearl River Delta region that has led the way, particularly when it comes to China's rise as a trading nation. And within the Greater Pearl River Delta region, it has been Hong Kong, or foreign companies operating through Hong Kong, that have brought the capital, technology, market knowledge, and managerial capabilities that have combined with labour and resources from all over China that has allowed the region to achieve such international prominence.

The combinations found in the Greater Pearl River Delta region mean that the question of how facilities in other countries can compete with 'China' in export markets is actually not the right question, especially when 'China' is framed as a third world nation with a low overall level of development. Instead, in the case of the Greater Pearl River Delta region they are competing with the resources and labour of China, combined with first world-level knowledge of markets, finance, technology, and management from Hong Kong or based in Hong Kong. In industries in which this combination can be brought to bear, it is very difficult for others to compete. It is also very difficult for other developing economies to create a Hong Kong to foster interaction with the rest of the world. While the relative importance of Hong Kong roles in China's development is diminishing, the absolute magnitude of its contribution is actually increasing. This will be particularly true in the context of China's WTO accession process, CEPA, and China's continued reforms.

The Greater Pearl River Delta region already is making itself felt on a global scale. However, when one realises that only around half the region has been developed to any great extent, it clearly has the potential to become much more important in the future. As the western part of the Delta is developed and infrastructure throughout the region is improved, its population could well go from around 50 million people to 70 million or 75 million. This would be larger than the populations of the United Kingdom and France. Moreover, it is likely to attract the right population for the economy, in the form of skilled professionals, as the Pearl River Delta region is under-populated at present compared to the Yangtze River Delta and Bohai regions. The completion of new transport infrastructure, the emergence of the Pan-Delta Region of Hong Kong, Macao, and nine provinces in south and south-west China (Pan-Pearl River Delta 9+2), plus the formation of ASEAN+1 (or ASEAN+2) will very substantially add to the Greater Pearl River Delta region's reach and linkages. By 2002, the size of the Greater Pearl River Delta region's GDP already exceeded that of all but 16 national economies in the world. At present growth rates, it will continue to move up the charts quickly.

THE FUTURE ECONOMIC TRAJECTORY OF THE PEARL RIVER DELTA REGION

The economic trajectory of the Guangdong portion of the Greater Pearl River Delta region over the next decade will be characterised by modernisation, deepening and broadening of the industrial base, urbanisation, and greater openness. Modernisation will take place across several dimensions. Traditional industries will see an upgrading based on the incorporation of modern technologies into the design and production process. Modernisation also will take place in management and commercial activities. Management, strategic planning, control, accounting, and financial systems within many, if not most, Pearl River Delta region companies still leave a great deal to be desired. Improved management education, recruitment of professional managers, improvements in professional services, and a more modern regulatory system are all likely to contribute to better practices in the future. So too will competition among local firms and between local and foreign firms. Links with Hong Kong, with its relatively advanced management capabilities, could be crucial in upgrading the management systems found in the region.

The Pearl River Delta region is likely to have a much deeper and broader economy in the future as input, component, capital goods, and service industries rise to serve its industrial base. The electronics and telecommunications sectors and the electrical appliances and machinery sectors will continue to lead, but they will be joined by the chemical and transportation equipment sectors as principal engines of growth and development. Even traditional industries, such as garments and textiles, are likely to receive a boost with the abolition of the international quota regime. The Pearl River Delta region's logistics and trade-related service industries will also deepen with substantial new investments in ports, airports, transportation networks, and logistics centres. As skills and capabilities improve in the region, more and more corporate activities will be shifted into the Pearl River Delta region.

In addition, we would expect the supply base for inputs and components to expand substantially and to see far more in the way of capital goods for industry being produced in the region. As the local industrial base reaches a critical mass, it will become economically feasible to start producing capital equipment close to the customers. This has been the trend in all of the Asian economies that have started with relatively simple export processing. As a result, we would expect value added in industry to increase substantially over the next decade. Along with the deepening of the Pearl River Delta region economy, we would expect to see a broadening as well. As the industrial markets of the region grow, there will be demand for a higher volume and greater variety of materials and heavy industrial goods. The development in Nansha will spearhead heavy industrial development, particularly in steel and chemical facilities designed to supply the markets of South China.

Although the Pearl River Delta is strong in many industries, it faces challenges in terms of value-added mix, industrial congestion, and potentially fixed costs, land in particular. Opening up the western side via a bridge between Hong Kong, Macao, and Zhuhai will double the land base for export-oriented production. What we would expect is a substantial portion of the Pearl River Delta's lower end manufacturing to move to the western side of the Pearl

River Delta. This will allow Guangzhou, Shenzhen, and Dongguan to reduce congestion and facilitate movement up the technology and value-added ladder, while extending and strengthening the region's position in its traditional and new manufacturing sectors. Opening up the western side will also alleviate cost pressures in Guangzhou, Shenzhen, and Dongguan. It should further enable the region to enhance the sophistication of its economy by serving the local export sectors with components, capital goods, and support services.

THE FUTURE ECONOMIC TRAJECTORY OF HONG KONG

Increasingly, Hong Kong's economy is focused on high value-added, knowledge-intensive activities involving management, coordination, finance, information, market development, and business services.[1] These activities return more per person and more per square metre than other corporate activities. This is why they tend to be concentrated in the centres of major cities, particularly those that are relatively expensive in terms of wages and land costs. In essence, these are the activities that can justify the highest costs and the activities that tend to crowd out other activities (such as manufacturing) that do not return the same value per person or per square metre. These activities are consistent with Hong Kong's goal to become Asia's world city, a city that has regional or even global reach. Other world cities, such as New York and London, have overall economic profiles similar to that of Hong Kong. They are also consistent with a cost gradient between Hong Kong and its hinterland that is substantially greater than that found in other major commercial cities around the world.

Hong Kong's economic trajectory is likely to include an extension of its position as a regional base for multinational firms. Hong Kong has long been the leading centre for regional headquarters of such firms.[2] The main shift in recent years has been Hong Kong gaining share at the expense of Singapore. This has been due to the shift of investment and interest from South-east Asia to North-east Asia, the continued superiority of Hong Kong in infrastructure, clear and transparent rules and regulations, international access, and proximity to large markets. Since the Asian Crisis, major international financial service firms increasingly are concentrating Asian regional activities into Hong Kong. The main activities that foreign multinationals undertake and plan to undertake in Hong Kong reflect the managerial, financial, information, coordination, and market development activities that Hong Kong firms also perform there. As indicated earlier, Hong Kong companies tend to perform the highest value-added activities in Hong Kong and expect to continue to do so in the future.

The emergence of the Pearl River Delta region has allowed Hong Kong companies to decentralise many activities out of the Hong Kong SAR and into the surrounding areas. This is exactly the type of development that one would expect once the economies of Hong Kong and the Pearl River Delta region were allowed to interact. The result has been a narrowing of the activity base of Hong Kong's economy even as the economy has grown. While the activity base of Hong Kong's economy is likely to continue to narrow, it is likely to perform high value-added activities for a wider range of industries than has been the case in the past. Despite the extensive interaction between Hong Kong and the Chinese mainland in general, and the Pearl River Delta region in particular, what is striking is how limited this interaction is when compared to that between other major economic cities and their surroundings. China's entry into the WTO and the development of the Pearl River Delta region into a wider range of industries, including not just light manufacturing, but also heavier industries and services, will provide greater scope for high-value activities linking these industries to the rest of the world through Hong Kong. They also will provide additional impetus for foreign investment and the location of management activities for a wider range of multinational companies in Hong Kong. Thus Hong Kong is likely to perform high value-added managerial, financial, coordination, and information activities across more industries. It also is likely to perform these activities for a wider range of firms, including foreign multinationals interested in accessing the region and Chinese firms seeking to access international markets.

The inescapable conclusion is that Hong Kong's economy will narrow in terms of the activities that it performs. Hong Kong is likely to see the range of activities that it performs narrow to many of the highest value-added management, coordination, financial, and information activities, while the number of firms and the number of types of firms performing such activities is likely to expand significantly. This is not necessarily good or bad. In many ways, as the Chinese mainland in general and the Pearl River Delta region in particular progress and open, Hong Kong's economy will start to look more and more like those of other major economic cities around the world. These cities, be they New York, London, Chicago, Zurich, or Tokyo, grew prosperous through their ability to be the nodes at which economic activities are managed, coordinated, and financed. Major economic cities thrive on controlling or handling flows of knowledge, information, goods, and finance. China's opening allows Hong Kong a much greater scope to perform precisely these activities. The question is whether Hong Kong will perform these activities for a large enough number of local, Chinese, and multinational firms to offset the employment impact of the loss of middle-class jobs. While the vast potential of the Pearl River Delta region,

China, and Asia as a whole, would seem to indicate that this is a distinct possibility, ultimately it will be an empirical question whose answer will only become clear over time.

Although concerns have been voiced about the impact of the Pearl River Delta region on Hong Kong,[3] the region's dynamism should represent more of an opportunity than a threat to the future development of Hong Kong's economy. Hong Kong is well positioned to benefit from the region's burgeoning and diversifying trade. Hong Kong's financial system and financial strength are well matched to the substantial investment requirements of the region. Hong Kong-based professionals are well placed to help meet the region's growing demand for management, accounting, marketing, and consulting expertise. Hong Kong's developers and infrastructure companies are likely to take leadership roles in several of the large-scale development projects in the region. Hong Kong-based distribution, logistics, and retailing companies will benefit from a rapid expansion in consumer demand. Of course, Hong Kong firms must rise to the challenge, expand their horizons, and improve their own competitiveness if they are to benefit from increasing interaction.

NEW MINDSETS AND STRATEGIES IN A POLYCENTRIC REGION

The Greater Pearl River Delta region is a polycentric region. There are multiple centres in the region and each has its strong points and weak points. The unique political and historical circumstances in the Greater Pearl River Delta region means that no single centre will dominate, as is the case in the Yangtze River Delta region. Guangzhou, with its political, administrative and distribution roles as the provincial capital of Guangdong, will always be an important centre. Hong Kong, with its wealth, international linkages, and special status also will be an important centre. Shenzhen also has emerged as a strong centre in its own right, as will other cities in the Greater Pearl River Delta region. In essence, the Pearl River Delta region is like the Randstadt region of the Netherlands, in which there is a political centre (The Hague), a business and commercial centre (Amsterdam), a port and logistics centre (Rotterdam), and an education centre (Utrecht), among others.

Given the historical circumstances of the Greater Pearl River Delta region, the major centres once focused on their own policies and programs without paying too much attention to their neighbours. Hong Kong and Macao were under foreign administration until 1997 and 1999 respectively, while the Special Economic Zone status of Shenzhen and Zhuhai gave them a great deal of autonomy. The fact that foreign investment drove the economies of Shenzhen and

Dongguan meant that they were not so much in the orbit of Guangzhou or even the Guangdong Provincial Government. For many years, the interactions within the Greater Pearl River Delta region occurred in a decentralised fashion, with linkages developing based on family, cultural, or business ties. While these linkages have allowed the Greater Pearl River Delta region to flourish, this very success has resulted in a situation in which each jurisdiction in the region will perhaps be more dependent on the other jurisdictions in the region than it has been in the past. Given the newness of this situation, it is not surprising that it is taking time for the relations between different jurisdictions to be worked out.

One of the major forces for development in the Greater Pearl River Delta region going forward is a change of mindsets and strategies of players in the region. The mindsets and strategies of the different jurisdictions that once tended to operate in isolation are changing. Several years of experience with 'one country, two systems' has helped people become accustomed to the arrangement in Hong Kong and Macao. There has been new interest within the Greater Pearl River Delta region in identifying joint business opportunities and potential. This shared mindset, combined with greater cross-boundary communication, and the advent of sources of information on the region,[4] is likely to act as a positive force for greater interaction in the future. The new mindset can be seen in the tremendous upswing in terms of the numbers of government-to-government meetings, seminars, cooperative research under-takings, study tours, professional visits, and other signs of interaction since 2002. Areas receiving particular attention have been infrastructure projects and flows of capital, talent, and information within the region.[5] The result of this trend will be a much more fluid interaction that allows for discussion of joint issues and joint undertakings.[6] The new mindset has been accelerated by the Closer Economic Partnership Arrangement (CEPA), which has brought about a dramatic shift in business mindset on both sides of the boundary. With the advent of CEPA, businesses and officials are much more open to new opportunities across the boundary in both directions. In 2003, conferences and seminars on CEPA attracted thousands of participants from Hong Kong, the Pearl River Delta region, and the rest of China. Officials from scores of jurisdictions all over the Chinese mainland travelled to Hong Kong to explore how CEPA might benefit their communities. The existence of CEPA has been bringing new groups together to interact in new ways. The shift in mindset is driving a new, broader business interaction than has been seen before, one that promises to transcend the actual provisions of the free trade agreement.

The shift towards a shared mindset is nowhere more evident than in the joint promotion efforts between Hong Kong, Macao, and several Pearl River Delta region jurisdictions that began in 2003. In that year, the Trade

Development Council and Invest Hong Kong carried out Hong Kong–Pearl River Delta investment promotion missions jointly with representatives from the Pearl River Delta region in a number of overseas locations. Joint promotion efforts between Hong Kong and Pearl River Delta region jurisdictions were not on the radar screen in 1997. The fact that they had become routine six years later reflects significant advances in understanding the Greater Pearl River Delta region as an integrated economic region. It also reflects an emerging desire to enhance the competitive position of the Greater Pearl River Delta region in relation to other regions of China. Even in areas in which cooperation has proven difficult, a greater awareness of the other jurisdictions in the region and their strategies is increasingly allowing jurisdictions in the Greater Pearl River Delta region to formulate their own plans in a better informed fashion.

NEW COMBINATIONS AND COMPLEMENTARITIES

The change in mindset and strategies has the potential to greatly expand the impact of the combinations and complementarities in the Greater Pearl River Delta region. In many, if not most, instances existing combinations have been built upon intra-regional complementarities on a company-by-company and industry-by-industry basis with little overall recognition of the economic inter-dependence of the different jurisdictions in the region. Recent developments have created a mindset in which governments in the Greater Pearl River Delta region are actively seeking out linkages to be made and obstacles to interaction to be removed. Meanwhile, companies from the region are starting to look for Greater Pearl River Delta region opportunities, placing different activities in different jurisdictions according to their underlying advantages, and increasingly tying these activities together through improved transportation and communications.

At the same time, major international companies and foreign governments are taking increasing notice of the Greater Pearl River Delta region. In an increasing range of industries, leading firms from all over the world are finding the region an indispensable production platform, or to put it more directly, firms that do not produce in the region run the risk of being out-competed by firms that do. Industrial, urban, and consumer-oriented development in the region are creating markets that cannot be ignored for any company serious about its China business. The result for many firms selling into China will be a re-balancing of activities and management structures to take into account the growing importance of the region. Many have, or will, set up South China management structures to manage the new opportunities.

For foreign governments, many are finding that in order to learn from China's rise, and in order to prepare their own economies to compete with China and to serve Chinese markets, an understanding of the dynamics of the Greater Pearl River Delta region is also indispensable. While such an understanding is crucial, it also provides some difficult conclusions. That is, it is very difficult for other nations, or other regions, to match the distinctive combinations and complementarities that have contributed to the growing competitiveness of the Greater Pearl River Delta region. It is these combinations and complementarities that are likely to continue to power the development of one of the world's most dynamic economic regions.

Notes

CHAPTER 1

1. Michael J. Enright, 'China and its Neighbours', paper presented at Wilton Park Conference 'China and its Neighbours', November 2001.
2. World Economic Forum, *World Competitiveness Report 2003*, Geneva: World Economic Forum, 2003.
3. D. Lu and V. F. S. Sit, 'China's Regional Development Policies: A Review', in *China's Regional Disparities: Issues and Policies*, D. Lu and V. F. S. Sit (eds), New York: Nova Science Publishers, 2001, pp. 19–37; Y. D. Wei, *Regional Development in China – States, Globalization, and Inequality*, London: Routledge, 2000, pp. 14–46; S. Démurger, J. D. Sachs, W. T. Woo, S. Bao, G. Chang, and A. Mellinger, 'Geography, Economic Policy and Regional Development in China', Discussion Paper Number 1950, Harvard Institute of Economic Research, March 2002.
4. D. L. Yang, *Beyond Beijing – Liberalization and the Regions in China*, London: Routledge, 1997, pp. 62–78; S. Démurger, J. D. Sachs, W. T. Woo, S. Bao, G. Chang, and A. Mellinger, 'Geography, Economic Policy and Regional Development in China', Discussion Paper Number 1950, Harvard Institute of Economic Research, March 2002; B. Zhao, *Embeddedness and Competitiveness: Regional Clusters in China*, PhD Thesis, The University of Hong Kong, 2003; Michael Enright and Vincent Mak, 'Regional Development in the Chinese Mainland', Centre for Asian Business Cases, University of Hong Kong, 2004.
5. The listed cities, which have provincial status in the PRC political hierarchy, are Beijing, Shanghai, Tianjin, and Chongqing.
6. See, for example, Ezra Vogel, *Canton under Communism: Programs and Politics in a Provincial Capital, 1949–1968*, New York: Harper & Row, 1971; Ezra Vogel, *One Step Ahead in China: Guangdong under Reform*, Cambridge, Mass.: Harvard University Press, 1989; Yun-wing

Sung, Liu Pak-wai, Richard Yue-chim Wong, and Lau Pui-king, *The Fifth Dragon: The Emergence of the Pearl River Delta*, Singapore: Addison Wesley Publishing Co., 1995.

7. World Health Organization, 'Summary of Probable SARS Cases with Onset of Illness from 1 November 2002 to 31 July 2003', 26 September 2003.

8. Hong Kong Tourism Board, 'Tourism Statistics – 2003', 8 March 2004.

9. Hong Kong Special Administrative Region Government, Census and Statistics Department, 'Frequently Asked Statistics', 10 March 2004.

CHAPTER 2

1. For further background on Hong Kong's historical development and the economic roles it has played over time, see Michael J. Enright, 'Globalization, Regionalization and the Knowledge-based Economy in Hong Kong', in John Dunning (ed.), *Globalization, Regions and the Knowledge Economy*, Oxford: Oxford University Press, 2002; Michael J. Enright, Edith E. Scott, and David Dodwell, *The Hong Kong Advantage*, Hong Kong: Oxford University Press, 1997; and Michael J. Enright, Edith E. Scott, and Edward Leung, *Hong Kong's Competitiveness Beyond the Asian Crisis*, Hong Kong: Hong Kong Trade Development Council, February 1999.

2. See, for example, Peter Y. W. Chiu, 'Economic Integration between Hong Kong and Mainland China: The Effect on Hong Kong of China's Entry into the WTO', *China Perspectives*, 40 (March–April 2002): 63-4; A. G. Eason, 'Planning of Hong Kong in the Pearl River Delta Region Context', in Anthony Gar-On Yeh (ed.), *Planning Hong Kong for the 21st Century: A Preview of the Future Role of Hong Kong*, Hong Kong: Centre of Urban Planning and Environmental Management, University of Hong Kong, 1996, pp. 6–8; and Ezra F. Vogel, *One Step Ahead in China: Guangdong Under Reform*, Cambridge, Mass.: Harvard University Press, 1989, pp. 43–75.

3. Michael J. Enright, 'Globalization, Regionalization and the Knowledge-based Economy in Hong Kong', in John Dunning (ed.), *Globalization, Regions and the Knowledge Economy*, Oxford: Oxford University Press, 2002.

4. Michael J. Enright, Edith E. Scott, and Edward Leung, *Hong Kong's Competitiveness Beyond the Asian Crisis*, Hong Kong: Hong Kong Trade Development Council, February 1999, pp. 30–1.

5. Hong Kong Special Administrative Region Government, Census and Statistics Department, various years.

6. Michael J. Enright, Edith E. Scott, and David Dodwell, *The Hong Kong Advantage*, Hong Kong: Oxford University Press, 1997, pp. 179–81.

7. *Guangdong Statistical Yearbook 2002* and Hong Kong Special Administrative Region Government, Census and Statistics Department, 2002.

8. For further discussion of Hong Kong's service economy, see Michael J. Enright, 'Globalization, Regionalization and the Knowledge-based Economy in Hong Kong', in John Dunning (ed.), *Globalization, Regions and the Knowledge Economy*, Oxford: Oxford University Press, 2002; Michael J. Enright, Edith E. Scott, and Edward Leung, *Hong Kong's Competitiveness Beyond the Asian Crisis*, Hong Kong: Hong Kong Trade Development Council, February 1999, pp. 3–10.

9. Michael J. Enright, Edith E. Scott, and Edward Leung, *Hong Kong's Competitiveness Beyond the Asian Crisis*, Hong Kong: Hong Kong Trade Development Council, February 1999,

pp. 7–10; see also Hong Kong Centre for Economic Research, *Made in PRD: The Changing Face of Hong Kong Manufacturers*, Hong Kong: Federation of Hong Kong Industries, June 2003; Sung Yun-wing, *Hong Kong and South China: The Economic Synergy*, Hong Kong: City University of Hong Kong Press, Hong Kong Economic Policy Study Series, 1998, pp. 109–14.

10. World Trade Organization, *International Trade Statistics 2003*, 5 November 2003, Table 1.7.

11. Hong Kong Trade Development Council, *Economic & Trade Information on Hong Kong*, 5 February 2004.

12. Michael J. Enright, Edith E. Scott, and David Dodwell, *The Hong Kong Advantage*, Hong Kong: Oxford University Press, 1997, pp. 53–4.

13. Michael J. Enright, Edith E. Scott, and David Dodwell, *The Hong Kong Advantage*, Hong Kong: Oxford University Press, 1997, pp. 57–61.

14. Michael J. Enright, Edith E. Scott, and David Dodwell, *The Hong Kong Advantage*, Hong Kong: Oxford University Press, 1997, p. 73; *Zhongguo duiwai jingji maoyi nianjian* (*Almanac of China Foreign Economic Relations and Trade*), Beijing: China Foreign Economic and Trade Press, various years.

15. Enright, Scott & Associates Ltd research.

16. See also Michael Enright and Edith Scott, 'The RHQ Question', in *Business Asia*, The Economist Intelligence Unit (11 December 2000): 1–6.

17. Michael Enright and Edith Scott, 'The RHQ Question', in *Business Asia*, The Economist Intelligence Unit (11 December 2000): 1–6; Edith Scott, *First Choice Hong Kong – Your Asia-Pacific Platform: A Practical Handbook for Businesses*, 2nd edn., Hong Kong: Hong Kong Trade Development Council and Invest Hong Kong, 2002. As of June 2003, 966 foreign firms had regional headquarters in Hong Kong, up from 948 one year earlier, while 2,241 had regional offices in Hong Kong. See Invest Hong Kong Website.

18. Enright, Scott & Associates Ltd research.

19. Michael J. Enright, Edith E. Scott, and David Dodwell, *The Hong Kong Advantage*, Hong Kong: Oxford University Press, 1997, p. 71.

20. Hong Kong Trade Development Council, *Economic & Trade Information on Hong Kong*, 7 January 2004.

21. Hong Kong Special Administrative Region Government Information Centre, 'Links between Hong Kong and the Mainland of China', November 2003; Hong Kong Special Administrative Region Government, Information Services Department, *Hong Kong Yearbook 2003*, p. 256.

22. For a discussion of regional clusters see Michael J. Enright, 'Regional Clusters What We Know and What We Should Know', in Johannese Bröcker, Dirk Dohse, and Rüdiger Soltwedel (eds), *Innovation Clusters and Interregional Competition*, Berlin: Springer Verlag, 2003, pp. 99–129; Michael J. Enright and Ifor Ffowcs-Williams, 'Local Partnerships, Clusters and SME Globalisation', in *Enhancing SME Competitiveness*, Paris: OECD, 2001, pp. 115–50; and Michael J. Enright, 'Globalization, Regionalization and the Knowledge-based Economy in Hong Kong', in John Dunning (ed.), *Globalization, Regions and the Knowledge Economy*, Oxford: Oxford University Press, 2002, pp. 381–406.

23. See also Michael J. Enright, Edith E. Scott, and David Dodwell, *The Hong Kong Advantage*, Hong Kong: Oxford University Press, 1997; pp. 119–66; Michael J. Enright, Edith E. Scott, and Edward Leung, *Hong Kong's Competitiveness Beyond the Asian Crisis*, Hong Kong: Hong Kong Trade Development Council, February 1999, pp. 3–7, 11–4.

24. Hong Kong Exchanges and Clearing data seconded by Hong Kong Trade Development Council, 'Profiles of Hong Kong Major Service Industries – Securities', 31 July 2003.
25. Invest Hong Kong, 'Corporate and Investment Banking', 2004.
26. Hong Kong Trade Development Council, 'Profiles of Hong Kong Major Service Industries – Banking', 5 August 2003.
27. Hong Kong Trade Development Council, 'Profiles of Hong Kong Major Service Industries – Banking', 5 August 2003.
28. Asian Venture Capital Journal, *The 2003 Guide to Venture Capital in Asia*, 14th edn, p. 27.
29. Bank for International Settlements, 'Triennial Central Bank Survey of Foreign Exchange and Derivatives Market Activity 2001 – Final Results', 18 March 2002.
30. Hong Kong Special Administrative Government, Information Services Department, 'Hong Kong Facts', February 2003; Hong Kong Trade Development Council, 'Profiles of Hong Kong Major Service Industries – Securities', 31 July 2003; and Hong Kong Trade Development Council, 'Advantage Hong Kong – International Financial Centre', 5 August 2003.
31. Michael J. Enright, Edith E. Scott, and David Dodwell, *The Hong Kong Advantage*, Hong Kong: Oxford University Press, 1997, pp. 99–101; Michael Enright, 'Even More Than Before, it's Worth Betting on Hong Kong', *Asian Business, Special Handover Issue* (June–August 1997): 8.
32. Hong Kong Special Administrative Region Government, Census and Statistics Department, 'Employment in Hong Kong's Major Service Sectors', September 2003; Hong Kong Special Administrative Region Government, Census and Statistics Department, 'Gross Domestic Product (GDP) by Economic Activity at Current Prices', September 2003.
33. Michael J. Enright, Edith E. Scott, and David Dodwell, *The Hong Kong Advantage*, Hong Kong: Oxford University Press, 1997, p. 100.
34. Edith Scott, *Hong Kong: Marketplace for the World*, Hong Kong: Hong Kong Trade Development Council, November 2003, pp. 30–1.
35. Hong Kong Trade Development Council, 'Profiles of Hong Kong Major Service Industries – Building & Construction', 4 July 2003.
36. Hong Kong Trade Development Council, 'Economic & Trade Information on Hong Kong', 2 December 2003; Hong Kong Port Development Council, 'Summary Statistics on Port Traffic of Hong Kong', August 2003, p. 14.
37. Hong Kong Special Administrative Region Government, Hong Kong International Airport, *Civil International Air Transport Movements of Aircraft, Passenger and Freight (1998–2003)*.
38. Hong Kong Trade Development Council, 'Profiles of Hong Kong Major Service Industries – Import and Export Trade', 21 August 2003.
39. Hong Kong Special Administrative Region Government, Census and Statistics Department, *Quarterly Report of Employment and Vacancies Statistics*, December 2003.
40. Hong Kong Special Administrative Region Government, Information Services Department, *Hong Kong Yearbook 2002*, p. 456; Hong Kong Special Administrative Region Government, Hong Kong Tourism Commission, 'Tourism Statistics'; and World Tourism Organisation, 'Tourism Highlights 2003'.
41. In comparison, the PRC attracted 36.8 million visitors, Malaysia 13.3 million, Singapore 7.0 million, and Thailand 10.9 million – Hong Kong Special Administrative Region, Census and Statistics Department, 'Statistical Digest of the Services Sector 2003', July 2003, p. 254; World Tourism Organisation, 'Tourism Highlights 2003'.

42. Arrivals from non-mainland markets fell 26.9% in 2003 and in 2004 returned close to levels recorded in 2002. Carrie Chan, 'Mainland Visitors Expected to Surge 32 pc', *The South China Morning Post* (24 February 2004): A-3; Grace Lam and Jonathan Tam, 'Record Visitor Arrivals Likely to Top 20m', *The Standard* (24 February 2004): A-6.

43. Edith Scott, *Hong Kong: Marketplace for the World*, Hong Kong: Hong Kong Trade Development Council, November 2003, p. 8.

44. Hong Kong Special Administrative Region Government, Office of the Telecommunications Authority, 'Capacity of External Telecommunications Facilities'.

45. Edith Scott, *Hong Kong: Marketplace for the World*, Hong Kong: Hong Kong Trade Development Council, November 2003, p. 32.

46. Edith Scott, *Hong Kong: Marketplace for the World*, Hong Kong: Hong Kong Trade Development Council, November 2003, p. 30.

47. Edith Scott, *First Choice Hong Kong – Your Asia-Pacific Platform: A Practical Handbook for Businesses*, 2nd edn, Hong Kong: Hong Kong Trade Development Council and Invest Hong Kong, 2002, p. 20; Gerald P. O'Driscoll, Edwin J. Feulner, and Anastasia O'Grady (eds), *2003 Index of Economic Freedom*, The Heritage Foundation and *The Wall Street Journal*; and James D. Gwartney and Robert A. Lawson (eds), *Economic Freedom of the World: 2003 Annual Report*, The Fraser Institute.

48. Michael J. Enright, Edith E. Scott, and David Dodwell, *The Hong Kong Advantage*, Hong Kong: Oxford University Press, 1997, pp. 29–34; J. Shen, D. K.Y. Chu, and K.Y. Wong, 'The Shenzhen Model: Forces of Development and Future Direction of a Mainland City Near Hong Kong', in S. Ye, Y. Niu, and C. Gu (eds), *Studies on the Regional Integration under the Model of One Country Two Systems* (in Chinese), Beijing: Sciences Press, 1999, p. 129.

49. Joseph Y. S. Cheng (ed.), *Political Development in the HKSAR*, Hong Kong: The Chinese University Press, 2001, p. 63.

50. For a historical account of Hong Kong's political system see Norman Miners, *The Government and Politics of Hong Kong*, 5th edn, New York: Oxford University Press, 2000.

51. Li Pang Kwong, 'The Executive–Legislature Relationship in Hong Kong: Evolution and Development', in Joseph Y. S. Cheng (ed.), *Political Development in the HKSAR*, Hong Kong: The Chinese University Press, 2001, pp. 85–100.

52. For a comprehensive critique of the Hong Kong Special Administrative Region Government's decision-making process under Tung Chee-hwa, see Lau Siu Kai (ed.), *The First Tung Chee-hwa Administration: The First Five Years of the Hong Kong Special Administrative Region*, Hong Kong: The Chinese University Press, 2002.

53. Enright, Scott & Associates Ltd research.

54. Michael J. Enright, Edith E. Scott, and Edward Leung, *Hong Kong's Competitiveness Beyond the Asian Crisis*, Hong Kong: Hong Kong Trade Development Council, February 1999, p. 29.

CHAPTER 3

1. Zhu Wen-hui and Jo Wilson made significant contributions to this chapter.

2. For more on the historical development of the Pearl River Delta region, see, for example, A. G. O. Yeh, Y. S. F. Lee, Tunney Lee, and Sze Nien Dak (eds), *Building a Competitive Pearl River Delta: Collaboration, Cooperation and Planning*, Hong Kong: Centre of Urban Planning

and Environmental Management, The University of Hong Kong, 2002, pp. 9–26; Stewart MacPherson and Joseph Y. S. Cheng (eds), *Economic and Social Development in South China*, Cheltenham: Edward Elgar, 1996, pp. 1–56; Ezra F. Vogel, *One Step Ahead in China: Guangdong Under Reform*, Cambridge, Mass.: Harvard University Press, 1989, pp. 161–95; and Wang Liwen, Yue Yue, and Yang Changzun, *Jianshe zhujiang sanjiao zhou jingji qu – cehuapian (Building the Pearl River Delta Economic Zone – the Planning)*, Guangzhou: Guangzhou Press, 1995, pp. 83–98.

3.   Zheng Tianxiang and Li Huan (eds), *Yuegangao jingji guanxi (The Guangdong – Hong Kong – Macao Economic Relationship)*, Guangzhou: Sun Yatsen University Press, 2001, p. 9; see also Ezra F. Vogel, *Canton under Communism; Programs and Politics in a Provincial Capital, 1949–1968*, New York: Harper & Row, 1971.

4.   Zheng Tianxiang and Li Huan (eds), *Yuegangao jingji guanxi (The Guangdong – Hong Kong – Macao Economic Relationship)*, Guangzhou: Sun Yatsen University Press, 2001, p. 9. See also Sung Yun-wing, Liu Pak-wai, Richard Yue-chim Wong, and Lau Pui-king (eds), *The Fifth Dragon*, Hong Kong: Addison Wesley, 1995; David K. Y. Chiu, 'Synthesis of Economic Reforms and Open Policy', in Y. M. Yeung and David K. Y. Chiu (eds), *Guangdong: Survey of a Province Undergoing Rapid Change*, Hong Kong: The Chinese University Press, 1998, pp. 485–504; and Di Changyun, *Guangdong gaige kaifang juece anli (Case Studies of Guangdong's Decision Making in Reform and Opening)*, Beijing: People's Daily Press, 1995.

5.   Chen Dezhao, 'Chinese Public Policy and the Southern China Growth Triangle', in Myo Thant, Min Tang, and Hiroshi Kakazu (eds), *Growth Triangles in Asia: A New Approach to Regional Cooperation*, Hong Kong: Asian Development Bank, 1998, pp. 103–22; and He Jiasheng and Wang Yingjie, *Maixiang xin shiji de Guangdong jingji tequ (The Guangdong Economic Zone Towards the New Century)*, Guangzhou: Guangdong Tertiary Education Press, 1999, pp. 12–6.

6.   Sung Yun-wing, *Hong Kong and South China: The Economic Synergy*, Hong Kong Economic Policy Study Series, City University of Hong Kong Press, 1998, pp. 31–47; Ezra F. Vogel, *One Step Ahead in China: Guangdong Under Reform*, Cambridge, Mass.: Harvard University Press, 1989, pp. 125–60.

7.   For more on the importance of Deng's 1992 southern tour for boosting investments into the Pearl River Delta region, see Sung Yun-wing, *Hong Kong and South China: The Economic Synergy*, Hong Kong Economic Policy Study Series, City University of Hong Kong Press, 1998, pp. 93–119.

8.   J. Shen, D. K. Y. Chu, and K. Y. Wong, 'The Shenzhen Model: Forces of Development and Future Direction of a Mainland City Near Hong Kong', in S. Ye, Y. Niu, and C. Gu (eds), *Studies on the Regional Integration under the Model of One Country Two Systems* (in Chinese), Beijing: Sciences Press, 1999, pp. 112–3.

9.   See, for example, George C. S. Lin, 'Region-based Urbanisation in Post-Reform China: Spatial Restructuring in the Pearl River Delta', in John R. Logan (ed.), *The New Chinese City*, United Kingdom: Blackwell Publishers, 2002, pp. 245–57.

10. Yang Qianqi, Deputy Director of the Development Research Centre, Guangdong Province, '*Fazhan tese gongye, tigao jingzheng youshi*' ('Developing Special Industries, Improving Competitive Advantages'), *Guangdong gaige kaifang ershi nian jinian wenji (A Collection of Commemorative Essays and Information for Guangdong's Twenty Years of Reform and Opening Up)*, Guangdong Provincial People's Government Development Research Centre, 1998, p. 182.

11. See William H. Overholt, *China: The Next Economic Superpower*, London: Weidenfeld & Nicolson, 1993, p. 118.
12. See Wang Liwen, Yue Yue, and Yang Changzun, *Jianshe zhujiang sanjiao zhou jingji qu – cehuapian (Building the Pearl River Delta Economic Zone – The Planning)*, Guangzhou: Guangzhou Press, 1995, pp. 137–51.
13. *Guangdong Statistical Yearbook 2001*, p. 340.
14. Ho Wainang, 'Individual Economy in the Pearl River Delta Region: A Study on Dongguan, Guangzhou, Zhongshan and Nanhai', in Stewart MacPherson and Joseph Y. S. Cheng (eds), *Economic and Social Development in South China*, Cheltenham: Edward Elgar, 1996, pp. 183–205.
15. The Centre for Urban and Regional Studies, Zhongshan University, '*Zhujiang sanjiao zhou fazhan licheng yanjiu*' ('A Study of the Development Trajectory of the Pearl River Delta'), *Xianggang yu zhujiang sanjiao zhou jingji hudong yanjiu (A Study of the Hong Kong – Pearl River Delta Economic Interaction)*, April 2002, p. 36.
16. Guangzhou and Shenzhen, in particular, have been singled out by analysts for their established positions as main commercial hubs in China. See Rosemary Reenan, Robin Goodchild, Jeffrey Havsy, Jeremy Kelly, Timothy Bellman, and Camilla Bastoni (analysts), *Rising Urban Stars – Uncovering Future Winners*, Jones Lang LaSalle, May 2003.
17. *Guangdong Statistical Yearbook 2003*, p. 519.
18. Guangzhou Statistical Bureau, *Zhujiang sanjiao zhou 12 shi (qu) shehui jingji zhibiao tongji zhiliao 2001 (Major Economic Indicators of 12 Cities in the Pearl River Delta 2001)*.
19. See Wu Zhiwen and Qiu Chuanying, *Guangzhou xiandai jingji shi (Modern Economic History of Guangzhou)*, Guangzhou: Guangdong People's Press, 2001, pp. 11–210; Wang Dingchang, *Guangzhou de zuotian, jintian, mingtian (The Yesterday, Today and Tomorrow of Guangzhou)*, Guangzhou: Guangzhou Press, 1998, pp. 105–28.
20. See Edward Leman, 'Can the Pearl River Delta Region Still Compete?' *The China Business Review* (May–June 2003): 6–17; see also Wu Zhiwen and Qiu Chuanying, *Guangzhou xiandai jingji shi (Modern Economic History of Guangzhou)*, Guangzhou: Guangdong People's Press, 2001, pp. 211–388.
21. *Guangdong Statistical Yearbook 2003*, pp. 102–3.
22. *Guangdong Statistical Yearbook 2003*, pp. 270–3.
23. Michael J. Enright and Edith E. Scott, *The Greater Pearl River Delta*, Hong Kong: Invest Hong Kong, June 2004.
24. Zheng Gong Zhengzheng and Liang Qiwen, 'Auto Maker Launches Engine Joint Venture', *China Daily* (26 February 2004): 10; Zheng Caixiong, 'Toyota Gears Up on Engine-making Factory', *China Daily* (9 October 2003): chinadaily.com; Zheng Caixiong, 'Schroeder Visits Pearl River Delta', *China Daily* (4 December 2003): 5; 'Nissan's China JV to set up R&D Centre in Guangzhou', 24 March 2004: WardsAuto.com.
25. Michael J. Enright and Edith E. Scott, *The Greater Pearl River Delta*, Hong Kong: Invest Hong Kong, June 2004.
26. The Publicity Department of the Guangdong Committee of Communist Party of China, *Zhujiang sanjiaozhou jingjiqu fazhan zhanlue yu guihua yanjiu (A Study of the Development Strategies and Planning of the Pearl River Delta Economic Zone)*, Guangzhou: Guangdong People's Press, 1995, pp. 76–119, 128–33, 147–52, and 296–303.
27. To learn more about Guangzhou's past economic achievements and future ambitions, see Wu Zhiwen and Qiu Chuanying, *Guangzhou xiandai jingji shi (Modern Economic History of*

Guangzhou), Guangzhou: Guangdong People's Press, 2001, pp. 391–410; Zhu Xiaodan (ed.), *Gaige kaifang ershi nian de Guangzhou* (*Guangzhou in the Past Twenty Years of Reform and Opening*), Guangzhou: Open Times, 1998.

28. J. Shen, D. K. Y. Chu, and K. Y. Wong, 'The Shenzhen Model: Forces of Development and Future Direction of a Mainland City Near Hong Kong', in S. Ye, Y. Niu, and C. Gu (eds), *Studies on the Regional Integration under the Model of One Country Two Systems* (in Chinese), Beijing: Sciences Press, 1999, pp. 112–4.

29. Wang Dingchang, *Shenzhen de zuotian, jintian, mingtian* (*The Yesterday, Today and Tomorrow of Shenzhen*), Guangzhou: Guangzhou Press, 2000, pp. 188–96.

30. *Guangdong Statistical Yearbook 2001*, p. 34.

31. Zhang Jinsheng, *Waizi yu Shenzhen chanye jiegou* (*Foreign Capital and Shenzhen's Industrial Structure*), Beijing: Central Literature Publishing House, 2000, pp. 73–115; Bien Perez, 'Kingdee Eyes HK Base to Compete with Giants', *South China Morning Post* (12 March 2003): B-2. Huawei Technologies, for example, a leading producer of telecommunications equipment, was established in 1988. By 2002, the company had sales of US$2.7 billion, research and development expenditures in excess of US$362 million, and a staff of 22,000 (85% of whom were university graduates and 10,000 of whom were researchers). Huawei, whose major product lines included fixed networks, mobile network equipment, data communications, and optical networks, has set up over 40 sales offices and customer support centres worldwide, as well as research centres in places including Silicon Valley, Bangalore, Stockholm, Moscow, Beijing, and Shanghai. See www.huawei.com.

32. *Shenzhen Statistical Yearbook 2003*, p. 186.

33. Jin Huikang, 'A Rising Star in China', *News Guangdong* (17 September 2003): newsgd.com.

34. *Guangdong Statistical Yearbook 2003*, pp. 270–3.

35. 'Shenzhen Container Making Up', *China Daily* (13 December 2001): chinadaily.com; Wu Zhong, 'Yuletide Cheer', *The Standard* (25 September 2003): A-17; and 'Shenzhen Hits Big Time as Clock Maker', *iMail* (22 February 2002): 13.

36. 'More Global Firms Sourcing in Shenzhen', *China Daily* (29 May 2003): chinadaily.com; 'Wal-Mart Asia President: I Hope to Retire in China', *People's Daily* (7 December 2003): peopledaily.com.

37. Michael J. Enright and Edith E. Scott, *The Greater Pearl River Delta*, Hong Kong: Invest Hong Kong, June 2004; see also The Shenzhen Museum, *Shenzhen Tequ Shi* (*History of the Shenzhen Special Economic Zone*), Beijing: People's Publishing House, 1999, pp. 312–26; Wang Dingchang, *Shenzhen de zuotian, jintian, mingtian* (*The Yesterday, Today and Tomorrow of Shenzhen*), Guangzhou: Guangzhou Press, 2000, pp. 160–87; and Wu Zhong, 'Happy Days for Insurers', *The Standard* (4 February 2004): A-17.

38. Thomas Chan and Zhu Wenhui, *Industrial Clusters and Regional Concentration, the Changes of Investment Behaviours of Taiwanese in the Chinese Mainland at the Turn of the Century*, Hong Kong: China Business Centre, Hong Kong Polytechnic University, 2000.

39. Dongguan City Government, *Dongguan diaoyan 1997* (*Dongguan Studies 1997*), pp. 1–2.

40. Thomas Chan and Zhu Wenhui, *Industrial Clusters and Regional Concentration, the Changes of Investment Behaviours of Taiwanese in the Chinese Mainland at the Turn of the Century*, Hong Kong: China Business Centre, Hong Kong Polytechnic University, 2000.

41. For more information on the economic development of Dongguan, see George Lin Chusheng, 'Intrusion of Global Forces and Transformation of a Local Chinese Economy: The Experience of Dongguan', in R. Watters (ed.), *Asia-Pacific: New Geographies of the Pacific*

Rim, London: Christopher Hurst, 1997, pp. 250–65; A. G. O. Yeh and X. Li, 'The Need for Compact Development in Fast Growing Areas of China: The Pearl River Delta', in M. Jenks and R. Burgess (eds), *Compact Cities: Sustainable Urban Forms for Developing Countries*, London: Spon Press, 2000, pp. 73–90; and Godfrey Yeung, 'Foreign Direct Investment and Investment Environment in Dongguan Municipality of Southern China', *Journal of Contemporary China*, 10, 26 (2001): 125–54.

42. *Dongguan Statistical Yearbook 2003*, p. 271; *Shenzhen Statistical Yearbook 2003*, p. 186; and *Shanghai Statistical Yearbook 2003*, p. 183.

43. Michael J. Enright and Edith E. Scott, *The Greater Pearl River Delta*, Hong Kong: Invest Hong Kong, June 2004.

44. *Guangdong Statistical Yearbook 2003*, pp. 270–3.

45. *Guangdong Statistical Yearbook 2003*, pp. 270–3.

46. Michael J. Enright and Edith E. Scott, *The Greater Pearl River Delta*, Hong Kong: Invest Hong Kong, June 2004.

47. *Guangdong Statistical Yearbook*, various years.

48. *Guangdong Statistical Yearbook 2003*, pp. 270–3.

49. Michael J. Enright and Edith E. Scott, *The Greater Pearl River Delta*, Hong Kong: Invest Hong Kong, June 2004; Enright, Scott & Associates Ltd research.

50. Calculated by dividing Zhuhai's GDP for 2002 by the latest Census figure from the year 2000.

51. *Guangdong Statistical Yearbook 2003*, pp. 270–3.

52. *Guangdong Statistical Yearbook 2003*, pp. 270–3.

53. Michael J. Enright and Edith E. Scott, *The Greater Pearl River Delta*, Hong Kong: Invest Hong Kong, June 2004.

54. *Guangdong Statistical Yearbook 2003*, pp. 270–3.

55. Michael J. Enright and Edith E. Scott, *The Greater Pearl River Delta*, Hong Kong: Invest Hong Kong, June 2004.

56. *Guangdong Statistical Yearbook 2003*, pp. 270–3.

57. Michael J. Enright and Edith E. Scott, *The Greater Pearl River Delta*, Hong Kong: Invest Hong Kong, June 2004; *Guangdong Statistical Yearbook 2003*, p. 270.

58. Michael J. Enright, 'Regional Clusters What We Know and What We Should Know' in Johannese Bröcker, Dirk Dohse, and Rüdiger Soltwedel (eds), *Innovation Clusters and Interregional Competition*, Berlin: Springer Verlag, 2003, pp. 99–129; Michael J. Enright and Ifor Ffowcs-Williams, 'Local Partnerships, Clusters and SME Globalisation', in *Enhancing SME Competitiveness*, Paris: OECD, 2001, pp. 115–50; and Michael J. Enright, 'Globalization, Regionalization and the Knowledge-based Economy in Hong Kong', in John Dunning (ed.), *Globalization, Regions and the Knowledge Economy*, Oxford: Oxford University Press, 2002, pp. 381–406.

59. See Long Guoqiang, '*Jiagong maoyi: quanqiuhua beijingxia gongyehua xindaolu*' ('Processing Trade: A New Road for Industrialisation Against the Background of Globalisation'), *Jingji qianyan (Forward Position in Economics)*, January 2003, pp. 8–9.

60. Zheng Caixiong, 'Toyota Gears Up on Engine-making Factory', *China Daily* (9 October 2003): chinadaily.com.

61. 'Denso Sets Up in Guangzhou', *South China Morning Post* (2 April 2003): scmp.com.

62. Gong Zhengzheng and Liang Qiwen, 'Auto Maker Launches Engine Joint Venture', *China Daily* (26 February 2004): 10; Zheng Caixiong, 'Toyota Gears Up on Engine-making Factory', *China Daily* (9 October 2003): chinadaily.com.

63. Reuters, 'Power Shortage Hits Honda Joint Venture', *South China Morning Post* (20 February 2004): B-3; Zhan Lisheng, 'US$1b JV on Steel Sheets', *China Daily* (23 September 2003): chinadaily.com.

64. 'Real Prosperity of Fake Village', *China Daily* (21 February 2002): chinadaily.com.

65. 'Time for Watch-Makers to Build Own Brands', *China Daily* (26 June 2003): chinadaily.com.

66. Quoted in Catholic Agency for Overseas Development (CAFOD), 'Clean up Your Computer: Working Conditions in the Electronics Sector', London, 26 January 2004.

67. Toh Han Shih, 'Delta Weaves a Success Story', *South China Morning Post* (8 March 2004): B-2.

68. 'Children's Garment Centre Completed', *China Daily* (30 January 2002): chinadaily.com.

69. Zheng Caixiong, 'Shunde Town Aims to Become Cowboy Country', *China Daily* (26 September 2003): chinadaily.com.

70. See the Nanhai Non-Ferrous Metal Industry website: www.nhtip.com; Zhan Lisheng, 'Aluminium Sector Seeks Sustained Growth', *China Daily* (8–14 March 2004): 17.

71. Michael J. Enright and Edith E. Scott, *The Greater Pearl River Delta*, Hong Kong: Invest Hong Kong, June 2004; Tom Mitchell, 'Casual-wear Capital Spinning up a Huge Profit', *South China Morning Post* (29 January 2002): scmp.com; Tom Mitchell, 'All Because of a Bright Spark', *South China Morning Post* (29 January 2002): scmp.com.

72. Li Siming, 'Pearl Riversville: A Survey of Urbanisation in the Pearl River Delta', in Joseph Y. S. Cheng (ed.), *The Guangdong Development Model and Its Challenges*, Hong Kong: City University of Hong Kong Press, 1988, p. 130.

73. See Wang Liwen, Yue Yue, and Yang Changzun, *Jianshe zhujiang sanjiao zhou jingji qu – cehuapian* (*Building the Pearl River Delta Economic Zone – The Planning*), Guangzhou: Guangzhou Press, 1995, pp. 189–97. For more on the history of economic planning in the Pearl River Delta, see M. K. Ng and W. S. Tang, 'Urban System Planning in China: A Case Study of the Pearl River Delta', *Urban Geography,* 20:7 (1999): 591–616; He Jiasheng and Wang Yingjie, *Maixiang xin shiji de Guangdong jingji tequ* (*The Guangdong Economic Zone Towards the New Century*), Guangzhou: Guangdong Tertiary Education Press, 1999, pp. 290–313.

CHAPTER 4

1. Zhu Wen-hui made significant contributions to this chapter.

2. For historical accounts of the economic interaction between Hong Kong and the Pearl River Delta until 1996, see Sung Yun-wing, *Hong Kong and South China: The Economic Synergy,* Hong Kong Economic Policy Study Series, City University of Hong Kong Press, 1998, pp. 81–7; J. Shen, 'Urban and Regional Development in Post-reform China: The Case of Zhujiang Delta', *Progress in Planning,* 57: 2 (2002): 91–140; Thomas P. Rohlen, *Hong Kong and the Pearl River Delta: One Country, Two Systems in the Emerging Metropolitan Context,* Asia Pacific Research Centre, July 2000; A. G. O. Yeh, 'Hong Kong and the Pearl River Delta: Competition or Cooperation?' *Built Environment,* 27, 2 (2001): 129–45; Joseph Y. S. Cheng and Zheng Peiyu, 'Hi-tech Industries in Hong Kong and the Pearl River Delta: Development Trends in Industrial Cooperation', *Asian Survey,* 41, 4 (2001): 584–610; and Wang Dengrong, '*Yuegang diqu quyu hezuo fazhan fenxi ji quyu guanzhi tuijin celue*' ('An Analysis of Regional Cooperation in the Hong Kong – Guangdong

Region and the Strategies for Promoting Regional Administration'), *Xiandai chengshi yanjiu* (*Modern Urban Studies*), (2002): 60–2.

3. *Guangdong Statistical Yearbook 2001*, p. 340, Table 12-2. See also Zheng Tianxiang and Li Huan (eds), *Yuegangao jingji guanxi* (*The Guangdong – Hong Kong – Macao Economic Relationship*), Guangzhou: Sun Yatsen University Press, 2001, pp. 39–41.

4. Michael J. Enright and Edith E. Scott, *The Greater Pearl River Delta*, Hong Kong: Invest Hong Kong, June 2004.

5. Zheng Tianxiang and Li Huan (eds), *Yuegangao jingji guanxi* (*The Guangdong–Hong Kong–Macao Economic Relationship*), Guangzhou: Sun Yatsen University Press, 2001, pp. 11, 26–30.

6. C. K. Leung, 'Personal Contacts, Subcontracting Linkages and Development in the Hong Kong–Zhujiang Delta Region', *Annals of the Association of American Geographers*, 83, 2 (1993): 272–302.

7. Wang Jun, 'Expansion of the Southern China Growth Triangle', in Myo Thant, Min Tang, and Hiroshi Kakazu (eds), *Growth Triangles in Asia: A New Approach to Regional Cooperation*, Hong Kong: Asian Development Bank, 1998, p. 169.

8. The Centre for Urban and Regional Studies, Zhongshan University, '*Xianggang yu zhujiang sanjiao zhou jingji guanxi yanjiu*' ('A Study of the Economic Relationship Between Hong Kong and the Pearl River Delta'), *Xianggang yu zhujiang sanjiao zhou jingji hudong yanjiu* (*A Study of the Hong Kong–Pearl River Delta Economic Interaction*), April 2002, p. 9.

9. Hong Kong Centre for Economic Research, *Made in PRD: The Changing Face of Hong Kong Manufacturers*, Hong Kong: Federation of Hong Kong Industries, June 2003, Appendix, Table A-8.

10. Hong Kong Centre for Economic Research, *Made in PRD: The Changing Face of Hong Kong Manufacturers*, Hong Kong: Federation of Hong Kong Industries, June 2003, p. 22.

11. The Centre for Urban and Regional Studies, Zhongshan University, '*Xianggang yu zhujiang sanjiao zhou jingji guanxi yanjiu*' ('A Study of the Economic Relationship Between Hong Kong and the Pearl River Delta'), *Xianggang yu zhujiang sanjiao zhou jingji hudong yanjiu* (*A Study of the Hong Kong–Pearl River Delta Economic Interaction*), April 2002, p. 8. The proportion of direct investment grew to 88% of the total of actual investment, while indirect investment and other forms of investment fell to 8% and 4%, respectively.

12. The figures above are generally consistent with other official sources that have quoted figures for Hong Kong investment into Guangdong Province. In June 2002, Lu Ruihua, Governor of Guangdong, claimed that Guangdong had used US$120 billion in foreign investment and that 70% (yielding a figure of US$84 billion) had come from Hong Kong. See 'Lu Ruihua Expects Guangdong's Exports to Increase 10% this Year', *Hong Kong Commercial Daily* (6 June 2002). In April 2002, Huang Ziqiang, Director of the Guangdong Provincial Foreign Affairs Office, said Guangdong had used US$78.9 billion in investment from Hong Kong, representing 70% of the total Hong Kong investment in the Chinese mainland. See 'Trade between Hong Kong and Guangdong Reaches US$38.7 Billion', *Ta Kung Pao* (10 April 2002). It has been reported that Hong Kong businesses had made actual investments of US$183.3 billion in the Chinese mainland by October of 2001 with the vast majority of this invested in Guangdong Province. See 'Hong Kong Businesses Prepare Domestic Sales', *Ta Kung Pao* (22 January 2002). The discrepancy is most likely due to the fact that most of the machinery and equipment, which typically represents the largest investment in export processing facilities and that enters China duty-free under export processing regulations, has not been included in the official foreign investment

statistics. In fact, by 2000, the *Guangdong Statistical Yearbook* showed the accumulative value of imported processing and assembly equipment between 1979 and 2000 to amount to only US$ 5.64 billion, of which less than one-fifth were subject to tax. See *Guangdong Statistical Yearbook 2001*, Table 15–16: Amount of Foreign Capital Actually Used, p. 543.

13.   Figures derived from Enright, Scott & Associates Ltd research; the Hong Kong Trade Development Council, *Profiles of Hong Kong Major Manufacturing Industries*, 4 November 2002.

14.   Hong Kong Centre for Economic Research, *Made in PRD: The Changing Face of Hong Kong Manufacturers*, Hong Kong: Federation of Hong Kong Industries, June 2003, p. 23.

15.   Ng and Tuan specifically stress the importance of Hong Kong SMEs in providing this investment and contributing to the development of the Pearl River Delta region. See Linda F. Y. Ng and Tuan Chyau, 'Location Decisions of Manufacturing FDI in China: Implications of China's WTO Accession', *Journal of Asian Economics*, North-Holland, 14 (2003): 51–72.

16.   The Centre for Urban and Regional Studies, Zhongshan University, '*Xianggang yu zhujiang sanjiao zhou jingji guanxi yanjiu*' (*A Study of the Economic Relationship Between Hong Kong and the Pearl River Delta*), *Xianggang yu zhujiang sanjiao zhou jingji hudong yanjiu* (*A Study of the Hong Kong – Pearl River Delta Economic Interaction*), April 2002, p. 10.

17.   'Hong Kong Businesses Prepare Domestic Sales', *Ta Kung Pao* (22 January 2002).

18.   Hong Kong Centre for Economic Research, *Made in PRD: The Changing Face of Hong Kong Manufacturers*, Hong Kong: Federation of Hong Kong Industries, June 2003, pp. 21, 23.

19.   Hong Kong Centre for Economic Research, *Made in PRD: The Changing Face of Hong Kong Manufacturers*, Hong Kong: Federation of Hong Kong Industries, June 2003, p. 21.

20.   Hong Kong Centre for Economic Research, *Made in PRD: The Changing Face of Hong Kong Manufacturers*, Hong Kong: Federation of Hong Kong Industries, June 2003, p. 26. Although the figures are for factory facilities in the mainland, the vast majority of the facilities were located in Guangdong Province.

21.   Enright, Scott & Associates Ltd research.

22.   Enright, Scott & Associates Ltd research; see also Hong Kong Centre for Economic Research, *Made in PRD: The Changing Face of Hong Kong Manufacturers*, Hong Kong: Federation of Hong Kong Industries, June 2003, p. 32.

23.   Hong Kong Trade Development Council, 'Why Hong Kong? – A Survey of Japanese Companies in the Pearl River Delta', *Economic Forum*, 21 November 2002.

24.   Dutch Chamber of Commerce in Guangzhou, 'Industrial Zone Survey in the Pearl River Delta', September 2002.

25.   Hong Kong Trade Development Council, 'Hong Kong as the Business Platform for Foreign Businesses Operating in the PRD with CEPA Agreement', *Economic Forum*, 12 November 2003.

26.   Hong Kong Trade Development Council, 'Hong Kong as the Business Platform for Foreign Businesses Operating in the PRD with CEPA Agreement', *Economic Forum*, 12 November 2003.

27.   Hong Kong Polytechnic University, China Business Centre, *The Characteristics of the Operation and Development of Taiwan-invested Enterprises in Hong Kong* (in Chinese), 2000.

28.   Hong Kong Trade Development Council, 'Hong Kong as a Service Platform for Taiwan Companies Investing in the Mainland', *Economic Forum*, 31 October 2002.

29.   Zheng Tianxiang and Li Huan (eds), *Yuegangao jingji guanxi* (*The Guangdong – Hong Kong – Macao Economic Relationship*), Guangzhou: Sun Yatsen University Press, 2001, p. 135–7.

30. Hong Kong Trade Development Council, *Hong Kong's Trade and Trade Supporting Services: New Developments and Prospects*, January 2002, p. iv.

31. The Centre for Urban and Regional Studies, Zhongshan University, '*Xianggang yu zhujiang sanjiao zhou jingji guanxi yanjiu*' ('A Study of the Economic Relationship Between Hong Kong and the Pearl River Delta'), *Xianggang yu zhujiang sanjiao zhou jingji hudong yanjiu* (*A Study of the Hong Kong–Pearl River Delta Economic Interaction*), April 2002, p. 21.

32. Enright, Scott & Associates Ltd research; Edith Scott, *Hong Kong Plus: Your Global Platform for Sourcing, Producing and Selling in China*, Hong Kong: Hong Kong Trade Development Council, October 2002, p. 22.

33. Enright, Scott & Associates Ltd research; Wang Jun, 'Expansion of the Southern China Growth Triangle', in Myo Thant, Min Tang, and Hiroshi Kakazu (eds), *Growth Triangles in Asia: A New Approach to Regional Cooperation*, Hong Kong: Asian Development Bank, 1998, pp. 172–3.

34. Hong Kong's strength in R&D is concentrated in these areas of design development, rather than research-intensive work. Author's interviews; see also Hong Kong Centre for Economic Research, *Made in PRD: The Changing Face of Hong Kong Manufacturers*, June 2003, pp. 46–63; and Joseph Y. S. Cheng and Zheng Peiyu, 'Hi-tech Industries in Hong Kong and the Pearl River Delta: Development Trends in Industrial Cooperation', *Asian Survey*, 41, 4 (2001): 596–7.

35. Enright, Scott & Associates Ltd research.

36. Enright, Scott & Associates Ltd research.

37. Hong Kong Trade Development Council, 'Hong Kong as a Service Platform for Taiwan Companies Investing in the Mainland', *Economic Forum*, 31 October 2002; Hong Kong Trade Development Council, 'A Survey of Korean Companies in the Pearl River Delta', *Economic Forum*, 7 April 2003; Hong Kong Trade Development Council, 'Why Hong Kong? – A Survey of Japanese Firms in the Pearl River Delta', *Economic Forum*, 21 November 2002; Hong Kong Trade Development Council, 'Why Hong Kong as a Business Platform? A Survey of US Companies in the Pearl River Delta', *Economic Forum*, 25 July 2003; and Hong Kong Trade Development Council, 'Why Choose Hong Kong as a Business Platform? A Survey of EU Companies in the Pearl River Delta', *Economic Forum*, 23 June 2003.

38. Sung Yun-wing, *Hong Kong and South China: The Economic Synergy*, Hong Kong Economic Policy Study Series, City University of Hong Kong Press, 1998, pp. 47–67, 119–35.

39. Enright, Scott & Associates Ltd research; see also Yeung Yueman, 'Infrastructure Development in the Southern China Growth Triangle', in Myo Thant, Min Tang, and Hiroshi Kakazu (eds), *Growth Triangles in Asia: A New Approach to Regional Cooperation*, Hong Kong: Asian Development Bank, 1998, pp. 149–50.

40. Zheng Tianxiang and Li Huan (eds), *Yuegangao jingji guanxi* (*The Guangdong–Hong Kong–Macao Economic Relationship*), Guangzhou: Sun Yatsen University Press, 2001, p. 41.

41. Zheng Tianxiang and Li Huan (eds), *Yuegangao jingji guanxi* (*The Guangdong–Hong Kong–Macao Economic Relationship*), Guangzhou: Sun Yatsen University Press, 2001, p. 89.

42. Claude Comtois and Brian Slack, 'Hong Kong: Adding Value to China – Transport Hub and Urban Super Region', *China Perspectives*, 29 (May–June 2000): 16.

43. See Hutchinson Port Holdings: hph.com.hk.

44. Samuel Lam, Oriental Trucking Hong Kong Ltd, 'Cross Border Trucking', Presentation to Hong Kong Amcham Transport and Logistics Committee, 29 May 2002, citing Hong Kong Special Administrative Region Government, Census and Statistics Department.

45. Hong Kong Special Administrative Region Government, Census and Statistics Department, *Annual Digest of Statistics 2003*, pp. 180–1.
46. Hong Kong Special Administrative Region Government, Planning Department, *Cross-boundary Travel Survey 2001*, published 2002.
47. The Centre for Urban and Regional Studies, Zhongshan University, '*Xianggang yu zhujiang sanjiao zhou jingji guanxi yanjiu*i, ('A Study of the Economic Relationship Between Hong Kong and the Pearl River Delta'), *Xianggang yu zhujiang sanjiao zhou jingji hudong yanjiu (A Study of the Hong Kong–Pearl River Delta Economic Interaction)*, April 2002, p. 23.
48. Hong Kong Business Professionals Association, *Impact of Cross Border Economic Activities on Hong Kong*, January 2002, p. 7; Hong Kong Special Administrative Region Government, Census and Statistics Department, 'Consumption Expenditure of Hong Kong Residents Travelling to the Mainland of China', in *Hong Kong Monthly Digest of Statistics*, April 2001.
49. Hong Kong Tourism Board, 'Visitor Arrival Statistics – Jan 2004'. Guangdong estimate based on tourist arrivals in August 2002. See 'More Records Set as August Visitor Arrivals Pass 1.5 Million', *Hong Kong Tourism Board News* (26 September 2002).
50. Hong Kong Tourism Board, 'Tourism Expenditure Associated to Inbound Tourism – January to December 2002'.
51. Hong Kong Special Administrative Region Government, Census and Statistics Department, *Hong Kong Monthly Digest of Statistics*, February 2004, p. 117; 'Mainland Visitors Now Top Spenders as Tourism Receipts Grow to HK$64 Billion', *Hong Kong Tourism Board News*, 5 March 2002.
52. Hong Kong Special Administrative Region Government, Trade and Industry Department, *Mainland/Hong Kong Closer Economic Partnership Arrangement*, Annex 4: Section 9.3 (29 September 2003); 'Hong Kong Is Boosted by Record Number of Visitors in First Week of October', *South China Morning Post* (22 October 2003): scmp.com.
53. Grace Lam and Jonathan Tam, 'Record Visitor Arrivals Likely to Top 20m', *The Standard* (24 February 2004): A-6; Grace Lam, 'Holidays will Attract 900,000,' *The Standard* (12 January 2004): A-3; Connie Bolland, Regional Economist, 'Building on the Growth Momentum in Place ... Despite Political Bickering', presentation at 'Regional Strategic Forecast for Q1 2004, a Year to Forget ... or Remember?', Economist Corporate Network Conference, Guangzhou, 9 March 2004.
54. The Centre for Urban and Regional Studies, Zhongshan University, '*Xianggang yu zhujiang sanjiao zhou jingji guanxi yanjiu*' ('A Study of the Economic Relationship Between Hong Kong and the Pearl River Delta'), *Xianggang yu zhujiang sanjiao zhou jingji hudong yanjiu (A Study of the Hong Kong–Pearl River Delta Economic Interaction)*, April 2002, p. 10; Zheng Tianxiang and Li Huan (eds), *Yuegangao jingji guanxi (The Guangdong–Hong Kong–Macao Economic Relationship)*, Guangzhou: Sun Yatsen University Press, 2001, pp. 42–3.
55. Hong Kong people were expected to buy 19,500 to 21,400 property units in 2002 and 50% of these units were expected to be purchased in Shenzhen. See also 'HK Eyes Mainland Investment Properties', *China Daily* (24 July 2002): chinadaily.com.
56. C.Y. Leung, 'HK & Guangdong: One Country, Two Systems and One Market?' Presentation to the American Chamber of Commerce in Hong Kong, 31 May 2001. Analysts at UBS Warburg noted that though 4% of Hong Kong residents owned property in the mainland in 2003, only 0.8% actually lived there. Most Hong Kong people that bought mainland property did so in Shenzhen, but 20% of the total properties bought by Hong Kong people

in China were not rented and remain vacant. See UBS Warburg Global Equity Research, Beatrice Ho, and Franklin Lam (analysts), *HK + The Pearl River Delta: Making a Two Way Street for Tourists & Homebuyers*, 13 January 2003.

57. Approximately 2.1 million people lived in public rental housing in Hong Kong at the start of 2003, according to the Housing Planning and Lands Bureau. See Hong Kong Special Administrative Region Government, Information Services Department, 'Hong Kong: The Facts – Housing, May 2003'.

58. The Centre for Urban and Regional Studies, Zhongshan University, '*Xianggang yu zhujiang sanjiao zhou jingji guanxi yanjiu*' ('A Study of the Economic Relationship Between Hong Kong and the Pearl River Delta'), Xianggang yu zhujiang sanjiao zhou jingji hudong yanjiu (A Study of the Hong Kong–Pearl River Delta Economic Interaction), April 2002, p. 11.

59. Enright, Scott & Associates Ltd research; see also Zheng Tianxiang and Li Huan (eds), *Yuegangao jingji guanxi* (*The Guangdong–Hong Kong–Macao Economic Relationship*), Guangzhou: Sun Yatsen University Press, 2001, p. 42.

60. Hong Kong Business Professionals Federation, *Impact of Cross Border Economic Activities on Hong Kong*, January 2002, p. 7.

61. UBS Warburg Global Equity Research, Beatrice Ho, and Franklin Lam (analysts), *HK + The Pearl River Delta: Making a Two Way Street for Tourists & Homebuyers*, 13 January 2003.

62. Enright, Scott & Associates Ltd research.

63. Enright, Scott & Associates Ltd research; see also Feng Xiaoyun, *Current Conditions and Analysis of Overseas Investment in the Service Industry in the Pearl River Delta*, Hong Kong: China Business Centre, Hong Kong Polytechnic University, 2002. It cites data from the Ministry of Foreign Trade and Economic Cooperation, Guangdong Province.

64. Enright, Scott & Associates Ltd research; see also Linda F. Y. Ng and Tuan Chyau, 'Location Decisions of Manufacturing FDI in China: Implications of China's WTO Accession', *Journal of Asian Economics*, North-Holland: 14 (2003): 51–72.

65. Similarly, Tuan and Ng's study on the impact of agglomerations on FDI flows found that the distance between the core and periphery area was a critical factor in investment decisions in the Pearl River Delta region. See Tuan Chyau and Linda F. Y. Ng, 'FDI Facilitated by Agglomeration Economies: Evidence from Manufacturing and Services Joint Ventures in China', *Journal of Asian Economics*, North-Holland: 13 (2003): 749–65.

66. Hong Kong Special Administrative Region Government, Planning Department, *Cross-boundary Travel Survey 2001*, published 2002.

67. Zheng Tianxiang and Li Huan (eds), *Yuegangao jingji guanxi* (*The Guangdong–Hong Kong–Macao Economic Relationship*), Guangzhou: Sun Yatsen University Press, 2001, p. 15.

CHAPTER 5

1. Jo Wilson made a significant contribution to this chapter.

2. Michael J. Enright, Edith E. Scott, and David Dodwell, *The Hong Kong Advantage*, Hong Kong: Oxford University Press, 1997, pp. 71–80; Edward K. Y. Chen and Joseph S. L. Lee, 'Southern China Growth Triangle: An Overview', in Myo Thant, Min Tang, and Hiroshi Kakazu (eds), *Growth Triangles in Asia: A New Approach to Regional Cooperation*, Hong Kong: Asian Development Bank, 1998, pp. 58–62, 81–8.

3. Enright, Scott & Associates Ltd research; see Guo Wanda and Ma Chunhui, '*Shengang jingji hezuo de yiyi, mubiao ji duice*' ('The Meanings, Goals and Strategies of Hong

Kong–Shenzhen Economic Cooperation'), *Kaifang daobao* (*China Opening Herald Monthly*), 3 (2003): 5.

4. V. F. S. Sit, 'Increasing Globalization and the Growth of the Hong Kong Extended Metropolitan Region', in F. Lo and P. Marcottullio (eds), *Globalization and the Sustainability of Cities in the Asia Pacific Region*, Tokyo: UNU Press, 2001, pp. 199–238; Zheng Tianxiang and Li Huan (eds), *Yuegangao jingji guanxi* (*The Guangdong–Hong Kong–Macao Economic Relationship*), Guangzhou: Sun Yatsen University Press, 2001, p. 12.

5. Reported in Hong Kong Trade Development Council, *Hong Kong's Trade and Trade Supporting Services: New Developments and Prospects*, January 2002; Hong Kong Trade Development Council, *The Rise in Offshore Trade and Offshore Investment*, August 1998. See also Tuan Chyau and Linda F. Y. Ng, 'Regional Division of Labour from Agglomeration Economies' Perspectives: Some Evidence', *Journal of Asian Economics*, 12 (2001): 65–85.

6. Similarly, a survey carried out by the Hong Kong Centre for Economic Research for the Federation of Hong Kong Industries found that almost 20% of Hong Kong-based manufacturers and traders active in the mainland spend 50% or more of their time there, mostly in the Pearl River Delta. See Hong Kong Centre for Economic Research, *Made in PRD: The Changing Face of Hong Kong Manufacturers*, Hong Kong: Federation of Hong Kong Industries, June 2003.

7. Hong Kong Trade Development Council, 'Competitiveness of the HK+ PRD Region: An Export Centre in the Global Supply Chain & Operational Base for Penetrating the China Market', PowerPoint Presentation, 2003: tdctrad.com; Zheng Tianxiang and Li Huan (eds), *Yuegangao jingji guanxi* (*The Guangdong–Hong Kong–Macao Economic Relationship*), Guangzhou: Sun Yatsen University Press, 2001, pp. 45–6.

8. Zheng Tianxiang and Li Huan (eds), *Yuegangao jingji guanxi* (*The Guangdong–Hong Kong–Macao Economic Relationship*), Guangzhou: Sun Yatsen University Press, 2001, p. 17.

9. Enright, Scott & Associates Ltd research; see also Huang Zhaoyong, '*Gangzi beiyi yu yuegang jingji yitihua yanjiu*' ('Studies of the Northward Shifting of Hong Kong Capital and the Economic Integration of Hong Kong and Guangdong'), *Diyu yanjiu yu kaifa* (*Areal Research and Development*), (June 2002): 18.

10. 'Toying with the Future', *Shanghai Star* (31 October 2002); Toy Industry Association, 'U.S. Imports of Toy Products, 2002': toy-tia.org; Toy Industry Europe, 'Facts and Figures 2003', July 2003; and Hong Kong Centre for Economic Research, *Made in PRD: The Changing Face of Hong Kong Manufacturers*, Hong Kong: Federation of Hong Kong Industries, 2003.

11. Enright, Scott & Associates Ltd research and calculations. A survey carried out in 2002 by the Hong Kong Centre for Economic Research for the Federation of Hong Kong Industries yielded a similar employment figure. See Hong Kong Centre for Economic Research, *Made in PRD: The Changing Face of Hong Kong Manufacturers*, Hong Kong: Federation of Hong Kong Industries, 2003, Appendix, Table A-7.

12. Enright, Scott & Associates Ltd research.

13. Carlos Moore, Senior Vice-President, American Textile Manufacturers Institute, written submission to the United States International Trade Commission, quoted in United States International Trade Commission, *Textiles and Apparel: Assessment of the Competitiveness of Certain Foreign Suppliers to the U.S. Market*, 1, USITC Publication 3671, January 2004, p. E–5.

14. United States International Trade Commission, *Textiles and Apparel: Assessment of the Competitiveness of Certain Foreign Suppliers to the U.S. Market*, 1, USITC Publication 3671, January 2004, pp. E–8 to E–9.

15. Hong Kong Special Administrative Region Government, Hong Kong Census and Statistics Department, *Hong Kong Annual Digest of Statistics 2003*, pp. 55, 59.
16. Hong Kong Centre for Economic Research, *Made in PRD: The Changing Face of Hong Kong Manufacturers*, Hong Kong: Federation of Hong Kong Industries, 2003, Appendix, Table A-7.
17. Liu Li, 'Incredible Journey Planned to Reach Distant Loved Ones', *China Daily* (1 February 2002): 5.
18. 'Children's Garment Centre Completed', *China Daily* (30 January 2002): 3.
19. Zhangcha was home to 1,600 knitting mills in 2003, producing fabric with an annual export value of nearly US$121 million. 'A Knitting Kingdom – Zhangcha', South China GC.comm (May 2003).
20. Global Sources, 'Sourcing Report: Denim Jeans', globalsources.com (20 October 2003).
21. Catholic Agency for Overseas Development (CAFOD), 'Clean up Your Computer: Working Conditions in the Electronics Sector', London, 26 January 2004.
22. 'China's Electronics Industry Registers Rapid Growth', *People's Daily* (10 January 2002): peopledaily.com.
23. LSI Logic, 'China: Centerpiece of a Winning Strategy for the Consumer Electronics Market and LSI Logic', 2004.
24. GK Goh, 'Consumer Electronics: China's Outsourcing Magnet Fuels Growth', 10 December 2003.
25. Booz, Allen, Hamilton, 'Electronics Manufacturing in Emerging Markets', 2 June 2003.
26. Quoted in Karl Shoenberger, 'Cheap Products' Human Cost', *Mercury News* (24 November 2002).
27. Enright, Scott & Associates Ltd research.
28. Hong Kong Centre for Economic Research, *Made in PRD: The Changing Face of Hong Kong Manufacturers*, Hong Kong: Federation of Hong Kong Industries, 2003, Appendix, Table A-7.
29. Hong Kong electronics producers tend to favour Shanghai over the Pearl River Delta region as a location for the development of China markets. However, for certain items such as mobile phones and security systems, the Pearl River Delta region is widely viewed as the mainland's most important market. Enright, Scott & Associates Ltd research.
30. For R&D in general, and particularly for software development, Shanghai is often favoured by many Hong Kong electronics producers.
31. Enright, Scott & Associates Ltd research.
32. Mike Patterson, 'China's Dongguan Transforms from Opium Battleground to Hi-tech Dragon', *Things Asian* (12 June 2002): thingsasian.com.
33. Hong Kong Trade Development Council, 'Hong Kong as a Service Platform for Taiwan Companies Investing in the Mainland', 31 October 2002.
34. Enright, Scott & Associates Ltd research; Hong Kong Trade Development Council, 'Hong Kong as a Service Platform for Taiwan Companies Investing in the Mainland', *Economic Forum*, 31 October 2002.
35. Jinn-yuh Hsu, 'From Transfer to Hybridization: The Changing Organizations of Taiwanese PC Investments in China', Department of Geography, National Taiwan University (undated).
36. Hong Kong Trade Development Council, 'Market Share of Famous Brand Names Grows', *Business Alert-China*, 15 February 2000; 'Nine Chinese TV Producers Face up to EU's Anti-dumping Complaint', *People's Daily* (24 July 2000): peopledaily.com.

37. Duncan Clark, 'Going Global, China's Handset Manufacturers Take on the World', *Eurobiz Magazine*, August 2003: sinomedia.net.
38. Federation of the Swiss Watch Industry, 'The Swiss Watch Industry in 2000', Bienne 2001; Federation of the Swiss Watch Industry, 'The Swiss Watch Industry in 2002', Bienne 2003.
39. Hong Kong Trade Development Council, 'Hong Kong's Watches & Clocks Industry', 1 March 2004.
40. Hong Kong Centre for Economic Research, *Made in PRD: The Changing Face of Hong Kong Manufacturers*, Hong Kong: Federation of Hong Kong Industries, 2003, Appendix, Table A-7.
41. Edith Scott, *First Choice Hong Kong – Your Asia-Pacific Platform: A Practical Handbook for Businesses*, 2nd edn, Hong Kong: Hong Kong Trade Development Council and Invest Hong Kong, 2002.
42. James J. Wang and Brian Slack, 'The Evolution of a Regional Container Port System: The Pearl River Delta', *Journal of Transport Geography*, 8, 4 (2000): 265.
43. For more on the history of port development in Hong Kong and the Pearl River Delta, see Claude Comtois and Brian Slack, 'Hong Kong: Adding Value to China – Transport Hub and Urban Super-Region', *China Perspectives*, 29 (May–June 2000): 11–8; James J. Wang and Brian Slack, 'The Evolution of a Regional Container Port System: The Pearl River Delta', *Journal of Transport Geography*, 8, 4 (2000): 263–75; and Sung Yun-wing, Liu Pak-wai, Richard Yue-chim Wong, and Lau Pui-king (eds), *The Fifth Dragon*, Hong Kong: Addison Wesley, 1995, pp. 193–8.
44. Hong Kong Port and Maritime Board, *Summary Statistics on Port Traffic in Hong Kong*, 2003.
45. Michael J. Enright, Edith E. Scott, and David Dodwell, *The Hong Kong Advantage*, Hong Kong: Oxford University Press, 1997, pp. 122–9; Liu Shaojian and Shi Yan, '*Yuegang hezuo tisheng*' ('The Promotion of Guangdong–Hong Kong Cooperation'), *Zhongguo wuliu yu caigou* (*China Logistics and Procurement*) (January 2003): 27; see also Zheng Tianxiang and Li Huan (eds), *Yuegangao jingji guanxi* (*The Guangdong–Hong Kong–Macao Economic Relationship*), Guangzhou: Sun Yatsen University Press, 2001, pp. 80–1.
46. Data received from the Hong Kong Shippers' Council, citing Hong Kong Special Administrative Region Government Census and Statistics Department and Marine Department, Hong Kong Port and Maritime Board, Shenzhen Municipal Transport Bureau, and the Shenzhen Municipal Port Authority.
47. Data received from the Hong Kong Shippers' Council; 'Shenzhen Loads Up 50pc', *The Standard* (15 January 2003): thestandard.com; and 'Mainland Ports Booming', *The Standard* (7 June 2002): thestandard.com. Data from Hong Kong Shippers' Council, citing Hong Kong Special Administrative Region Government Census and Statistics Department and Marine Department, Hong Kong Port and Maritime Board, Shenzhen Municipal Transport Bureau, and the Shenzhen Municipal Port Authority.
48. See Zheng Tianxiang and Li Huan (eds), *Yuegangao jingji guanxi* (*The Guangdong–Hong Kong–Macao Economic Relationship*), Guangzhou: Sun Yatsen University Press, 2001, pp. 75–9.
49. Research and Statistics Team, Hong Kong Shippers' Council.
50. Enright, Scott & Associates Ltd research.
51. Enright, Scott & Associates Ltd research. In a survey carried out by the Hong Kong Centre for Economic Research of 2,597 Hong Kong-based manufacturers, 70% of companies surveyed chose Yantian in addition to Hong Kong to ship products. The most

important reason for this was overseas buyers' requests, followed by transportation costs and transportation time. (Hong Kong Centre for Economic Research, *Made in PRD: The Changing Face of Hong Kong Manufacturers*, Hong Kong: Federation of Hong Kong Industries, June 2003, p. 29.)

52. James J. Wang and Brian Slack, 'The Evolution of a Regional Container Port System: The Pearl River Delta', *Journal of Transport Geography*, 8, 4 (2000): 272.

53. Hong Kong Trade Development Council, *Hong Kong's Trade and Trade Supporting Services: New Developments and Prospects*, January 2002, pp. 8–9.

54. 'Technology Holds the Key to Keep Cargo Moving', *South China Morning Post* (5 July 2002): scmp.com.

55. *Hong Kong International Airport Annual Report, 2002.*

56. Hong Kong International Airport: hkairport.com.

57. *Guangdong Statistical Yearbook* 2003, p. 380; see also 'Rival Airports Pose a Threat to Chek Lap Kok', *South China Morning Post* (14 May 2002): scmp.com.

58. *Shenzhen Statistical Yearbook 2003*, p. 111.

59. FedEx Press Releases, 'FedEx Pioneers International Air-Express Service in Shenzhen', 2 November 1999.

60. Macao International Airport: macau-airport.gov.mo.

61. Gary Cheung, 'Regional Airport Chiefs Set to Discuss Coordination of Services', *South China Morning Post* (16 June 2003): scmp.com.

62. Hong Kong Special Administrative Region Government, Census and Statistics Department, *Quarterly Report of Employment and Vacancies Statistics*, 2001 and 2002; Hong Kong Trade Development Council, 'Profile of Hong Kong's Major Service Industries – Import and Export Trade, 21 August 2003; Tuan Chyau and Linda F. Y. Ng, 'FDI Facilitated by Agglomeration Economies: Evidence from Manufacturing and Services Joint Ventures in China', *Journal of Asian Economics*, 13 (2003): 753; see also Sung Yun-wing, Liu Pak-wai, Richard Yue-chim Wong, and Lau Pui-king (eds), *The Fifth Dragon*, Hong Kong: Addison Wesley, 1995, pp. 92–7.

63. Edith Scott, *Hong Kong: Marketplace for the World*, November 2003, pp. 16–7.

64. Enright, Scott & Associates Ltd research; see also Hang Seng Bank Economic Research Department, 'Strengthening Economic Integration with the Pearl River Delta' (in Chinese), *Hang Seng Economic Monthly*, May 2001.

65. Edith Scott, *Hong Kong: Marketplace for the World*, November 2003, pp. 13–7; Edith Scott, *Hong Kong Plus: Your Global Platform for Sourcing, Producing and Selling in China*, October 2002, pp. 17–8.

66. For a discussion of CEPA's provisions in logistics and transportation, see Chapter 7.

67. See Liu Shaojian and Shi Yan, '*Yuegang hezuo tisheng*' ('The Promotion of Guangdong–Hong Kong Cooperation') *Zhongguo wuliu yu caigou* (*China Logistics and Procurement*) (January 2003): 26–7; Tan Gang, '*Zhusanjiao: goujian shijie gongchang yu fazhan xiandai wuliuye – jianlun shenzhen yu xianggang wuliuye hezuo*' ('The Pearl River Delta: Building the World's Factory and Developing a Modern Logistics Industry – A Discussion of Shenzhen–Hong Kong Cooperation in the Logistics Industry') *Kaifang daobao* (*China Opening Herald Monthly*) 5 (2003): 19.

68. Enright, Scott & Associates Ltd research.

69. 'The Ministry of Justice of the People's Republic of China Notice (2002 No. 10 and No. 11)', *China Daily* (20 and 21 September 2002): chinadaily.com.

70. Enright, Scott & Associates Ltd research; see also Hang Seng Bank Economic Research Department, 'Strengthening Economic Integration with the Pearl River Delta' (in Chinese), *Hang Seng Economic Monthly,* May 2001.

CHAPTER 6

1. See Zuo Liancun, Wang Hongliang, and Huang Guoxian, '*Zhongguo giaru* WTO *dui yueganggao jingji de yingxiang*' ('The Impact of China's WTO Entry on the Economies of Guangdong, Hong Kong and Macao') *Guoji jingji hezuo* (*International Economic Cooperation*), 11 (2000): 3; Feng Xiaoyun, 'WTO *kuangjia xia yuegang jingji hezuo de chuangxin yu tupo*' ('Innovations and Breakthroughs in Guangdong-Hong Kong Economic Cooperation under the WTO Framework'), *Kaifang daobao* (*China Opening Herald Monthly*), 12 (2002): 16–7.
2. Office of the United States Trade Representative, *2004 National Trade Estimate Report on Foreign Trade Barriers,* 1 April 2004; European Commission, Directorate General for External Relations, 'EU–China Sectoral Agreements and Dialogue', External Relations Website.
3. Guangdong Government Development Research Centre, *Rushi hou de Guangdong jingji yunzuo – 'Zhongguo rushi yu Guangdong jingji' xupian* (*Guangdong's Economy after China's Entry into the WTO – A Sequel to 'China's WTO Entry and Guangdong's Economy'*), Guangzhou: Guangdong Economic Press, 2002, pp. 76–84. See also Zuo Liancun, Wang Hongliang, and Huang Guoxian, '*Zhongguo giaru* WTO *dui yuegang jingji de yingxiang*' ('The Impact of China's WTO Entry on the Economies of Guangdong, Hong Kong and Macao'), *Guoji jingji hezuo* (*International Economic Cooperation*), 11 (2000); Feng Xiaoyun, 'WTO *kuangjia xia yuegang jingji hezuo de chuangxin yu tupo*' ('Innovations and Breakthroughs in Guangdong-Hong Kong Economic Cooperation under the WTO Framework'), *Kaifang daobao* (*China Opening Herald Monthly*), 12 (2002): 16; and Hong Kong Trade Development Council, *China's WTO Entry and its Implications for Hong Kong,* 22 November 2001.
4. CEPA is technically speaking a free trade arrangement, not an agreement, as it is not between two sovereign nations. For the text of CEPA, see Hong Kong Special Administrative Region Government, Trade and Industry Department, *Mainland/Hong Kong Closer Economic Partnership Arrangement,* 29 June 2003 and 29 September 2003.
5. Hong Kong General Chamber of Commerce, *CEPA Business Assessment,* November 2003, pp. 39–40.
6. Stephen Fletcher, Partner, Linklaters Hong Kong, 'CEPA Definition of Hong Kong Companies', Hong Kong General Chamber of Commerce Roundtable Workshop, 24 November 2003.
7. See Hong Kong Special Administrative Region Government, Trade and Industry Department, *Mainland/Hong Kong Closer Economic Partnership Arrangement,* Annex 5 (29 September 2003).
8. See Hong Kong Special Administrative Region Government, Trade and Industry Department, *Mainland/Hong Kong Closer Economic Partnership Arrangement,* Annex 5, Footnote to Section 3.1.2(2) (29 September 2003).
9. Hong Kong Trade Development Council, 'CEPA to Drive Co-operation of Logistics Industry in the Chinese Mainland and Hong Kong', (May 2004): tdctrade.com; 'Cepa Helps Japanese Logistics Firm Expand in China', *Hong Kong Trader* (8 March 2004): hktrader.net.
10. 'Luxury Goods Group Sees CEPA as a Business Generator', *Hong Kong Trader* (1 April 2004): hktrader.net.

11. 'World Banks Localise for First-mover Advantage in China', *Hong Kong Trader* (28 April 2004): hktrader.net.
12. International Monetary Fund, *World Economic Outlook Database*, September 2003.
13. 'GNI per Capita 2002, Atlas Method and PPP', World Development Indicators Database, World Bank, July 2003.
14. 'Rise of the Bourgeoisie', *Asia Inc* (July 2003): 8.
15. 'Behind the Mask', *The Economist*, 370, 8367, special section (20 March 2004): 3–4.
16. 'Patriot's Paradox: for China's Youth Internationalism is Desired Destination', *Journal of the American Chamber of Commerce in Hong Kong* (February 2004): 31.
17. Mario Cavolo, 'China Decade Pt II' (23 September 2002): shanghaiexpat.com.
18. Hong Kong Trade Development Council, 'Shenzhen', tdctrade.com.
19. Marcal Joanilho, 'Private-car Sales Soar in Shenzhen', *South China Morning Post* (29 June 2003): scmp.com.
20. 'Emerging Opportunities in Auto Service Sector', *Business Alert – China* (1 June 2003): tdctrade.com.
21. 'Patriot's Paradox: for China's Youth Internationalism is Desired Destination', *Journal of the American Chamber of Commerce in Hong Kong* (February 2004): 31.
22. James Kynge, 'How Long can China Continue to Boom?', *Financial Times* (23 March 2004): FT.com.
23. *Guangdong Statistical Yearbook 2001*.
24. A study by Seto and Kaufmann found urban expansion in the Pearl River Delta to be driven by foreign investment and the relative rates of return on the land, as well as off-farm wage rates and the influx of migrant workers into the delta region. See Karen C. Seto and Robert Kaufmann, 'Modeling the Drivers of Urban Land Use Change in the Pearl River Delta, China: Integrating Remote Sensing with Socioeconomic Data', *Land Economics*, 79, 1 (February 2003): 106–21. Similarly, a study by Yeh and Li concludes that much of the urban development in the Pearl River Delta has been the unplanned result of economic development. See A. G. O. Yeh and X. Li, 'The Need for Compact Development in Fast Growing Areas of China: The Pearl River Delta', in M. Jenks and R. Burgess (eds), *Compact Cities: Sustainable Urban Forms for Developing Countries*, London: Spon Press, 2000, pp. 73–90.
25. Alberto Nogales and Graham Smith, 'China's Evolving Transport Sector', *The China Business Review*, 31, 2 (March/April 2004): 26.
26. On the east–west axis, the highway between Shanghai and Chengdu completed by year-end 2003 has cut travel time from five or more days to three to four days.
27. Dr Victor K. Fung, Chairman, Hong Kong Airport Authority, 'A New Road Map for Hong Kong', Speech to the Swiss Business Council/Swiss Association, 8 March 2004.
28. Alberto Nogales and Graham Smith, 'China's Evolving Transport Sector', *The China Business Review*, 31, 2 (March/April 2004): 26, 29.
29. Pamela Pun, 'Guangzhou Plans Largest Asia Rail Hub', *The Standard* (13 February 2004): A-8.
30. 'Traffic Woes to Ease with Express Thoroughfares', *People's Daily* (17 November 2003): peopledaily.com; 'Eight Railways to Bring Vitality into GPRD', China.Org. (15 March 2004): china.org.cn.
31. See also Hong Kong Special Administrative Region Government, Planning Department, 'Development Interface between Hong Kong and Mainland', in *Hong Kong 2030 Planning Vision and Strategy*, Working Paper 18, January 2002; Hong Kong Trade

Development Council, *China's WTO Entry and its Impact on Hong Kong*, January 2000, p. 40; and Report by the Hong Kong General Chamber of Commerce, *The Impact of China's WTO Entry on Hong Kong's Businesses, a View from the Business Sector* (in Chinese), June 2000.

32. Pamela Pun, '"9+2" Bloc Moves to Co-ordinate Development', *The Standard* (12 February 2004): A-7; Leu Siew Ying, 'Close Co-operation Best Remedy for Region', *South China Morning Post* (16 February 2004): A-4.

33. Leu Siew Ying, 'Close Co-operation Best Remedy for Region', *South China Morning Post* (16 February 2004): A-4.

34. Liu Zhijun, Railways Minister of the People's Republic of China, as quoted in Chow Chung-yan, 'Overhaul of Delta Transport Links to Slash Travel Times', *South China Morning Post* (1 June 2004): A-3.

35. By comparison, US–ASEAN bilateral trade was $120 billion in 2003. ASEAN–China Expert Group on Economic Cooperation, 'Forging Closer ASEAN–China Economic Relations in the Twenty-first Century', October 2001.

36. ASEAN–China Expert Group on Economic Cooperation, 'Forging Closer ASEAN–China Economic Relations in the Twenty-first Century', October 2001.

37. Inkyo Cheong, 'Korea's FTA Policy', Pacific Economic Cooperation Council Trade Forum, 25 May 2003.

38. Siaou-Sze Lien, Senior Vice-President of HP Services Asia-Pacific, as quoted in 'China Becoming New Engine for World Economy: Forbes', *People's Daily* (18 September 2003): peopledaily.com.

39. Ron Spithill, President of Alcatel Asia-Pacific Region, as quoted in 'China to Become Largest Market for Computer Equipments in 5 Years: Intel CEO', *People's Daily* (3 March 2004): peopledaily.com.

40. Andrew Grove, CEO of Intel, as quoted in 'China to Become Largest Market for Computer Equipments in 5 Years: Intel CEO', *People's Daily* (3 March 2004): peopledaily. com.

41. American Chambers of Commerce in Shanghai and Beijing, *2003 White Paper: American Business in China*, 2003.

42. 'We are the Champions', *The Economist: Special Section*, 370, 8367 (20 March 2004): 13–15.

43. 'We are the Champions', *The Economist: Special Section*, 370, 8367 (20 March 2004): 13–15.

44. 'We are the Champions', *The Economist: Special Section*, 370, 8367 (20 March 2004): 13–15.

45. 'We are the Champions', *The Economist: Special Section*, 370, 8367 (20 March 2004): 13–15.

46. Ray Brooks and Ran Tao, 'China's Labor Market Performance and Challenges', IMF Working Paper #WP/03/210, November 2003.

47. 'On the Capitalist Road', *The Economist*, 370, 8367, special section (20 March 2004): 15–17.

48. 'Haier's Purpose', *The Economist*, 370, 8367 (20 March 2004): 72.

49. 'Huawei–3Com Union Makes Sense', *South China Morning Post: Business Post* (19 November 2003): 2.

50. 'CNOOC Outlines Oil, Natural Gas Output Targets', *People's Daily* (9 March 2004): peopledaily.com.

51. 'China's Largest Semi-trailer Production Base Operational', *Asia Pulse* (7 April 2004): au.news.yahoo.com.

52. Zheng Xianling, auto analyst with China Securities Co., quoted in 'Logistics Company Seeks IPO this Year', *People's Daily* (17 March 2004): peopledaily.com.

53. Daniel Chan, Baker & McKenzie, 'CEPA Trading/Distribution/Retail WOFE', Presentation to the Dutch Business Association of Hong Kong, 12 February 2004.

54. Enright, Scott & Associates Ltd research.

55. Enright, Scott & Associates Ltd research.

56. DTZ Research, 'Asia Pacific Property Market Overview 2004', February 2004, p. 8.

57. *Guangdong Statistical Yearbook 2003*, pp. 36, 46.

58. Numbers taken from statistical yearbooks of Hong Kong, Guangzhou, and Guangdong. See also A. G. O. Yeh, *The Hong Kong–Pearl River Delta Producer Services Linkages*, Hong Kong: Centre for Urban Planning and Environmental Management, University of Hong Kong, 2002.

59. 'Tung Urges Fast Track for New Bridge', *South China Morning Post* (29 August 2003): scmp.com.

60. '24-Hour Border Beats Forecast', *The Standard* (6 February 2003): thestandard. com.; Leu Siew Ying, 'Western Corridor Border to Operate around the Clock', *South China Morning Post* (16 February 2004): A-1.

61. Louisa Yan, 'Border Crossings up by 10 pc to 128m People', *South China Morning Post* (6 January 2004): A-4.

62. Hong Kong Special Administrative Region Government, Environment, Transport and Works Bureau, *The Hong Kong–Zhuhai–Macau Bridge*, 6 August 2003; 'Authorities Back HK Bridge Design', *South China Morning Post* (22 July 2003): scmp.com.

63. 'HK Sea Bridge Could Start in Mid-2004', *China Daily* (29 July 2003): chinadaily.com.

64. See also One Country Two Systems Research Institute, *Background Information for the Guangdong–Hong Kong–Macau Bridge – Consensus and Dissension* (in Chinese), September 2002; One Country Two Systems Research Institute, *A Comprehensive Coordination Solution for the Guangdong–Hong Kong–Macau Bridge* (in Chinese), September 2002; and One Country Two Systems Research Institute, *An Assessment of the Cost and Benefits of the Guangdong–Hong Kong–Macau Bridge* in Chinese, December 2002.

65. Pamela Pun, 'Wen to Rein in Economy', *The Standard* (15 March 2004): A-1; Wang Xiangwei, 'Critical Year for the Economy: Premier', *South China Morning Post* (15 March 2004): A-1; and Wu Zhong, 'Shift in Focus', *The Standard* (9 March 2004): A-33.

66. The Research Team of the Guangdong Government Development Research Centre, '*Guangdong jingji mianlin de xin xingshi yu duice fenxi*' ('An Analysis of the New Situation Facing the Guangdong Economy and Related Strategies') *Guangdong Jingji* (*Guangdong Economy*), (January 2001): 11–12. As of mid-2003, work was starting on Guangdong Province's Eleventh Five-year Plan under the leadership of Governor Huang Huahua who assumed office in January 2003.

67. Guangdong Government State Development Planning Commission, *Tuijin xiandaihua, kaichuang xinjiyuan: Guangdong sheng guomin jingji he shehui fazhan shiwu jihua* (*Pushing Forward Modernisation, Opening up a New Era: The Tenth Five-year Plan for the Economic and Social Development of Guangdong*), Guangzhou: Guangdong Economic Press, 2001, pp. 473–508. Chen Mingde, Vice-Mayor of Guangzhou, has stressed the importance of cooperation with Hong Kong for Guangzhou's future development, particularly in light of the Closer Economic Partnership Arrangement (CEPA). Guangzhou is keen to develop the logistics and financial sectors, as well as automobile and related industries, and intends to capitalise on increased opportunities for Hong Kong involvement in Guangzhou afforded by CEPA. Chen Mingde, Vice-Mayor of Guangzhou, *South China Morning Post*/Hong Kong

General Chamber of Commerce, *The Second Pearl River Delta Conference: Charging Ahead to a New Pearl River Super Zone*, 'Cities Forum: Panel Discussion', 17 October 2003, Hong Kong.

68. The Publicity Department of the Guangdong Committee of the Communist Party of China, *Zhujiang sanjiaozhou jingjiqu fazhan zhanlue yu guihua yanjiu* (*A Study of the Development Strategies and Planning of the Pearl River Delta Economic Zone*), Guangzhou: Guangdong People's Press, 1995, pp. 76–119, 128–33, 147–52, and 296–303.

69. Guangdong Government State Development Planning Commission, *Tuijin xiandaihua, kaichuang xinjiyuan: Guangdong sheng guomin jingji he shehui fazhan shiwu jihua* (*Pushing Forward Modernisation, Opening up a New Era: The Tenth Five-year Plan for the Economic and Social Development of Guangdong*), Guangzhou: Guangdong Economic Press, 2001, pp. 509–39.

70. Hong Kong Special Administrative Region Government, Planning Department, *Note on the Planning Implications of Mainland's Tenth Five-year Plan*, Working Paper 22, May 2002.

71. Remarks by Wang Zhile, Researcher, Economic Academy, Ministry of Foreign Trade and Economic Co-operation, at the South China Morning Post Conference, *Pearl River Delta: Forging a New Force*, special session on 'Multinational Companies' Development in Shenzhen', 9 July 2002, Hong Kong.

72. The Shenzhen Museum, *Shenzhen Tequ Shi* (*History of the Shenzhen Special Economic Zone*), Beijing: People's Publishing House, 1999, pp. 380–623; Enright, Scott & Associates Ltd research.

73. Enright, Scott & Associates Ltd research.

74. Guangdong Government State Development Planning Commission, *Tuijin xiandaihua, kaichuang xinjiyuan: Guangdong sheng guomin jingji he shehui fazhan shiwu jihua* (*Pushing Forward Modernisation, Opening up a New Era: The Tenth Five-year Plan for the Economic and Social Development of Guangdong*), Guangzhou: Guangdong Economic Press, 2001, pp. 680–704.

75. Wang Liwen, Yue Yue, and Yang Changzun, *Jianshe zhujiang sanjiao zhou jingji qu – cehuapian* (*Building the Pearl River Delta Economic Zone – The Planning*), Guangzhou: Guangzhou Press, 1995, pp. 64–7.

76. For more detailed information on the economic development plans and economies of the different jurisdictions in the Pearl River Delta, see Michael Enright and Edith Scott, *The Greater Pearl River Delta*, Hong Kong: Invest Hong Kong, June 2004.

77. Guangdong Government State Development Planning Commission, *Tuijin xiandaihua, kaichuang xinjiyuan: Guangdong sheng guomin jingji he shehui fazhan shiwu jihua* (*Pushing Forward Modernisation, Opening up a New Era: The Tenth Five-year Plan for the Economic and Social Development of Guangdong*), Guangzhou: Guangdong Economic Press, 2001, pp. 540–53.

78. Michael J. Enright, Edith E. Scott, and David Dodwell, *The Hong Kong Advantage*, Hong Kong: Oxford University Press, 1997, pp. 29–34.

79. Hong Kong Special Administrative Region Government, Information Services Department, 'Hong Kong: The Facts–Housing', May 2003.

80. Hong Kong Special Administrative Region Government, Commission on Strategic Development, 'Bringing the Vision to Life – Hong Kong's Long Term Development Needs and Goals', February 2000, pp. 5, 18, and 24–33.

81. See Hong Kong Special Administrative Region Government, Planning Department, 'Hong Kong 2030 Planning Vision and Strategy: Stage 3 Public Consultation', Consultation

Booklet; see also Cheung Chifai, 'More Space, Fewer People in HK's Future View', *South China Morning Post* (26 November 2003): A-1; Chloe Lai, 'Suggestions for HK's Future Mapped Out', *South China Morning Post* (22 November 2003): A-3; and Joseph Lo, Russell Barling, and Carrie Chan, 'Need for a Third Runway is Signalled', *South China Morning Post* (26 November 2003): A-3.

CHAPTER 7

1. 'Trade between Hong Kong and Guangdong Reaches US$ 38.7 Billion', *Ta Kung Pao* (10 April 2002).
2. Hong Kong Centre for Economic Research, *Made in PRD: The Changing Face of Hong Kong Manufacturers*, Hong Kong: Hong Kong Federation of Industries, June 2003, Appendix, Table A-8.
3. Zheng Tianxiang and Li Huan (eds), *Yuegangao jingji guanxi* (*The Guangdong–Hong Kong–Macao EconomicRelationship*), Guangzhou: Sun Yatsen University Press, 2001, p. 55; Chen Lijun and Lin Jiang, *Jiuqi hou de tantao – xianggang jingji ji qi yu neidi jingji guanxi* (*A Discussion of the Post-1997 Hong Kong Economy and its Relationship with the Economy of the Chinese Mainland*), Hong Kong: Cosmos Books Limited, 2000, pp. 317–21.
4. Hong Kong Trade Development Council, *Hong Kong as an International Commercial and Financial Centre – From the Perspective of Mainland Private Enterprises*, June 2002.
5. Edith Scott, *Hong Kong Plus: Your Global Platform for Sourcing, Producing and Selling in China*, Hong Kong: Hong Kong Trade Development Council, October 2002.
6. Hong Kong Trade Development Council, *Hong Kong's Trade and Trade Supporting Services: New Developments and Prospects*, January 2002.
7. See also Hong Kong Special Administrative Region Government, Planning Department, 'Development Interface between Hong Kong and Mainland', in *Hong Kong 2030 Planning Vision and Strategy*, Working Paper 18, January 2002; Hong Kong Trade Development Council, *China's WTO Entry and its Impact on Hong Kong*, January 2000, p. 40; The Hong Kong General Chamber of Commerce, *The Impact of China's WTO Entry on Hong Kong's Businesses, a View from the Business Sector* (in Chinese), June 2000; and Zuo Liancun, Wang Hongliang, and Huang Guoxian, 'Zhongguo giaru WTO dui yuegangao jingji de yingxiang' ('The Impact of China's WTO Entry on the Economies of Guangdong, Hong Kong and Macao') *Guoji jingji hezuo* (*International Economic Cooperation*), 11 (2000): 3.
8. Firms are subject to a threshold requirement of US$ 10 million average trade volume with the mainland in the previous three years. Hong Kong Special Administrative Region Government, Trade and Industry Department, *Mainland/Hong Kong Closer Economic Partnership Arrangement*, Annex 4: Table 1, Section 4.3 (29 September 2003).
9. Raymond Ma, 'Manufacturers Weigh up Moving Back to Hong Kong', *South China Morning Post* (29 September 2003): B1.
10. Hong Kong General Chamber of Commerce, *Closer Economic Partnership Arrangement: Business Assessment*, November 2003, pp. 33–4.
11. Enright Scott & Associates Ltd research.
12. Hong Kong Special Administrative Region Government, Trade and Industry Department, *Mainland/Hong Kong Closer Economic Partnership Arrangement*, Annex 4: Table 1, Section 1.F (29 September 2003); see also Hong Kong General Chamber of Commerce, *Closer Economic Partnership Arrangement: Business Assessment*, November 2003, p. 62.
13. Paul Woodward, Principal, Business Strategies Group.

14.   'Pearl River Delta Becomes the Biggest Hi-Tech Industry Base in China', *Hong Kong Economic Journal* (20 June 2002).
15.   See also Zheng Tianxiang and Li Huan (eds), *Yuegangao jingji guanxi* (*The Guangdong–Hong Kong–Macao Economic Relationship*), Guangzhou: Sun Yatsen University Press, 2001, pp. 54–5.
16.   Enright, Scott & Associates Ltd research.
17.   As of late 2003, there were indications that under CEPA, some Taiwanese firms were exploring the possibility of selectively moving certain high-tech manufacturing operations into Hong Kong in order to benefit from zero tariff access to the mainland (Enright, Scott & Associates Ltd research).
18.   See also Guo Wanda and Ma Chunhui, '*Shengang jingji hezuo de yiyi, mubiao ji duice*' ('The Meanings, Goals and Strategies of Hong Kong–Shenzhen Economic Cooperation'), *Kaifang daobao* (*China Opening Herald Monthly*), 3 (2003): 6–7; and Chen Lijun and Lin Jiang, *Jjiuqi hou de tantao – xianggang jingji ji qi yu neidi jingji guanxi* (*A Discussion of the Post-1997 Hong Kong Economy and its Relationship with the Economy of the Chinese Mainland*), Hong Kong: Cosmos Books Limited, 2000, pp. 312–17, 322–3.
19.   Enright, Scott & Associates Ltd research.
20.   Enright, Scott & Associates Ltd research.
21.   See Duan Jie and Yan Xiaopei, '*Yuegang shengchan xing fuwu ye hezuo fazhan yanjiu*' ('A Study of the Development of Cooperation Between Hong Kong and Guangdong in the Producer Services Sector'), *Diyu yanjiu yu kaifa* (*Areal Research and Development*), (June 2003): 26–30; Zuo Liancun, Wang Hongliang, and Huang Guoxian, '*Zhongguo giaru WTO dui yuegangao jingji de yingxiang*' ('The Impact of China's WTO Entry on the Economies of Guangdong, Hong Kong and Macao'), *Guoji jingji hezuo* (*International Economic Cooperation*), 1 (2000): 3; and Feng Xiaoyun, '*WTO kuangjia xia yuegang jingji hezuo de chuangxin yu tupo*' ('Innovations and Breakthroughs in Guangdong–Hong Kong Economic Cooperation under the WTO Framework'), *Kaifang daobao* (*China Opening Herald Monthly*), 12 (2002): 16.
22.   Enright, Scott & Associates Ltd research; see also Bank of East Asia Economic Research Department, 'Hong Kong: City for Mainland Entrepreneurs', *Economic Analysis*, July 2002. This report maintains that entrepreneurs and affluent individuals from mainland China will play a key role in positioning Hong Kong as the business centre for the mainland.
23.   Hong Kong Special Administrative Region Government, Transport Department, *Monthly Traffic and Transport Digest* (December 2003): Table 8.1 (d).
24.   Hong Kong Special Administrative Region Government, Trade and Industry Department, *Mainland/Hong Kong Closer Economic Partnership Arrangement*, Annex 4: Table 1, Section 11.F (29 September 2003).
25.   C. Y. Leung, 'Social Implications of Pearl River Delta Integration: Livelihood Issues and Social Welfare', Speech to the Hong Kong General Chamber of Commerce/South China Morning Post Pearl River Delta Forum, 8 July 2002.
26.   'Authorities Back HK Bridge Design', *South China Morning Post* (22 July 2003): scmp.com.
27.   Ian Petersen, KCRC, Presentation to the Hong Kong AmCham Transportation and Logistics Committee, 24 April 2002; Hong Kong Special Administrative Region Government, Planning Department, 'Development Interface between Hong Kong and Mainland', in *Hong Kong 2030 Planning Vision and Strategy*, Working Paper 18, January 2002.
28.   Hong Kong Special Administrative Region Government, Trade and Industry Department, *Mainland/Hong Kong Closer Economic Partnership Arrangement*, Annex 4: Table 1, Section 11.A.H (29 September 2003).

29. Hong Kong Special Administrative Region Government, Planning Department, 'Hong Kong 2030 Planning Vision and Strategy: Stage 3 Public Consultation', Consultation Booklet.
30. 'Airport Authority Eyes Shenzhen Stake', *The Standard* (19 September 2002): thestandard.com.
31. Russell Barling, 'Dragonair Expands Services to Delta', *South China Morning Post: Business Post* (25 November 2003): 2.
32. 'Helicopter Service Offers Zhuhai in 17 Minutes', *South China Morning Post* (20 March 2002): scmp.com.
33. 'OBI Moves Asian Hub to Shenzhen', *South China Morning Post* (10 November 2003): scmp.com.
34. Hong Kong Special Administrative Region Government, Trade and Industry Department, *Mainland/Hong Kong Closer Economic Partnership Arrangement*, Annex 4: Table 1, Section 12 (29 September 2003).
35. 'Scanner Checks at Border Likely for 2004' *South China Morning Post* (3 September 2004): scmp.com; 'Shenzhen Plans Giant Checkpoint', *The Standard* (11 September 2003): thestandard.com.
36. Hong Kong Special Administrative Region Government, Trade and Industry Department, *Mainland/Hong Kong Closer Economic Partnership Arrangement*, Annex 6: Section 4 (29 September 2003).
37. 'Hactl to Improve Cargo Flows', *South China Morning Post* (29 March 2002): scmp.com.
38. Russell Barling, 'Hactl Gains Mainland Foothold', *South China Morning Post: Business Post* (4 October 2003): 1.
39. Hong Kong Special Administrative Region Government, Planning Department, 'Hong Kong 2030 Planning Vision and Strategy: Stage 3 Public Consultation', Consultation Booklet.
40. Hong Kong Special Administrative Region Government, Trade and Industry Department, *Mainland/Hong Kong Closer Economic Partnership Arrangement*, Annex 4: Table 1, Section 9.3 (29 September 2003). Hong Kong authorities were aiming for extension of this arrangement to Guangdong Province by May 2004, ahead of the CEPA deadline. See 'Hong Kong is Boosted by Record Number of Visitors in First Week of October', *South China Morning Post* (22 October 2003): scmp.com.
41. Hong Kong Special Administrative Region Government, Trade and Industry Department, *Mainland/Hong Kong Closer Economic Partnership Arrangement*, Annex 4: Table 1, Section 9.2 (29 September 2003).
42. Chen Lijun and Lin Jiang, *Jiuqi hou de tantao – xianggang jingji ji qi yu neidi jingji guanxi* (*A Discussion of the Post-1997 Hong Kong Economy and its Relationship with the Economy of the Chinese Mainland*), Hong Kong: Cosmos Books Limited, 2000, pp. 325–6.
43. Enright, Scott & Associates Ltd research; Sung Yun-wing, Liu Pak-wai, Richard Yue-chim Wong, and Lau Pui-king (eds), *The Fifth Dragon*, Hong Kong: Addison Wesley, 1995, pp. 163–84.
44. Business and Professional Federation of Hong Kong, *Impact of Cross Border Economic Activities on Hong Kong*, January 2002.
45. CEPA also allows Hong Kong service providers 'to provide, in the form of wholly-owned operations, high standard real estate project services in the Mainland'. Hong Kong Special Administrative Region Government, Trade and Industry Department, *Mainland/Hong Kong Closer Economic Partnership Arrangement*, Annex 4: Table 1, Section 1.D (29 September 2003).

46. Hong Kong Special Administrative Region Government, Trade and Industry Department, *Mainland/Hong Kong Closer Economic Partnership Arrangement*, Annex 4: Table 1, Section 3 (29 September 2003); see also Hong Kong General Chamber of Commerce, *Closer Economic Partnership Arrangement: Business Assessment*, November 2003, pp. 57–8.

47. Hong Kong General Chamber of Commerce, *Closer Economic Partnership Arrangement: Business Assessment*, November 2003, p. 66.

48. The minimum average annual sales value in the previous three years is US$100 million. For minimum asset and registered capital requirements that also apply, see Hong Kong Special Administrative Region Government, Trade and Industry Department, *Mainland/ Hong Kong Closer Economic Partnership Arrangement*, Annex 4: Table 1, Section 4.C (29 September 2003).

49. Hong Kong Trade Development Council, 'Hong Kong Chinese Nationals May Register Individual Businesses In Guangdong', *Business Alert China*, 6 November 2003. Shenzhen had pioneered similar measures in Luohu Commercial City with considerable success.

50. CEPA lowers the threshold requirements for wholesale businesses as well, setting a three-year, US$30 million average sales value requirement. For minimum asset and registered capital requirements that also apply, see Hong Kong Special Administrative Region Government, Trade and Industry Department, *Mainland/Hong Kong Closer Economic Partnership Arrangement*, Annex 4: Table 1, Section 4.C (29 September 2003). This threshold will be too high for many Hong Kong small- and medium-sized enterprises. Hong Kong General Chamber of Commerce, *Closer Economic Partnership Arrangement: Business Assessment*, November 2003, pp. 69–70.

51. The penetration of ICT services in Guangdong, at roughly 7% of GDP, is more advanced than most other places in China. See Ericsson (China) and Enright, Scott & Associates Ltd, 'Telecommunications and Information Infrastructure in Guangdong's Competitiveness and Development', paper for the Guangdong Governors' International Advisory Council Meeting, November 2003, p. 8; see also Hong Kong Trade Development Council, *Business Alert China*, 1 March 2003.

52. 'Telcos in Cepa Head Start', *The Standard* (30 September 2003): thestandard.com.

53. Hong Kong General Chamber of Commerce, *Closer Economic Partnership Arrangement: Business Assessment*, November 2003, pp. 83–4.

54. Hong Kong General Chamber of Commerce, *Closer Economic Partnership Arrangement: Business Assessment*, November 2003, pp. 85–6.

55. For more on the history of China's capital flow into Hong Kong, particularly from the Pearl River Delta region, see Cheng Yukshing, Lu Weigou, and C. Findlay, 'Hong Kong's Economic Relationship with China', *Journal of the Asia Pacific Economy*, 3:1 (1998): 123–6; Sung Yun-wing, *Hong Kong and South China: The Economic Synergy*, Hong Kong Economic Policy Study Series, Hong Kong: City University of Hong Kong Press, 1998, pp. 100–17.

56. Enright, Scott & Associates Ltd research.

57. CEPA made only modest inroads into the mainland's highly protected securities sector for Hong Kong, allowing the Hong Kong Exchanges and Clearing Limited to set up a representative office in Beijing and making it easier for Hong Kong professionals to obtain securities qualifications in the mainland. See Hong Kong Special Administrative Region Government, Trade and Industry Department, *Mainland/Hong Kong Closer Economic Partnership Arrangement*, Annex 4: Table 1, Section 7.B (29 September 2003).

58. 'Funds Forming Group to Boost Bargaining Power,' *South China Morning Post* (2 May 2002): scmp.com. In a separate agreement, Hong Kong licensed stock and futures brokers who pass a mainland exam will be permitted to work for mainland brokerages. Mainland brokers who pass a Hong Kong exam will be permitted to work for Hong Kong brokerages. This is seen as a first step towards permitting mainland residents 'to invest in Hong Kong through a Qualified Domestic Institutional Investor (QDII) scheme'. Enoch Yiu, 'Mainland Opens up to HK Brokers', *South China Morning Post* (22 November 2003): A1.

59. Zhang Jinsheng, *Waizi yu Shenzhen chanye jiegou (Foreign Capital and Shenzhen's Industrial Structure)*, Beijing: Central Literature Publishing House, 2000, pp. 116–54.

60. Hong Kong General Chamber of Commerce, *Closer Economic Partnership Arrangement: Business Assessment*, November 2003, pp. 75–6.

61. Hong Kong Special Administrative Region Government, Trade and Industry Department, *Mainland/Hong Kong Closer Economic Partnership Arrangement*, Annex 4: Table 1, Section 7.B (29 September 2003).

62. Hong Kong General Chamber of Commerce, *Closer Economic Partnership Arrangement: Business Assessment*, November 2003, p. 78.

63. 'Shops Welcome Yuan Credit Card Plan', *South China Morning Post* (19 November 2003): scmp.com.

64. 'One Country, Two Currencies Boosts Economic Integration', *South China Morning Post* (19 November 2003): scmp.com; 'Shops Welcome Yuan Credit Card Plan', *South China Morning Post* (19 November 2003): scmp.com. Guangdong business people have been allowed to conduct business transactions using Hong Kong dollar denomination cheques.

65. Enright, Scott & Associates Ltd research.

66. Hong Kong Special Administrative Region Government, Trade and Industry Department, *Mainland/Hong Kong Closer Economic Partnership Arrangement*, Annex 4: Table 1, Section 7.A.1 (29 September 2003).

67. Hong Kong General Chamber of Commerce, *Closer Economic Partnership Arrangement: Business Assessment*, November 2003, pp. 79–81.

68. Hong Kong Special Administrative Region Government, Trade and Industry Department, *Mainland/Hong Kong Closer Economic Partnership Arrangement*, Annex 4: Section 1.A.1 (29 September 2003).

69. Enright, Scott & Associates Ltd research; Hong Kong Trade Development Council, 'Opportunities for Hong Kong in Accounting Sector', *Inside PRD*, 5 (1 May 2003).

70. Hong Kong General Chamber of Commerce, *Closer Economic Partnership Arrangement: Business Assessment*, November 2003, p. 54.

71. Hong Kong Special Administrative Region Government, Trade and Industry Department, *Mainland/Hong Kong Closer Economic Partnership Arrangement*, Annex 4: Section 1.F.a (29 September 2003).

72. 'SAR in TCL Picture', *The Standard* (7 June 2002): thestandard.com.

73. Hong Kong Special Administrative Region Government, Trade and Industry Department, *Mainland/Hong Kong Closer Economic Partnership Arrangement*, Annex 4: Table 1, Section 1.F.c (29 September 2003); Hong Kong General Chamber of Commerce, *Closer Economic Partnership Arrangement: Business Assessment*, November 2003, p. 56.

74. Hong Kong Special Administrative Government, Census and Statistics Department, *Hong Kong Population Projections 2002–2031: Announcement of Results*, 7 May 2002.

75. 'Shenzhen the Focus of SAR Investors', *South China Morning Post* (24 April 2002): scmp.com.
76. Hong Kong Special Administrative Region Government, Trade and Industry Department, *Mainland/Hong Kong Closer Economic Partnership Arrangement*, Annex 4: Table 1, Section 1.A.h (29 September 2003).
77. Hong Kong General Chamber of Commerce, *Closer Economic Partnership Arrangement: Business Assessment*, November 2003, pp. 58–60.

CHAPTER 8

1.   Enright, Scott & Associates Ltd research.
2.   Enright, Scott & Associates Ltd research.
3.   Guangdong Government Development Research Centre, *Rushi hou de Guangdong jingji yunzuo – 'Zhongguo rushi yu Guangdong jingji' xupian* (*Guangdong's Economy after China's Entry into the WTO – A Sequel to 'China's WTO Entry and Guangdong's Economy'*), Guangzhou: Guangdong Economic Press, 2002, pp. 100–12; '*Zuo Liancun, Wang Hongliang, and Huang Guoxian, Zhongguo giaru WTO dui yuegang jingji de yingxiang*' ('The Impact of China's WTO Entry on the Economies of Guangdong, Hong Kong and Macao'), *International Economic Cooperation*, 11 (2000).
4.   United States International Trade Commission, *Textiles and Apparel: Assessment of the Competitiveness of Certain Foreign Suppliers to the U.S. Market*, Inv. No. 332-448, USTIC Pub. 3671, January 2004, pp. 3–10.
5.   Hong Kong Trade Development Council, 'Hong Kong's Clothing Industry', 6 January 2004.
6.   Enright, Scott & Associates Ltd research.
7.   Regional Technology Strategies research, private communication; see Andrew Higgins, 'Power and Peril: America's Supremacy and its Limits', *The Asian Wall Street Journal* (2 February 2004): global.factiva.com.
8.   Lehman Brothers, Global Equity Research, 'Fourth Annual EMS/ODM/OEM Asia Tour, China is the Place; Tech Demand has Legs', 18 December 2003, p. 1.
9.   Lehman Brothers, Global Equity Research, 'Fourth Annual EMS/ODM/OEM Asia Tour, China is the Place; Tech Demand has Legs', 18 December 2003, pp. 11–3, 15.
10. Enright, Scott & Associates Ltd research; see also Zuo Zheng, '*Zhujiang sanjiaozhou liyong waizi fazhan gaoxin chanye de yanjiao*' ('A Study of the Development of New and Hi-tech Industries by Utilising Foreign Capital in the Pearl River Delta Region'), *Nanfang Jingji* (*Southern Economics*), 6 (2002): 39–40; Li Jianping, Yan Xiaopei, and Zhou Chunshan, '*Kuaguo gongsi zai zhujiang sanjiaozhou de touzi xianzhuang yu fazhan qushi tanxi*' ('An Investigation into the Current Situations and Development Trends of MNC Investment in the Pearl River Delta Region') *Guangdong Fazhan Daokan* (*Guangdong Development Magazine*), 1 (2002): 43; and Publicity Department of the Guangdong Committee of the Communist Party of China, *Zhujiang sanjiaozhou jingjiqu fazhan zhanlue yu guihua yanjiu* (*A Study of the Development Strategies and Planning of the Pearl River Delta Economic Zone*), Guangzhou: Guangdong People's Press, 1995, pp. 342–6.
11. Lehman Brothers, Global Equity Research, 'Fourth Annual EMS/ODM/OEM Asia Tour, China is the Place; Tech Demand has Legs', 18 December 2003, p. 12.
12. Hong Kong Trade Development Council, 'Hong Kong as a Service Platform for Taiwan Companies Investing in the Mainland', 31 October 2002.

13. Cai Haizhi, '*Lun zhusanjiao chanye zhuanyi*,' ('A Discussion of the Industrial Shifts in the Pearl River Delta Region') *Lingnan xuekan* (*Lingnan Academic Journal*), (January 2003): 70.
14. Enright, Scott & Associates Ltd research.
15. Hong Kong Trade Development Council, 'Hong Kong's Watches and Clocks Industry', 1 March 2004: asia.news.yahoo.com.
16. Tom Walsh, 'GM's China Bonanza', *Detroit Free Press* (30 March 2004): freep.com.
17. 'China Production Soars Again in November', *Automotive News* (8 December 2003): autonews.com.
18. 'GM Profits in China Triple in 03', *Automotive News* (22 March 2004): autonews.com.
19. Zheng Caixiong, 'Toyota Gears Up on Engine-making Factory', *China Daily* (9 October 2003): chinadaily.com; The Japan Society of Mechanical Engineers, *Engineering News in Brief*, October 2003.
20. 'Toyota Launches Engine Joint Venture in China's Guangzhou', *AsiaPulse*, 1 April 2004: asia.news.yahoo.com.
21. BDA Business Development Asia, *Asian Automotive Newsletter*, 30, April 2002.
22. Gong Zhengzheng and Liang Qiwen, 'Auto Maker Launches Engine Joint Venture', *China Daily* (26 February 2004): 10; Zheng Caixiong, 'Toyota Gears up on Engine-making Factory', *China Daily* (9 October 2003): chinadaily.com.
23. 'On a Roll', *The Economist Global Agenda* (27 June 2003): economist.com.
24. 'JV to Help Meet Sheet Steel Demand', *People's Daily* (16 January 2004): peopledaily.com.
25. Research and markets, *China Chemical Industry Newsletter 2003*.
26. Research and markets, *China Chemical Industry Newsletter 2003*.
27. While Shanghai handled 26% of China's container throughput, this share had held steady since 1996. Charles de Trenck, Citigroup Smith Barney, quoted in 'We Can See Clearly Now', *South China Morning Post: Special Supplement* (2 April 2004): S-7.
28. Nomura Asian Equity Research, K. Y. Ng, *Hong Kong and China Ports* (5 March 2003): 1.
29. Russell Barling, 'CT10 Decision Tempers Runaway Ambitions', *South China Morning Post* (10 March 2004): B-5.
30. GHK Consultants, *HK Port – Master Plan 2020*, cited in Russell Barling, 'Costs Cripple HK Port Growth', *South China Morning Post* (25 March 2004): B-1.
31. GHK Consultants, *HK Port – Master Plan 2020*, cited in Russell Barling, 'Costs Cripple HK Port Growth', *South China Morning Post* (25 March 2004): B-1.
32. 'Port Throughput Continues to Rise', *Hong Kong Looking Ahead*, 19 November 2003.
33. Russell Barling, 'CT10 Decision Tempers Runaway Ambitions', *South China Morning Post* (10 March 2004): B-5.
34. Russell Barling, 'CT10 Decision Tempers Runaway Ambitions', *South China Morning Post* (10 March 2004): B-5.
35. Alexandra Harney, 'Guangdong's Handshake with Hong Kong Could Prove a Bone-crusher for the Territory', *Financial Times* (30 December 2003): FT.com.
36. 'Shenzhen Port Upgrades Volume Forecast', *South China Morning Post* (5 November 2003): scmp.com.
37. Christine Loh, *Ports, Airports and Bureaucrats: Restructuring Hong Kong and Guangdong*, CLSA Emerging Markets, October 2002, pp. 23–4.
38. 'Port Throughput Continues to Rise', *Hong Kong Looking Ahead*, 19 November 2003.
39. Chow Chung-yan, 'Guangzhou Says Nansha Port Will Boost HK Shipping Role', *South China Morning Post* (17 March 2004): A-3; Tom Mitchell, 'Nature Will Have a Say in Port Development', *South China Morning Post* (16 January 2003): scmp.com.

40. 'We Can See Clearly Now', *South China Morning Post: Special Supplement* (2 April 2004): S-7.

41. The Centre for Urban and Regional Studies, Zhongshan University, '*Xianggang yu zhujiang sanjiao zhou jingji guanxi yanjiu*' ('A Study of the Economic Relationship between Hong Kong and the Pearl River Delta'), *Xianggang yu zhujiang sanjiao zhou jingji hudong yanjiu* (*A Study of the Hong Kong–Pearl River Delta Economic Interaction*), Guangzhou: April 2002, p. 32.

42. Sidney Luk, 'Airport Freight Traffic Soars', *South China Morning Post* (15 March 2004): B-7.

43. Hong Kong Airport Authority, *Hong Kong International Airport Master Plan 2020*, October 2001, p. 3.

44. Hong Kong Trade Development Council, 'Profile of Hong Kong Major Service Industries', 'Air Transport', tdctrade.com.

45. Hong Kong Airport Authority.

46. Zheng Caixiong, 'New Airport to Heighten City's Role', *China Business Weekly* (8–14 March 2004): 17.

47. Federation of American Scientists, 'Guangzhou Baiyun International Airport 23°11'N 113°16'E', fas.org.

48. Zheng Caixiong, 'Guangzhou Spreads its Wings with Bigger Airport', *China Daily* (1 April 2004): 18.

49. 'FedEx Moves Asia Hub to Guangzhou', *People's Daily* (5 January 2004): peopledaily.com.

50. Russell Barling, 'FedEx Keeps its Asia-Pacific Hub in Philippines', *South China Morning Post* (31 March 2004): scmp.com.

51. Annette Chiu, 'Shenzhen Seeks HKAA Investment', *South China Morning Post* (13 February 2004): B-1.

52. 'Macau Proves Recession Proof', *Airsider Commercial Aviation News and Reports*, airsider.net; Macau International Airport website, www.macau-airport.gov.mo/.

53. Enright, Scott & Associates Ltd research.

54. Jonathan Tam and Keith Wallis, 'Airport Chiefs Head for Zhuhai Takeover', *The Standard* (2 March 2004): 2.

55. Zheng Tianxiang and Li Huan (eds), *Yuegangao jingji guanxi* (*The Guangdong–Hong Kong–Macao Economic Relationship*), Guangzhou: Sun Yatsen University Press, 2001, pp. 101–3.

56. 'China's Shenzhen Airport in Talks with Hong Kong Investor', *Reuters*, 12 February 2004; Francesco Guerrera and Alexandra Harney, 'HK in Talks to Buy Chinese Airport Stake', *Financial Times* (London Edition) (25 March 2004): 29.

57. Guangdong Government Development Research Centre, *Rushi hou de Guangdong jingji yunzuo – 'Zhongguo rushi yu Guangdong jingji' xupian* (*Guangdong's Economy after China's Entry into the WTO – A Sequel to China's WTO Entry and Guangdong's Economy*), Guangzhou: Guangdong Economic Press, 2002, pp. 158–65.

58. Chen Hong, 'More Global Firms Sourcing in Shenzhen', *China Daily* (29 May 2003): chinadaily.com; 'Wal-mart's Push North Will Not Hurt Delta', *The Standard* (27 January 2003): thestandard.com.

59. Hong Kong Trade Development Council, 'Products on Air', *HK Enterprise*, 9 (2000): 30.

60. Enright, Scott & Associates Ltd research.

61. Enright, Scott & Associates Ltd research; see also Liu Shaojian and Shi Yan, '*Yuegang hezuo tisheng*' ('The Promotion of Guangdong–Hong Kong Cooperation'), *Zhongguo wuliu yu caigou* (*China Logistics and Procurement*), (January 2003): 26–7.

62. For further discussion on the cooperation in the logistics sector between Hong Kong and Shenzhen see Guo Wanda and Ma Chunhui, '*Shengang jingji hezuo de yiyi, mubiao ji duice*'

('The Meanings, Goals and Strategies of Hong Kong–Shenzhen Economic Cooperation'), *Kaifang daobao (China Opening Herald Monthly)*, 3 (2003): 7; and Tan Gang, 'Zhusanjiao: Goujian shijie gongchang yu fazhan xiandai wuliuye – jianlun shenzhen yu xianggang wuliuye hezuo' ('The Pearl River Delta: Building the World's Factory and Developing a Modern Logistics Industry – A Discussion of Shenzhen–Hong Kong Cooperation in the Logistics Industry'), *Kaifang daobao (China Opening Herald Monthly)*, 5 (2003): 19–20.

63. See Guangdong Government Development Research Centre, *Rushi hou de Guangdong jingji yunzuo – 'Zhongguo rushi yu Guangdong jingji' xupian (Guangdong's Economy after China's Entry into the WTO – A Sequel to 'China's WTO Entry and Guangdong's Economy')*, Guangzhou: Guangdong Economic Press, 2002, pp. 152–7.

64. Zhang Jinsheng, *Waizi yu Shenzhen chanye jiegou (Foreign Capital and Shenzhen's Industrial Structure)*, Beijing: Central Literature Publishing House, 2000, pp. 188–223.

65. Joel Baglole, 'In a Major Shift, Equities Replace Debt as Favourite of Asian Investors', *The Asian Wall Street Journal* (19 April 2004): A-6.

66. Guangdong Government Development Research Centre, *Rushi hou de Guangdong jingji yunzuo – 'Zhongguo rushi yu Guangdong jingji' xupian (Guangdong's Economy after China's Entry into the WTO – A Sequel to 'China's WTO Entry and Guangdong's Economy')*, Guangzhou: Guangdong Economic Press, 2002, pp. 125–30.

67. See Governo da Região Administrativa Especial de Macau Gabinete de Comunicação Social, *Basic Information on Macao's Gaming Concessions*, September 2002.

CHAPTER 9

1. Shi Jiangtao, 'Sucked Dry, Guangdong Casts Nets for Energy', *South China Morning Post* (30 March 2004): A-4.

2. Liu Weifeng, 'Guangdong Continues to Buy HK Electricity', *China Daily* (21 April 2004): 19.

3. Pamela Pun, 'Shenzhen to Pull the Plug on Power Grid Gluttons', *The Standard* (15 April 2004): A-6.

4. Liu Weifeng, 'Guangdong Continues to Buy HK Electricity', *China Daily* (21 April 2004): 19.

5. Liu Weifeng, 'Guangdong Continues to Buy HK Electricity', *China Daily* (21 April 2004): 19.

6. 'Power Shortage Hits Honda Joint Venture', *South China Morning Post* (20 February 2004): B-3.

7. Enright, Scott & Associates Ltd research.

8. Priscilla Lau, Associate Professor, Hong Kong Polytechnic University, quoted in Olivia Chung, 'Guangdong Plans to Move 8 Million Farmers into Cities', *The Standard* (14 April 2004): A-11.

9. Liu Weifeng, 'Guangdong Continues to Buy HK Electricity', *China Daily* (21 April 2004): 19.

10. Chow Chung-yan, 'Power Shortages to Put Guangzhou in the Dark', *South China Morning Post* (10 March 2004): A-8; 'Several Nuclear-power Plants to Quench Energy Thirst', *People's Daily* (9 April 2003): peopledaily.com.

11. Chow Chung-yan, 'Power Shortages to Put Guangzhou in the Dark', *South China Morning Post* (10 March 2004): A-8.

12. Denise Tsang, 'CKI Seeks Expansion in Zhuhai', *South China Morning Post* (25 September 2003): scmp.com; Denise Tsang, 'Hopewell Powering into Guangdong', *South China Morning Post* (1 May 2004): B-1.

13. Thomas P. Rohlen, *Hong Kong and the Pearl River Delta: 'One Country, Two Systems' in the Emerging Metropolitan Context*, Asia Pacific Research Centre, July 2000, p. 20.

14. Cheung Chi-fai, 'Nasa Gives Clear Picture of Smog from Guangdong', *South China Morning Post* (1 March 2004): A-2.
15. Cheung Chi-fai, 'Mountains Offer Pollution Protection', *South China Morning Post* (4 March 2002): scmp.com.
16. Cheung Chi-Fai and Quinton Chan, 'Cleaner Air on Horizon by Year's End: Liao', *South China Morning Post* (24 February 2004): A-1.
17. Hong Kong Special Administrative Region Government, Environment, Transport and Works Bureau, 'Improving Air Quality in PRD Region', ACE Paper 15/2002, 29 April 2002.
18. Hong Kong Special Administrative Region Government, Environment, Transport and Works Bureau, 'Improving Air Quality in PRD Region', ACE Paper 15/2002, 29 April 2002.
19. Hong Kong Special Administrative Region Government, Environment, Transport and Works Bureau, 'LCQ3: Progress of Emissions Trading Pilot Scheme', Press Release, 10 December 2003.
20. 'No Place for Clouded Vision on Pollution', *South China Morning Post* (3 November 2003): scmp.com.
21. Wu Zhong, 'Guangdong Targets 9pc GDP Growth', *The Standard* (12 January 2004): A-6.
22. Cheung Chi-fai and Quinton Chan, 'SAR Faces Mainland Water Battle', *South China Morning Post* (16 December 2002): A-1.
23. Liu Weifeng, 'Project to Clean up Waterway', *China Daily* (11 March 2003): chinadaily.com.
24. Tom Mitchell, 'Clean-up Bill for $41b Should Bring Fisherman Cleaner Dinner', *South China Morning Post* (8 October 2002): scmp.com.
25. 'Environmental Protection in Guangdong', GC.Comm, December 2001–January 2002.
26. Sarah Liao, Hong Kong Environment Minister, as quoted in Cheung Chi-fai, 'Benefits of Pearl River Clean-up in Doubt', *South China Morning Post* (14 October 2002): scmp.com.
27. Alyssa Lau, 'Firms Could Buy Pollution Solution', *South China Morning Post* (5 July 2002): A-6; Cheung Chi-fai, 'Benefits of Pearl River Clean-up in Doubt', *South China Morning Post* (14 October 2002): scmp.com.
28. Zhan Lisheng, 'Fund to Improve Water Quality', *China Daily* (11 March 2004): 5.
29. Liu Weifeng, 'Project to Clean Up Waterway', *China Daily* (11 March 2003): 4; Zhan Lisheng, 'Exhibition Floats High-tech Water Quality Improvements', *China Daily* (11 March 2003): 4.
30. Liu Weifeng, 'City Tackles Water Pollution', *China Daily* (30 April 2004): 4.
31. Liu Weifeng, 'Project to Clean up Waterway', *China Daily* (11 March 2003): 4.
32. 'Let's Find a Way to Pay for Full Waste Treatment', *South China Morning Post* (27 December 2003): scmp.com; Heike Phillips, 'Need for Urgent Action on Scheme', *South China Morning Post* (8 September 2003): scmp.com.
33. Olivia Chung, 'Guangdong Plans to Move 8 Million Farmers into Cities', *The Standard* (14 April 2004): A-11.
34. Chow Chung-yan, 'Shenzhen Sees Population Growing Too Fast', *South China Morning Post* (19 February 2004): A-4.
35. Yang Lixun, member of the Shenzhen Communist Party Committee, quoted in Chow Chung-yan, 'Shenzhen Sees Population Growing Too Fast', *South China Morning Post* (19 February 2004): A-4.
36. 'Guangzhou to Zhuhai in just 48 Minutes', *South China Morning Post* (2 March 2004): A-4.

37. Zheng Caixiong, 'Maglev an Option for New Guangzhou–HK Line', *China Daily* (15 April 2004): chinadaily.com.
38. Zheng Caixiong, 'Railway Pursues Int'l Aid', *China BusinessWeekly Review* (16 March 2004): chinadaily.com; 'A Dreamland of Future', *NewsGuangdong* (17 September 2003): newsgd.com.
39. 'University Town Opens', *NewsGuangdong* (17 September 2003): newsgd.com.
40. Zhan Lisheng, 'Cityscape Receiving Big Facelift', *China Daily* (9 April 2004): 4.
41. Wang Linsheng, Deputy Party Secretary, Guangzhou Urban Planning and Gardening Bureau, as quoted in Zhan Lisheng, 'New Garden Projects Give City a Facelift', *China Daily* (22 April 2004): 4.
42. Qiu Quanlin, 'Eager Guangzhou Eyes 2010 Asian Games', *China Daily* (19 April 2004): 5.
43. Yeung Yueman, 'Infrastructure Development in the Southern China Growth Triangle', in Myo Thant, Min Tang, and Hiroshi Kakazu (eds), *Growth Triangles in Asia: A New Approach to Regional Cooperation*, Hong Kong: Asian Development Bank, 1998, p. 156.
44. Wang Dengrong, '*Yuegang diqu quyu hezuo fazhan fenxi ji quyu guanzhi tuijin celue*' ('An Analysis of Regional Cooperation in the Hong Kong–Guangdong Region and the Strategies for Promoting Regional Administration'), *Xiandai chengshi yanjiu* (*Modern Urban Studies*), (2002): 62; Zheng Tianxiang and Li Huan (eds), *Yuegangao jingji guanxi* (*The Guangdong–Hong Kong–Macao Economic Relationship*), Guangzhou: Sun Yatsen University Press, 2001, pp. 91–3.
45. See Feng Xiaoyun, 'WTO *kuangjia xia yuegang jingji hezuo de chuangxin yu tupo*' ('Innovations and Breakthroughs in Guangdong–Hong Kong Economic Cooperation under the WTO Framework'), *Kaifang dabao* (*China Opening Herald Monthly*), 12 (2002): 18.
46. See also Yang Qinqi (ed.), '*Zhujiang sanjiaozhou chengshihua yanjiu*' ('A Study of the Urbanisation of the Pearl River Delta'), *Guangdong Jingji* (*Guangdong Economy*), (June 2002): 25; Zheng Tianxiang and Li Huan (eds), *Yuegangao jingji guanxi* (*The Guangdong–Hong Kong–Macao Economic Relationship*), Guangzhou: Sun Yatsen University Press, 2001, p. 128.
47. 'Hong Kong, Mainland and Macau Unite to Fight Drugs', Hong Kong Special Administrative Region Government Press Release, 20 February 2003.
48. Lynne Curry, 'Dungeons and the Dragon', *CFO Asia* (28 March 1999): cfoasia.com.
49. Joseph Y. S. Cheng (ed.), *Political Development in the HKSAR*, Hong Kong: City University of Hong Kong, 2001, p. 63.
50. Lau Siu-Kai, 'Tung Chee-hwa's Governing Strategy: The Shortfall in Politics', in Lau Siu Kai (ed.), *The First Tung Chee-hwa Administration*, Hong Kong: Chinese University Press, 2002, p. 1. See also http://www.legco.gov.hk/english/index.htm.
51. Hong Kong Special Administrative Region Government Press Release, 'CE's Opening Remarks on Basic Law Article 23', 5 September 2003.
52. Standing Committee of the National People's Congress, 'Full Text of the Standing Committee Decision', *South China Morning Post* (27 April 2004): A-4.
53. 'Tracking Toronto's SARS Deaths': thestar.com.
54. Figures are from the World Health Organization, 'Summary of Probable SARS Cases with Onset of Illness from 1 November 2002 to 31 July 2003'.
55. Nils Pratley, Andrew Clark, and Jon Chinery, 'The Impact: Sars Effects Underline Fragility of Fast East Economies', *Guardian Unlimited* (25 April 2003): guardian.co.uk.
56. 'Life Will Never be the Same in Singapore after SARS', (4 July 2003): smh.com.au.

57. 'SARS Inflicts Nearly US$2bn Loss on Beijing's Tourism', *People's Daily* (18 June 2003): peopledaily.com.
58. Lawrence Chung, '$10m Campaign to Revive Taiwan Tourism', *The Straits Times* (19 June 2003).
59. Lau Siu-kai, Hong Kong Central Policy Unit, as quoted in 'The Crisis Infecting Cross-border Relations', *South China Morning Post* (7 May 2003): scmp.com.
60. Chris Yeung, 'Healthy Co-operation', *South China Morning Post* (24 March 2003): scmp.com.
61. Ella Lee, 'Guangdong "Ready to Work with HK"', *South China Morning Post* (4 October 2003): scmp.com; Hong Kong SAR Government, SARS Expert Committee Report, 'SARS in Hong Kong: From Experience to Action': sars-expertccm.gov.hk; Ella Lee, 'Hong Kong "Kept in the Dark" Over Outbreak', *South China Morning Post* (3 October 2003): scmp.com.
62. Ella Lee, 'Guangdong "Ready to Work with HK"', *South China Morning Post* (4 October 2003): scmp.com.
63. Frank Ching, 'Saving Lives', *South China Morning Post* (3 February 2004): scmp.com.
64. Mary Ann Benitez and Ella Lee, 'Guangdong Seeks to Gag HK Health Authorities', *South China Morning Post* (10 February 2004): scmp.com.
65. Chow Chung-yan, 'Better Reporting Promised on Spread of Disease', *South China Morning Post* (12 February 2004): scmp.com.
66. Mary Ann Benitez and Ella Lee, 'Guangdong Seeks to Gag HK Health Authorities', *South China Morning Post* (10 February 2004): scmp.com.
67. Leu Siew Ying, 'Province Asks for Help to Fight Bird Flu', *South China Morning Post* (21 January 2004): scmp.com.
68. Chow Chung-yan, 'Guangdong Official Threatens HK Media Over "Irresponsible" Bird Flu Coverage', (9 February 2004): scmp.com.
69. Hong Kong SAR Government, SARS Expert Committee Report, 'SARS in Hong Kong: From Experience to Action': sars-expertccm. gov.hk.
70. Lau Siu-kai, Hong Kong Central Policy Unit, as quoted in 'The Crisis Infecting Cross-border Relations', *South China Morning Post* (7 May 2003): scmp.com.
71. See Qi Huaiyang, '*Cong touzi huanjing kan zhujiang sanjiaozhou yu changjiang sanjiaozhou zhijian de jingzheng he fazhan*' ('Competition and Development Between the Pearl River Delta Region and the Yangtze River Delta Region – An Investment Perspective'), *Guangdong Fazhan Daokan (Guangdong Development Magazine)*, 4 (2001): 43.
72. The Research Team of the Guangdong Government Development Research Centre, '*Guangdong jingji mianlin de xin xingshi yu duice fenxi*' ('An Analysis of the New Situation Facing the Guangdong Economy and Related Strategies'), *Guangdong Jingji (Guangdong Economy)*, (January 2001): 7–9.
73. See also Wei Dazhi, '*Yitihua shiye xia de shengang guanxi*' ('The Shenzhen–Hong Kong Relationship Under the Vision of Integration'), *Kaifang daobao (China Opening Herald Monthly)*, 6 (2003): 18; The Research Team of the Guangdong Government Development Research Centre, '*Guangdong jingji mianlin de xin xingshi yu duice fenxi*' ('An Analysis of the New Situation Facing the Guangdong Economy and Related Strategies'), *Guangdong Jingji (Guangdong Economy)*, (January 2001): 9–10.
74. The Publicity Department of the Guangdong Committee of the Communist Party of China, *Zhujiang sanjiaozhou jingjiqu fazhan zhanlue yu guihua yanjiu (A Study of the Development Strategies and Planning of the Pearl River Delta Economic Zone)*, Guangzhou: Guangdong People's Press, 1995, pp. 5561; Michael J. Enright, 'Regional Clusters: What We Know And

What We Should Know', in Johannes Bröcker, Dirk Dohse, and Rüdiger Soltwedel (eds), *Innovation Clusters and Interregional Competition*, Berlin: Springer Verlag, 2003, p. 99–129; Wang Jun, '*Chanye zuzhi de wangluohua fazhan – Guangdong zhuanyezhen jingji de lilun fenxi*' ('Network Development of Industrial Organisations – An Economic Analysis of the Professional Towns in Guangdong'), in *Journal of Sun Yatsen University (Social Science Edition)*, 1 (2002): 89–95.

75. 'Shanghai Municipality', 'Market Profiles on Chinese Cities and Provinces', January 2004: tdctrade.com.

76. C. K. Lau and Joseph Lo, 'Regional Links "Vital to Delta's Economy"', *South China Morning Post* (27 February 2004): A-2.

77. Pamela Pun, '9+2 Block Moves to Co-ordinate Development', *The Standard* (12 February 2004): A-7.

78. See panel discussion proceedings, 'China–Taiwan: The Cross Strait Relationship', A Panel Discussion with Steven Goldstein, Yasheng Huang, Dwight Perkins, Alan Romberg, William Kirby (Moderator), Dean, Faculty of Arts and Sciences, Harvard University, ARCO Forum, Kennedy School of Government, 6 December 2002.

79. 'Implications for Hong Kong: If There are Direct Links between the Chinese Mainland and Taiwan', Economic Forum, July 2000: tdctrade.com/ econforum/tdc/tdc000701.htm.

80. James Dorn, 'Risky . . . or Worthy WTO Bid?', CTPS Articles, 26 July 1999, http://www.freetrade.org.

81. Dan Ikeson, 'The Stealth Trade War', Cato Institute, 2 March 2004: www.cato.org.

82. Dan Ikeson, 'The Stealth Trade War', Cato Institute, 2 March 2004, www.cato.org.

83. 'Anti-dumping Ruling Drags Down Exports', *China Daily* (9 February 2004): chinadaily.org.

84. 'Oxfam Response to European Commission's Comments on *Rigged Rules and Double Standards*': www.intermonoxfam.org.

85. John Authers and Alson Maitland, 'The Human Cost of the Computer Age', *The Financial Times* (25 January 2004): FT.com.

86. Catholic Agency for Overseas Development (CAFOD), 'Clean up Your Computer: Working Conditions in the Electronics Sector', London, 26 January 2004, pp. 1–2.

87. Catholic Agency for Overseas Development (CAFOD), 'Clean up Your Computer: Working Conditions in the Electronics Sector', London, 26 January 2004, p. 34.

88. *Toys of Misery: a Report on the Toy Industry in China*, New York: The National Labor Committee, December 2001, pp. 6–7.

89. 'How Hasbro, McDonald's, Mattel and Disney Manufacture their Toys: Report on the Labor Rights and Occupational Safety and Health Conditions of Toy Workers in Foreign Investment Enterprises in Southern Mainland China', Hong Kong Christian Industrial Committee: Hong Kong, December 2001, pp. 1–2.

90. Joseph Kahn, 'When Chinese Workers Unite, the Bosses Often Run the Union', *New York Times* (29 December 2003): Global Policy Forum: globalpolicy.org.

CHAPTER 10

1. Michael J. Enright, Edith E. Scott, and Edward Leung, *Hong Kong's Competitiveness Beyond the Asian Crisis*, Hong Kong: Hong Kong Trade Development Council, February 1999.

2. Michael J. Enright and Edith E. Scott, 'The RHQ Question', *Business Asia*, The Economist Intelligence Unit (11 December 2000): 1–6.

3. Thomas Chan, *Restructuring in Hong Kong and the Pearl River Delta*, (in Chinese), internal discussion paper for the China Business Centre, Hong Kong Polytechnic University, October 2001.
4. See Michael J. Enright and Edith E. Scott, *The Greater Pearl River Delta*, Hong Kong: Invest Hong Kong, June 2004.
5. Chow Chung-yan and Ambrose Leung, 'Cities Urged to Team up or Lose Out', *South China Morning Post* (31 July 2003): scmp.com.
6. See D. K. Y. Chu, Shen Jianfa, and K. Y. Wong, 'Trans-Border Complications and Regional Governance, the Case of Hong Kong and Guangdong', Proceedings of the Conference on Cities in Transition: The Face of Our City in the Next 20 Years, Hong Kong Institute of Planners and Centre of Urban Planning and Environmental Management, University of Hong Kong, 1999, p. 23; Peter Y. W. Chiu, 'Economic Integration between Hong Kong and Mainland China: The Effect on Hong Kong of China's Entry into the WTO', *China Perspectives*, 40 (March–April 2002): 62–74.

Bibliography

Airsider Commercial Aviation News and Reports, 'Macau Proves Recession Proof': airsider.net.

American Chambers of Commerce in Shanghai and Beijing 2003, *2003 White Paper: American Business in China.*

ASEAN–China Expert Group on Economic Cooperation 2001, 'Forging Closer ASEAN–China Economic Relations in the Twenty-first Century', October.

Asia Inc 2003, 'Rise of the Bourgeoisie', 8 July.

Asia Pulse 2004a, 'Toyota Launches Engine Joint Venture in China's Guangzhou', 1 April: asia.news.yahoo.com.

Asia Pulse 2004b, 'China's Largest Semi-trailer Production Base Operational', 7 April: au.news.yahoo.com.

Asian Venture Capital Journal 2003, *The 2003 Guide to Venture Capital in Asia,* 14th edition, p. 27.

Authers, John and Alson Maitland 2004, 'The Human Cost of the Computer Age', *The Financial Times,* 25 January: FT.com.

Automotive News 2003, 'China Production Soars Again in November', 8 December: autonews.com.

Automotive News 2004, 'GM Profits in China Triple in '03', 22 March: autonews.com.

Baglole, Joel 2004, 'In a Major Shift, Equities Replace Debt as Favourite of Asian Investors', *The Asian Wall Street Journal,* 19 April, p. A6.

Bank for International Settlements 2002, 'Triennial Central Bank Survey of Foreign Exchange and Derivatives Market Activity 2001 – Final Results', 18 March.

Bank of East Asia Economic Research Department 2002, 'Hong Kong: City for Mainland Entrepreneurs', *Economic Analysis,* July.

Barling, Russell 2003a, 'Hactl Gains Mainland Foothold', *South China Morning Post,* 4 October, p. B1.

Barling, Russell 2003b, 'Dragonair Expands Services to Delta', *South China Morning Post,* 25 November, p. B2.

Barling, Russell 2004a, 'CT10 Decision Tempers Runaway Ambitions', *South China Morning Post,* 10 March, p. B5.

Barling, Russell 2004b, 'Costs Cripple HK Port Growth', *South China Morning Post*, 25 March, p. B1.

Barling, Russell 2004c, 'FedEx Keeps its Asia-Pacific Hub in Philippines', *South China Morning Post*, 31 March: scmp.com.

BDA Business Development Asia 2002, *Asian Automotive Newsletter*, 30 April.

Benitez, Mary Ann and Ella Lee 2004, 'Guangdong Seeks to Gag HK Health Authorities', *South China Morning Post*, 10 February: scmp.com.

Bolland, Connie 2004, Regional Economist, 'Building on the Growth Momentum in Place Despite Political Bickering', presentation at 'Regional Strategic Forecast for Q1 2004, a Year to Forget or Remember?', Economist Corporate Network Conference, Guangzhou, 9 March.

Booz, Allen, Hamilton 2003, 'Electronics Manufacturing in Emerging Markets', 2 June.

Brooks, Ray and Ran Tao 2003, 'China's Labor Market Performance and Challenges', IMF Working Paper #WP/03/210, November.

Business Alert – China 2003, 'Emerging Opportunities in Auto Service Sector', 1 June: tdctrade.com.

Business and Professional Federation of Hong Kong 2002, *Impact of Cross Border Economic Activities on Hong Kong*, January.

Cai Haizhi 2003, '*Lun zhusanjiao chanye zhuanyi*' ('A Discussion of the Industrial Shifts in the Pearl River Delta Region'), *Lingnan xuekan (Lingnan Academic Journal)*, January, p. 70.

Catholic Agency for Overseas Development 2004, 'Clean up Your Computer: Working Conditions in the Electronics Sector', London, 26 January.

Cavolo, Mario 2002, 'China Decade Pt II', 23 September: shanghaiexpat.com.

Centre for Urban and Regional Studies 2002a, Zhongshan University, *Xianggang yu zhujiang sanjiao zhou jingji hudong yanjiu (A Study of the Hong Kong–Pearl River Delta Economic Interaction)*, April, pp. 1, 34, and 37.

Centre for Urban and Regional Studies 2002b, Zhongshan University, '*Zhujiang sanjiao zhou fazhan licheng yanjiu*' ('A Study of the Development Trajectory of the Pearl River Delta'), *Xianggang yu zhujiang sanjiao zhou jingji hudong yanjiu (A Study of the Hong Kong–Pearl River Delta Economic Interaction)*, April, p. 36.

Chan, Carrie 2004, 'Mainland Visitors Expected to Surge 32 pc', *The South China Morning Post*, 24 February, p. A3.

Chan, Daniel, Baker & McKenzie 2004, 'Logistics Company Seeks IPO this Year', Presentation to the Dutch Business Association of Hong Kong, 12 February.

Chan, Thomas 2001, *Restructuring in Hong Kong and the Pearl River Delta* (in Chinese), internal discussion paper for the China Business Centre, Hong Kong Polytechnic University, October.

Chan, Thomas and Zhu Wenhui 2000, *Industrial Clusters and Regional Concentration, the Changes of Investment Behaviours of Taiwanese in the Chinese Mainland at the Turn of the Century*, Hong Kong: China Business Centre, Hong Kong Polytechnic University.

Chen Dezhao 1998, 'Chinese Public Policy and the Southern China Growth Triangle', in Myo Thant, Min Tang, and Hiroshi Kakazu (eds), *Growth Triangles in Asia: A New Approach to Regional Cooperation*, Hong Kong: Asian Development Bank, pp. 103–22.

Chen, Edward K. Y. and Joseph S. L. Lee 1998, 'Southern China Growth Triangle: An Overview', in Myo Thant, Min Tang, and Hiroshi Kakazu (eds), *Growth Triangles in Asia: A New Approach to Regional Cooperation*, Hong Kong: Asian Development Bank, pp. 58–62 and 81–8.

Chen Hong 2003, 'More Global Firms Sourcing in Shenzhen', *China Daily*, 29 May: chinadaily.com.

Chen Lijun and Lin Jiang 2000, *Jiuqi hou de tantao – xianggang jingji ji qi yu neidi jingji guanxi* (*A Discussion of the Post-1997 Hong Kong Economy and its Relationship with the Economy of the Chinese Mainland*), Hong Kong: Cosmos Books Limited.

Cheng, Joseph Y. S. (ed.) 2001, *Political Development in the HKSAR*, Hong Kong: City University of Hong Kong, The Chinese University Press, p. 63.

Cheng, Joseph Y. S. and Zheng Peiyu 2001, 'Hi-tech Industries in Hong Kong and the Pearl River Delta: Development Trends in Industrial Cooperation', *Asian Survey*, Vol. 41, No. 4, pp. 584–610.

Cheng Yukshing, Lu Weigou, and C. Findlay 1998, 'Hong Kong's Economic Relationship with China', *Journal of the Asia Pacific Economy*, Vol. 3, No. 1, pp. 123–6.

Cheong, Inkyo 2003, 'Korea's FTA Policy', Pacific Economic Cooperation Council Trade Forum, 25 May.

Cheung Chi-fai 2002a, 'Mountains Offer Pollution Protection', *South China Morning Post*, 4 March: scmp.com.

Cheung Chi-fai 2002b, 'Benefits of Pearl River Clean-up in Doubt', *South China Morning Post*, 14 October: scmp.com.

Cheung Chi-fai 2003, 'More Space, Fewer People in HK's Future View', *South China Morning Post*, 26 November, p. A1.

Cheung Chi-fai 2004, 'NASA Gives Clear Picture of Smog from Guangdong', *South China Morning Post*, 1 March, p. A2.

Cheung Chi-fai and Quinton Chan 2002, 'SAR Faces Mainland Water Battle', *South China Morning Post*, 16 December, p. A1.

Cheung Chi-fai and Quinton Chan 2004, 'Cleaner Air on Horizon by Year's End: Liao', *South China Morning Post*, 24 February, p. A1.

Cheung, Gary 2003a, 'Regional Airport Chiefs Set to Discuss Coordination of Services', *South China Morning Post*, 16 June: scmp.com.

Cheung, Gary 2003b, 'Authorities Back HK Bridge Design', *South China Morning Post*, 22 July: scmp.com.

China Daily 2001, 'Shenzhen Container Making Up', 13 December: chinadaily.com.

China Daily 2002a, 'Children's Garment Centre Completed', 30 January: chinadaily.com.

China Daily 2002b, 'Real Prosperity of Fake Village', 21 February: chinadaily.com.

China Daily 2002c, 'HK Eyes Mainland Investment Properties', 24 July: chinadaily.com.

China Daily 2002d, 'The Ministry of Justice of the People's Republic of China Notice 2002 No. 10 and No. 11)', 20–21 September: chinadaily.com.

China Daily 2003a, 'Time for Watch-Makers to Build Own Brands', 26 June: chinadaily.com.

China Daily 2003b, 'HK Sea Bridge Could Start in Mid-2004', 29 July: chinadaily.com.

China Daily 2004, 'Anti-dumping Ruling Drags Down Exports', 9 February: chinadaily.com.

China Foreign Economic and Trade Press (various years), *Zhongguo duiwai jingji maoyi nianjian* (*Almanac of China Foreign Economic Relations and Trade*), Beijing.

China Information Center 2004, 'Eight Railways to Bring Vitality into GPRD', 15 March: china.org.cn.

China State Statistical Bureau 2003a, 'International Trade, Second Quarter 2003', September.

China State Statistical Bureau 2003b, *China Industrial Economy Statistical Yearbook 2003*, Beijing.

China State Statistical Bureau (various years), *China Statistical Yearbook*, Beijing.

China Statistics Press (various years), *Dongguan Statistical Yearbook*, Beijing.

China Statistics Press (various years), *Guangdong Statistical Yearbook*, Beijing.

China Statistics Press (various years), *Jiangsu Statistical Yearbook*, Beijing.

China Statistics Press (various years), *Shanghai Statistical Yearbook*, Beijing.

China Statistics Press (various years), *Shenzhen Statistical Yearbook*, Beijing.

China Statistics Press (various years), *Zhejiang Statistical Yearbook*, Beijing.

Ching, Frank 2004, 'Saving Lives', *South China Morning Post*, 3 February: scmp.com.

Chiu, Annette 2004, 'Shenzhen Seeks HKAA Investment', *South China Morning Post*, 13 February, p. B1.

Chiu, David K. Y. 1998, 'Synthesis of Economic Reforms and Open Policy', in Y. M. Yeung and David K. Y. Chiu (eds), *Guangdong: Survey of a Province Undergoing Rapid Change*, Hong Kong: The Chinese University Press, pp. 485–504.

Chiu, Peter Y. W. 2002, 'Economic Integration between Hong Kong and Mainland China: The Effect on Hong Kong of China's Entry into the WTO', *China Perspectives*, Vol. 40, March/April, pp. 62–74.

Chow Chung-yan 2004a, 'Guangdong Official Threatens HK Media Over "Irresponsible" Bird Flu Coverage', *South China Morning Post*, 9 February: scmp.com.

Chow Chung-yan 2004b, 'Better Reporting Promised on Spread of Disease', *South China Morning Post*, 12 February: scmp.com.

Chow Chung-yan 2004c, 'Shenzhen Sees Population Growing Too Fast', *South China Morning Post*, 19 February, p. A4.

Chow Chung-yan 2004d, 'Power Shortages to Put Guangzhou in the Dark', *South China Morning Post*, 10 March, p. A8.

Chow Chung-yan 2004e, 'Guangzhou Says Nansha Port Will Boost HK Shipping Role', *South China Morning Post*, 17 March: p. A3.

Chow Chung-yan 2004f, 'Overhaul of Delta Transport Links to Slash Travel Times', *South China Morning Post*, 1 June, p. A3.

Chow Chung-yan and Ambrose Leung 2003, 'Cities Urged to Team up or Lose Out', *South China Morning Post*, 31 July: scmp.com.

Chu, D. K. Y., Shen Jianfa, and K. Y. Wong 1999, 'Trans-border Complications and Regional Governance, the Case of Hong Kong and Guangdong', Proceedings of the Conference on Cities in Transition: The Face of Our City in the Next 20 Years, Hong Kong Institute of Planners and Centre of Urban Planning and Environmental Management, University of Hong Kong, p. 23.

Chung, Lawrence 2003, '$10m Campaign to Revive Taiwan Tourism', *The Straits Times*, 19 June: thestraitstimes.com.

Chung, Olivia 2004, 'Guangdong Plans to Move 8 Million Farmers into Cities', *The Standard*, 14 April, p. A11.

Clark, Duncan 2003, 'Going Global, China's Handset Manufacturers Take on the World', *Eurobiz Magazine*, August: sinomedia.net.

Comtois, Claude and Brian Slack 2000, 'Hong Kong: Adding Value to China – Transport Hub and Urban Super-Region', *China Perspectives*, Vol. 29, May/June, pp. 11–8.

Curry, Lynne 1999, 'Dungeons and the Dragon:', *CFO Asia*, 28 March: cfoasia.com.

Démurger S., J. D. Sachs, W. T. Woo, S. Bao, G. Chang, and A. Mellinger 2002, 'Geography, Economic Policy and Regional Development in China', Discussion Paper Number 1950, Harvard Institute of Economic Research, March.

Di Changyun 1995, *Guangdong gaige kaifang juece anli (Case Studies of Guangdong's Decision Making in Reform and Opening)*, Beijing: People's Daily Press.

Dongguan City Government 1997, *Dongguan diaoyan 1997* (*Dongguan Studies 1997*), pp. 1–2.

Dorn, James 1999, 'Risky . . . or Worthy WTO Bid?', CTPS Articles, 26 July: freetrade.org.

DTZ Research 2004, 'Asia Pacific Property Market Overview 2004', February, p. 8.

Duan Jie and Yan Xiaopei 2003, '*Yuegang shengchan xing fuwu ye hezuo fazhan yanjiu*' ('A Study of the Development of Cooperation Between Hong Kong and Guangdong in the Producer Services Sector'), *Diyu yanjiu yu kaifa* (*Areal Research and Development*), June, pp. 26–30.

Dutch Chamber of Commerce in Guangzhou 2002, 'Industrial Zone Survey in the Pearl River Delta', September.

Eason, A. G. 1996, 'Planning of Hong Kong in the Pearl River Delta Region Context', in Anthony Gar-On Yeh (ed.), *Planning Hong Kong for the 21st Century: A Preview of the Future Role of Hong Kong*, Hong Kong: Centre of Urban Planning and Environmental Management, University of Hong Kong, pp. 6–8.

Economic Forum 2000, 'Implications for Hong Kong: If There are Direct Links between the Chinese Mainland and Taiwan', July: tdctrade.com.

The Economist 2004a, 'Behind the Mask', Vol. 370, No. 8367, special section, 20 March, pp. 3–4.

The Economist 2004b, 'We are the Champions', Vol. 370, No. 8367, special section, 20 March, pp. 13–15.

The Economist 2004c, 'On the Capitalist Road', Vol. 370, No. 8367, special section, 20 March, pp. 15–17.

The Economist 2004d, 'Haier's Purpose', Vol. 370, No. 8367, 20 March, p. 72.

The Economist Global Agenda 2003, 'On a Roll', 27 June: economist.com.

Enright, Michael J. 1997, 'Even More Than Before, it's Worth Betting on Hong Kong', *Asian Business, Special Handover Issue*, June/August, p. 8.

Enright, Michael J. 2001, 'China and its Neighbours', paper presented at Wilton Park Conference 'China and its Neighbours', November.

Enright, Michael J. 2002, 'Globalization, Regionalization and the Knowledge-based Economy in Hong Kong', in John Dunning (ed.), *Globalization, Regions and the Knowledge Economy*, Oxford: Oxford University Press, pp. 381–406.

Enright, Michael J. 2003, 'Regional Clusters What We Know and What We Should Know', in Johannese Bröcker, Dirk Dohse, and Rüdiger Soltwedel (eds), *Innovation Clusters and Interregional Competition*, Berlin: Springer Verlag, pp. 99–129.

Enright, Michael J. and Edith E. Scott 2000, 'The RHQ Question', *Business Asia*, The Economist Intelligence Unit, 11 December, pp. 1–6.

Enright, Michael J. and Edith E. Scott 2004, *The Greater Pearl River Delta*, Hong Kong: Invest Hong Kong, June.

Enright, Michael J. and Ifor Ffowcs-Williams 2001, 'Local Partnerships, Clusters and SME Globalisation', in *Enhancing SME Competitiveness*, Paris: OECD, pp. 115–50.

Enright, Michael J. and Vincent Mak 2004, 'Regional Development in the Chinese Mainland', Centre for Asian Business Cases, University of Hong Kong.

Enright, Michael J., Edith E. Scott, and David Dodwell 1997, *The Hong Kong Advantage*, Hong Kong: Oxford University Press, pp. 29–34.

Enright, Michael J., Edith E. Scott, and Edward Leung 1999, *Hong Kong's Competitiveness Beyond the Asian Crisis*, Hong Kong: Hong Kong Trade Development Council, February.

Ericsson (China) and Enright, Scott & Associates Ltd 2003, 'Telecommunications and Information Infrastructure in Guangdong's Competitiveness and Development', paper for the Guangdong Governors' International Advisory Council Meeting, November, p. 8.

European Commission, Directorate General for External Relations, 'EU–China Sectoral Agreements and Dialogue', External Relations Website.

Federation of American Scientists, 'Guangzhou Baiyun International Airport 23°11'N 113°16'E': fas.org.

Federation of the Swiss Watch Industry 2003, 'The Swiss Watch Industry in 2002', Bienne: Federation of the Swiss Watch Industry.

FedEx Press Releases 1999, 'FedEx Pioneers International Air-Express Service in Shenzhen', 2 November.

Feng Xiaoyun 2002a, *Current Conditions and Analysis of Overseas Investment in the Service Industry in the Pearl River Delta*, Hong Kong: China Business Centre, Hong Kong Polytechnic University.

Feng Xiaoyun 2002b, 'WTO *kuangjia xia yuegang jingji hezuo de chuangxin yu tupo* ('Innovations and Breakthroughs in Guangdong–Hong Kong Economic Cooperation under the WTO Framework'), *Kaifang daobao (China Opening Herald Monthly)*, Vol. 12, pp. 16–8.

Fletcher, Stephen 2003, Partner, Linklaters Hong Kong, 'CEPA Definition of Hong Kong Companies', at Hong Kong General Chamber of Commerce Roundtable Workshop, 24 November.

Fung, Victor K. 2004, Chairman, Hong Kong Airport Authority, 'A New Road Map for Hong Kong', Speech to the Swiss Business Council/Swiss Association, 8 March.

GC.Comm 2001–2002, 'Environmental Protection in Guangdong', December 2001–January 2002.

Global Sources 2003, 'Sourcing Report: Denim Jeans', 20 October: globalsources.com.

GK Goh Research 2003, 'Consumer Electronics: China's Outsourcing Magnet Fuels Growth', 10 December.

Gong Zhengzheng and Liang Qiwen 2004, 'Auto Maker Launches Engine Joint Venture', *China Daily*, 26 February, p. 10.

Governo da Região Administrativa Especial de Macau Gabinete de Comunicação Social 2002, *Basic Information on Macao's Gaming Concessions*, September.

Guangdong Government Development Research Centre 2002, *Rushi hou de Guangdong jingji yunzuo – 'Zhongguo rushi yu Guangdong jingji xupian' (Guangdong's Economy after China's Entry into the WTO – A Sequel to 'China's WTO Entry and Guangdong's Economy')*, Guangzhou: Guangdong Economic Press, pp. 76–84, 100–12, 125–30, and 152–7.

Guangdong Government State Development Planning Commission 2001, *Tuijin xiandaihua, kaichuang xinjiyuan: Guangdong sheng guomin jingji he shehui fazhan shiwu jihua (Pushing Forward Modernisation, Opening up a New Era: The Tenth Five-year Plan for the Economic and Social Development of Guangdong)*, Guangzhou: Guangdong Economic Press, pp. 473–508.

Guangdong Provincial People's Government, Development Research Centre 1998, *Guangdong gaige kaifang ershi nian jinian wenji (A Collection of Commemorative Essays and Information for Guangdong's Twenty Years of Reform and Opening Up)* (monograph).

Guangdong Provincial Statistics Bureau 1995, *Zhujiang sanjiao zhou jingji qu tongji ziliao, 1980–1994 (The Pearl River Delta Statistical Data, 1980–1994)*, Guangdong: Zhong gong Guangdong Sheng Wei ban Gong ting Zong he Chu, Guangdong Sheng tong ji ju Zong he Chu bian.

Guangzhou Statistical Bureau 2001, *Zhujiang sanjiao zhou 12 shi (qu) shehui jingji zhibiao tongji ziliao 2001 (Major Economic Indicators of 12 Cities in the Pearl River Delta 2001)* Guangzhou: Zhujiang Sanjiao Zhou 12 Shi (qu) Shi tong ji ju.

Guerrera, Francesco and Alexandra Harney 2004, 'HK in Talks to Buy Chinese Airport Stake', *Financial Times* (London Edition), 25 March, p. 29.

Guo Wanda and Ma Chunhui 2003, '*Shengang jingji hezuo de yiyi, mubiao ji duice*' ('The Meanings, Goals and Strategies of Hong Kong–Shenzhen Economic Cooperation'), *Kaifang daobao (China Opening Herald Monthly)*, Vol. 3, pp. 5–7.

Gwartney, James D. and Robert A. Lawson (eds) 2003, *Economic Freedom of the World: 2003 Annual Report*, The Fraser Institute.

Hang Seng Bank Economic Research Department 2001, 'Strengthening Economic Integration with the Pearl River Delta' (in Chinese), *Hang Seng Economic Monthly*, May.

Harney, Alexandra 2003, 'Guangdong's Handshake with Hong Kong Could Prove a Bone-crusher for the Territory', *Financial Times*, 30 December: FT.com.

He Jiasheng and Wang Yingjie 1999, *Maixiang xin shiji de Guangdong jingji tequ* (*The Guangdong Economic Zone Towards the New Century*), Guangzhou: Guangdong Tertiary Education Press, pp. 12–6 and 290–313.

Higgins, Andrew 2004, 'Power and Peril: America's Supremacy and its Limits', *The Asian Wall Street Journal*, 2 February: global. factiva.com.

Ho, Beatrice and Franklin Lam (analysts) 2003, *HK + The Pearl River Delta: Making a Two Way Street for Tourists & Homebuyers*, UBS Warburg Global Equity Research, 13 January.

Ho Wainang 1996, 'Individual Economy in the Pearl River Delta Region: A Study on Dongguan, Guangzhou, Zhongshan and Nanhai', in Stewart MacPherson and Joseph Y. S. Cheng (eds), *Economic and Social Development in South China*, Cheltenham: Edward Elgar, pp. 183–205.

Hong Kong Airport Authority 2001, *Hong Kong International Airport Master Plan 2020*, October, p. 3.

Hong Kong Business Professionals Federation 2002, *Impact of Cross Border Economic Activities on Hong Kong*, January, p. 7.

Hong Kong Centre for Economic Research 2003, *Made in PRD: The Changing Face of Hong Kong Manufacturers*, Hong Kong: Federation of Hong Kong Industries, June.

Hong Kong Christian Industrial Committee: Hong Kong 2001, 'How Hasbro, McDonald's, Mattel and Disney Manufacture their Toys: Report on the Labor Rights and Occupational Safety and Health Conditions of Toy Workers in Foreign Investment Enterprises in Southern Mainland China', December, pp. 1–2.

Hong Kong Economic Journal 2002, 'Pearl River Delta Becomes the Biggest Hi-tech Industry Base in China', 20 June, p. 23.

Hong Kong General Chamber of Commerce 2000, *The Impact of China's WTO Entry on Hong Kong's Businesses, a View from the Business Sector* (in Chinese), June.

Hong Kong General Chamber of Commerce 2003, *CEPA: Business Assessment*, November.

Hong Kong International Airport Annual Report 2002: hkairport.com.

Hong Kong Looking Ahead 2003, 'Port Throughput Continues to Rise', 19 November: sc.info. gov.hk/gb/www.hklookingahead.gov.hk/news.

Hong Kong Polytechnic University, China Business Centre 2000, *The Characteristics of the Operation and Development of Taiwan-invested Enterprises in Hong Kong* (in Chinese).

Hong Kong Port Development Council 2003, 'Summary Statistics on Port Traffic of Hong Kong', August: pdc.gov.hk.

Hong Kong Special Administrative Region Government Information Centre 2003, 'Links between Hong Kong and the Mainland of China', November.

Hong Kong Special Administrative Region Government Press Release 2003a, 'Hong Kong, Mainland and Macau Unite to Fight Drugs', 20 February.

Hong Kong Special Administrative Region Government Press Release 2003b, 'CE's Opening Remarks on Basic Law Article 23', 5 September.

Hong Kong Special Administrative Region Government, Census and Statistics Department 2001a, 'Consumption Expenditure of Hong Kong Residents Travelling to the Mainland of China', *Hong Kong Monthly Digest of Statistics*, April.

Hong Kong Special Administrative Region Government, Census and Statistics Department 2001b, *Quarterly Report of Employment and Vacancies Statistics*.

Hong Kong Special Administrative Region Government, Census and Statistics Department 2002a, *Hong Kong Population Projections 2002–2031: Announcement of Results*, 7 May.

Hong Kong Special Administrative Region Government, Census and Statistics Department 2002b, *Quarterly Report of Employment and Vacancies Statistics*.

Hong Kong Special Administrative Region Government, Census and Statistics Department 2003a, 'Statistical Digest of the Services Sector 2003', July, p. 254.

Hong Kong Special Administrative Region Government, Census and Statistics Department 2003b, 'Employment in Hong Kong's Major Service Sectors', September.

Hong Kong Special Administrative Region Government, Census and Statistics Department 2003c, 'Gross Domestic Product (GDP) by Economic Activity at Current Prices', September.

Hong Kong Special Administrative Region Government, Census and Statistics Department 2003d, 'Hong Kong Residents Working in the Mainland of China', *Social Data Collected via the General Household Survey: Special Topics Report No. 35*.

Hong Kong Special Administrative Region Government, Census and Statistics Department 2003e, *Annual Digest of Statistics 2003*, pp. 55, 59, and 180–1.

Hong Kong Special Administrative Region Government, Census and Statistics Department 2003f, *Quarterly Report of Employment and Vacancies Statistics*, December.

Hong Kong Special Administrative Region Government, Census and Statistics Department 2004a, *Hong Kong Monthly Digest of Statistics*, February, p. 117.

Hong Kong Special Administrative Region Government, Census and Statistics Department 2004b, *Statistics on Labour Force, Unemployment and Underemployment*, 19 February.

Hong Kong Special Administrative Region Government, Census and Statistics Department 2004c, 'Frequently Asked Statistics', 10 March.

Hong Kong Special Administrative Region Government, Census and Statistics Department 2004d, *Gross Domestic Product, Implicit Price Deflator of GDP and Per Capita GDP*, 10 March.

Hong Kong Special Administrative Region Government, Commission on Strategic Development 2000, 'Bringing the Vision to Life – Hong Kong's Long Term Development Needs and Goals', February, pp. 5, 18, and 24–33.

Hong Kong Special Administrative Region Government, Environment, Transport and Works Bureau 2002, 'Improving Air Quality in PRD Region', ACE Paper 15/2002, 29 April.

Hong Kong Special Administrative Region Government, Environment, Transport and Works Bureau 2003a, *The Hong Kong–Zhuhai–Macau Bridge*, 6 August.

Hong Kong Special Administrative Region Government, Environment, Transport and Works Bureau 2003b, 'LCQ3: Progress of Emissions Trading Pilot Scheme', Press Release, 10 December.

Hong Kong Special Administrative Region Government, Hong Kong International Airport 1998–2003, *Civil International Air Transport Movements of Aircraft, Passenger and Freight*.

Hong Kong Special Administrative Region Government, Information Services Department 2002, *Hong Kong Yearbook 2002*, pp. 256 and 456.

Hong Kong Special Administrative Region Government, Information Services Department 2003a, 'Hong Kong Facts', February.

Hong Kong Special Administrative Region Government, Information Services Department 2003b, 'Hong Kong: The Facts – Housing', May.

Hong Kong Special Administrative Region Government, Office of the Telecommunications Authority 2004, 'Capacity of External Telecommunications Facilities', June.

Hong Kong Special Administrative Region Government, Planning Department 2002a, 'Development Interface between Hong Kong and Mainland', *Hong Kong 2030 Planning Vision and Strategy*, Working Paper 18, January.

Hong Kong Special Administrative Region Government, Planning Department 2002b, *Cross-boundary Travel Survey 2001*.

Hong Kong Special Administrative Region Government, Planning Department 2003, 'Hong Kong 2030 Planning Vision and Strategy: Stage 3 Public Consultation', Consultation Booklet, November.

Hong Kong Special Administrative Region Government, SARS Expert Committee Report, 'SARS in Hong Kong: From Experience to Action': sars-expertccm.gov.hk.

Hong Kong Special Administrative Region Government, Trade and Industry Department 2003, *Mainland/Hong Kong Closer Economic Partnership Arrangement*, 29 June and 29 September.

Hong Kong Tourism Board 2002a, 'Tourism Expenditure Associated to Inbound Tourism – January to December 2002'.

Hong Kong Tourism Board 2002b, 'Visitor Arrival Statistics – Jan 2004'.

Hong Kong Tourism Board 2004, 'Tourism Statistics – 2003', 8 March.

Hong Kong Tourism Board News 2002a, 'Mainland Visitors Now Top Spenders as Tourism Receipts Grow to HK$64 Billion', 5 March.

Hong Kong Tourism Board News 2002b, 'More Records Set as August Visitor Arrivals Pass 1.5 Million', 26 September.

Hong Kong Trade Development Council 1998, *The Rise in Offshore Trade and Offshore Investment*, 2nd edition, August.

Hong Kong Trade Development Council 2000a, *China's WTO Entry and its Impact on Hong Kong*, January, p. 40.

Hong Kong Trade Development Council 2000b, 'Market Share of Famous Brand Names Grows', *Business Alert–China*, 15 February.

Hong Kong Trade Development Council 2000c, 'Products on Air', *HK Enterprise*, Vol. 9, p. 30.

Hong Kong Trade Development Council 2001, *China's WTO entry and its Implications for Hong Kong*, 22 November.

Hong Kong Trade Development Council 2002a, *Hong Kong's Trade and Trade Supporting Services: New Developments and Prospects*, January.

Hong Kong Trade Development Council 2002b, *Hong Kong as an International Commercial and Financial Centre – From the Perspective of Mainland Private Enterprises*, June.

Hong Kong Trade Development Council 2002c, 'Hong Kong as a Service Platform for Taiwan Companies Investing in the Mainland', *Economic Forum*, 31 October.

Hong Kong Trade Development Council 2002d, 'Profiles of Hong Kong Major Service Industries– Air Transport': tdctrade.com.

Hong Kong Trade Development Council 2002e, *Profiles of Hong Kong Major Manufacturing Industries*, 4 November.

Hong Kong Trade Development Council 2002f, 'Why Hong Kong? – A Survey of Japanese Companies in the Pearl River Delta', *Economic Forum*, 21 November.

Hong Kong Trade Development Council 2002g, *Economic & Trade Information on Hong Kong*, 29 November.

Hong Kong Trade Development Council 2003a, *Business Alert China*, 1 March.

Hong Kong Trade Development Council 2003b, 'A Survey of Korean Companies in the Pearl River Delta', *Economic Forum*, 7 April.

Hong Kong Trade Development Council 2003c, 'Opportunities for Hong Kong in Accounting Sector', *Inside PRD*, Vol. 5, 1 May.

Hong Kong Trade Development Council 2003d, 'Why Choose Hong Kong as a Business Platform? A Survey of EU Companies in the Pearl River Delta', *Economic Forum*, 23 June.

Hong Kong Trade Development Council 2003e, 'Profiles of Hong Kong Major Service Industries–Building & Construction', 4 July.

Hong Kong Trade Development Council 2003f, 'Why Hong Kong as a Business Platform? A Survey of US Companies in the Pearl River Delta', *Economic Forum*, 25 July.

Hong Kong Trade Development Council 2003g, 'Profiles of Hong Kong Major Service Industries–Securities', 31 July.

Hong Kong Trade Development Council 2003h, 'Advantage Hong Kong – International Financial Centre', 5 August.

Hong Kong Trade Development Council 2003i, 'Profiles of Hong Kong Major Service Industries–Banking', 5 August.

Hong Kong Trade Development Council 2003j, 'Profiles of Hong Kong Major Service Industries–Import and Export Trade', 21 August.

Hong Kong Trade Development Council 2003k, 'Hong Kong Chinese Nationals May Register Individual Businesses in Guangdong', *Business Alert China*, 6 November.

Hong Kong Trade Development Council 2003l, 'Hong Kong as the Business Platform for Foreign Businesses Operating in the PRD with CEPA Agreement', *Economic Forum*, 12 November.

Hong Kong Trade Development Council 2003m, 'Competitiveness of the HK+PRD Region: An Export Centre in the Global Supply Chain & Operational Base for Penetrating the China Market', PowerPoint Presentation: tdctrad.com.

Hong Kong Trade Development Council 2003n, *Economic & Trade Information on Hong Kong*, 2 December.

Hong Kong Trade Development Council 2004a, 'Shanghai Municipality-Market Profiles on Chinese Cities and Provinces', January: tdctrade.com.

Hong Kong Trade Development Council 2004b, 'Hong Kong's Clothing Industry', 6 January.

Hong Kong Trade Development Council 2004c, *Economic & Trade Information on Hong Kong*, 7 January and 5 February.

Hong Kong Trade Development Council 2004d, 'Hong Kong's Watches and Clocks Industry', 1 March.

Hong Kong Trade Development Council 2004e, 'CEPA to Drive Co-operation of Logistics Industry in the Chinese Mainland and Hong Kong', May: tdctrade.com.

Hong Kong Trade Development Council, 'Shenzhen': tdctrade.com.

Hong Kong Trader 2004a, 'CEPA Helps Japanese Logistics Firm Expand in China', 8 March: hktrader.net.

Hong Kong Trader 2004b, 'Luxury Goods Group Sees CEPA as a Business Generator', 1 April: hktrader.net.

Hong Kong Trader 2004c, 'World Banks Localise for First-mover Advantage in China', 28 April: hktrader.net.

Hong Kong Transport Department 2003, *Monthly Traffic and Transport Digest*, December, Table 8.1 (d).

Hsu, Jinn-yuh (undated), 'From Transfer to Hybridization: The Changing Organizations of Taiwanese PC Investments in China', Department of Geography, National Taiwan University.

Huang Zhaoyong 2002, '*Gangzi beiyi yu yuegang jingji yitihua yanjiu*' ('Studies of the Northward Shifting of Hong Kong Capital and the Economic Integration of Hong Kong and Guangdong'), *Diyu yanjiu yu kaifa (Areal Research and Development)*, June, p. 18.

Hutchinson Port Holdings: hph.com.hk.

Ikeson, Dan 2004, 'The Stealth Trade War', Cato Institute, 2 March: cato.org.

iMail 2002, 'Shenzhen Hits Big Time as Clock Maker', 22 February, p. 13.

Intermon Oxfam 2002, 'Oxfam Response to European Commission's Comments on Rigged Rules and Double Standards', 17 April: intermonoxfam.org.

International Monetary Fund 2003, *World Economic Outlook Database*, September.

Invest Hong Kong 2004, 'Corporate and Investment Banking': investhk.gov.hk.

Invest Hong Kong: investhk.gov.hk.

Japan Society of Mechanical Engineers 2003, Engineering News in Brief, October.

Jiangmen Statistical Bureau 2003, *Zhujiang sanjiao zhou 12 shi (qu) shehui jingji zhibiao tongji zhiliao 2002 (Major Socio-Economic Indicators of 12 Cities in the Pearl River Delta)*, pp. 12–3, 16–7, 96–7, 112–3, and 120–1.

Jin Huikang 2003, 'A Rising Star in China', *News Guangdong*, 17 September: newsgd.com.

Joanilho, Marcal 2003, 'Private-car Sales Soar in Shenzhen', *South China Morning Post*, 29 June: scmp.com.

Journal of the American Chamber of Commerce in Hong Kong 2004, 'Patriot's Paradox: For China's Youth Internationalism is Desired Destination', February, p. 31.

Kahn, Joseph 2003, 'When Chinese Workers Unite, the Bosses Often Run the Union', Global Policy Forum, *New York Times*, 29 December: globalpolicy.org.

Kynge, James 2004, 'How Long can China Continue to Boom?', *Financial Times*, 23 March: FT.com.

Lai, Chloe 2003, 'Suggestions for HK's Future Mapped Out', *South China Morning Post*, 22 November, p. A3.

Lam, G. 2004, 'Holidays will Attract 900,000', *The Standard*, 12 January, p. A3.

Lam, G. and Jonathan Tam 2004, 'Record Visitor Arrivals Likely to Top 20m', *The Standard*, 24 February, p. A6.

Lam, Samuel 2002, Oriental Trucking Hong Kong Ltd, 'Cross Border Trucking', Presentation to Hong Kong Amcham Transport and Logistics Committee, citing Hong Kong Special Administrative Region Government, Census and Statistics Department, 29 May.

Lau, Alyssa 2002, 'Firms Could Buy Pollution Solution', *South China Morning Post*, 5 July, p. A6.

Lau, C. K. and Joseph Lo 2004, 'Regional Links "Vital to Delta's Economy"', *South China Morning Post*, 27 February, p. A2.

Lau Siu-Kai 2002, 'Tung Chee-hwa's Governing Strategy: The Shortfall in Politics', in Lau Siu Kai (ed.), *The First Tung Chee-hwa Administration*, Hong Kong: Chinese University Press, p. 1.

Lau Siu-Kai (ed.) 2002, *The First Tung Chee-hwa Administration: The First Five Years of the Hong Kong Special Administrative Region*, Hong Kong: The Chinese University Press.

Lee, Ella 2003a, 'Hong Kong "Kept in the Dark" Over Outbreak', *South China Morning Post*, 3 October: scmp.com.

Lee, Ella 2003b, 'Guangdong "Ready to Work with HK"', *South China Morning Post*, 4 October: scmp.com.

Legislative Council: legco.gov.hk.

Lehman Brothers 2003, Global Equity Research, 'Fourth Annual EMS/ODM/OEM Asia Tour, China is the Place; Tech Demand has Legs', 18 December, p.1.

Leman, Edward 2003, 'Can the Pearl River Delta Region Still Compete?', *The China Business Review*, May/June, pp. 6–17.

Leu Siew Ying 2004a, 'Province Asks for Help to Fight Bird Flu', *South China Morning Post*, 21 January: scmp.com.

Leu Siew Ying 2004b, 'Western Corridor Border to Operate around the Clock', *South China Morning Post*, 16 February, p. A1.

Leu Siew Ying 2004c, 'Close Co-operation Best Remedy for Region', *South China Morning Post*, 16 February, p. A4.

Leung, C. K. 1993, 'Personal Contacts, Subcontracting Linkages and Development in the Hong Kong–Zhujiang Delta Region', *Annals of the Association of American Geographers*, Vol. 83, No. 2, pp. 272–302.

Leung, C. Y. 2001, 'HK & Guangdong: One Country, Two Systems and One Market?', Presentation to the American Chamber of Commerce in Hong Kong, 31 May.

Leung, C. Y. 2002, 'Social Implications of Pearl River Delta Integration: Livelihood Issues and Social Welfare', Speech to the Hong Kong General Chamber of Commerce/South China Morning Post Pearl River Delta Forum, 8 July.

Li Jianping, Yan Xiaopei, and Zhou Chunshan 2002, '*Kuaguo gongsi zai zhujiang sanjiaozhou de touzi xianzhuang yu fazhan qushi tanxi*' ('An Investigation into the Current Situations and Development Trends of MNC Investment in the Pearl River Delta Region'), *Guangdong Fazhan Daokan* (*Guangdong Development Magazine*), Vol. 1, p. 43.

Li Pang Kwong 2001, 'The Executive–Legislature Relationship in Hong Kong: Evolution and Development', in Joseph Y. S. Cheng (ed.), *Political Development in the HKSAR*, Hong Kong: The Chinese University Press, pp. 85–100.

Li Siming 1988, 'Pearl Riversville: A Survey of Urbanisation in the Pearl River Delta', in Joseph Y. S. Cheng (ed.), *The Guangdong Development Model and Its Challenges*, Hong Kong: City University of Hong Kong Press, p. 130.

Lin, George C. S. 1997, 'Intrusion of Global Forces and Transformation of a Local Chinese Economy: The Experience of Dongguan', in R. Watters (ed.), *Asia-Pacific: New Geographies of the Pacific Rim*, London: Christopher Hurst, pp. 250–65.

Lin, George C. S. 2002, 'Region-based Urbanisation in Post-reform China: Spatial Restructuring in the Pearl River Delta', in John R. Logan (ed.), *The New Chinese City*, United Kingdom: Blackwell Publishers, pp. 245–57.

Liu Li 2002, 'Incredible Journey Planned to Reach Distant Loved Ones', *China Daily*. 1 February, p. 5.

Liu Shaojian and Shi Yan 2003, '*Yuegang hezuo tisheng*' ('The Promotion of Guangdong–Hong Kong Cooperation'), *Zhongguo wuliu yu caigou* (*China Logistics and Procurement*), January, pp. 26–7.

Liu Weifeng 2003, 'Project to Clean Up Waterway', *China Daily*. 11 March, p. 4.

Liu Weifeng 2004a, 'Guangdong Continues to Buy HK Electricity', *China Daily*. 21 April, p. 19.

Liu Weifeng 2004b, 'City Tackles Water Pollution', *China Daily*. 30 April, p. 4.

Lo, Joseph, Russell Barling, and Carrie Chan 2003, 'Need for a Third Runway is Signalled', *South China Morning Post*, 26 November, p. A3.

Loh, Christine 2002, *Ports, Airports and Bureaucrats: Restructuring Hong Kong and Guangdong*, CLSA Emerging Markets, October, pp. 23–4.

Long Guoqiang 2003, '*Jiagong maoyi: quanqiuhua beijingxia gongyehua xindaolu*' ('Processing Trade: A New Road for Industrialisation Against the Background of Globalisation'), in *Jingji qianyan* (*Forward Position in Economics*), January, pp. 8–9.

LSI Logic 2004, 'China: Centerpiece of a Winning Strategy for the Consumer Electronics Market and LSI Logic'.

Lu, D. and V. F. S. Sit 2001, 'China's Regional Development Policies: A Review', in D. Lu and V. F. S. Sit (eds), *China's Regional Disparities: Issues and Policies*, New York: Nova Science Publishers, pp. 19–37.

Luk, Sidney 2004, 'Airport Freight Traffic Soars', *South China Morning Post*, 15 March, p. B7.

Ma, Raymond 2003, 'Manufacturers Weigh up Moving Back to Hong Kong', *South China Morning Post*, 29 September, p. B1.

Macau International Airport website: macau-airport.gov.mo.

MacPherson, Stewart and Joseph Y. S. Cheng (eds) 1996, *Economic and Social Development in South China*, Cheltenham: Edward Elgar, pp. 1–56.

Mitchell, Tom 2002a, 'All Because of a Bright Spark', *South China Morning Post*, 29 January: scmp.com.

Mitchell, Tom 2002b, 'Casual-wear Capital Spinning up a Huge Profit', *South China Morning Post*, 29 January: scmp.com.

Mitchell, Tom 2002c, 'Clean-up Bill for $41b Should Bring Fisherman Cleaner Dinner', *South China Morning Post*, 17 October: scmp.com.

Mitchell, Tom 2003, 'Nature Will Have a Say in Port Development', *South China Morning Post*, 16 January: scmp.com.

Nanhai Non-Ferrous Metal Industry website: nhtip.com.

New York: The National Labor Committee 2001, 'Toys of Misery: A Report on the Toy Industry in China', December, pp. 6–7.

NewsGuangdong 2003a, 'A Dreamland of Future', 17 September: newsgd.com.

NewsGuangdong 2003b, 'University Town Opens', 17 September: newsgd.com.

Ng, K. Y. 2003, *Hong Kong and China Ports*, 5 March, p. 1.

Ng, Linda F. Y. and Tuan Chyau 2003, 'Location Decisions of Manufacturing FDI in China: Implications of China's WTO Accession', *Journal of Asian Economics*, Vol. 14, pp. 51–72.

Ng, M. K. and W. S. Tang 1999, 'Urban System Planning in China: A Case Study of the Pearl River Delta', *Urban Geography*, Vol. 20, No. 7, pp. 591–616.

Nogales, Alberto and Graham Smith 2004, 'China's Evolving Transport Sector', *The China Business Review*, Vol. 31, No. 2, March/April, pp. 26 and 29.

Norman Miners 2000, *The Government and Politics of Hong Kong*, 5th edition, New York: Oxford University Press.

O'Driscoll, Gerald P., Edwin J. Feulner, and Anastasia O'Grady (eds), *2003 Index of Economic Freedom*, The Heritage Foundation and The Wall.

Office of the United States Trade Representative 2004, *2004 National Trade Estimate Report on Foreign Trade Barriers*, 1 April.

One Country Two Systems Research Institute 2002a, *A Comprehensive Coordination Solution for the Guangdong–Hong Kong–Macau Bridge* (in Chinese), September.

One Country Two Systems Research Institute 2002b, *Background Information for the Guangdong–Hong Kong–Macau Bridge – Consensus and Dissension* (in Chinese), September.

One Country Two Systems Research Institute 2002c, *An Assessment of the Cost and Benefits of the Guangdong–Hong Kong–Macau Bridge* (in Chinese), December.

Overholt, William H. 1993, *China: The Next Economic Superpower,* London: Weidenfeld & Nicolson, p. 118.

Panel discussion proceedings 2002, 'China–Taiwan: The Cross Strait Relationship', A Panel Discussion with Steven Goldstein, Yasheng Huang, Dwight Perkins, Alan Romberg, William Kirby (Moderator), Dean, Faculty of Arts and Sciences, Harvard University, ARCO Forum, Kennedy School of Government, 6 December.

Patterson, Mike 2002, 'China's Dongguan Transforms from Opium Battleground to Hi-tech Dragon', *Things Asian,* 12 June: thingsasian.com.

People's Daily 2000, 'Nine Chinese TV Producers Face up to EU's Anti-dumping Complaint', 24 July: peopledaily.com.

People's Daily 2002, 'China's Electronics Industry Registers Rapid Growth', 10 January: people daily.com.

People's Daily 2003a, 'SARS Inflicts Nearly US$2bn Loss on Beijing's Tourism', 18 June: people daily.com.

People's Daily 2003b, 'Several Nuclear-power Plants to Quench Energy Thirst', 4 September: peopledaily.com.

People's Daily 2003c, 'China Becoming New Engine for World Economy: Forbes', 18 September: peopledaily.com.

People's Daily 2003d, 'Traffic Woes to Ease with Express Thoroughfares', 17 November: people daily.com.

People's Daily 2003e, 'Wal-Mart Asia President: I Hope to Retire in China', 7 December: people daily.com.

People's Daily 2004a, 'FedEx Moves Asia Hub to Guangzhou', 5 January: peopledaily.com.

People's Daily 2004b, 'JV to Help Meet Sheet Steel Demand', 16 January: peopledaily.com.

People's Daily 2004c, 'China to Become Largest Market for Computer Equipment in 5 Years: Intel CEO', 3 March: peopledaily.com.

People's Daily 2004d, 'CNOOC Outlines Oil, Natural Gas Output Targets', 9 March: peopledaily.com.

People's Daily 2004e, 'Logistics Company Seeks IPO this Year', 17 March: peopledaily.com.

Perez, Bien 2003, 'Kingdee Eyes HK Base to Compete with Giants', *South China Morning Post,* 12 March, p. B2.

Petersen, Ian, KCRC 2002, Presentation to the Hong Kong AmCham Transportation and Logistics Committee, 24 April.

Phillips. H. 2003, 'Need for Urgent Action on Scheme', *South China Morning Post,* 8 September: scmp.com.

Pratley, Nils, Andrew Clark, and Jon Chinery 2003, 'The Impact: SARS Effects Underline Fragility of Fast East Economies', *Guardian Unlimited,* 25 April: guardian.co.uk.

The Publicity Department of the Guangdong Committee of Communist Party of China 1995, *Zhujiang sanjiaozhou jingjiqu fazhan zhanlue yu guihua yanjiu (A Study of the Development Strategies and Planning of the Pearl River Delta Economic Zone),* Guangzhou: Guangdong People's Press, pp. 76–119, 128–33, 147–52, and 296–303.

Pun, Pamela 2004a, '"9+2" Bloc Moves to Co-ordinate Development', *The Standard,* 12 February, p. A7.

Pun, Pamela 2004b, 'Guangzhou Plans Largest Asia Rail Hub', *The Standard,* 13 February, p. A8.

Pun, Pamela 2004c, 'Wen to Rein in Economy', *The Standard,* 15 March, p. A1.

Pun, Pamela 2004d, 'Shenzhen to Pull the Plug on Power Grid Gluttons', *The Standard,* 15 April, p. A6.

Qi Huaiyang 2001, '*Cong touzi huanjing kan zhujiang sanjiaozhou yu changjiang sanjiaozhou zhijian de jingzheng he fazhan*' ('Competition and Development Between the Pearl River Delta Region and the Yangtze River Delta Region – An Investment Perspective'), *Guangdong Fazhan Daokan (Guangdong Development Magazine)*, Vol. 4, p. 43.

Qiu Quanlin 2004, 'Eager Guangzhou Eyes 2010 Asian Games', *China Daily*, 19 April, p. 5.

Reenan, Rosemary, Robin Goodchild, Jeffrey Havsy, Jeremy Kelly, Timothy Bellman, and Camilla Bastoni (analysts) 2003, *Rising Urban Stars – Uncovering Future Winners*, Jones Lang LaSalle, May.

Research Team of the Guangdong Government Development Research Centre 2001, '*Guangdong jingji mianlin de xin xingshi yu duice fenxi*' ('An Analysis of the New Situation Facing the Guangdong Economy and Related Strategies'), *Guangdong Jingji (Guangdong Economy)*, January, pp. 11–2.

Researchandmarkets 2003, *China Chemical Industry Newsletter 2003*: researchand markets.com.

Reuters 2004a, 'China's Shenzhen Airport in Talks with Hong Kong Investor', 12 February.

Reuters 2004b, 'Power Shortage Hits Honda Joint Venture', *South China Morning Post*, 20 February, p. B3.

Rohlen, Thomas P. 2000, *Hong Kong and the Pearl River Delta: One Country, Two Systems in the Emerging Metropolitan Context*, Asia Pacific Research Centre, July.

Scott, Edith 2002a, *First Choice Hong Kong – Your Asia-Pacific Platform: A Practical Handbook for Businesses*, 2nd edition, Hong Kong: Hong Kong Trade Development Council and Invest Hong Kong.

Scott, Edith 2002b, *Hong Kong Plus: Your Global Platform for Sourcing, Producing and Selling in China*, Hong Kong: Hong Kong Trade Development Council, October.

Scott, Edith 2003, *Hong Kong: Marketplace for the World*, Hong Kong: Hong Kong Trade Development Council, November, pp. 30–1.

Seto, Karen C. and Robert Kaufmann 2003, 'Modeling the Drivers of Urban Land Use Change in the Pearl River Delta, China: Integrating Remote Sensing with Socioeconomic Data', *Land Economics*, Vol. 79, No. 1, February, pp. 106–21.

Shanghai Star 2002, 'Toying with the Future', 31 October: shanghaistar.com.

Shen, J. 2002, 'Urban and Regional Development in Post-reform China: The Case of Zhujiang Delta', *Progress in Planning*, Vol. 57, No. 2, pp. 91–140.

Shen, J., D. K. Y. Chu, and K. Y. Wong 1999, 'The Shenzhen Model: Forces of Development and Future Direction of a Mainland City Near Hong Kong', in S. Ye, Y. Niu, and C. Gu (eds), *Studies on the Regional Integration under the Model of One Country Two Systems* (in Chinese), Beijing: Sciences Press, p. 129.

Shenzhen Museum 1999, *Shenzhen Tequ Shi (History of the Shenzhen Special Economic Zone)*, Beijing: People's Publishing House, pp. 312–26.

Shi Jiangtao 2004, 'Sucked Dry, Guangdong Casts Nets for Energy', *South China Morning Post*, 30 March, p. A4.

Shih, Toh Han 2004, 'Delta Weaves a Success Story', *South China Morning Post*, 8 March, p. B2.

Shoenberger, Karl 2002, 'Cheap Products' Human Cost,' *Mercury News*, 24 November: mercurynews.com.

Sit, V. F. S. 2001, 'Increasing Globalization and the Growth of the Hong Kong Extended Metropolitan Region', in F. Lo and P. Marcottullio (eds), *Globalization and the Sustainability of Cities in the Asia Pacific Region*, Tokyo: UNU Press, pp. 199–238.

South China GC.comm 2003, 'A Knitting Kingdom – Zhangcha', May.

South China Morning Post 2002a, 'Helicopter Service Offers Zhuhai in 17 Minutes', 20 March: scmp.com.

South China Morning Post 2002b, 'Hactl to Improve Cargo Flows', 29 March: scmp.com.

South China Morning Post 2002c, 'Shenzhen the Focus of SAR Investors', 24 April: scmp.com.

South China Morning Post 2002d, 'Funds Forming Group to Boost Bargaining Power', 2 May: scmp.com.

South China Morning Post 2002e, 'Rival Airports Pose a Threat to Chek Lap Kok', 14 May: scmp.com.

South China Morning Post 2002f, 'Technology Holds the Key to Keep Cargo Moving', 5 July: scmp.com.

South China Morning Post 2003a, 'Denso Sets Up in Guangzhou', 2 April: scmp.com.

South China Morning Post 2003b, 'The Crisis Infecting Cross-border Relations', 7 May: scmp.com.

South China Morning Post 2003c, 'Tung Urges Fast Track for New Bridge', 29 August: scmp.com.

South China Morning Post 2003d, 'Hong Kong is Boosted by Record Number of Visitors in First Week of October', 22 October: scmp.com.

South China Morning Post 2003e, 'No Place for Clouded Vision on Pollution', 3 November: scmp.com.

South China Morning Post 2003f, 'Shenzhen Port Upgrades Volume Forecast', 5 November: scmp.com.

South China Morning Post 2003g, 'OBI Moves Asian Hub to Shenzhen', 10 November: scmp.com.

South China Morning Post 2003h, 'Huawei-3Com Union Makes Sense', 19 November, p. B2.

South China Morning Post 2003i, 'Shops Welcome Yuan Credit Card Plan', 19 November: scmp.com.

South China Morning Post 2003j, 'One Country, Two Currencies Boosts Economic Integration', 19 November: scmp.com.

South China Morning Post 2003k, 'Let's Find a Way to Pay for Full Waste Treatment', 27 December: scmp.com.

South China Morning Post 2004a, 'Power Shortage Hits Honda Joint Venture', 20 February, p. B3.

South China Morning Post 2004b, 'Guangzhou to Zhuhai in Just 48 Minutes', 2 March: p. A4.

South China Morning Post 2004c, 'We Can See Clearly Now', Special Supplement, 2 April, p. S7.

South China Morning Post 2004d, 'Scanner Checks at Border Likely for 2004', 3 September: scmp.com.

South China Morning Post/Hong Kong General Chamber of Commerce 2003, *The Second Pearl River Delta Conference: Charging Ahead to a New Pearl River Super Zone*, Cities Forum: Panel Discussion, 17 October, Hong Kong.

The Standard 2002a, 'Mainland Ports Booming', 7 June: thestandard.com.

The Standard 2002b, 'SAR in TCL Picture', 7 June: thestandard.com.

The Standard 2002c, 'Airport Authority Eyes Shenzhen Stake', 19 September: thestandard.com.

The Standard 2003a, 'Shenzhen Loads Up 50pc', 15 January: thestandard.com.

The Standard 2003b, 'Wal-mart's Push North Will Not Hurt Delta', 27 January: thestandard.com.

The Standard 2003c, '24-Hour Border Beats Forecast', 6 February: thestandard.com.

The Standard 2003d, 'Shenzhen Plans Giant Checkpoint', 11 September: thestandard.com.

The Standard 2003e, 'Telcos in Cepa Head Start', 30 September: thestandard.com.

Standing Committee of the National People's Congress 2004, 'Full Text of the Standing Committee Decision', *South China Morning Post*, 27 April, p. A4.

Sung Yun-wing 1998, *Hong Kong and South China: The Economic Synergy*, Hong Kong Economic Policy Study Series, City University of Hong Kong Press, pp. 100–17.

Sung Yun-wing, Liu Pak-wai, Richard Yue-chim Wong, and Lau Pui-king 1995a, *The Fifth Dragon: The Emergence of the Pearl River Delta*, Singapore: Addison Wesley Publishing Co.

Sydney Morning Herald 2003, 'Life Will Never be the Same in Singapore after SARS', 4 July: smh.com.au.

Ta Kung Pao 2002a, 'Hong Kong Businesses Prepare Domestic Sales', 22 January, p. C4.

Ta Kung Pao 2002b, 'Trade between Hong Kong and Guangdong Reaches US$ 38.7 Billion', 10 April, p. A8.

Tam, Jonathan and Keith Wallis 2004, 'Airport Chiefs Head for Zhuhai Takeover', *The Standard*, 2 March, p. 2.

Tan Gang 2003, 'Zhusanjiao: goujian shijie gongchang yu fazhan xiandai wuliuye – jianlun shenzhen yu xianggang wuliuye hezuo' ('The Pearl River Delta: Building the World's Factory and Developing a Modern Logistics Industry – A Discussion of Shenzhen–Hong Kong Cooperation in the Logistics Industry'), *Kaifang daobao (China Opening Herald Monthly)*, Vol. 5, pp. 19–20.

Toronto Star 2003, 'Tracking Toronto's SARS Deaths', September: thestar.com.

Toy Industry Association 2002, 'U.S. Imports of Toy Products, 2002': toy-tia.org.

Toy Industry Europe 2003, 'Facts and Figures 2003', July.

Tsai, Nasa Hsiung 2002, 'China Market', paper presented at the SEMI International Trade Partners Conference, November.

Tsang, Denise 2003, 'CKI Seeks Expansion in Zhuhai', *South China Morning Post*, 25 September: scmp.com.

Tsang, Denise 2004, 'Hopewell Powering into Guangdong', *South China Morning Post*, 1 May, p. B1.

Tuan Chyau and Linda F. Y. Ng 2001, '"Regional Division of Labour from Agglomeration Economies", Perspectives: Some Evidence', *Journal of Asian Economics*, Vol. 12, pp. 65–85.

Tuan Chyau and Linda F. Y. Ng 2003, 'FDI Facilitated by Agglomeration Economies: Evidence from Manufacturing and Services Joint Ventures in China', *Journal of Asian Economics*, North-Holland, Vol. 13, pp. 749–65.

UNCTAD 2003, *World Investment Report 2003*, Geneva: UNCTAD.

United States International Trade Commission 2004, *Textiles and Apparel: Assessment of the Competitiveness of Certain Foreign Suppliers to the U.S. Market*, Inv. No. 332–448, USTIC Pub. 3671, January, pp. 3–10, E5, and E8–E9.

Vogel, Ezra F. 1971, *Canton under Communism; Programs and Politics in a Provincial Capital, 1949–1968*, New York: Harper & Row.

Vogel, Ezra F. 1989, *One Step Ahead in China: Guangdong under Reform*, Cambridge, Mass.: Harvard University Press.

Walsh, Tom 2004, 'GM's China Bonanza', *Detroit Free Press*, 30 March: freep.com.

Wang Dengrong 2002, 'Yuegang diqu quyu hezuo fazhan fenxi ji quyu guanzhi tuijin celue' ('An Analysis of Regional Cooperation in the Hong Kong–Guangdong Region and the Strategies for Promoting Regional Administration'), *Xiandai chengshi yanjiu (Modern Urban Studies)*, pp. 60–2.

Wang Dingchang 1998, *Guangzhou de zuotian, jintian, mingtian (The Yesterday, Today and Tomorrow of Guangzhou)*, Guangzhou: Guangzhou Press, pp. 105–28.

Wang Dingchang 2000, *Shenzhen de zuotian, jintian, mingtian (The Yesterday, Today and Tomorrow of Shenzhen)*, Guangzhou: Guangzhou Press, pp. 160–96.

Wang, James J. and Brian Slack 2000, 'The Evolution of a Regional Container Port System: The Pearl River Delta', *Journal of Transport Geography*, Vol. 8, No. 4, pp. 265 and 272.

Wang Jun 1998, 'Expansion of the Southern China Growth Triangle', in Myo Thant, Min Tang, and Hiroshi Kakazu (eds), *Growth Triangles in Asia: A New Approach to Regional Cooperation*, Hong Kong: Asian Development Bank, pp. 169–73.

Wang Jun 2002, '*Chanye zuzhi de wangluohua fazhan – Guangdong zhuanyezhen jingji de lilun fenxi*' ('Network Development of Industrial Organisations – An Economic Analysis of the Professional Towns in Guangdong'), *Journal of Sun Yatsen University* (Social Science Edition), Vol. 1, pp. 89–95.

Wang Liwen, Yue Yue, and Yang Changzun 1995, *Jianshe zhujiang sanjiao zhou jingji qu – cehuapian* (*Building the Pearl River Delta Economic Zone – the Planning*), Guangzhou: Guangzhou Press, pp. 137–51.

Wang Xiangwei 2004, 'Critical Year for the Economy: Premier', *South China Morning Post*, 15 March, p. A1.

Wang Zhile 2002, Researcher, Economic Academy, Ministry of Foreign Trade and Economic Co-operation, at the South China Morning Post Conference, *Pearl River Delta: Forging a New Force*, special session on 'Multinational Companies Development in Shenzhen', Hong Kong, 9 July.

Ward's 2004, 'Nissan's China JV to set up R&D Centre in Guangzhou', 24 March: WardsAuto.com.

Wei Dazhi 2003, '*Yitihua shiye xia de shengang guanxi*' ('The Shenzhen–Hong Kong Relationship under the Vision of Integration'), *Kaifang daobao* (*China Opening Herald Monthly*), Vol. 6, p. 18.

Wei, Y. D. 2000, *Regional Development in China – States, Globalization, and Inequality*, London: Routledge, pp. 14–46.

Wenweipo 2002, 'Guangdong's Exports to Increase 10% Annually', 6 June, p. B08.

World Bank 2003, *World Development Indicators 2003*, Washington, D.C.

World Development Indicators Database 2003, 'GNI per Capita 2002, Atlas Method and PPP', World Bank, July.

World Economic Forum 2003, *World Competitiveness Report 2003*, Geneva.

World Health Organization 2003, 'Summary of Probable SARS Cases with Onset of Illness from 1 November 2002 to 31 July 2003', 26 September.

World Tourism Organization 2003, 'Tourism Highlights 2003', Geneva: world-tourism.org.

World Trade Organization 2003, *International Trade Statistics 2003*, Geneva.

Wu Zhiwen and Qiu Chuanying 2001, *Guangzhou xiandai jingji shi* (*Modern Economic History of Guangzhou*), Guangzhou: Guangdong People's Press, pp. 11–210.

Wu Zhong 2003, 'Yuletide Cheer', *The Standard*, 25 September, p. A17.

Wu Zhong 2004a, 'Guangdong Targets 9pc GDP Growth', *The Standard*, 12 January, p. A6.

Wu Zhong 2004b, 'Happy Days for Insurers', *The Standard*, 4 February, p. A17.

Wu Zhong 2004c, 'Shift in Focus', *The Standard*, 9 March, p. A33.

Xinmin, Bu, Ye Jianfu, Huang Defa, Zhang Hanchang, Ma Jianqiang, Meng Shenbao, and Chen Lifen 2001, '*Chuangxin zhusanjiao – Jianyu changjiang sanjiaozhou bijiao yanjiu*' ('Creating a New Pearl River Delta: A Comparative Study with the Yangtze River Delta'), *Guangdong Statistical Yearbook 2001*, pp. 34–52.

Yan, Louisa 2004, 'Border Crossings up by 10 pc to 128m People', *South China Morning Post*, 6 January, p. A4.

Yang, D. L. 1997, *Beyond Beijing – Liberalization and the Regions in China*, London: Routledge, pp. 62–78.

Yang Qianqi 1998, Deputy Director of the Development Research Centre, Guangdong Province, '*Fazhan tese gongye, tigao jingzheng youshi*' ('Developing Special Industries, Improving

Competitive Advantages'), *Guangdong gaige kaifang ershi nian jinian wenji (A Collection of Commemorative Essays and Information for Guangdong's Twenty Years of Reform and Opening Up)*, Guangdong Provincial People's Government Development Research Centre, p. 182.

Yang Qinqi (ed.) 2002, '*Zhujiang sanjiaozhou chengshihua yanjiu*' ('A Study of the Urbanisation of the Pearl River Delta'), *Guangdong Jingji (Guangdong Economy)*, June, p. 25.

Yeh, A. G. O. 2001, 'Hong Kong and the Pearl River Delta: Competition or Cooperation?', *Built Environment*, Vol. 27, No. 2, pp. 129–45.

Yeh, A. G. O. 2002, *The Hong Kong–Pearl River Delta Producer Services Linkages*, Hong Kong: Centre for Urban Planning and Environmental Management, University of Hong Kong.

Yeh, A. G. O. and X. Li 2000, 'The Need for Compact Development in Fast Growing Areas of China: The Pearl River Delta', in M. Jenks and R. Burgess (eds), *Compact Cities: Sustainable Urban Forms for Developing Countries*, London: Spon Press, pp. 73–90.

Yeh, A. G. O., Y. S. F. Lee, Tunney Lee, and Sze Nien Dak (eds) 2002, *Building a Competitive Pearl River Delta: Collaboration, Cooperation and Planning*, Hong Kong: Centre of Urban Planning and Environmental Management, The University of Hong Kong, pp. 9–26.

Yeung, Chris 2003, 'Healthy Co-operation', *South China Morning Post*, 24 March: scmp.com.

Yeung, Godfrey 2001, 'Foreign Direct Investment and Investment Environment in Dongguan Municipality of Southern China', *Journal of Contemporary China*, Vol. 10, No. 26, pp. 125–54.

Yeung Yueman 1998, 'Infrastructure Development in the Southern China Growth Triangle', in Myo Thant, Min Tang, and Hiroshi Kakazu (eds), *Growth Triangles in Asia: A New Approach to Regional Cooperation*, Hong Kong: Asian Development Bank, p. 156.

Yiu, Enoch 2003, 'Mainland Opens up to HK Brokers', *South China Morning Post*, 22 November, p. A1.

Zhan Lisheng 2003a, 'Exhibition Floats High-tech Water Quality Improvements', *China Daily*, 11 March, p. 4.

Zhan Lisheng 2003b, 'US$ 1b JV on Steel Sheets', *China Daily*. 23 September: chinadaily.com.

Zhan Lisheng 2004a, 'Aluminium Sector Seeks Sustained Growth', *China Daily*. 8–14 March, p. 17.

Zhan Lisheng 2004b, 'Fund to Improve Water Quality', *China Daily*. 11 March, p. 5.

Zhan Lisheng 2004c, 'Cityscape Receiving Big Facelift', *China Daily*. 9 April, p. 4.

Zhan Lisheng 2004d, 'New Garden Projects Give City a Facelift', *China Daily*. 22 April, p. 4.

Zhang Jinsheng 2000, *Waizi yu Shenzhen chanye jiegou (Foreign Capital and Shenzhen's Industrial Structure)*, Beijing: Central Literature Publishing House, pp. 116–54.

Zhao, B. 2003, *Embeddedness and Competitiveness: Regional Clusters in China*, PhD Thesis, The University of Hong Kong.

Zheng Caixiong 2003a, 'Shunde Town Aims to Become Cowboy Country', *China Daily*. 26 September: chinadaily.com.

Zheng Caixiong 2003b, 'Toyota Gears Up on Engine-making Factory', *China Daily*. 9 October: chinadaily.com.

Zheng Caixiong 2003c, 'Schroeder Visits Pearl River Delta', *China Daily*. 4 December, p. 5.

Zheng Caixiong 2004a, 'New Airport to Heighten City's Role', *China Business Weekly*. 8–14 March, p. 17.

Zheng Caixiong 2004b, 'Railway Pursues Int'l Aid', *China Business Weekly Review*, 16 March: chinadaily.com.

Zheng Caixiong 2004c, 'Guangzhou Spreads its Wings with Bigger Airport', *China Daily*. 1 April, p. 18.

Zheng Caixiong 2004d, 'Maglev an Option for New Guangzhou–HK Line', *China Daily*. 15 April: chinadaily.com.

Zheng Gong Zhengzheng and Liang Qiwen 2004, 'Auto Maker Launches Engine Joint Venture', *China Daily*. 26 February, p. 10.

Zheng Tianxiang and Li Huan (eds) 2001, *Yuegangao jingji guanxi (The Guangdong–Hong Kong–Macao Economic Relationship)*, Guangzhou: Sun Yatsen University Press, pp. 12 and 45–6.

Zhu Xiaodan (ed.) 1998, *Gaige kaifang ershi nian de Guangzhou (Guangzhou in the Past Twenty Years of Reform and Opening)*, Guangzhou: Open Times.

Zuo Liancun, Wang Hongliang, and Huang Guoxian 2000, 'Zhongguo jiaru WTO dui yuegang jingji de yingxiangao' ('The Impact of China's WTO Entry on the Economies of Guangdong, Hong Kong, and Macao'), *Guoji jingji hezuo (International Economic Cooperation)*, Vol. 11, p. 3.

Zuo Zheng 2002, 'Zhujiang sanjiaozhou liyong waizi fazhan gaoxin chanye de yanjiao' ('A Study of the Development of New and Hi-tech Industries by Utilising Foreign Capital in the Pearl River Delta Region'), *Nanfang jingji (Southern Economics)*, Vol. 6, pp. 39–40.

Index